Erasmus in the Twentieth Century:

Interpretations c 1920–2000

Erasmus of Rotterdam is one of the most studied and published literary figures and religious thinkers in western culture. Yet despite the considerable attention paid to him and his work, scholarly opinion of his intellectual and historical importance is diverse and often ambivalent. In this study, Bruce Mansfield shows how changing interpretations and critical assessments of Erasmus and his work reflect cultural shifts of the last century.

Placing the development of Erasmus studies in the context of religious movements as well as trends in humanities scholarship throughout the century, Mansfield looks at the increasing awareness of the impact of Erasmus' thought on religion and politics, the growing regard for Erasmus as a serious religious and theological thinker, and the revival of interest in his role in the rhetorical tradition.

Controversy about Erasmus' influence nevertheless remains. The theological and rhetorical approaches differ in their assessments of Erasmus as an 'orthodox' thinker, and recent literary and critical theory has contributed further to the debate. Differences of opinion also remain about his personal and political influence. In *Erasmus in the Twentieth Century*, Mansfield shows that to this day the subject of Erasmus' influence on his own and later ages continues to be of vital interest.

This is the final volume in Mansfield's trilogy examining Erasmus' reputation from his death to the present day. It follows his two earlier studies, *Phoenix of His Age: Interpretations of Erasmus c 1550–1750* (1979) and *Man On His Own: Interpretations of Erasmus c 1750–1920* (1992).

BRUCE MANSFIELD is Emeritus Professor, Macquarrie University, and an Honorary Research Associate at the University of Sydney.

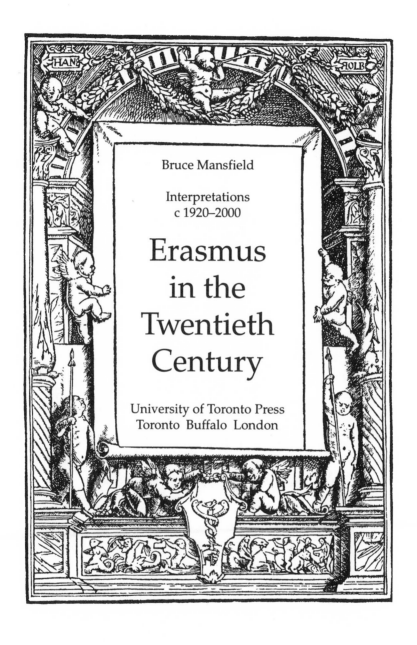

Bruce Mansfield

Interpretations
c 1920–2000

Erasmus in the Twentieth Century

University of Toronto Press
Toronto Buffalo London

© University of Toronto Press Incorporated 2003
Toronto Buffalo London
Printed in Canada

ISBN 0-8020-3767-4

Printed on acid-free paper

Erasmus Studies

National Library of Canada Cataloguing in Publication

Mansfield, Bruce, 1926–
Erasmus in the twentieth century : interpretations c 1920–2000 /
Bruce Mansfield.

(Erasmus studies)
Final vol. in the trilogy which includes Phoenix of his age, published
1979, and Man on his own, published 1992.
Includes bibliographical references and index.
ISBN 0-8020-3767-4

1. Erasmus, Desiderius, d. 1536 – Criticism and interpretation –
History – 20th century.   I. Series.

PA8518.M353 2003   199'.492   C2002-905538-5

This book has been published with the assistance of grants from The
Australian Academy of the Humanities and the University of Sydney.

University of Toronto Press acknowledges the financial assistance to
its publishing program of the Canada Council for the Arts and the
Ontario Arts Council.

University of Toronto Press acknowledges the financial support for its
publishing activities of the Government of Canada through the Book
Publishing Industry Development Program (BPIDP).

FOR EMMA, OSKAR, AND MATHILDE

Contents

✺

Preface

In a sense, this book is a sequel to *Phoenix of His Age* and *Man On His Own*. Like them, it is a study of the essays, articles, books, and monographs written about Erasmus of Rotterdam in a given period. Chronologically, it takes up where *Man On His Own* left off, in the 1920s. In other ways, it cannot be a sequel. It has become a book of a different character. Certainly, as with its predecessors, its subject is the history of Erasmus' image, fame, and reputation. They were, however, as much interested (or nearly so) in the writers on Erasmus, their social positions, intellectual moorings, religious convictions, and stances in contemporary controversies, as in Erasmus himself. Or, rather, their quest was for the intersections between these things and the authors' views on Erasmus. Such a quest would not readily be profitable for the writers of the twentieth century.

Most have been professional academics. The profession has expanded enormously in the twentieth century and – one dares to say – has grown more alike across the world. At least the contributions of specialists on their chosen topic have been to something more like a continuous, invisible seminar than the outbursts of controversy about him that marked the history of Erasmus' reputation up to the late nineteenth century. This is not to say that there have not been, among the writers on him, distinctive personalities whose individual flair comes out in their works.

In assembling interpretations of Erasmus, we can use broadbrush categories – Catholic, Protestant, liberal – but, in twentieth-century circumstances, this does not carry us very far. One may touch lightly the national chord, but speaking of a 'German tradition' or a 'French school' of interpretation brings us quickly to a dead end. There are 'schools' in the sense of concentrations of scholars, in Liège, Tours, or Toronto, but it is misleading to give them too specific a scholarly, let alone an ideological, character. The result of all this is that the material here is organized, not (as in the previous volumes) by the ideologies and commitments of the writers, but thematically. Hence the presentation of chapters 2, 3, 5, and 6.

There is another and obvious problem, the sheer magnitude of the field to be surveyed. The aim in the previous volumes was to be complete, or at least comprehensive (one, of course, fell short). That is impossible for the twentieth century. The aim of this book is to bring out the main themes of Erasmus scholarship in that century. Authors are drawn into the discussion as they illustrate these or advance them. I must say bluntly that I have not achieved, or perhaps even attempted, even-handed justice. Space is not always commensurate with importance. I have not wished to replicate the admirable bibliographies of J.-C. Margolin, an indispensable tool for all Erasmus scholarship. Again, this book is not a collection of reviews. All the books and monographs mentioned here were no doubt reviewed in their time. If points are raised here with individual works, it is not so much to make a critique as to elucidate themes and make progress towards a personal, synthetic view. These things are said against the background of the author's limitations, which force him at times into mere reference or at best reportage. Further, the subject 'Erasmus' shades into other subjects, his life into other lives, issues about him into the problems of his age. Generally, a cut-off comes at the literature which is predominantly about those other subjects.

Three chapters (1, 4, and 7) deal with the Erasmus commemorations (1936, 1967–70, and 1986). They have a double purpose: to evoke, for each occasion, the cultural and social setting, the mood, in which Erasmus scholarship was being carried on; to make a sounding, as it were, into the scholarship of the time by analysing the contents of the major commemorative volumes (most derived from meetings and conferences). It is a fair assumption that the essays and papers published there represent the contemporary state of play.

The audience for this work may well be made up of students, and perhaps non-specialists or general readers, wanting an orientation to the Erasmus literature of the century. Erasmus scholars themselves may, as they pursue their own tracks, be glad of a reminder of the broader landscape. The humble mapmaker may be of service to experienced and enterprising explorers, and even the simple flow-chart has its uses.

There is a more fundamental justification for this kind of study. It is now hardly possible to go directly to the sources and arrive at a fresh, defensible view of Erasmus. The vocabulary of possible interpretations is used up. This does not mean that he can be understood only through his interpreters; rather, they provide a register of possibilities on which the new investigator can draw. Any dialogue with Erasmus must be a dialogue also with his interpreters. A breakthrough to something fresh requires breaking out of, transcending, that register. This cannot happen in ignorance or unawareness of previous interpreters.

I conclude with a brief survey of the character and principal findings of the thematic chapters of this book. Those in the first half (chapters 2 and 3) deal with subjects of continuous interest through the twentieth century: the political thought of Erasmus and his appeal to various European audiences. The first treats the literature at three levels suggested by Quentin Skinner's approach to the history of political thought: Erasmus' intellectual debts; his responsiveness to the political context; the 'normative vocabulary' of politics in his time. Writings on this theme showed the effects of contemporary events, the tensions of the Cold War, for example. They traced, even so, a more or less consistent course, towards an appreciation of the seriousness, and even the realism, of Erasmus' political thought. The audiences treated in the other thematic chapter in this half are national, as the nature of the literature on this theme requires. That literature could be defined as a development of, or a response to or, more recently, a reaction against, Marcel Bataillon's classic work of 1937 on Erasmus and Spain. A key to understanding Bataillon's book is the concept of 'Préréforme,' a broad complex of spiritual and reforming movements to which Reformation and Catholic Reformation were subsidiary, and in which Erasmus was a central figure. Writings in the twentieth century on Erasmus and his audiences demonstrate the fruitfulness and then the fragmentation of this idea: various audiences took Erasmus in different, some in radically different, ways. 'Préréforme' as a concept is not strong enough to encompass the contradictory forces at work, though it has not lost all usefulness.

The thematic chapters of the second half (5 and 6) deal with the two major developments in Erasmus interpretation in the twentieth century, his final emergence as a serious religious thinker (many would say theologian) and the recovery of his relation to the classical rhetorical tradition. There is a chronological pattern to these developments. In the 1950s, the view that Erasmus had a very open, pre-Enlightenment kind of religion found still attractive expressions, whether put in the form of a 'third church' or a 'second Reformation' or otherwise. By then, however, a rival view, that Erasmus was essentially an orthodox Christian (indeed Catholic) was in the field and receiving scholarly exposition. By the mid-1960s, he was claimed formally for the theology discipline and, in the next decade, there followed a series of substantial studies developing the argument. A host of tributary questions pressed forward, all headed in the same direction and all receiving attention: Erasmus and the Fathers, Erasmus and the scholastics, Erasmus and the Reformers, Erasmus on the church, Erasmus on the Bible. But, with orthodoxy itself being reframed through Vatican 2, the simplicities of measuring him against a set of fixed standards were outdated. In any case, he always somehow escapes the net.

Around 1980, the historical discipline took a linguistic turn. That went with a revival of intense interest in the rhetorical tradition, which in turn revitalized old interests in Erasmus scholarship, his attitude to language and discourse in various forms, written and spoken. From this quarter came one work on a grand scale (Jacques Chomarat's *Grammaire et rhétorique chez Erasme*) and other important studies. With these developments, the old, and apparently superseded, view that Erasmus had an unusual openness of mind came back in another form. To treat issues rhetorically was to see them from different points of view. Finally, after 1990 this theme underwent further refinement, the application to Erasmus of contemporary literary and critical theory. Studies in that field were proliferating at the end of the century. Judgments remained finely balanced between Erasmus theologian and Erasmus master of the rhetorical tradition.

Acknowledgments

Ron Schoeffel and James McConica have encouraged my work through its whole course, and I am grateful. I have had the encouragement also, and the hospitality, of good friends in the Erasmus business: Marjorie Boyle, the late regretted John Olin, and Dominic Baker-Smith. Of conversations with other eminent Erasmians, I must mention comments, at the Rotterdam symposium of 1986 and after, from Cornelis Reedijk, Erika Rummel, and Johannes Trapman. I was honoured by the invitation of the Executive Committee of the Erasmus of Rotterdam Society, through Richard DeMolen, to deliver the Erasmus Birthday Lecture at Leiden in 1993. I am ever in the debt of my colleagues in the Australian historical profession and think especially, in connection with this work, of Brian Fletcher, Edwin Judge, Barry O'Dwyer, Roslyn Pesman, and Deryck Schreuder. I must recall also the late Robert Scribner, once my student at the University of Sydney, and later a leader in the social and cultural history of the German Reformation, to whose thesis on the social thought of Erasmus I still turn for illumination. I also appreciate the work, relevant to chapter 2, of my student of a later time, Glenn Richardson. I obtained indispensable microfilm from the Erasmuscollectie of the Gemeentebibliotheek Rotterdam, through the kind offices of Dr J.J.M. van de Roer-Meyers. The bulk of this work has been done in the Fisher Library, University of Sydney, and the Macquarie University Library. I thank library staffs for their help and think especially of the Interlibrary Loans section of Fisher Library. I am grateful for grants in support of publication made by The Australian Academy of the Humanities, under its Publication Subsidy Scheme, and by the School of Philosophical and Historical Inquiry, University of Sydney (Head, Professor Richard Waterhouse). I have always had the interest and support of friends, my three sons (my son Martin helped greatly in the preparation of the bibliography), and, above all, my wife Joan, and again express my gratitude.

The work is dedicated to my grandchildren, Emma, Oskar, and Mathilde.

Erasmus in the Twentieth Century

ONE

Prologue:
Quatercentenary (1936)

꽃

In 1598 a Dutch fleet sailed from Rotterdam for the Pacific. A member of the fleet, once called *Erasmus* and now *De Liefde*, carried the wooden statuette of a man in a scholar's cap and holding a book in one hand and a banderole in the other. The fleet came to grief on the coasts of Japan, and the Japanese received the wooden figure as that of a god or saint. Only in the twentieth century did scholars in Japan and the Netherlands identify it with Erasmus of Rotterdam, though some defended an association with St Erasmus, patron saint of sailors. On its identification, the figure was installed in the Imperial Museum in Tokyo. From there, in July 1936, it came on loan to the Boymans Museum in Rotterdam for the exhibition marking the quatercentenary of Erasmus' death. Both the burgomaster of Rotterdam and the Japanese ambassador spoke at its reception.[1] The outbreak of the Pacific war and the Japanese occupation of the Dutch empire in the east was just over five years away.

Rotterdam was naturally a centre of commemoration in 1936. The great humanist had incorporated the name of the city in his own. The house in the Wijde Kerkstraat taken to be his birthplace had been restored in 1896. Hendrik de Keyzer's elegant statue of 1622 stood in the busy Groot Marktplaats. A scholarly conference, the publishing of a catalogue of the Municipal Library's precious holdings of Erasmiana, a students' presentation of scenes from Erasmus' life (devised by Garmt Stuiveling) were among the city's tributes in 1936.[2] Less than four years lay ahead for Rotterdam before its destruction by blitzkrieg on 14 May 1940, when Erasmus' birthplace and thousands of other dwellings were to disappear.

Nineteen-thirty-six was a sombre year for celebrating Erasmus. On his birthday in October, schoolchildren filed past his statue, and passages were read from his writings on peace. The hopes attached to such readings in 1936 were sometimes active, sometimes forlorn. There were more grotesque conjunctures. The commemorative advertisement of a Berlin publishing house which bore Erasmus' name (Erasmusdruck GMBH) carried a text of Adolf Hitler's on its front page. Flemish nationalists, someone said, could relate to Erasmus as the German National Socialists related to Goethe.[3]

Pacifists indeed made much of his execration of war, and scholarship registered their anxieties. Erasmus on politics and war featured in the two main scholarly conferences of the year, at Rotterdam and Basel. How did Erasmus stand to nations and nationalism? Were his political hopes naïve, did he lack a sense for the realities of power? What did he make of the traditional theory of just war?[4] The European experience of war and nationalism since the late nineteenth century posed such questions to Erasmus scholarship. An article in the liberal Protestant periodical *Kerk en Wereld* made 'transparent allusions' to the Italo-Abyssinian conflict and referred to Schweitzer's shame at the fratricide of European Christians in 1914–18.[5]

A calmer, less agitated light is shed on the celebration of Erasmus' quatercentenary by essays and papers that recalled the places where he had lived or with which he had strong attachments. It was as though European observers, sensing the threat of destruction to these places, wanted to capture for posterity the material and specific character of their association with Erasmus. This was, in more recent terminology, the heritage Erasmus. Leaders in this sphere were Daniel van Damme, founder and curator of the Erasmus museum at Anderlecht near Brussels, and Emil Major, curator of the historical museum at Basel. In the Netherlands, beside Rotterdam, there was Gouda, where Erasmus was conceived and went to school and where, or at least nearby in the Emmaus cloister at Steyn, he spent, unhappily so he says, his monastic years. The last of the Netherlands celebrations of 1936 was the fixing of a marble plaque to a wooden gate of 1519 on the farm "'t Klooster,' which occupies the site of the Emmaus house: 'Hic domicilium habuit Erasmus 1488–1493. Gouda 1936.'[6] At Gouda and other places in the Netherlands, not least in Zeeland, where, as a young man, he had friends and

patrons and where the humanist studies he would come to represent were already putting down roots, there was emphasis on
Erasmus' bonding to his native country; he drew on popular
beliefs and customs there for his *Colloquia* and other writings, he
understood its political structures and suffered its civil wars, he
absorbed and continued its distinctive religious traditions, a continuity about which Dutch scholars had been writing since early
in the nineteenth century.[7]

Erasmus spent the summer of 1521 at Anderlecht, in the house
called 'The Swan' ('de Zwane') of canon Pieter Wichmans. By the
standard of his stressful and controversial life, the time was rest-
ful, even idyllic. In writings of 1936 and later, Daniel van Damme
represented with exactness the house and garden which Erasmus
knew and the neighbouring structures, the late-Gothic parish
church of St Peter and St Guidon, to whose chapter Wichmans
belonged, and a thirteenth-century *béguinage*. Van Damme was at
pains to establish the authenticity of the heritage status accorded
the house in 1931.[8] As in Holland, commemorations in Belgium
in 1936 claimed Erasmus for the Netherlands and, in particular,
for Brabant, of which, when elsewhere, he spoke nostalgically,
honouring his printers, friends, and colleagues at Antwerp and
even at Louvain, despite the hostility of its theologians.[9]

Basel was as important as these northern centres in Erasmus'
story, and the physical evidences of his residence there were considerable. The scholars of Basel did not neglect these material
remains in their commemoration of 1936. The city archivist
depicted the three houses where he had lived in, respectively,
1514–16, 1522–9, and 1535–6; they were cultural sites of European
significance linked to the history of humanism and the Reformation and, since they all belonged to the Froben family, to the blos-
soming of the printing industry. Emil Major wrote about various
objects of Erasmus' – some he had sketched himself in the margins of manuscripts – and, above all, about his burial place in the
minster, a site not free of disturbance (in 1855, for example, by the
installation of conduits for heating) or, even now, of controversy.
The Basel exhibition of 1936 displayed the Erasmian treasures of
the university library, including what had come, by various
routes, from Erasmus' friend and heir, Bonifacius Amerbach. The
legacy of Erasmus also belongs to the history of Basel, since he
intended it to support students, the poor and frail, and girls without dowries in the city; in 1586 the administration of the legacy,

as an essay of 1936 shows, passed from the Amerbach family to the city and the university.[10]

Erasmus was very sensitive to place, primarily but not only because of the circles of friends (and, in some cases, of enemies) he met in his various stopping-places, beginning with the Paris of his student days in the 1490s. This is justification for the almost local studies of his activity and influence. An issue was made in his lifetime of his national connections (did he, or his homeland for that matter, belong to Germany or to France?) and more so in the nationalistic eras that followed. Studies of his sympathetic or problematic relations with the various nationalities appeared in 1936, as we have already seen for Holland and Belgium. Those on Erasmianism in Spain anticipated the great work of Marcel Bataillon, *Erasme et l'Espagne* (1937). England had, so it was said, a special relationship with Erasmus. The claim rested in part on the abiding influence of the nineteenth-century book by Frederic Seebohm, *The Oxford Reformers*, which carried remarkable, if somewhat misplaced, authority, and which contributed also to the continuing vitality of the liberal Enlightenment understanding of Erasmus. For some, he was a kind of founding father of the Anglican tradition. Cambridge, where on his longest stay in England, 1511–14, he taught Greek and theology and left lasting impressions on scholars and students, joined Anderlecht and Basel as a place whose physical spaces, notably the precincts of Queens' College, evoked the presence of Erasmus.[11]

It is curious that, in a commemorative year when so much was said about Erasmus' connections with places and his attachments to people, his friends and associates throughout Europe, the most influential biography of the man should remain one that emphasized his isolation and his solitary, even footloose character. Johan Huizinga's *Erasmus* had its third Dutch and its second German edition in 1936, the latter aimed at a more popular audience than its predecessor of 1928.[12] The widespread influence of Huizinga's seductive portrait was apparent in 1936. His views on Erasmus were finely balanced, at times bordering on paradox, but he set a precedent in the psychological study of Erasmus that attracted less subtle minds. John Joseph Mangan's, as it had been revealed in his massive biography of 1927, was a less subtle mind.

Two obsessions, Mangan says, drove Erasmus. First, he would keep concealed his illegitimacy, while freeing himself of its legal or canonical consequences, aims not always reconcilable. Secondly, he would undo what an imprudent step in his youth had done, tied him to a monastery. Much in his personal history arose from his desire desperately to evade recall to the monastery. Mangan contends that his writings against the monks, like the 'blasphemous' *Praise of Folly,* belonged to that campaign. To keep his own freedom, he would destroy monasticism; he was 'a cautious and calculating Samson.' A physician, Mangan pronounces the personality shaped by these obsessions 'neurasthenic' (Luther, by contrast, he calls a 'psychopath'). Mangan's Erasmus was restless, variable, querulous, hypersensitive, voluble, petulant, indiscreet. He was at ease only when giving free rein to his rhetorical flair.[13]

Mangan's was not a particularly theological work, but its vantage-point is clear, Catholic orthodoxy of the early twentieth century. Erasmus, he says, was not intentionally heretical – he could, in his little handbook the *Enchiridion,* for example, produce a work of 'real fervor' and he ended his life a Catholic – but his writings on religion were shallow and limited. He led his humanist colleagues into a 'pronounced latitudinarianism.' In the Luther affair, he would pare Catholic doctrine down to accommodate the dissidents; in this, as in his whole life, he referred everything to his own interest and safety. He was 'supremely egoistic.'[14]

In 1936 there were articles, in medical journals and elsewhere, resuming Mangan's psychological quest and, especially when centred on reactions to Holbein's late portraits of Erasmus, giving him a character little different from that evoked by John Caspar Lavater's essays in physiognomy of 170 years before: he was sharp, penetrating, supple, delicate, prudent, anxious, in a conventional sense unheroic, and, one could by 1936 frankly speculate, bisexual.[15] Huizinga himself, in his commemorative speech at the peak of the Basel celebrations, while conceding to his friend the Basel historian Werner Kaegi that events since the first appearance of his biography in 1924 had given Erasmus a new topicality, stood by his portrait of 1924: a smallness of character in Erasmus stood in the way of his greatness of mind, a mind which prefigured the Enlightenment; his world of books shielded him from real life, though he persisted in a drive for moral and social betterment, and that remains an inspiration.[16]

The intellectual link Huizinga made between Erasmus and the Enlightenment and the liberal interpretation of his thought pre-

eminent in the nineteenth century had defenders in 1936: Erasmus broke the rigidities of medieval culture and religion and
prepared the way for liberty of mind. Some, shaken by the
authoritarian tendencies of the time, sought a libertarian and
anarchist Erasmus.[17] The liberal view of his mental world carried
most conviction when related to his writings on the education of
children. Erasmus, it was said, combined a clear vision of social
realities, a capacity, based on classical precedents, for rational
reflection on what he observed, sympathy for the human subject,
especially the child, a recognition of the bond between intellect
and character, and strong convictions about the receptiveness of
the mind and spirit to leading and instruction. A plausible connection could then be made between Erasmus and Locke, Rous-
seau, and Pestalozzi. In this way the pedagogical journals of 1936
celebrated Erasmus. His pedagogy, said one lecturer, had a 'rational, practical and unmystical character' and formed a tradition,
especially in Holland.[18]

Huizinga inspired the most popular book about Erasmus in
this era, Stefan Zweig's *Triumph und Tragik des Erasmus von Rotterdam* of 1934.[19] Spanish and Polish translations appeared in 1936,
complementing the English and French translations of the year of
original publication in German in Vienna, and others were to follow.[20] Huizinga's paradox of an unheroic, small-spirited individual who yet promoted ideas of great purity and nobility is
repeated in Zweig, who also echoes Lavater. Erasmus lacked
robustness; he and his fellow-humanists were isolated from the
life of the people. Yet, the vigour and vitality missing from his
physique and social relations were present in full measure in his
mind and writings. Like Huizinga, Zweig gives Erasmus a liberal's cast of mind; he was the enemy of every kind of fanaticism
and bigotry. He set Erasmus at the head of a line of sceptical, libertarian thinkers: Montaigne, Spinoza, Diderot, Voltaire, Lessing.
Erasmus' place in such a succession had been associated by liberal writers since Gibbon with the idea of a 'second Reformation,'
rival to that of Luther and Calvin. Nevertheless, Zweig, whose
historical biographies rest on serious, if necessarily shallow and
incomplete, research, is not blind to the Christian element in his
subject. Erasmus wanted 'a renewal of the Christian ideal by a
return to its Nazarene purity.' In putting the matter that way,
Zweig was following an early twentieth-century school of Protestant theologians who sought to recover the pristine religion of

Jesus from the dogmatic accretions of later centuries and thought Erasmus shared their aims.[21]

What gives point and poignancy to Zweig's *Triumph und Tragik* is his recognition of himself in Erasmus and the analogy he makes between his and Erasmus' historical predicaments. Erasmus, he says, valued above all his independence and refused to make common cause with other actors on the scene. Of himself he says: 'From my earliest youth my strongest instinct was to remain free and independent,' attributing this in part to reaction against the conformist Austrian education system in which he had been brought up. The 'urge to be untrammelled by fixed responsibilities' had deep roots in his character as in Erasmus.' The man who saw the *Vaterlandsideal* as too limiting and, under the most unpromising conditions, longed and appealed for the cultural unity of Europe as a first step to world understanding saw in Erasmus the first European and the apostle of humanity. The succession from Erasmus through Montaigne to Lessing was completed by the line of peace propagandists from Kant through Tolstoy to Gandhi and Romain Rolland.[22]

Zweig is caught between sharing the humanist hope of concord and condemning it as facile optimism. 'Reason,' he begins, 'is eternal and patient, and can afford to bide her time,' but his conclusion is more tenuous: only ideals which have so far failed have the capacity to recur. At a more intimate level, the analogy was tragic. Here was a world-famous Jewish author living in 1934 at Salzburg within sight of Berchtesgaden and writing of one who for a time was the most prominent of European scholars but who was soon to be overtaken by the cataclysm of the German Reformation. Later Zweig was to compare the experience of writing *Erasmus* with that of composing his play *Jeremias* during the Great War, which he opposed: 'In my effort to help others, I had helped myself towards my most personal, most intimate work besides *Erasmus*, by means of which in 1934, in the days of Hitler, I extricated myself from a similar crisis. From the moment when I attempted to shape them, I no longer suffered so greatly from the tragedy of the times.' The crisis arose from Zweig's refusal publicly to denounce the new regime in Germany. There was in him a deep reluctance to embroil himself in the politics of the day. He believed that he shared this evasiveness with Erasmus: 'I had to accept, perhaps justly, the reproach of indecision that was so often made to my revered master of an earlier century, Erasmus of Rotterdam.' He was consoled by Thomas Mann: you are writing, Mann wrote, 'to some extent the myth of our existence. ... and the justification of the apparent ambiguity under which we suffer and which has made me, at least, almost as hated by the émigrés as by those "in there."'[23]

Zweig recognizes the 'apparent ambiguity' in Erasmus' confrontation with Luther and brings it out. Temperamentally, the two men were a complete contrast. Their historical action was different, the one addressing the learned, the other penetrating at a stroke 'to the depths of folk-feeling and folk-passion.' Yet at a critical moment on the eve of the Diet of Worms, Erasmus protected Luther before the monk's own prince, Frederick of Saxony, but then, as later at the Diet of Augsburg in 1530, failed to follow through and tie conciliation down by his own presence and action. The world in 1521 (as in 1934) looked for a clear stand. In such circumstances, Zweig writes wryly, personal fame is both an obligation and a curse.[24]

In letters to friends, he defended his own position, referring to *Erasmus*, which he finished in London in the first stages of his exile. 'For me,' he wrote to Hermann Hesse at the end of 1933, 'it was a small consolation to see ... that one is not alone in tormenting oneself in all decency over difficult decisions, instead of making oneself comfortable by jumping at one leap on the back of a party.' The book, he said to René Schickele, was grossly misunderstood when seen as raising neutrality to the status of a principle; rather it showed by an example 'what enormous moral demands [neutrality] can make on a man and to what a tragic position a man of independence must come in times of mob madness.' Erasmus was defeated by Luther as humane Germans by Hitler (a comparison rejected by Thomas Mann for unworthily dignifying Hitler). His book, Zweig had written earlier to Klaus Mann, would be 'a hymn on defeat.' Defeat settled on Zweig's mind in the following years, often with reference to Erasmus. 'We are too Erasmian,' he wrote in 1938, 'to prevail against these men who have a battering-ram in place of forehead and brain. Against those possessed by the mania of nationalism only those themselves possessed can stand: we are poisoned by our humanity.'[25] The end came with his suicide in Brazil in 1942.

Behind the celebrations of 1936 brooded the dark visage of Adolf Hitler, and much said and written then made nervous reference to the menaces of the moment. At the same time, old issues and old controversies continued to receive an airing, especially those about Erasmus' religion and theology. The proposition that Erasmus was not truly Catholic and did not think or feel with the church was of long standing, and Catholic journals reiterated it in 1936. That the author of a short piece putting the contrary view – Erasmus' attitude was profoundly religious and his influence in the church good – should entitle it 'The unknown Erasmus' ('De onbekende Erasmus') suggests that the weight of opinion was on the critical side. In a Catholic Church still tense from its nineteenth-century struggles to recover ground lost to the Revolution and from the more recent controversies over modernism, Erasmus was suspect to majority opinion. Nevertheless, various reviews of Catholic opinion in 1936 suggested that the balance was changing, and some nuanced researches foreshadowed a new Catholic consensus: Erasmus theologian and Catholic reformer.[26]

The issue of Catholic substance or otherwise in Erasmus' ideas had always been tied to that of his attitude to the Middle Ages, especially their characteristic intellectual form, scholasticism. Discussion of that matter was advanced notably in 1936 itself by the publication of *Die Stellung des Erasmus von Rotterdam zur scholastischen Methode*, which Christian Dolfen, a Redemptorist teacher and archivist at Osnabrück, presented as a doctoral dissertation to the old Catholic theological faculty at Münster. Dolfen held to the received view that Erasmus was an opponent of scholasticism, essentially because it overvalued dialectic and made Christianity captive to philosophy. However, he made distinctions: Erasmus was sharp against Scotus, but not so sharp against Aquinas. Dolfen seems unsure about the character of late-medieval scholasticism and Erasmus' relation to it. His main conclusion is that Erasmus' critique was not revolutionary. Erasmus' master Jerome had resisted the infiltration of philosophy; his call not to run to speculation beyond what is in scripture, his emphasis on the practical in religion rather than the dialectical can be heard in the Fathers and in theologians of the conciliar movement like Jean Gerson only a century before his time.[27] Characteristically, he did not reject the scholastic method entirely but sought to moderate its use. Dolfen's thesis of 1936 was a refinement on all that had gone before on Erasmus and scholasticism.

On another debt of Erasmus to the medieval, his formation by the fifteenth-century pietistic movement called the *Devotio moderna*, there was less need for refinements, since a sophisticated

literature had appeared in the early years of the twentieth century. Nevertheless, there were confusing cross-currents. The book
by Frederic Seebohm on the 'Oxford Reformers,' which con-
tended for a singular intellectual dependence of Erasmus on his
older English friend John Colet, kept its reputation still in 1936,
but its argument received a full frontal battery from the American
historian Albert Hyma. Hyma (born 1893) was from a Dutch family settled in the Midwest and of the Reformed religion. His student years and his academic career were spent mostly at the
University of Michigan, but his accomplishments rested on
researches made back in the Netherlands in the 1920s.[28] His contribution to the commemorative conference at Rotterdam in 1936
was characteristic. His 'Erasmus and the Oxford Reformers 1493–
1503' argued that the humanist could not have been weaned by
the devout Colet away from a medieval form of Christianity,
grounded in scholasticism and monasticism, and turned towards
a more critical, personal, and evangelical form. That is what various scholars, all ultimately dependent on Seebohm and his
English contemporary John Lupton, had argued. But, says Hyma,
Erasmus had never been interested in scholasticism; if not openly
hostile to monasticism at the time of his meeting with Colet
(1499), he did not share the monastic ideal in any serious way
and, as for the mysticism of the Italian Neoplatonists, which,
some said, was mediated to him by Colet, this was always
beyond his range. Those who affected him most were the more or
less irreverent Italian humanists like Lorenzo Valla. If any current
of piety touched him, it came from his early teachers and associates in the Brethren of the Common Life and was of the sober,
earnest, practical, northern kind, the *Devotio moderna*.[29]

   In his first work, *The Christian Renaissance: A History of the
'Devotio Moderna'* (1924), Hyma had put this last point categorically: Erasmus was a child of the *Devotio moderna* and could no
more slough off its ideals than change the colour of his skin. Not
Colet, but the Brethren led him to Paul, Augustine, and Jerome.
Hyma had a penchant for summary judgments and used his
sources in a very positivist way. Even so, he qualified the conclusions of 1924 in his major work of 1930, *The Youth of Erasmus*, at
the cost of a certain confusion. He reiterates that Erasmus was a
child of the movement; in his last year of schooling at Deventer,
he was 'strongly affected' by the teachings of the Brethren and
later he imbibed Thomas à Kempis' *Imitatio Christi*; as a result, he

was 'fully prepared' to renounce worldly ambitions and enter on the monastic life. Yet, there is a cautionary note: 'All that one can say with assurance is that when his mind was absorbing knowledge and was plastic, he was subjected for several years to a course of training which reflected the ideas and methods of the Brethren of the Common Life and their friends.' Such influences had to contend, not only with the attractions of a secularizing Italian humanism, but also with serious flaws of character. Erasmus was moved, not by imitation of the lowly Jesus, as commended to him by the Brethren, but by longings for fame and honour, to be won by triumphs of scholarship and an inimitable grace of style.[30]

Hyma's treatment of Erasmus' early development ends in an impasse. He wants to make the *Devotio moderna* the primary, if not the exclusive, influence on Erasmus' spirituality; he sees the Brethren, admittedly of a later generation, as forerunners of Erasmus' most important work, that on the Fathers and the Bible. Yet, he depicts in his Erasmus a temperament and a personality profoundly unsympathetic to the outlook of the Brethren. His own evangelical religion was not unconnected to this conclusion. The Cross, he says at one point, had no significance for Erasmus. Kenneth Strand underestimates the tensions in Hyma's writing when he says that in it his Christian commitment and the historical discipline are combined 'in beautiful harmony.' Hyma's way out of the impasse is a periodization by which Erasmus began by concentrating on the Christian literature under the influence of the Brethren; then (1490–5), secularized by the Italian humanists, he became absorbed in the classical and the pagan; finally, he drifted back towards his starting-point.[31] This is not a convincing solution. The question of Erasmus' early development, first seriously canvassed by the young German scholar Paul Mestwerdt on the eve of World War 1, would remain on the agenda of Erasmus scholarship.[32]

So would the issue, alive since the controversies of Erasmus' lifetime, of his relations with Luther and the other Reformers. For most commentators in 1936, Luther and Erasmus represented contrasting and conflicting principles, the one the absoluteness of revelation and the response of faith, the other cooperation between grace and nature, God and man. Liberal Protestants acknowledged both claims but inclined towards Erasmus, as they had done since the nineteenth century. A Barthian voice retorted that, not human values or spiritual qualities, but the *nudum verbum* of God constituted the church. Scholarly progress in understanding the fraught relationship of Luther and Erasmus depended on a recognition, not only of the differences of temperament and principle that made them enemies in the end, but also of the common, or at least the neighbouring, sources of their reform programs: the biblicism of the late Renaissance, moral revulsion against abuses in the church, the practical mysticism of the *Devotio moderna* and its German counterparts. The ecumenical climate favourable to this recognition was still distant in 1936.[33]

Already by then, nevertheless, the theologically sophisticated or astute were able to distinguish Erasmus from the flat moralist (Mangan's 'latitudinarian') depicted by both Catholic and Protestant controversialists: for him, too, Christ was an object of trust and confidence, not an ethical teacher alone. At the same time they recognized, as the more perceptive writers in the Enlightenment tradition had done, the bond he made between religion and life, faith and *praxis*. He had from the Fathers and the gospel of St John a theology of the *Logos*. It represented an earthing, an incarnation of the divine which persisted in the lives of believers and the renewal of the world. Walter Köhler, speaking at Rotterdam in 1936 of Erasmus 'als religiöse Persönlichkeit,' found in his rediscovery of the *Logos* theology the source of the dialectic, characteristic of his religious outlook, between unity and diversity: each stage of life, each religious expression, each cultural form may be a step in the divine pedagogy. Here is the source of his plea for tolerance. Writers on the theology of mission recognized ahead of others the dynamic, evangelical character of Erasmus' Christianity, identifying the passages in his late writings, especially the *Ecclesiastes* of 1535, which appealed for missions to the Indies.[34]

Erasmus was remembered in many different ways in 1936. Amid wars and rumours of wars his name was attached to values that were manifestly under threat: peace, toleration, liberal education, even democracy. Often the mood bordered on desperation, as in Stefan Zweig's popular biography. There was a fund of earlier writing on which observers in 1936 could draw, culminating in Huizinga's study, which left in its train a scatter of reflections on the more neurasthenic traits in Erasmus' personality. Huizinga's depiction of his mind, which had most in common with the liberal tradition of interpretation, portraying Erasmus as a precursor of the Enlightenment, remained authoritative in 1936. One major cultural shift could, however, be discerned; the signs were apparent, above all, in Holland. Erasmus was being taken seriously as Christian thinker and theologian. The long stand-off among Catholic writers about his religious thought, and indeed his spiritual being, continued, but the balance was changing in favour of those who saw him as heir to late-medieval spirituality and a source of Catholic reform.

Since the late nineteenth century, Erasmus studies had been moving into an era of more exact scholarship; a great explosion of scholarly publications was to follow on the expansion of universities in Western countries after World War 2. By 1936 the Allen edition of Erasmus' letters had reached July 1530 (volume 8 1934), and numerous pieces, especially for the commemorative exercises at Rotterdam and Basel, drew on the new resources. Study of Erasmus' relations with places and people, collaborators and patrons, friends and enemies depended above all on the letters. So did more exact work on Erasmus' writings.[35] More precise scholarship did not simply cancel out the patterns of interpretation, long established and reiterated in 1936, deriving from the Reformation controversies, the Enlightenment, romanticism, and the nineteenth-century debates over secularism and liberalism. Long-standing disagreements persisted. 'For so great a man,' wrote W.G. Moore, 'the esteem in which he is generally held is curiously uncertain.' Some of the best scholarship of 1936 went into essays on differing perceptions of Erasmus in different periods and cultural settings.[36] Progress required, not only more dependable narrative and a closer scrutiny of texts, but also entering into a dialogue with the interpreters of the past, including the recent past. Inescapable was dialogue with Erasmus himself, since interpreting him, understanding him, and listening to him were intertwined. Studies of his political writings demonstrate the point.

TWO

Erasmus' Liberation Theology

'The Utopian preferential option for the poor against the rich.'
That, says Brendan Bradshaw, is the core of what Erasmus had to
say about government in his most formal and substantial writing
on the subject, the *Institutio principis christiani* (1516). The stance
was populist. Erasmus undermined shibboleths of the time: 'the
inviolable rights of property and heredity, the divinely ordained
wisdom of lineage and social hierarchy, the axiomatic morality of
severe justice and dynastic warfare.' The ideology, Bradshaw
says, was identical with Thomas More's in *Utopia*. Erasmus' task
was to apply it to sixteenth-century structures, transforming
them through a reshaping of the values of those destined for
power and responsibility.[1]

How had Erasmus' political ideas come, by 1991, when Bradshaw was writing for the *Cambridge History of Political Thought*, to
have this significance? It had not always been so. A nineteenth-
century biographer thought those ideas 'tolerably obvious.'[2] By
1914 only a handful of serious essays had appeared on the subject. J.W. Allen's *History of Political Thought in the Sixteenth Century*
(1928) has nothing of substance on Erasmus. By then, nevertheless, there were signs of quickening interest. The purpose of this
chapter is to follow the course from Allen to Bradshaw.

The history of political thought may be treated at different levels. It can be the study of intellectual influences, dependence on
predecessors and influence on successors. This can require some
abstraction from historical realities and suggest what Quentin
Skinner, adopting an expression of Peter Gay's, has called, in a
famous essay, 'spurious persistence.' Nevertheless, intellectual
dependencies exist. Even practical problems of the day may be

pictured or imagined in terms set by sources from the past. This kind of study is necessary but of limited value. Its weakness may be corrected by proceeding to the next level, by introducing historical context and treating political thought as essentially responsive. 'For I take it,' Skinner says, 'that political life itself sets the main problems for the political theorist, causing a certain range of issues to appear problematic, and a corresponding range of questions to become the leading subjects of debate.' Of course, the 'main problems' may be misconceived, the response may be to pseudo-problems or non-problems. Misconception may be the result of the intellectual tools the thinker employs, which make a third level. So, Skinner again: 'It is evident that the nature and limits of the normative vocabulary available at any given time will also help to determine the ways in which particular questions come to be singled out and discussed.'[3] This is not just a matter of limitations and distortions. Broaching the 'normative vocabulary' also introduces the larger scheme, philosophical, ethical, or religious, to which the political ideas attach. For Erasmus, whose thought is, on the face of it, ethically and religiously determined, exploring this connection is inescapable. Finally, we can consider a body of political ideas at the level of action. To what extent have they stimulated or guided political action in the past? Are they versatile enough to be turned to new issues and situations? Evidence may be thin or lacking. At least one might ask: how far do they escape the trap of abstraction and have realism and actuality?[4]

I

Writers who concentrate on intellectual sources adopt one of two models. Either they think in a linear way, assuming a line of descent in ideas, or they see their text as a pattern of sources, sometimes simple, sometimes intricate. The first path was taken by L.K. Born, of Chicago and Western Reserve Universities, who pioneered the study of Erasmus' political ideas by producing an English version of the *Institutio*, with preliminary studies and accompanying notes (1936). He describes the book's sources, especially its classical sources, as 'its lineal ancestors.' His whole emphasis is on continuity. At times, continuity becomes identity. For Born, there was, from Greek antiquity to the twentieth century, a common fund of ideas on the moral order in politics. Erasmus drew on that fund.[5] This approach at least saves Born from overstating Erasmus' dependence on any one thinker. Erasmus' model was the *To Nicocles* of Isocrates (c 372 BC), who himself had said: 'we should not seek novelties ... but, rather we should regard that man as the most accomplished in this field who can collect the greatest number of ideas scattered among the thoughts of all the rest and present them in the best form.' Otherwise, Born says, Erasmus' debts were to Plato, Cicero, Seneca, and Plutarch.[6]

Born does not deny that Erasmus' political writings included a 'frank study of current problems' or carried 'the stamp of his own genius,' but his interest is not there. In one note, he rejects the contextualist approach 'in view of the wealth of precedent in antiquity for almost all that Erasmus discussed.'[7] The difficulty is that precedents for almost anything are notoriously easy to find as long as one remains at the intellectualist level. Historically interesting is the use to which the common fund of ideas is put in a particular historical situation, and identifying that requires reading from context to text as well as from text to context.

Roland Bainton, who was to write the most important Erasmus biography of the 1960s, earlier demonstrated the pattern approach in a search for the sources of Erasmus' *Complaint of Peace* (1517). He describes this work as an 'artistic weave' blending the classical and the Christian. Though the fusion of the two heritages, he goes on, had been familiar since Augustine, Erasmus' acquaintance with the literature was fresh and original, and his zeal was 'quickened through circumstance.' The result is 'so well integrated that the sources are lost to view and the plea sweeps to an impassioned climax as if springing unpremeditated from the author's mind and pen.' Even Erasmus' prudential arguments for peace have, Bainton adds, counterparts in classical literature. He considers Erasmus' biblical sources obvious (the Sermon on the Mount and the Pauline injunctions) and changes front by asking which of three Christian options Erasmus chooses: pacifism, just war, or crusade. He moved 'within the framework of the traditional just-war theory,' but his scepticism threatened to dissolve it from within.[8] Bainton's change of front defines the limit to the usefulness of the search for sources. At some point, the discussion has to turn from where the words come from to how they are used in argument, as between various options. Circumstances give these options their seriousness. Erasmus, who grew up in a country brutalized by civil war, hardly

needed classical sources to convince him of the prudential considerations for peace.

The author and his ancient source are, in any case, not two
fixed points between which a line of influence can be plotted
once for all. The ancient source itself is not a set quantity but has
been understood differently from time to time and from setting to
setting. In a long and complex essay, 'Isokrates, Erasmus und die
Institutio principis christiani,' Otto Herding has asked what
made Isocrates (436–338 BC), whose *To Nicocles* was, as we know,
the classical model for Erasmus' *Institutio*, attractive to late-
medieval learned circles and government officials, especially
those around the Habsburg emperor. He answers: first, Isocrates
vindicated the collections of moral maxims, as in the 'mirror of
princes' literature, to which the *Institutio* belonged; but, secondly,
he went beyond casuistry and 'moralische Technik' and thought
about life in community and reciprocity between ruler and people. He was optimistic about the outcomes of education, saying:
'education and diligence are in the highest degree potent to
improve our nature.'[9] All this, Isocrates' whole pedagogical
approach, appealed to the essentially pedagogical northern
humanist movement, to which these scholars, teachers, and
bureaucrats belonged and of which Erasmus was a luminary.
Herding here goes beyond the pattern model or, at least, the pattern becomes dynamic; the reception of Isocrates was active, he
met the needs and reinforced the assumptions of the northern
humanists.[10]

The bulk of Herding's essay addresses the question: how
could Erasmus relate this ancient, secular, religiously indifferent
writing to his own Christian program? Herding warns against
a methodology which ticks off with a red pencil Christian-
sounding expressions and so measures the theological content of
a work like the *Institutio*. In many places, he concludes, the Christian element is 'relatively superficial.' Erasmus' writing on the
practical aspects of ruling hardly required theological reference.
On some issues, like the severity of the criminal code, he was
indeed a forerunner of the Enlightenment. Over much of his text
the ethical predominated over the theological. In these parts, the
Institutio did not break from Isocrates and the classical guidance
to rulers. At three points, nevertheless, Erasmus reoriented the
whole tradition towards the Christian; they were decisive. Herding identifies three key words: *libertas, caritas, crux*. The relation

of ruler and people is defined by the freedom won for both by Christ's death, and by Christian love which mediates between them. The ruler, by becoming a Christian, does not lose his power but holds it in another way (*aliter possidet*). To rule is to bear a cross.[11]

II

In contrasting these ideas to late-medieval notions of kingship, especially in Burgundy, to which Erasmus himself belonged, Herding's essay becomes contextualist. Contextualist studies, studies at our second level, to which we now come, have seen Erasmus, above all, as a critic of aristocratic culture and the language and values of chivalry in decay. In his *The Better Part of Valor: More, Erasmus, Colet, and Vives on Humanism, War, and Peace, 1496–1535* (1962), Robert P. Adams associates him in this cause with the English humanists. His critique and theirs, Adams says, was of the illusions in policy-makers nurtured by the chivalric romances published by Caxton and issuing in the destructive military adventures of Henry VIII. Behind such adventurism lurked the threat of tyranny. James D. Tracy touches on the same chivalric ethos but as part of a study, the most complete so far, of Erasmus' relationship with the Netherlands-Burgundian court and government. The prince whom Erasmus acknowledged as his own was, after all, Charles of Burgundy, heir to a court where the language and values of chivalry were especially cultivated. Tracy brings out the moral rivalry between the aristocratic tutors of the young prince, who nurtured him on Arthurian romance and romanticized depictions of the conquerors of the ancient world, and Erasmus' Christian version of kingship.[12]

For Adams, writing in the Cold-War era, Erasmus and the English humanists opposed to chivalric illusions a 'critical realism,' modern in character. Their hopes and anxieties were finely balanced: favourable circumstances around 1516, including the presence of a pacific pope, Leo X, led Erasmus to hope for the restoration of the medieval *pax ecclesiae*; a bad outcome was, however, always possible, as in the modern Cold War. By the French war of 1523, all hope was gone in the triumph of *Realpolitik*.[13]

It is a weakness of Adams' study that he associates Erasmus too exclusively with English humanism. Can the *Institutio*, written for Charles of Burgundy, be fairly described as 'a part of

English humanist literature'? Adams' subjects are, in fact, Seebohm's group from his *Oxford Reformers* (Colet, More, and Erasmus), with the young Spaniard Juan Luis Vives added in. The
difficulty is not overcome by renaming the group the 'London
Reformers.' Colet and Erasmus were friends and intermittent correspondents from 1499; More and Erasmus were close when
Erasmus was writing his *Institutio* and More his *Utopia* (1515–16).
They had temporarily pinned their hopes on Henry VIII and the
English government, but their work of social criticism and propaganda for peace was far from making a 'unified whole' over the
long period, 1497–1530, as Adams suggests.[14]

Tracy demonstrates that, in the years after 1516, when, for
Adams, Erasmus and his English friends were still hoping for a
golden age of peace in Europe, Erasmus was attending closely to
military events in the Netherlands, and his comments were
mostly gloomy. He tacitly supported the unwillingness of the
Netherlands towns, and the estates which represented them, to
meet the fiscal demands of the Habsburg government and shared
their suspicions about its handling of the savage mercenary
bands, on which it traditionally relied, and its whole conduct of
the long-running war against Guelders. These suspicions, as
Tracy shows in a more recent work, were exaggerated, even
somewhat paranoid, as can happen with intellectuals in politics.
The exaggeration came in part from Erasmus' anti-chivalric
ideology, which mistrusted governors steeped, as he thought, 'in
the tyrannous traditions of an otiose aristocracy.'[15]

One might well ask whether, in the light of recent literature on
the subject, the whole humanist view of the aristocracy was not
an exaggeration. The historian of chivalry acknowledges the
horrible realities of late-medieval warfare as Erasmus and other
critics depicted them. Only the spoils of the countryside could
recompense fighting men whom the rulers used but could not
pay. Yet, attempts at reform often called on the very same stock of
chivalric ideas as justified the depredations. Reform turned the
marauder and freebooter into an officer of the prince under his
discipline.[16] At the same time, there was a shift towards intellectual pursuits and serious education among the aristocracy. The
picture of a European aristocracy unskilled, boorish, philistine,
marginalized, or in economic decline is now seen to be a distortion. Among the French nobility, royal service and patronage
were, by the sixteenth century, the surest way of securing family

interests. In Erasmus' own country, the nobility, though small in numbers, was in 1500 active and prominent in administration, both local and central; more remarkably, it did not thereafter disappear from the scene, despite the upheavals of the sixteenth century and the emergence of the bourgeois republic in the seventeenth.[17] Over all, the nobility was surviving as an energetic element in the body politic; its energy, along with its skills and values, including certainly its military values, were being harnessed by government. At that point criticism by Erasmus and his friends was cogent. Rulers, who through better administration were capable of more efficient, economical, and equitable government, were endangering those gains by subordinating domestic peace to foreign war. Of this the young Henry VIII, initially so attractive to the humanists as Adams shows, was the perfect example.[18]

The strengthening of the bureaucratic state, for both war and peace, was the main political event of early modern times. Any contextual reading of Erasmus' political thought should relate it to this development, but, surprisingly, little has been said on this theme. Too often Erasmus' ideas have been written off as abstract and moralistic, and the contrast of Erasmus and Machiavelli has been too ready to hand. Resisting these clichés, Wilhelm Maurer in a work of 1930 argued that Erasmus' moralizing itself enhanced the prospects of the territorial state, especially in post-Reformation Germany. The ethical demand on the ruler was to serve the state and be the educator of the people in their responsibilities to the *publica utilitas*. So he prepared the way for enlightened despotism and was predecessor to Frederick the Great.[19] Furthermore, since he made ruling a Christian calling not inferior to the monks,' he surrounded the state with a religious aura. This prefigured the subordination of church to state in the German territories.[20] There is a true perception in Maurer's monograph, Erasmus' positive acceptance of bureaucratic rulership, but there is also exaggeration. The way from the *Institutio* to enlightened despotism is long.

The one extended sequel to Maurer's monograph, James M. Estes' '*Officium principis christiani*: Erasmus and the Origins of the Protestant State Church' (1992), confirms and elaborates his demonstration of Erasmus' influence on the development of the territorial state. Estes, like Maurer, recognizes that for Erasmus, and notably in his *Institutio*, rule is a Christian calling and rulers have moral, indeed religious and spiritual, functions. His aim, he says, is 'not to provide a judicious assessment of Erasmus' political thought considered for its own sake but rather to show what others could take from that thought for their own purposes.'[21] It is, in fact, too much to say, as Estes does, that Erasmus described a relationship so intimate that 'the distinction between priest and prince, church and state, sacred and profane all but disappears.' Erasmus held, I believe, to distinctions between the gospel and keeping the worldly peace, between the Christian community of love and government, which must often settle for the lesser evil.[22] But the moral and religious responsibility of the ruler is the element in Erasmus' political thought which the Reformers in the German territorial states seized upon, and the significance of Estes' article as a contribution to German Reformation history lies in demonstrating that. Thus, they not only took up his idea of the prince as father to his people, providing for their welfare and keeping them in peace, but they extended his statement of the prince's religious duties to include the bringing in and preservation of right doctrine and pure worship.[23]

Maurer and Estes, in showing that Erasmus' model of the ethical, Christian ruler was determining for Reformers and rulers in the German territorial states, put paid to the notion that Erasmus' political thought was purely ethereal and had no influence on political realities. Indeed, these states and the free cites of the German Empire appealed to Erasmus because their relatively modest scale made possible a more personal bond between rulers and people. What of the larger political constructions of the time, above all the vast *monarchia* of the prince for whom the *Institutio* was written, Emperor Charles V, uniting under one ruler peoples diverse and remote? Writings in the 1950s in particular present Erasmus as universalist, cosmopolitan, and internationalist. 'Erasmus became,' wrote C.R. Thompson in 1955, 'and still remains, a symbol of the bond that links men of learning across parochial, national, and ideological boundaries.' Thompson's preferred expression for this side of Erasmus' thought is cosmopolitanism. Its sources lay in 'temperament, experience, reading, reflection, religion,' but especially the last. Politically, it inclined towards nostalgia for the lost *pax Romana* but, with the weakness of the actual German Empire in Erasmus' time, he advocated a 'policy of enlightened isolationism' for the independent states.[24]

Hans Treinen, in a doctoral dissertation prepared in one of

Europe's borderlands (the Saarland), links Erasmus to a political universalism, beginning with Dante, in which the empire was not dependent on church and papacy but immediate to God. Erasmus' universalism was apparent, negatively, in his rejection of nationalism and, positively, in his struggle for moral and social reform on the basis of a universalist ethic. He clung, says Treinen, to the hope of a general reform through empire and papacy, but his realistic awareness of the fragmentation of his time and his recognition that success depended on the behaviour of actual rulers left him sceptical. Treinen does not clinch the case for seeing Erasmus as a supporter of the universal empire of Charles V. He moves on to study Erasmus' critique of late-medieval society, where group egoisms shattered the sense of community and entrenched themselves behind a prevailing formalism and materialism, and his plan for restoring moral order by a return to the sources, biblical and classical. Church and state could advance this restoration only if each in its own sphere recognized Christian love as the supreme end and guide of its activity.[25] This approach, Treinen concludes, did not lead to the conflation of church and state as Maurer thought but to a recognition of the claims of the citizens, lay people, high and low, rich and poor, on the rulers of both state and church.[26] This conclusion is fair to Erasmus' commitment to social justice and perceptively presents him as a critic, in a fundamental way, of late-medieval culture.

If Treinen's study, which sets out to link Erasmus with the idea of universal empire, cannot make its case but finishes elsewhere, not surprisingly writers who begin more sceptically reach negative conclusions. In summary, those conclusions are: the religious function Erasmus attributed to the emperor, of guiding the people in the ways of the gospel, was in fact a critique of the instrumental and absolutist values propagated by the court jurists; Habsburg foreign policy was actually remote from Erasmus' admonitions; the association of Erasmus and Charles V was not close, the main intermediary being the Grand Chancellor Mercurino Gattinara, who was certainly affected by humanism but subordinated it and all else to the revival and restoration of the Christian empire, a priority foreign to Erasmus. Erasmus' dedication of his Suetonius to the dukes of Saxony (1517) expressed, not the imperial idea, but disenchantment with the old empire and complete scepticism about its revival. Gattinara failed to persuade Erasmus to prepare an edition of Dante's *Monarchia*, the handbook of world monarchy. In the late 1520s they agreed on the need to accommodate the Lutherans in Germany; the influence of Erasmus was strong on the imperial government's attempt, after Gattinara's death, at a compromise at the Diet of Augsburg (1530). On the universal empire, however, the two were always 'diametrically opposed.'[27]

Although a universal monarchy was not the best, or even a sure, way of securing it, peace was of supreme value to Erasmus, as everybody knows. His writings on war and peace were, more than those on any other subject, charged with emotion. In her edition of the *Querela pacis* of 1924, Elise Constantinescu Bagdat called this the least noticed of Erasmus' works. She could hardly say so today. Among the many authors on the subject, a fair consensus exists about Erasmus' views on war and peace: Erasmus may justly be called a pacifist, but his pacifism was not absolute. One can find expressions asserting radical non-violence and others accepting defensive or protective war. J.-C. Margolin says that his thought was essentially consistent, if not systematic, for he returned constantly to the same themes, using the same expressions 'drawn from his personal lexicon or that of his great models' in Christian or classical antiquity. By contrast, Pierre Brachin finds here incoherence and ambiguity. These, together with Erasmus' too rapid analyses and the lack of realism in his solutions, explain the failure of his initiatives for peace. Nevertheless, Brachin recognizes that circumstances helped determine his various responses.[28]

Erasmus faced a dilemma familiar in Christian history. He wanted rulers to accept the ideal of Christian community, formed by Word and sacrament and ruled by the norm of Christian love alone; at the same time, he was aware of the realities of political life and the hard choices they impose. The issue of just war encapsulated this dilemma, which was not mere intellectual incoherence. Writing in 1936, when the issue was urgent for many, Robert Regout saw in Erasmus' pure pacifist expressions deliberate exaggeration for bringing his readers over at least to middle ground. In fact, says Regout, Erasmus accepted the idea of just war in language that could have come from Vitoria or Grotius. This acceptance, José Fernandez has since said, was real but reluctant; the reluctance was due above all to the brutal nature of mercenary warfare, which Erasmus knew by experience. He resisted calling that kind of warfare Christian under any circumstances. He also, adds Rudolf Padberg, rejected Augustine's defence of war to protect or advance the Christian religion.[29]

The test-case was, of course, the war against the Turks, and essays by A.G. Weiler, together with his editing of Erasmus' *Utilissima consultatio de bello Turcis inferendo* (1530), elucidate Erasmus' response. He advocated armed defence against the Turks; otherwise, Christians conquered or threatened by conquest would be left without hope. But armed defence would be useless without a moral renewal within Christendom itself. That might even make Christianity, now disfigured by a barbarism equal to the Turks,' attractive and winning to the enemy. Thus Erasmus linked his response on the Turkish war to his hopes for Christian renewal and restoration. And underneath lay his characteristic fears: that the princes and warlords would use the emergency to further oppress the people and break down the institutions that protected them.[30]

His work on the Turkish war would be enough in itself to refute the assertion that Erasmus was remote from the struggles of his age. His thinking about peace had a more immediate context, the experience he shared of war and civil war in his own country. It is possible to fit his writings into the controversies over foreign policy and the factional conflicts within the Netherlands court and government. He supported the peace party. In her work of 1924, Elise Constantinescu Bagdat wrote about this in a tone of postwar disenchantment with peace programs tied to political factions and interests. Erasmus' patrons at the time of his writing the *Querela pacis*, she says, had ulterior motives in seeking for the Netherlands a peace with France. Charles of Burgundy (soon to be Emperor Charles V) inherited Spain on the death of his maternal grandfather, Ferdinand of Aragon, in 1516, and Spain offered glittering prizes to his Netherlands courtiers, if only they could secure peace with France. This was 'an ambiguous and insincere policy, a strange peace which gave the appearance of a conspiracy against the tranquillity of the people rather than the prospect of an easing of their lot.'[31]

Ferdinand Geldner's *Staatsauffassung und Fürstenlehre des Erasmus von Rotterdam* of 1930, which dismisses Constantinescu Bagdat as a 'doctrinaire pacifist,' judges Erasmus' orientation in Netherlands' politics from the standpoint of a hard doctrine of the state. Erasmus, Geldner says, adopted the wish of the Netherlands estates, the cities and the provinces, to protect their ancient privileges against the centralizing policies of the Burgundian dukes and their Habsburg successors. In this, he took over, not only their aspirations, but also their lack of political judgment (*Unverstand*), since, Geldner assumes, the future belonged to state-building in the interest of the whole people and not to the particularisms of the past. There is more than a touch of anachronism here.[32]

We can track Erasmus' connections in Netherlands politics through James Tracy's *Politics of Erasmus: A Pacifist Intellectual and His Political Milieu* (1978). Erasmus' first patron, Henry of Bergen, belonged to a family which supported the cause of the Habsburgs, introduced to the Netherlands by the marriage of Maximilian, emperor from 1493, to Mary, heiress of Burgundy. That cause became identified with enmity to France and an ambition to recover the Duchy of Guelders, once held by Burgundy, in short with a war policy. By the time Erasmus delivered his *Panegyricus* to Philip the Fair, Maximilian's and Mary's son, in 1504, he had moved to support the anti-imperial faction with its policy of restraint over Guelders and peace with France. By 1515, the peace party was in control of the Netherlands government, and Erasmus was close to it through his friend and patron the legist Jean Sauvage, Chancellor of Burgundy. He wrote *Querela pacis* on its behalf. But, Tracy concludes, Erasmus was not a mere hack, as Constantinescu Bagdat would have it, a naïve mouthpiece for his masters. He may for a time have overestimated their policy's chances of success, but his contemporary writings were full of criticisms, not least of their Spanish ambitions.[33] Those criticisms, as Tracy goes on to show, were bound up with his critique of the whole chivalric ethos already discussed. They were also related to crucial elements in his theology and ethics, Herding's liberty, love, and the cross. There were, it is obvious, theological and ethical determinants of Erasmus' responses to current events. We come to the edges of the 'normative vocabulary' of the time, of which Skinner speaks. We turn to studies which set Erasmus' political ideas within broader moral and intellectual frameworks, studies at the third level mentioned above.

III

Pride of place in most senses belongs to Pierre Mesnard (1900–69) and his *L'Essor de la philosophie politique au XVIe siècle*, first published in the anniversary year of 1936, a vast panorama of political thought from Machiavelli to Althusius. Erasmus follows Machiavelli in the second chapter of the work. Mesnard begins by rejecting the image of Erasmus as mere critic and pale sceptic and by setting himself to seek 'the moving import of his message and witness.' He finds this in what he calls, after Jacques Maritain, whose *Humanisme intégral* also appeared in 1936, 'integral humanism.'[34] The language of integration, synthesis, harmonization runs through Mesnard's whole account. Thus Erasmus' aim throughout his life was to base classical wisdom in Christian revelation, 'its true sustenance, its true climate.' Within historiography the link is with Pierre Imbart de la Tour and his definition of 'evangelism,' which Mesnard also calls 'reformism,' the pre-Reformation movement for the renewal of the church and culture, the regeneration of mankind by 'purifying religion and baptizing culture.'[35] This program of total renewal naturally embraced politics, on which Erasmus reflected throughout his life.

Integration is the theme of Mesnard's account of Erasmus' literary sources. There is mention of Cicero and of Plato through Cicero, of Lucian on tyrannicide and Aristotle's *Politics*, but, above all, of Seneca. On the other side were the gospels and other scriptures. The two influences very nearly balanced one another, the classical texts slightly more numerous, the religious texts more dynamic. The whole history of Erasmus' editions, mixing the profane and the sacred, demonstrates 'the manifest accord of these borrowings and the real unity to which they certainly tended in humanist politics.'[36]

Mesnard recognizes the other source of Erasmus' politics, the affairs of his own country, which, Mesnard appreciates, was the Burgundian Netherlands. Here integration enters in another form, the integration of theory and practice or, in language closer to that of Erasmus, the application of the gospel ideals to political reality. Mesnard uses the *Complaint of Peace* in particular to identify the behaviours which were the source of Peace's and Erasmus' complaints and the solutions he proposed. Among the constitutional options, Erasmus had, Mesnard says, decided for elective monarchy.[37]

In another context shortly, we will touch on Mesnard's view that Erasmus' understanding of law was deficient, but, for the moment, let us praise this classic presentation for its wholeness of view. A contemporary critic said of the book, into which we have taken only one narrow sounding – into the chapter on Erasmus – that 'the spirit of Erasmus traverses this vast work from one end to the other.'[38] Yet 'integral humanism' is a problematic concept. It cloaks with an expression tensions and cross-purposes, ambiguities and contradictions in humanism, the constant threat of fragmentation, which was especially real in the political sphere. One thinks of the distance between Erasmus and the imperial humanists, of court humanists and civic humanists, of the disunity sown by patriotisms of various kinds and, eventually, by the confessional divisions. And we must consider the tensions in Erasmus' thought itself, between the Christian community of love and the Christian duty of the ruler.

Eberhard von Koerber's *Die Staatstheorie des Erasmus von Rotterdam* of 1967, the most complete study of its subject to that time, applies a different vocabulary to Erasmus' political thought. The book belongs to a series on constitutional history, and Koerber makes clear in his foreword that its relation to Erasmus studies is of secondary interest; primary is establishing the sixteenth-century foundations, in humanism and, of course, in Erasmus, of the great age of *Staatsphilosophie* in the seventeenth century.[39] A chapter on 'Elements of Erasmus' thought about the state' demonstrates that Koerber's interest and Erasmus' thought are, in a sense, at oblique angles to one another.

Koerber recognizes that Erasmus was no philosopher and that speculative, abstract thought was foreign to him. Yet he organizes his own discussion under headings like 'idea of the state,' 'origin and end of the state,' 'justification of state power,' 'form of the state.' His purpose is to determine Erasmus' understanding of the state, its form, function, powers, and limits. Koerber himself sees an immediate difficulty. For an obvious reason, Erasmus never uses the word *Staat*. Its Latin 'equivalents' *respublica, civitas, patria* are not strictly equivalents and, in any case, Erasmus never defined them in relation to one another or indeed in a way that makes Koerber's attempt realizable. One cannot, Koerber concludes, determine, from his use of these terms, whether Erasmus was or was not foreshadowing the modern impersonal state. Koerber overcomes one difficulty, Erasmus' preference for a universal *respublica christiana* and his indifference to burgeoning nationalisms, by saying that each of the territorial states of his time was, for Erasmus, a *respublica christiana* in miniature.[40]

Koerber's approach, therefore, in beginning with definitions and structures and not with gospel imperatives, moral demands, and social values, gives a skewed view of Erasmus' thought. Despite that, it has the great virtue of correcting a widely held prejudice that Erasmus was anti-institutional and promoted a kind of gospel anarchy. In canvassing ideas like separation of powers   and representation, Erasmus was moving away from, though not leaving wholly behind, a personal conception of rule; indeed, in what he said about property and taxes, he drew a clear distinction between the private interest of the ruler and the public good. Erasmus was no mere moralist. 'For the practical thinker Erasmus, the pedagogue and psychologist, the concrete, the form and undogmatic pragmatism were much too important for his thought to be limited to Christian ethical attitudes.' There is here a true perception. For Koerber, Erasmus stood on the threshold of modern political thought, but, unlike the thinkers of the next two centuries, he had still to struggle free of the theocratic and scholastic structures of the Middle Ages. He recognized the ruler as office-holder but not yet the state as a 'legal and moral personality in institutional form.'[41] In developing this scheme, Koerber relies, not on empirical histories of the transition from medieval to modern political forms, but on writers in the German legal-historical tradition, especially Otto von Gierke with his idea of group personality and of the state itself as a form of legal personality; to the early modern period Gierke applied the 'concept of sovereign power' which, in Germany between 1525 and 1806, either absorbed or overrode the rights of corporations or fellowships within the state.[42]

In what follows, Koerber demonstrates a characteristic mixture of distortion, through too abstract and formal a presentation of the material, and a true sense for the practical thrust in Erasmus' thinking about policy and rule. Thus he surprisingly deals with Erasmus' peace thinking under the heading 'Legal foundations of the respublica christiana.' The key relationship, he argues, is between peace and law; with war comes lawlessness. This approach naturally allows Koerber to treat at length the question of just war, on which he considers Erasmus a political realist. It also brings him to the heart of Erasmus' social doctrine. War is especially the enemy of the weak and powerless, whose interests, Koerber has acknowledged in many places, Erasmus was committed to defend. Peace was ultimately a matter of social justice.[43]

In this way he comes, in this most formal of studies of Erasmus' political thought, to that 'preferential option for the poor' which Bradshaw later identifies as its core.

There are idealist foundations to what both Mesnard and Koerber have to say about the wider dimensions of Erasmus' political thought. The first links Erasmus to a humanism which seamlessly wove together classical wisdom and Christian revelation, without any of the rough edges of the historical reality. The second begins from an idea of the state, which, in its fullness at least, belonged to a later period, and presents it in a fairly formal and abstract way. R.W. Scribner's essay of 1970 on 'The Social Thought of Erasmus,' which seeks to relate Erasmus to the social values of his time, does not move away entirely from these foundations. Erasmus, Scribner argues, had a historical understanding of society and culture as subject to both development and decay. 'More, this is an awareness of man as living in a *saeculum*, a historically conditioned age created by the values and manner of life of the men who live in it.'[44] Thus the decline into barbarism after the classical age and the contemporary cultural revival, the descent into war and the struggle for peace have been events in human history, and the outcomes have been determined by the dominant values of the historical epochs concerned. The emphasis on values Erasmus owed to the *Devotio moderna*, the interest in cultural decay and restoration to Italian humanism, a double influence already much studied in the twentieth century.[45] Scribner links these ideas to a theory of the social itself which comes from Durkheim: truly social phenomena are 'the collective aspects of the beliefs, tendencies, and practices of a group.' Scribner, who later did pioneering work on the social character of the German Reformation, seems, without saying so explicitly, to take this definition of the 'Social Fact' as applying especially to the early modern era. 'It is clear that Erasmus has no concept of society in any modern sense. If his thought is directed towards the communal and the cultural, this should not surprise us. ... Rather than adopting the modern habit of seeking a classification of society according to economic or social relationships, we must take the more general notion of society as constituted by a common structure of values within which the relationships of its members are regulated. This common structure of values and presuppositions creates an impersonal area which sets the framework of conditions and behaviour against which individual lives are measured.'[46]

This notion of the social Erasmus shared with his contemporaries. He, and Thomas More for that matter, did not look predominantly for structural reforms. Rather they were recalling Christian society 'to fidelity to the values on which it was ostensibly based.' Erasmus demanded a sharp distinction between the private interests of the ruler, sexual, familial, and financial, and the public welfare, and he used his skills as a publicist to make his point. His action, Scribner concludes, was realistic on two counts: the shift from personal politics was a powerful tendency of the time; the appeal to a broad reading public recognized the emergence of a 'new social realm created by the press.'[47]

Scribner's views might be considered idealist because of the place he gives to values in defining societies. The paradox is that they make it possible for him to argue that Erasmus' call for a 'transvaluation of values' was the realistic way of going about reform in his society. Both Koerber and Scribner, from within their respective frameworks, the one starting from *Staatsphilosophie*, the other from a Durkheimian understanding of early modern society, conclude that, as a political thinker, Erasmus was a realist, above all because he sensed the main political trend of his age. This is to go against a strong tendency in Erasmus interpretation, as we shall see.

Closest to Skinner's concept of 'normative vocabulary' are the studies which link Erasmus' political thought to accepted literary and linguistic conventions, deriving in his time from the rhetorical tradition, classical and Christian. To this we will return at greater length in a later chapter. Marjorie O'Rourke Boyle has studied Erasmus' dedication to Henry VIII of his paraphrase of Luke, composed in 1523 on the eve of the French war which, for R.P. Adams, marked the collapse of humanist hopes for peace and reconstruction in Europe. Erasmus employed the metaphor of illness and therapy; he would cure the English king of the disease of war-mongering. The remedy was logotherapy, the humanizing and reconciling work of speech and conversation, which, said a Greek proverb, 'is the medicine for a burdened spirit.' Present, too, is the Christian doctrine of the *Logos*: 'The living conversation of the Father is Christ.'[48]

In an essay of 1982, 'The Literary Conventions of Erasmus' *Education of a Christian Prince*: Advice and Aphorism,' Richard F. Hardin has argued that the *Institutio* must be read, not, as Born and others had read it, as a continuous treatise, but as a collection of aphorisms, like the classical anthologies of proverbs or the wisdom books of the Bible. One may not look here for originality. The more ready-made the advice, the more easily could it be imbibed by those too busy or too distracted to take in anything subtle or complex. 'Each aphorism is a discrete observation; there is no necessary logic to the ordering of the whole, though it is possible to detect sequences of thought here and there. It is thus a method suitable for the rough-hewn "science" of kingship in the early sixteenth century.' This way of reading the book, Hardin says, puts claims about Erasmus' political naïvety in a new light. The aphoristic form brought out his scepticism over the pretensions of princes, which was part and parcel of his wish to go below the surface of things and discern the true realities.[49]

IV

The relation of Erasmus' ideas to political realities remains an issue, and their lack of political realism the most persistent charge against them. Ferdinand Geldner framed the charge in its most systematic form in his *Staatsauffassung und Fürstenlehre* (1930). His first sentence put the cards on the table: 'The state is the most important fact of historical life.' Thus Erasmus will be judged by his handling of political institutions and the place he gives to power. Geldner rightly sees that Erasmus rejected rule as domination; rather it was 'a stewardship, a benefit, a guardianship.' But, Geldner goes on, he could not get beyond that assertion, either in theory or in practice. In theory, he could find no reconciliation between the necessity for a coercive state and the gospel's 'anarchy of love.' He believed that the injunctions of the Sermon on the Mount applied without subtraction to the ruler but, says Geldner, to believe that is to break up the state. In practice, Erasmus could not envisage the institutional forms his moral preferences required. Indeed, he was caught in contradictions. He preferred a mixed constitution, but the demands he made of the ruler could be met only by an absolute monarch in a spirit of *christliche Patriarchalismus*. He accepted the idea of popular consent but could not give it force or content. The root of the difficulty was his moralizing of politics: 'For him the disposition is everything, the institution nothing.' In the Netherlands case, this ended in a 'maze': the absolute moral demands on the ruler, defence of the privileges of the ancient, exclusive estates, and a call for popular consent.[50]

Geldner is asking a lot in wanting from Erasmus an 'organic' bond between his acceptance of the state with its police powers and his insistence on the absolute demands of love. Pierre Mesnard has questioned Geldner's assumption of a 'necessary contradiction' here, though he concedes that the two planes are not easily aligned and the bridge in Erasmus' thought between Caesar's authority and Christ's is fragile. The difficulty in Mesnard's view arises from Erasmus' weak conception of law, as evidenced by his cavalier treatment of established rights, contracts, and treaties. Mesnard himself links this with Erasmus' indifference to institutions; on that point he and Geldner agree.[51] There is also common ground between Mesnard's remarks and the fuller study of Erasmus and the law by Guido Kisch: *Erasmus und die Jurisprudenz seiner Zeit* (1960). Kisch begins from Erasmus' reflection on the ancient dictum *Summum ius, summa iniuria* (greatest right, greatest wrong) in the *Adagia*. Erasmus' reading of this passage, Kisch says, conformed to his general moral and theological position: do not remain bound by the letter of the law but act in its spirit and according to the intention of the lawgiver. The standpoint is not juridical, but ethical. Human justice must realize the divine law. In this appreciation of Erasmus, Kisch is in line with Geldner. His understanding of Erasmus' mind has been shaped by the liberal Protestant writers Paul Wernle and Ernst Troeltsch, who identified Erasmus' *philosophia Christi* with the Sermon on the Mount, and by Walter Köhler and Augustin Renaudet with their conflation of the Christian and the humanist-classical in his idea of *humanitas*. General ethical considerations controlled Erasmus' handling of legal forms and institutions. 'Erasmus,' Kisch concludes, 'was no jurist.'[52]

If, as I will shortly argue, the anti-institutional bias in Erasmus' thought has been exaggerated, there already is a correction to the claimed contradiction between his pragmatism and his moral absolutism. Besides, is not the dilemma of love and power built into Christianity itself? Erasmus, like other Christian thinkers, must resolve the dilemma by one strategy or another. One strategy is the doctrine of the lesser evil. That was present in Erasmus as, more positively, was 'a sense of what can be achieved through the political order.'[53]

Nevertheless, the legend of Erasmus' political naïvety has lived sturdily on since Geldner's time. Those who, in line with a long tradition associating him with the Enlightenment, have seen him essentially as a rationalist, have accused him of overestimating the influence of rationality and enlightenment in politics. In a Basel commemorative essay of 1936, Rudolf Liechtenhan pictures him among the struggling statesmen 'like a schoolmaster.' His hopes in their peaceful initiatives around 1517 were excessive; by the 1520s disappointments had led to gloom, even despair. Only his grappling with the problem of the Turkish war in his last years produced a more sober realism. Johan Huizinga in another anniversary essay thought his mood swings evidence of an essentially apolitical spirit: 'He belonged to those who make their political judgments by giving free rein, on the one side, to their moral indignation and, on the other, to their idyllic vision of perfect happiness.'[54]

This line continued after World War 2. Indeed it could hardly be taken further than by Fritz Caspari in a well-known essay of 1947, 'Erasmus on the Social Functions of Christian Humanism.' Caspari shrewdly observes that, for all his sanguine claims, Erasmus is not able, finally, to harmonize the classical and Christian traditions, leaving a 'thinly veiled dichotomy.' But his expressions on Erasmus as a social thinker are sweeping. Erasmus' vision was 'abstract,' conveying a 'general impression of idealistic detachment,' and his optimism about human educability and rationality was unlimited. He did not face the problem of love and force; he was vague about institutions, subordinating the organizational to the ethical, as in his Platonist view of social hierarchy.[55] There is a lack of depth and, ultimately, of seriousness about this mind as Caspari depicts it.

The undermining of judgments like these came from various directions, some already indicated in this chapter: Erasmus' closeness, from time to time, to political affairs, especially in the Netherlands; his passionate critique of the warrior class; the grounding of his thought in value systems and social philosophies accepted as authoritative in his time. One not so far mentioned is his association with Thomas More's *Utopia*, whose depth and seriousness are not in doubt. In his famous introduction to *Utopia*, J.H. Hexter demonstrates the solidarity between More and Erasmus about everything that mattered. Between 1515 and 1520, in the years surrounding the publication of *Utopia* and the *Institutio*, More was Erasmus' 'most pertinacious and combative defender.'[56] The doctrine of *Utopia* was the doctrine of Erasmus, that religion was a matter of the heart, of the inner being, and a way of life, not a mere assent of the mind or a ritualistic observance. But to go so far is not to lay to rest the issue of Erasmus' political effectiveness or ineffectiveness, percipience or naïvety.

At that point Hexter himself separates sharply the Erasmus of the *Institutio* from the More of *Utopia*. Erasmus, he says, swung moodily between hope in and despair at the rulers he was exhorting through his writings. By contrast, More spoke, through his fictional traveller Raphael Hythlodaeus, in the clear, consistent tones of the Hebrew prophets. More saw the connections between the various social ills from which Europe suffered and proffered the vision of a society which removed the social pathology, above all by abolishing private property and making all wealth common. By contrast, Erasmus' 'social observations are invertebrate; they are unconnected, particular responses to social malaises, because he has only a very slight awareness of the interpenetration of social institutions and social structures.'[57] To this Richard Hardin has responded in his fashion.[58] One might also ask a more general question: why should an attempt to persuade actual rulers to behave responsibly be considered less realistic than the depiction of an imaginary society? Explaining the difference between the *Institutio* and *Utopia* requires something more subtle than Hexter's simple dichotomy between the platitudinous and the prophetic.

The most common solution has been to interpret *Utopia* in its two parts, the dialogue over the counselling of princes and Hythlodaeus' account of Utopian society itself, as a critique of the social thought of Christian or northern humanism, addressed by a humanist to his fellow-humanists. For Quentin Skinner, the weak point lay in the way Erasmus and his fellows handled the nobility. They recognized, in line with their Italian forebears, that virtue not lineage was the true source of nobility, but fudged the issue by claiming that the virtues were to be found naturally in the old nobility of birth. More cut across this comforting non sequitur, pressing the humanist criticism of the predominance of private over public interests to its radical conclusion and envisaging a society where lineage and wealth were entirely removed and equality prevailed. In sealing his case Skinner exaggerates; Erasmus, he says, adopted 'a thoroughly genial attitude towards the ruling classes.'[59] This is flatly contradicted by the forcefulness, even the savagery, of his criticism of those classes.

The bona fides of this line of argument has been enhanced by adding to it the contention that even the unpalatable features of Utopia as Hythlodaeus described it, the uniformity, lack of privacy, moral regulation, bureaucratic surveillance, ruthlessness in war, were used by More to demonstrate to his fellows the consequences of their moral and social prescriptions. *Utopia* was an exercise in applying Christian humanist values to the social system, and it produced both pleasing and unpleasing results. There are, More was saying, limits to ideal state-building and no straightforward application of moral norms to existing societies. On this showing, More's thinking was more analytical, his proposals more systematic, Erasmus' whole approach looser and more rhetorical.[60]

When put like that, the contrast is convincing. Nevertheless, Geldner's remark, repeated in different forms down to the time of Hexter and beyond, that, for Erasmus, disposition was everything and institutions nothing, cannot stand. In his introduction to the text of the *Institutio* in ASD, Otto Herding identifies as basic to Erasmus' political thought the distinction between the true prince and the tyrant. This was an ethical distinction of long standing in the Christian and classical literature. But, Herding goes on, in the last sections of the *Institutio* it was worked out on the practical issues of contemporary government. Thus, at a time of review and reform in the Netherlands tax system, Erasmus argued for reducing expenditure, restraining the excesses of the revenue agents and tax farmers, limiting taxes on the necessities of the poor (the reference was to the *accijns*, excises on beer, wine and grain milling), and increasing them on imported luxuries. The prescriptions were debatable, especially in their effects on the great port of Antwerp, but they did not come from a mind barely in touch with political and economic realities. They were aimed at counteracting inordinate inequalities of wealth.[61] Greater equality was a practical political program for Erasmus; community of goods, which he accepted for a long time as a Platonic and apostolic ideal, was not.[62] He was well capable of distinguishing between the two. The tasks he ascribed to the ruler met precisely the needs of a country prey to the sea and devastated four times by storms in the eight years before he wrote the *Institutio*: protecting vulnerable cities, diverting rivers, draining swamps, building public works. Fulfilling these tasks required, not moral platitudes, but technical and organizational skills.[63]

V

Although he directed his political writings mostly at the rulers of his time, Erasmus did not see social and political problems exclusively from their point of view. In his essay of 1936 Rudolf Liechtenhan speaks of a 'warm social feeling' breaking through Erasmus' writing on war; in war the weak, poor, and defenceless suffer most. This is the justification for Brendan Bradshaw's attributing to him a 'biblical populism' and liberation theology's 'preferential option for the poor against the rich.' Yet, studies of his social thought suggest that it had other sides. In the 1930s Augustin Renaudet argued that, while Erasmus condemned hoarders and cornerers and monopolies, including the colonial monopoly, he did not reject the newer forms of interest-taking; while he was suspicious of fraud and abuse among the merchants, he yet favoured enterprise of the kind he saw in the capitalist printers among whom he worked: 'Christ did not forbid ingenious activity, but the tyrannical care for gain.' Erasmus wished the state to intervene to check abuse and correct inequality but not to hamper productive work, as it often did, arbitrarily and ruinously, with tricks like the debasement of the coinage. He was conservative in seeking preference for agriculture and the necessary, rather than the luxurious, industries. The old urban economy was closest to his ideal. Thirty years after Renaudet, Jean-Claude Margolin gave a more reserved account. On the money question, he agrees with Renaudet that Erasmus did not condemn riches in themselves. He and the humanists could not master the money problem intellectually; they could only draw on their feelings and the Christian ethic, which condemned exploitation, while reflecting the equivocations of their own struggles for material support. On another social question, the position of women, Margolin says that Erasmus shared the prejudice of his time against women in leadership, but he did look for a more equal and open partnership in marriage, the foundation of lay society.[64]

On this question, only one book of importance had appeared up to the time when Margolin was writing (1973), and he was indebted to it. That was Elisabeth Schneider's *Das Bild der Frau im Werk des Erasmus von Rotterdam* of 1955. Schneider's mentor was the eminent Erasmian of Basel, Werner Kaegi, and the book reflected something of a consensus, emerging at that time, about how to interpret Erasmus. He was seen as the proponent of an essentially lay piety which corrected the medieval bias in favour of the monk's vocation over that of the lay people, and of celibacy and virginity over the married state. Erasmus' views on a particular social question, like the position of women, should be read in light of that statement of his significance. The consensus owed something to Renaudet, who in many studies attributed to Erasmus an alternative, very open, form of Christianity, and to Huizinga, who would have applauded Schneider's remark: 'In the first place, Erasmus was a religiously and morally sensitive man, in second place, a philologist; he was never a politician.' If she underestimates his sense for practicalities, Schneider rightly discerns Erasmus' starting-point: the world, civil society, with its various vocations, was the place where the Christian faith was lived out.[65]

Later studies, influenced by the rediscovery of the rhetorical tradition, have emphasized the ambiguities in Erasmus' position. Schneider's sources, the *Colloquies* and the treatises on marriage and widowhood, can, it is said, no longer be read as a straightforward expression of Erasmus' own attitudes. The form, in one case the dialogue and in the other the exposition of conventional opinions, 'muffles and disguises the authorial voice.' The ambiguities were, in part, of Erasmus' own contriving. Where he used female personifications, as of Folly in the *Moria* and of Peace in the *Querela pacis*, he produced a 'gender blurring' which at least opened the door to a fresh understanding of women's roles. What can be said otherwise about his views does not contradict Schneider and Margolin: he shared many contemporary prejudices about female character but saw marriage as a partnership and a kind of equality and rejected the double standard in sexual behaviour. He wrote his pedagogical works exclusively for boys but praised the liberal education of women. We see the liberalizing tendency of his mind breaking through the convenional crust.[66]

The liberalizing or progressive tendencies in Erasmus' social thought were treated in two essays representing rival standpoints of the Cold-War era, and with these we might draw the threads together. The one, Albert Salomon's 'Democracy and Religion in the Work of Erasmus' (1950), emanated from the religion and democracy section of the Columbia University Seminar on Religion, whose theme captured something of the mood of post-war America, the other, Günther Rudolph's 'Das sozialökonomische Denken des Erasmus von Rotterdam' (1969), from a research group on the history of German economic thought, which built on the entrenched Marxism of the old East Germany. Both associated Erasmus with the productive classes of early modern Europe, Salomon attributing to them and to him the 'inner-worldly asceticism' which Max Weber had seen as a source of modernization, Rudolph locating them at the turning-point between feudalism and early capitalism and depicting him as an antifeudal ideologist. In his rejection of serfdom, says Rudolph, he anticipated the peasant revolution of 1525 and the greater revolution of 1789. Salomon insists that Erasmus' social criticism and his utilitarianism and constitutionalism derived from his religious principles, which mean little to Rudolph, as well as from his observation of actual societies, especially the Netherlands. His religion, for Salomon as for Renaudet, was comprehensive, non-hierarchical, and free, with roots in late-medieval mysticism and lay piety. Rudolph's historiography lands Erasmus in a contradiction: in one sense apologist for the emerging bourgeoisie, who pilloried the misuse of private property rather than the institution itself, he was, in another sense, already its enemy, through his criticism of contemporary merchants, his attachment to the early Christian community of goods, and his connection with *Utopia*. Both Salomon and Rudolph have Erasmus pointing to a distant future, Salomon to democracy and free citizenship and Rudolph to the proletarian revolution. These claims are both implausible, though Rudolph's strains credulity more.[67]

VI

In the twentieth century, in the time between J.W. Allen's neglect of the subject and Brendan Bradshaw's startling claim to its contemporary relevance, Erasmus' political thought has been studied, more or less systematically, along three main lines, and fair measures of agreement have been reached. Since Born, scholarship has known of his literary sources; now there is a more subtle recognition of the rhetorical forms and conventions of discourse, which possibly makes our readings more uncertain or ambiguous. At the same time, research has illuminated the points of contact between his writings and contemporary events, the conflict of factions, the policy decisions, even the actual workings of public institutions. The *Institutio*, the *Querela pacis*, the political *Adagia*, the commentary on the Turkish war were not, it must by now be generally agreed, the work of a mere bookworm. To say that is not to contest that, for Erasmus, the starting-point was always ethical and theological, and the Christian affirmations had to be worked out in the political sphere, too. In my view, he was not unaware of the dilemmas this posed, of the exigencies of power and institutional inertia.

Every attempt at synthesis between these three lines, the literary and intellectual, the political and contextual, the ethical and theological, is bound to remain unstable, since tensions are unavoidable and probably unresolvable. In Christian terms, there is the tension between love and power, in Platonist terms that between the ideal and the actual. The edginess in Erasmus' political writings arises from the ambiguity of his relations, as a theologian, as a public intellectual, what Caspari calls a 'columnist,' with power.[68] Naturally, one beginning from the ethics of Jesus was stressed by daily awareness of how far his world was falling short. His own moral system was structured around the distinction between appearance and reality, shadow and substance. From tha arose his ferocious attacks on those elements in the social order that covered gross and brutal reality with the fairest or most glittering appearances. One can fairly link Erasmus to biblical populism, *Utopia*, and even a classic of liberation theology, as Bradshaw does, though the same man was, without strain of conscience, counsellor and correspondent of princes, heir to the sober moralists of the *Devotio moderna*, and admirer of Cicero, orator-philosopher-statesman of the dying Roman Republic.

THREE

Erasmus and His Audiences

❧

I

From late in the nineteenth century, there had been studies of Erasmus' influence in the different countries of Europe, of circles of his friends and admirers there, of the distribution of his books, especially in translation. They corrected the picture, common in the nineteenth century, of Erasmus as a solitary figure. Through the various Erasmian circles, the new works suggested, he became a force in European intellectual and cultural life. Accompanying this fresh view of Erasmus and his influence went an adjustment to how the lead-in to the Reformation should be seen. It crystallized in the idea of 'Préréforme,' a cluster of movements and influences aimed at religious reform and renewal. This idea entered the literature powerfully in Augustin Renaudet's work *Préréforme et humanisme à Paris pendant les premières guerres d'Italie (1494–1517)* of 1916. It involved humanism intimately with the religious aspirations of the time, while recognizing the latter's diversity; it defined a period in intellectual and cultural history of great interest in itself, though one preparatory also to the age of religious revolution that was to come, the age of Reformation and Counter-Reformation.

The idea was crucial to the work which, by its scale and elegance, validated the approach and encouraged new endeavours, Marcel Bataillon's *Erasme et l'Espagne*. Although later the idea became debatable and itself problematical, for Bataillon it was liberating.[1] That was because it recognizes reforming movements distinct from Protestantism. Christian Europe was not, so to speak, holding its breath for Luther's appearance. Similarly,

Catholic reform was not the work exclusively of the party of resistance to Protestantism, the negative, defensive Counter-Reformation party. Indeed, the spiritual movements of the beginning of the sixteenth century demonstrated the 'profound unity' of 'Préréforme,' Reformation, and Counter-Reformation. The connections were below the surface; the metaphor of depth appeals to Bataillon. The monastic reformers, he says, had 'deep affinities' with the Protestant Reformers that the word 'Counter-Reformation' obscures.[2]

The religious revival, the 'rénovation du sentiment religieux' of the sixteenth century, Bataillon adds, is not adequately captured by the word 'reform,' which is more applicable to change in the ecclesiastical or monastic institution. So he uses a broader terminology in his book, revealing the influence of Lucien Febvre's famous article of 1929, 'Une question mal posée: Les origines de la réforme française et le problème des causes de la réforme,' which argued the inadequacy of church abuses as an explanation of the great spiritual upheaval of the Reformation. Bataillon speaks rather of the European religious revolution of the sixteenth century of which the spiritual movements at the beginning of the century, Protestantism, and the Catholic Reformation were all aspects. To those early sixteenth-century spiritual movements he applies the name *évangélisme*, a term first used for movements of religious reform in France but applied generally by Bataillon. This was the powerhouse from which flowed the spiritual energies of the century. For Bataillon, the opening sixteenth century was a charged, expansive moment in the spiritual history of the West; from it came 'the most formidable thrust of the evangelical spirit since the formation of the church.' The form the movement took in Spain was illuminism, the movement of the *alumbrados*. It had two strains, the one more mystical, the other more biblical, but in both there was a rejection of religious formalism and a feeling of joy in free grace. At a key point in his discussion, Bataillon says that the solidarity of illuminism with the European religious revolution was beyond doubt. It made Spain ready for the grafting of Erasmian ideas. Metaphors of mobility or fluidity, the flow of currents or of sap, are favourites with Bataillon, but he recognizes that they have difficulties.[3]

Bataillon depicts a Spain open to the influence of Erasmus and also a Spain always resistant to outsiders, the Spain of antibodies. Of these two Spains much was to be said in the discussions

Bataillon's book aroused. Institutional reform was led from the top by Cardinal Jiménez de Cisneros, archbishop of Toledo and primate of Spain. From the University of Alcalá, a new foundation under his patronage, came the Polyglot Bible, a massive achievement of cooperative scholarship. European manuals of spirituality in translation were in vogue. They found audiences among women, Jewish converts (the 'new Christians'), the reformed orders, especially the Franciscans, and the high nobility. This was a spirituality 'avide de révelations' and touched with messianism. Erasmus received an eager hearing from the same audiences. Yet, barely had his New Testament arrived in Spain than a worker on the Polyglot, López Zúñiga, denounced as a heretic 'the idol of scholarly Europe,' a denunciation tinged with Spanish patriotism.[4]

Bataillon's Erasmus, who powerfully attracted some Spaniards and aroused enmity among others, was not Huizinga's Erasmus, an Enlightenment man before his time. This was not the Erasmus above all of the *Folly* or *Colloquies* but the Erasmus of the little devotional books and the biblical and patristic studies. Renaudet influenced Bataillon: Erasmus taught a religion of the spirit, of the free gifts of the spirit, with its consequences of tolerance and, to a degree, of religious liberty. Its enemies were formalism, ceremonialism, and dogmatism. For Bataillon this Christianity was Pauline, and he saw its distinctive motif in Paul's image of the body of Christ. Luther's condemnation in 1521, Bataillon says, did not force Erasmus into silence or neutrality. From Basel he wrote in many different forms on behalf of the gospel as he understood it; this was an 'évangélisme au-dessus de la mêlée.'[5]

The book is an exploration on a vast scale of the spiritual map of Spain in the sixteenth century. Like all great works of history, it poses questions of method, as we shall shortly see. Bataillon was convinced when he wrote it that only by entering into the detail could he capture the truth of his subject. He worked on it for fifteen years, from his late twenties to his early forties. Let us briefly follow the story from the time of Erasmus' first success in Spain. That success came, for Erasmus, suddenly and as a surprise, since Spain did not attract him. He became aware around 1524 of the enthusiasm of a Spanish elite for him. Already elsewhere the Luther affair was dividing the society and his own disciples and associates. Bataillon's analysis recognizes this fragmentation; the broad evangelical movement has become a third party, the Erasmian third party, holding to the unity of the church while keeping in touch with the moderate Lutherans. The Spanish Erasmians were a staunch support for this party. Deeper impulses were expressed by the publication in 1525 of a sensitive Castillian translation of Erasmus' work of personal piety, the *Enchiridion*, with its raising of interior religion over all that was formal and ceremonial and its challenge: 'Monachatus non est pietas,' the monkish is not the only form of piety. No book, Bataillon reports, had been such a publishing success since the coming of printing to Spain. Further, 'no book was better fitted to meet that need of religious and moral renewal which had come to light in illuminism.' Through it illuminism ceased to be a merely local movement and became linked to the European religious revolution.[6]

Before the end of the 1520s the opposition had rallied. At a conference of monks and theologians at Valladolid in 1527 the critics and supporters of Erasmus were evenly divided. Valladolid makes a kind of hinge in Bataillon's analysis. For a time the Erasmian influence persisted strongly in Spain; there was a spate of translations, with amendments protective of the monks and the ecclesiastical hierarchy. It provided Spain with an Erasmian literature well beyond what was available in France, where the Sorbonne was savage on Erasmian as well as Lutheran books. In the entourage of Charles V, Gattinara and Alfonso de Valdés joined the imperial idea, to which, as we have seen, Erasmus himself was cold, to proposals for church reform inspired by Erasmus. By the early 1530s, however, the Erasmians had disappeared from the court and the government, and the persecution of Erasmians in the Spanish church had begun. Few, Bataillon says, who played a role in what he calls 'la révolution érasmienne' escaped pursuit by or denunciation to the Inquisition. The few years of almost complete freedom, when the 'spiritual fermentation' of Erasmism carried the illuminist movement forward and gave it a new character, a 'pietism impregnated with reason,' gave way to a time of trouble when the Erasmians were suspected of being Lutherans, without Erasmus himself yet being officially condemned.[7]

Even the frank condemnation of Erasmus and the substantial suppression of his name and influence around 1560 did not mean an end to Erasmism. Bataillon knows the difficulty of tracing subterranean currents. In a broad movement in favour of interior religion over ritualism, which was alive still in the second half of the sixteenth century when Erasmus himself was no longer recognized, how may one separate out the Erasmian strand? Bataillon is confident enough to say about the continuing influence of Erasmus' *Modus orandi*: 'He exercised a positive influence in showing how to pray in spirit.' The difficulty is greater still for secular literature, but Bataillon believed, and continued to believe, that Cervantes drew a thinned Erasmism from the Spanish ambience of his time.[8]

In a challenging sentence of his 'Conclusion,' Bataillon sums up the larger themes of his work, with a justification of both his title *Erasme et l'Espagne* and his subtitle 'Recherches sur l'histoire spirituelle du XVIe siècle': 'It is not at all surprising if Erasmus, interpreter of the best aspirations of the "Préréforme," has been adopted by the *illuminés* of Castile, if Erasmism has taken the place here of Protestant Reformation, if some of the greatest Spanish *spirituels* of the Counter-Reformation – an Arias Montano, a Luis de Léon – have forgiven Erasmus his "Monachatus non est pietas" in gratitude for the lessons in interior religion he gave to so many monks.' For the late-medieval spiritual movements, calling both lay and clerical people away from ritualism to a Christianity of the inner life, Erasmus was both conduit and source. The sap (a favourite metaphor, as we have seen) flowing in illuminism and drawing vigour above all from the 'new Christians' bound the Erasmian graft, brought from the north, to the Spanish trunk. This mix of Erasmism and illuminism was the counterpart in Spain of the Protestant Reformation of the north. It also fed the spirituality of the Counter-Reformation. On this account, Bataillon might well conclude that there came from Erasmus as he understood him 'un profond mouvement culturel' which carried far.[9]

Bataillon's great work, published when Spain was riven by a cruel civil war, won both admiration and critical appraisal, although commentators as late as the second half of the 1980s regretted a lack of fundamental criticism.[10] Erasmians who, in Menéndez y Pelayo's massive *Historia de los heterodoxos españoles* (second edition, seven volumes, Madrid 1911–32), appeared as heterodox and alien were now brought close to the heart of Spanish spirituality, without losing their centrality in the European religious renovation. Critics asked above all these questions. Did Bataillon give too dominant or too exclusive a position to Erasmism? Did he shift the balance of influences too far in Erasmus' direction? Had he understated the other possibilities? In prefaces to later editions, the Spanish editions of 1950 and 1966 and an unrealized second French edition, and in other writings, Bataillon responded, in what he sometimes called 'un examen de conscience,' to critics and commentators, so that the history of his book became a continuing soliloquy by the author and dialogue with others, all the pieces now being brought together posthumously by Daniel Devoto and Charles Amiel in a final three-volume edition of 1991 (Droz, Geneva).[11] In later years, Bataillon referred frequently to a long review article of 1952 on the first Spanish edition, in which his friend Eugenio Asensio had spelled out a case which Bataillon's examination of conscience, reported in his preface to that edition, had already accepted, that he had attributed to Erasmism ideas not particular to Erasmus: 'I ran the risk of confusions in placing the name of Erasmus in the title of a book where I dealt with Erasmus and other things: Erasmus and co.' His subject was like a frontier zone where the frontiers were imprecise.[12]

Asensio recognizes the distinctiveness in its time of Bataillon's view of Erasmus – this was an 'Erasmo pietista' – and largely accepts it. The problem comes from unpicking the skein of history to identify and give prominence to a single strand, Erasmus and Erasmism. The aim should be to restore the whole skein and give religious history 'its natural complexity.' So Asensio's article weaves Erasmus in with three other spiritual lineages, the biblicism found among Jews, *conversos*, and old Christians in fifteenth- and sixteenth-century Spain, Franciscan spirituality, and religious ideas come from the Italy of the Renaissance. On the first, Asensio says that Erasmus' biblical criticism found in Spain disciples 'more timid than the master' and, in any case, there was in the peninsula a long-standing, essentially Hebraic, tradition of biblical study. This is a reminder that the attitudes of men like Arias Montano and Luis de Léon, for all their strong attachment to Erasmus, 'could be learned from many masters.' The Pauline image of Christ's mystical body, which Bataillon saw as typically Erasmian and as, possibly, a reaction against the exclusiveness of old Christians, could, Asensio comments, be given different uses, including exclusivist ones.[13] On the second, the Franciscan influence, Asensio considers it 'much more powerful and abundant' than the Erasmian one in the unfolding of the illuminist movement. Some branches of illuminism had no contact with Erasmus, others were in touch with both Erasmus and Franciscan or other forms of late-medieval spirituality. On the third, Asensio sums up: 'The Erasmians mixed without scruple their taste for Italy and their taste for Erasmus.' Savonarola had special attraction. So the countless ramifications of the Erasmian tree intertwined themselves with neighbouring plants of many kinds.[14]

Asensio's article corrected Bataillon's singular emphasis on Erasmus by attending, on the one hand, to longer-standing, medieval influences and, on the other, to problems and situations peculiar to Spain. Already in his preface of 1950, Bataillon had acknowledged the justice of the first claim: more and more he accepted that the roots of 'le modernisme érasmien' were in the fifteenth century or even earlier. He had meant his cross-section of the spiritual history of the sixteenth century to be open to both the past and the future. In his much later (1970s) notes for a new edition, he confessed that when in 1936, as professor of Spanish in Algiers, he was putting the finishing touches to his work, he did not notice the moves already begun, especially by Etienne Gilson, to associate humanism and Erasmus with medieval culture, that of the twelfth century in particular, and, indeed, to question fixed entities like 'Middle Ages' and 'humanism' altogether.[15] As for the second claim, Bataillon was engaged, also in 1950, in dialogue with the Spanish historian Américo Castro over the 'vertical' (ie the Spanish) and the 'horizontal' (ie the European) dimensions of the Erasmian incursion into Spain. For Castro, it was not simply a matter of discovering the further sources of the religion called 'Erasmian.' He also argued that, in face of the essential structures of the Spanish historical experience, Erasmism could be only an episode in Spanish history, brief and transient. In response, Bataillon vigorously defended the European references of his subject. Not only nations, whose historic structures can in any case be problematical, but also historical periods have a characteristic unity. He stood by the linking of Erasmus and Spanish Erasmianism to the larger European religious renovation, with its aversion to the hierarchical and merely external and ceremonial, and its drive for inner renewal.[16]

This debate led Bataillon to a deeper introspection. He recognized, as he could not have done in 1937 when he still believed that, in plunging into the sources (books, letters, inquisitorial records) in all their multiplicity, he could arrive at an objective, definite picture of the Spanish Erasmians and their opponents, that 'my vision of that past was governed by *our* present and by *my* position in that present.' He had been influenced by Raymond Aron's *Introduction à la philosophie de l'histoire: Essai sur les limites de l'objectivité historique* of 1938. He was sensitive to the suggestion that he wrote 'in common cause' with the Erasmians. He did not deny that his sympathy was with Erasmus and the Erasmians rather than with the intolerant theocrats, their adversaries. Raised on the margins of Catholicism, he had at twenty been prepared to respond to Erasmian Paulinism by a teacher of Greek enthusiastic about Paul and the transition from Hellenism to Christianity. He was writing his book when the ancient conflicts between Protestant and Catholic were being assuaged and Christianity was reviving as a spiritual force, not merely as 'force de tradition et de police.' He was as a young man ready for his encounter with Erasmus. He liked to quote a remark of Renan, whom he admired and to whom he consecrated later studies: 'One should write only of what one loves.'[17]

Despite his revisions and introspections, which are themselves a tribute to his 'unbending intellectual honesty' and a relentless self-questioning learned from Montaigne, Bataillon held unshaken to the two main foundations of his work, his view of Erasmus as, not rationalist, sceptical, or indifferent, but deeply religious, and his contention that this man stood 'at the centre of the living currents of Christianity in his time.'[18] A later debate tested these propositions further. In 1970 J.C. Nieto published a study of Juan de Valdés, a profound influence on evangelical circles in both Spain and Italy, whom Bataillon had included among his Erasmians. In 1925 Bataillon himself had discovered and published in facsimile a copy of Valdés' first work, the *Diálogo de doctrina cristiana*, and had emphasized its rejection of external religiosity, remarking that such rejection was not specifically illuminist, Lutheran, or Erasmian but 'common to all religions of the spirit.' The expression, which Nieto questioned and Bataillon regretted, recalls Renaudet, but Bataillon thought he might have taken it from the title of a book by the French liberal Protestant Auguste Sabatier, *Les religions d'autorité et la religion de l'esprit*. Bataillon's regret was over the phenomenology of religion implied in the expression, but he stood by what he had said in *Erasme et l'Espagne* about the solidarity of Spanish illuminism with the wider European religious revolution, and that included a responsiveness to Erasmus.[19] This is what Nieto denies in the influential case of Juan de Valdés. He attributes to Valdés a matured and well-structured theology, a radical theocentrism, reminiscent of but not dependent on Luther's, in which lost humanity is wholly dependent on free grace. Previous writers have, he says, made Valdés a spiritualist, subjective, individualist, mystical. On that basis, he could be linked to Erasmus. For Nieto, Valdés' theological affinities were not with Erasmus but with a strain of thought within illuminism that was scriptural, centred on grace and, in effect, espousing justification by faith, even before Luther. On this view, Valdés owed nothing to Erasmus, though, at a time when he was widely in favour in Spain, using his name to disguise Valdés' more radical and dangerous ideas. That represents a marked diminishing of Erasmus' purported influence.[20]

Nieto's case depends in part on a certain interpretation of Erasmus, based in turn on a certain reading of the *Enchiridion* and some of the *Colloquies*. The religious thought of this Erasmus is subjectivist, anthropocentric, spiritualizing in a Neoplatonist way. Naturally, the robust biblicism of Nieto's Valdés could not come from this quarter.[21] The case also turns on argument about the contacts of individuals and the demonstrable influence of books. At that level Carlos Gilly gave a new twist by demonstrating that passages in Valdés' *Diálogo* were taken directly from works of Luther and, possibly, other Reformers. Gilly was provoked by Nieto's reluctance even to consider the possibility of Lutheran influence on Valdés and the *alumbrados*. He suggests arguments for the latter possibility; the effect is to reduce the independence and, to a degree, the importance of the illuminist movement in Spain. Naturally, Gilly's argument, like Nieto's, also diminishes the influence of Erasmus and the influence of Spanish Erasmism, although he recognizes in Valdés what smacks of Erasmus' 'Monachatus non est pietas' and his indifference to external things. Gilly acknowledges that Bataillon had been prepared to give ground but without surrendering the substance of his case.[22]

Erasmus' influence in Spain has remained an open question for Spanish historians and Hispanicists.[23] Criticism, suggesting that Bataillon split the Spanish intellectual world too simply into two camps, the humanist, Erasmian, and progressive and the anti-Erasmian, scholastic, and reactionary, carries conviction. Rather,

Spanish intellectuals discriminated among the Erasmian influences, most sympathizing with his pietistic ideals, on the one
hand, and remaining suspicious of his philological criticism of the
Bible, on the other.[24] Thus, his Spanish readers were active and dis-
criminating, not merely receptive. Our interest is, of course, in the
view of Erasmus that the different arguments represent. Bataillon
did not altogether reject the spiritualizing Erasmus depicted by
Nieto. But the Paulinism of Bataillon's Erasmus had not been
drained off into subjectivism and an optimistic, man-centred spirituality. Bataillon's Erasmus centred his religion on Christ; all, lay
people as well as clerics, participated in the life of his body and
shared his grace. Why might not, therefore, this vision of union
with Christ have provided for a thinker like Valdés a way to his
eventual positions? Bataillon preserved for Erasmus wider possibilities of influence than Nieto's more pallid figure allowed.[25]

II

A cluster or constellation would be an apt image for Bataillon's
understanding of the religious revolution of the sixteenth century. For him, Erasmus was close to the centre of the cluster. A
work, more or less contemporary with his and also influenced by
Renaudet, adopted the rival image of linear development. This
was *Erasme et les débuts de la Réforme française (1517–1536)* by the
young English graduate student Margaret Mann. The image of a
line of development was in part determined by the purpose of
her study, which was to assess the character and limits of Erasmus' influence on the French Reformers. In its way, it was a traditional question, defined by the end-point of the development, the
Reformed religion. Mann's conclusions are foreshadowed in her
early remark: the Reformers all learned from Erasmus, but they
also asked from him more than he could give.[26]

Following Henri Hauser's *Etudes sur la Réforme française*, Mann
accepts that between French humanism and the impulse for religious reform there was a close alliance, up to the 1530s. She
adopts Renaudet's idea of 'Préréforme' more or less as he presents it. But, she says, early differences between Erasmus and
Lefèvre d'Etaples, especially over biblical exegesis, prefigured
the eventual break between humanism and the Reformation.
Erasmus' bold and clear annotations to the New Testament
'obliged the reader to look at the text with the eyes of reason.'

Lefèvre's approach to the scriptures was more mystical and more theological and, initially, more traditionalist. Mann has produced a paradox: Erasmus, with his search for a simple, rational faith for lay people, appeared the more revolutionary; yet, it was Lefèvre who anticipated the Reformers. The conclusion of her account of a textual controversy between Erasmus and Lefèvre finds a resemblance between Lefèvre's and Luther's responses to Erasmus. For both he remained on the surface of the text, unresponsive to the deeper levels of inspiration. In this controversy, therefore, lay 'the germ of some great divergences.'[27]

Certainly, in his approach to scripture, Lefèvre drew, over time, closer to Erasmus. Yet, even at the moment of their greatest convergence, Mann sees between them still differences which would, under the impact of the Reformation in Germany and Switzerland, grow ever wider. The core difference, Mann considers, was on the question of human nature. In Erasmus' approach to the Bible, there was, for Lefèvre and the Reformers, a 'pride of knowing' which betrayed an overconfidence in human capacities. By the mid-1520s Luther's influence was, she concludes, apparent on Lefèvre and his patron Margaret of Angoulême. For the mystic Margaret, Erasmus' practical, undogmatic religion was too dry and unspiritual. She and Lefèvre were preparing the ground for the coming of Luther to France, though, one must say, their religion, as Mann depicts it, mystical, Neoplatonic, avid for sinking into the love of God, was very un-Lutheran.[28]

First with Guillaume Farel, zealous missioner for the Reformation, and then with Calvin the break between humanism and Reformation was complete. Mann entitles her final chapter 'Erasmus and Calvin: Humanism Judged by the Reformation (1530–1536).' Calvin was formed by Erasmian humanism but, by the time of the first publication of his *Institutes* in 1536, he would accept from Erasmus only the fruits of his erudition. On all matters of religion and theology, he had broken from him. Against humanist relativism, there stood 'la magnifique certitude de Calvin.'[29] There is a kind of teleology in this account: the break was inevitable, embedded in the story from the beginning. Or, one might say: the story took its meaning from its ending.

Mann's account rests on a view of Erasmus which she owes, above all, to Renaudet. Erasmus, she says, never diverged from the faith he stated early in the *Enchiridion*, 'a faith lively, peaceable and simple which, essentially intellectual, takes its source in ancient and evangelical wisdom and is expressed through love.' His bent was towards the rational and logical. At one point, Mann uses language familiar from liberal theology: 'Modern man, he tries to be guided by the facts.'[30] This image of Erasmus, popular in nineteenth-century liberalism and the Enlightenment, has been overshadowed in recent scholarship.

Mann's book has retained respect (reinforced by the distinction of her later contributions, as Margaret Mann Phillips, to Erasmus studies), although both the view of Erasmus in her 1936 book and her way of linking him to the Reformation have become problematical. In a lecture of 1986, J.-C. Margolin pays tribute to the book and to Renaudet's inspiration. Margolin accepts and reformulates Mann's distinction between Lefèvre, 'spiritual son of Platonists and Neoplatonists, but also of neo-Pythagoreans at home with abstract ideas,' and Erasmus, 'spiritual son of the Brothers of the Common Life and the *Devotio moderna*,' who always remained attached, 'even in his purest spiritual transports, to the sensual reality of the world and of men.' Margolin speaks even of 'un humanisme chrétien à la française' and 'un humanisme chrétien à la néerlandaise.' Theologically, the difference was between exalting the divinity of Christ and clinging to his humanity. The idea of the imitation of Christ was more important to Erasmus than to Lefèvre.[31]

Yet, between Mann's book and Margolin's essay there have been changes. Renaudet's scheme has fragmented and the idea of 'Préréforme' has been eclipsed. Margolin's interest is not the somewhat teleological one of seeing where Erasmus stood in relation to an end-point, the French Reformation of Farel and Calvin. Rather it is in Erasmus' connections with political and cultural circles in France and his significance for French culture. This interest extends to literary figures of later generations, beginning with Rabelais and Montaigne. Margolin discerns an Erasmian stream in French culture, an ethical and empirical tradition counterbalancing tendencies towards abstraction and system in French thought.[32]

The pattern in Mann's book is a sequential one: humanism and 'Préréforme,' then Reformation. It has been readily applicable to other countries like Germany, perhaps too readily applicable. In an address at Freiburg in 1937, Gerhard Ritter, Luther biographer and student of late-medieval humanism and scholasticism, frankly avowed his intention of assessing Erasmus from a Lutheran standpoint. Ritter presents Erasmus' aspirations sympathetically without sharing them or believing them realizable in sixteenth-century circumstances. It was courageous, in the Freiburg of 1937, to show sympathy for ideas Ritter reckoned to be sources of modern liberalism. Erasmus' hopes, he says, were in the recovery of an early Christianity which caught up the best values and aspirations of the ancient pagan world. He goes on: the religious content of his writings, not his more technical scholarly work, made Erasmus attractive to the German intellectuals and humanists, but they did not fully grasp his subtle combining of the Christian and the antique. They associated him with the yearnings of the German people for the simplification and purification of contemporary Christianity. Ritter's question is determined by his starting-point, which is really the end-point of his story, Luther's emergence as Reformer: was the turbulence of German life to be stilled by reforms defined by Erasmus' classical-Christian humanism? Or, could a profoundly secularized church be healed through a humanist revision of the theological curriculum? Ritter's answer lies in his adoption of the familiar periodization: at the moment of Erasmus' greatest prominence, Luther appeared. Unlike Luther, Erasmus had no understanding of German nationalism. Following Ferdinand Geldner, Ritter sees in Erasmus' political thought a critique of absolutism, determined partly by the straightforward application of Christian principles to political life, which Luther would have condemned as *Schwärmerei*, and partly by the political outlook of the Netherlands bourgeoisie, a seed-bed of modern liberalism.[33]

Later writers, without adopting Ritter's starting-point that all was preparatory to, while falling short of, Luther's meeting of Germany's religious needs, confirmed that Erasmus' sharing in their campaign for religious renewal was the key to his acceptance by the German intellectuals. Closest to Ritter's is Lewis Spitz's model of a German humanist movement in its maturity covering three generations. To this, in line with Margaret Mann, he finds parallels in France, and also in England. The third generation passed beyond its predecessors' longing for religious renewal and for liberation from Italian cultural domination to rally around Luther and become 'the defenders and builders of the Protestant church,' just as Farel and Calvin had 'superseded' the generation of Budé and Lefèvre.[34] A more thoroughgoing version of this insight contends that, while Luther's initial prominence, which was decisive for the eventual success of his

Reformation, depended on the vigorous support of the German humanists and their sodalities, the humanists soon split, some following Luther into religious revolution, others rediscovering their attachment to the old church. This split was along generational lines. Placed in this framework, Erasmus is seen, along with others of his generation like Pirckheimer and Mutianus Rufus, as committed essentially to a literary and scholarly vocation, with a religiosity genuine and appealing – in its dependence on the Fathers, for example – yet lacking in robustness.[35]

It has proved impossible to disentangle Erasmus' influence and standing in Germany from the ramifications of the Luther affair. Reading back from Luther's domination of German public opinion to Erasmus' brief time of prominence has been unavoidable. Luther's German Bible, for example, is seen as the end-point of the development which began with Erasmus' New Testament of 1516 and his argument for the vernacular scriptures. Even a prudent student of this development can say that Luther's New Testament is not a mere version but 'the pure gospel in German, no German interpretation but the Bible itself for the Germans.'[36] The famous title-page of 1521, 'The Divine Mill,' illustrates the sequential view of their relationship: Erasmus gathers the flour milled from the grain of the gospel and Luther bakes it, that is, issues through his books the truths first brought out by Erasmus.[37]

Only a study of the spread of Erasmus' writings in German translation can provide a sober estimate of his place in German history in the critical and turbulent years around 1520. Since 1983 we have had this, for translations of his biblical and polemical works, in Heinz Holeczek's *Erasmus Deutsch*. Erasmus' showing was surprisingly strong. Here is empirical support for those historians who, a hundred years before Holeczek, spoke of Erasmus as a power in the land. As an author in German, he was outstripped only by Luther. Strikingly, the curves in the publishing histories of the two ran parallel, each peaking at 1521–2. Of vernacular editions of Erasmus' works during his lifetime, the German outnumbered those of all other nations combined.[38]

Holeczek notes certain concentrations – in time (the years 1520–2, as we have seen), in places, and in people. The spread was strongest in the south Rhineland from Mainz to Freiburg, in the hinterlands of imperial cities, like Augsburg and Nuremberg, and in Saxony. Names recur – for example, those of Georg Spalatin, the associate of Luther and the Elector Frederick of Saxony, and Leo Jud, the Zürich Reformer. Naturally, translators tailored editions to meet their own objectives. The effort of translating Erasmus belonged to a fluid and diverse reforming movement with broad public appeal, which split into diverging streams only in the mid-1520s. Holeczek's scheme is a sequential one in a limited sense only. Rather he depicts a pattern of reforming impulses, different but interacting with one another. The whole movement was biblicist. Why, Holeczek asks, did Jud begin his translatios of Erasmus' *Paraphrases* with the Pauline epistles? Already, he replies, Luther had made Paul central to the theological discussion and reforming work of the time.[39]

As the German Reformation passed through various stages, Erasmus remained an influential figure, if not so central as in 1520–1. Three contributions to a colloquium at Amsterdam in 1996 (by Eugène Honée, Heribert Smolinsky, and Barbara Henze, respectively) illustrate the point. Participants in the German Reichstags between 1521 and 1530 (Honée's article shows) sought his advice. The aim initially was, through a commission of learned men, to discriminate between what was sound and what unsound in Luther's teaching. Then, after the formation of religious parties in the Empire around 1526, the search was for an accommodation between them. The influence, direct or indirect, of Erasmus' writings of the early 1520s can be traced all through.

The values he represented in these difficult and long-unresolved negotiations – moderation and mildness, readiness to let go what was not essential to Christian piety, fairness and reasonableness (*aequitas*) – appeared also in the influence he exercised in a particular Catholic territory, the united duchies of Jülich, Cleves, and Berg on the lower Rhine. The point of Smolinsky's article in this collection is to show how the administration of the duchies used those ideas as a defence against the disintegration which, in sixteenth-century circumstances in and around the duchies, always threatened. They were part and parcel of the politics of the time. Erasmian values, aimed above all at removing the causes of disunity and disaffection, helped shape, as has long been recognized, the church ordinances of 1532–3 in the duchies. The same was true of their attempted revision in the 1560s, but circumstances, German and European, had by then so changed, more confrontational and less irenic attitudes were so coming to prevail, that the new ordinances were never implemented. The Erasmian generation had passed.

The more philosophical or theological underpinnings of Erasmian irenicism (we come to Henze's article) were developed by
Georg Cassander (1513/15–66) and Georg Witzel (1501–73), the
first of whom in particular had a hand in the Cleves ordinances.
The key virtue on their way to church reunion, as with Erasmus
himself, was *moderatio*, which required of the parties mutual
accommodation. Distinguishing between the essential and the
inessential in faith should come, not by the assertion of authority,
but by a common search for consensus, guided by Christian love
and the Holy Spirit. In these German Catholic circles, solutions
were sought for religious conflict that can fairly be called 'Erasmian.' In their search for unity, they had something in common
with the Reformers and rulers in the Protestant territories studied
by Maurer and Estes. There is an intersection between these
inquiries, if not identity.[40]

III

Prominent in the literature on Erasmus' audiences in Spain,
France, and Germany has been a certain view of the movements
for religious reform and renewal in the years around Luther's
first appearance on the public stage in 1517. Despite notable differences from national setting to national setting, they have been
given a common character and, for a time at least, the common
name of 'Préréforme,' to which Renaudet's thesis of 1916 gave
currency. Included is a reaction against excessive formalism and
ceremonialism, a drive for greater inwardness and authenticity, a
trust in the biblical record and testimony, whether it be handled
critically or conservatively.

Before Renaudet, Dutch historians had claimed for the pre-
Reformation Netherlands, however defined, a distinctive form of
religious life, biblical rather than scholastic, lay rather than clerical, ethical rather than dogmatic, and moderate, even tolerant.
Erasmus could easily be associated with this Netherlandish religious atmosphere. The claim was, further, that it and he helped
determine the distinctive character of the Dutch Reformation,
which was by some too exclusively connected to Calvinism. The
Netherlands were, it was said, the pioneer in the movements later
called the 'Préréforme,' and Dutch historians pioneered the
studying of them.

Modern scholarship has not erased this picture entirely, but it is much faded and viewed mostly with scepticism. Historians have demonstrated the continuing strength of the medieval structures, intellectual and ecclesiastical, and of traditional piety. The shock to those structures and that piety came, not from native figures and forces around 1500, but from Luther after 1520. Yet, as Holeczek showed for Germany itself, the situation was fluid in the 1520s and confessional divisions and definitions still lay far in the future. Lucien Febvre's article of 1929, which had inspired Bataillon, criticized both a nationalist and a prematurely confessional interpretation of the French Reformation; it supported the case also for a Netherlands Reformation drawing on many sources not yet sharply distinguished from one another. Erasmus had an influence, interwoven with that of others. Reformers could call on the *Enchiridion* and his satirical or biblical works as well as on Luther's writings on Christian freedom or the Babylonian captivity of the church. Earlier movements, embedded in medieval culture and spirituality, could be reinterpreted and given a new character. In that way a reformist tradition could be created and even the historiography of a much later time anticipated. In an article on 'Erasmus en de nederlandse Reformatie' (1969), G.J. Hoenderdaal has suggested that there was, in the manner of the modern flow-chart, not a direct, but a dotted line between Erasmus' anti-ceremonialism and the 'sacramentarian' questioning of the sacraments and between his defence of free will and the Anabaptist teachings on holiness.[41]

The nature of the *Devotio moderna* and its expression above all through the Brothers of the Common Life has been an important issue in these debates. Before World War 1 Paul Mestwerdt had written of Italian humanism and the *Devotio moderna* as together shaping the mind of Erasmus. Despite the apparent radicalism of the one and the apparent conservatism of the other, they had common features: biblicism, a certain individualism, a practical and ethical rather than a dogmatic or institutional understanding of Christianity. Albert Hyma made large claims for the Brethren's cultural and religious significance. More recent scholarship has moderated these claims and has given the *Devotio moderna* a more conservative, sober, and backward-looking character, with its clerical and monastic elements growing stronger, not weaker. In particular, R.R. Post has warned against temptations like giving the movement a uniform character over its long history from the fourteenth to the sixteenth centuries and attributing to it the views of individuals whose connections with it might be loose or problematic. An assessment must be built on concrete studies of people and institutions. Post's own conclusion is that, while in the late fifteenth and early sixteenth centuries, the Brethren showed an increased interest in education, they were not notably proponents of change or pioneers of humanism in the Nether-lands. For his distinctive melding of the Christian and the classi-cal, Erasmus' debt was not to the Brethren. The outcome of Post's big book on *The Modern Devotion: Confrontation with Reformation and Humanism* is depressingly negative. It certainly removes the lynch-pin of the argument for a native Dutch Reformation with roots in the fifteenth century.[42]

Some, without returning to the large claims of the past, con-tinue to give a more positive turn to the story of Erasmus' rela-tions with the Brethren.[43] Erasmus and the Brethren converged in their concern for the inner life in religion, distinct from ecclesias-tical structures and external observances. But interiority had dif-ferent meanings. The Brethren worked to an 'inward-directed conception of the true Christian life, to be built up, to be con-structed by disciplining the body and the mind,' a regime of inner control and enclosure. For Erasmus, inward encounter with Christ released the powers of the self, allowing for self-realization and unconstrained dealings with the surrounding culture.[44]

The issue of a Netherlands 'Préréforme' has been in effect side-lined in recent writing about Erasmus and his homeland. In an essay for the quincentenary of 1969, 'Erasme, homo batavus,' Aloïs Gerlo shows that, despite Erasmus' claimed cosmopolitan-ism and a disaffection for his countrymen expressed from time to time, his bond with them grew stronger as the years passed.[45] Later writers have moved to another question, that of just who his countrymen were. It is curious that, at a time when national-ism is on the wane in Western Europe and the interest in Erasmus himself might be seen as a reflection of this, defining exactly what his nationality was should become an interest of historians. A summary of their conclusions follows. Erasmus had an attach-ment to the province or, more exactly, the County of Holland, although he could express towards its people by turns affection and aversion. He was also loyal to the Netherlands, the lands of diverse language and ethnicity ruled in his time by the Habsburgs. He was not then strictly a 'cosmopolitan.' He also accepted that he was a German, since his country, however defined, lay within the German Empire. Harassed by German nationalists like Ulrich von Hutten, he hedged over the German origins of his people and in fact gladly took up Hutten's dismissive epithet 'Gallogerman,' which had a certain historical justification and kept open his lines of communication with France. There was a pattern to Erasmus' various and apparently conflicting descriptions of himself. While never denying his origins, he responded to the pressures of the moment, seeking always to avoid too stifling an embrace from any direction and to preserve his precious personal freedom.[46]

IV

Bataillon's book had been a high-point in the Erasmus literature of the first half of the twentieth century. His Erasmus was a figure of genuine moral stature. Bataillon was correcting those who found him, as a religious thinker, shallow or flaccid. He was leading the way in the study of Erasmus' audiences, in this case the intellectually curious and religiously sensitive of Spain. Bataillon was also, without having this as a primary aim of his own, preparing for the Catholic reclaiming of Erasmus. The orthodoxy of the second half of the century, that Erasmus was to be taken seriously as a Christian, essentially Catholic, thinker, had among its foundations Bataillon's rediscovery of Erasmus as mentor and leader in Christian spirituality.[47]

The high-point in the study of Erasmus and his audiences in the second half of the century is a work equally massive, equally a scholarly and intellectual *tour de force* as Bataillon's. It is in part a continuation of Bataillon's work, in part a challenge to the assumptions on which that work rested. It reflects changes in the historical discipline in the last decades of the century, especially, but not exclusively, the prominence of social history and the quest for history from below. It is also in certain respects a challenge to the orthodoxy about Erasmus in these years. That comes from a question of method. How is Erasmus to be read? Whose reading is privileged? This book is Silvana Seidel Menchi's *Erasmo in Italia* (Turin, 1987).[48]

For the Spanish collection of 1986, *El Erasmismo in España*, Seidel Menchi formulated, in an essay entitled 'La fortuna di Erasmo in Italia: Confronto metodologico con la ricerca di Marcel Bataillon,' the differences between the Spanish and Italian experiences and the distinctiveness of her approach from Bataillon's. On the face of it, the Spanish and Italian cases should be alike; in both there was a Catholic monopoly enforced by an Inquisition. But in the one, as depicted by Bataillon, Erasmus had a receptive, enthusiastic audience, in the other, so far as Seidel Menchi's predecessors in the study of Erasmus' influence in Italy could discover, but a tenuous and transient interest. Seidel Menchi says that, in Bataillon's understanding of them, the two sides of the encounter, Erasmus and Spain, are mutually reinforcing. Erasmus' popularity in Spain becomes a kind of Ariadne's thread for penetrating the heart of Spanish spirituality; the Spanish understanding of Erasmus is an Ariadne's thread in reverse for discovering the true Erasmus, who was a religious figure, and for diverging from earlier writers' picture of him as a sceptic. The effect is that Erasmus' ideas emerge as a 'coherent system of thought,' more coherent than the evidence warrants, and the thinking of his Spanish followers is dignified and elevated by association with him. This is the methodological problem of 'levelling up.' Bataillon makes Erasmians of people who are anything but 'erasmiani puri.' Seidel Menchi does not hesitate to call a betrayal of Erasmus those Spanish translations which removed or diluted the radical elements in his writings, for the sake of safeguarding Catholic orthodoxy. By contrast, the Italian reception of Erasmus seems fragmented. Furthermore, in Italian minds, as we will see, Erasmus was securely tied to Luther and the Reformers. Bataillon maintains a sharp distinction between 'erasmismo' and 'luteranesimo,' and on this he even corrects his sources, for in Spain, as in Italy, there is evidence that contemporaries did not routinely discriminate between them. At this point, Seidel Menchi's critique, cogent so far, takes a false step; she criticizes Bataillon's reluctance to accept the fluidity of the borders between the different reforming streams and the existence of a common ideological patrimony on which all forms of dissent could draw. But that is to overlook what Bataillon says about the solidarity of the Spanish Erasmians with the European religious revolution and his use of the idea of 'Préréforme' itself, in which a variety of reforming impulses was caught up. Lucien Febvre had taught Bataillon and his generation of historians the openness and the theological imprecision of the early Reformation. It is true, nevertheless, that Bataillon's perception of these connections is essentially intellectual, whereas for Seidel Menchi they belong to the life of the people and emerge unmistakably from the archival sources. The inquisitorial records make clear that fine theological distinctions between the 'Erasmian' and the 'Lutheran' were not made by either the victims or the agents of the Inquisition. Faithful to these sources, Seidel Menchi integrates Erasmus with the 'vast movement of ideas' which was the Reformation in its pre-confessional phase.[49]

Seidel Menchi's predecessors on the subject of Erasmus' Italian connections had stopped at the periphery of the territory she has explored. Many who have written under the rubric 'Erasmus and Italy' have been concerned with Italian influences on him and have in effect followed in the steps of Pierre de Nolhac in his luminous study of Erasmus' visit to Italy in 1506–9 and the friendships it brought him, *Erasme en Italie: Etude sur un épisode de la Renaissance*.[50] Renaudet's *Erasme et l'Italie* of 1954, though paying tribute to Bataillon's *Erasme et l'Espagne*, in fact reverses Bataillon's question. He asks, not what did Italy owe to Erasmus, but what did Erasmus owe to Italy? This is a more conventional question, and Renaudet's depiction of Erasmus in these pages is essentially that of his earlier studies: this Erasmus stood, amid the turmoil of the early Reformation, for a kind of spiritualized Rome, a Roman church disburdened of many of its dogmas and practices. Renaudet calls it a 'third church.'[51]

In two late chapters, Renaudet studies Erasmus' reception among the Italian humanists. The first recalls his friends and correspondents, including the first translator of the *Enchiridion*, Emilio dei Migli of Brescia, and the second his enemies, Aleander, Alberto Pio, and the egregious Pietro Corsi, author of a *Defensio pro Italia ad Erasmum Roterodamum*, defending the military prowess of Italians against an Erasmian slight.[52] In these passages Renaudet comes closest to Bataillon's method and approach. Otherwise, his study is a straining out of the Italian element from the mix of associations influencing Erasmus at different stages of his life. Thus, his early development is encompassed by chapters headed 'L'italianisme des Pays-Bas' (on his first acquaintance with Italian humanism), 'L'italianisme parisien' (his contacts with Italian humanists while studying in Paris), and 'L'Angleterre italien.' This last exposes the difficulty in Renaudet's approach. His case turns on the contention that the mind of Erasmus' English friend John Colet, met first at Oxford in 1499, was formed by Italian humanism and Florentine Neoplatonism. The Italy which shaped Erasmus' reform program was, says Renaudet, mediated to him by Colet. But we now see that the range of intellectual interests Colet brought back from his own Italian journey was limited; he did not learn Greek, he had little sympathy for· the pagan classics, his Neoplatonism tilted away from the human and towards divine omnipotence. On the broad horizon of Renaudet's work has appeared a mirage: 'l'Angleterre florentine et vénitienne d'Oxford.' For Renaudet, this vision set the direction for what followed, Erasmus' engagement with the biblical criticism of Lorenzo Valla and the experiences of his Italian journey: 'He remained, at Rome, the pupil of John Colet and the Oxford reformers' (Renaudet's debt to Frederic Seebohm's work of eighty years before remained unqualified). Through the conflicts of the last years of Erasmus' life, with Luther and his Catholic enemies, he held to the reform program which Renaudet calls 'italianisme érasmien,' a program at once critical and spiritual. The regular reiteration of this expression in a narrative of Erasmus' life produces a strained effect and seems at times ritualistic. In one respect Renaudet's Erasmus anticipates the Erasmus received by the dissident groups whose archival traces Seidel Menchi has followed. He was nonconformist, 'volontiers dissident, hostile à tout conformisme d'église, d'ordre ou d'école.'[53]

At the time when Seidel Menchi's first papers were appearing, Myron Gilmore and Paul and Marcella Grendler wrote essays on questions her researches were addressing: how was Erasmus read, how was he taken in Italy? In both, the answers were largely negative. Erasmus had followers and supporters among the Catholic reformers, but mostly the church authorities and the dominant religious culture rejected him, his books were proscribed and many burnt. Gilmore has some pages on Erasmus' attractiveness to radicals of various kinds, and the Grendlers suggest that the virulence of official attacks upon him was in itself evidence of his popularity at levels, social and cultural, which scholarship had yet to explore.[54] Dissident groups that saw him, together with Luther, as symbols of radical change were Seidel Menchi's main subject. Earlier, her teacher and doyen of studies on the Italian Reformation, Delio Cantimori, had, in a paper for the Basel celebration of 1936, pointed the way for future researchers. Scholarship to that time had seen Erasmus' significance for Italy as essentially literary; in doing so, it virtually accepted the Counter-Reformation annihilation of him as a moral and religious figure. By contrast, Cantimori highlights the translations of his religious writings in the first half of the sixteenth century and, in the second, his continuing influence on the Italian exiles, heretics, and radicals, whose thought was at an oblique angle to his but who, even so, recognized him as, in some sense, their master. But what of the nonconformists who stayed at home? Seidel Menchi's was a search, which Cantimori had been unable to pursue, for Erasmus' traces among them.[55]

Her basic move is from intellectual history to social history. The images useful for depicting the reception of ideas from literary sources or in literary form – model and copy, origin and derivation – are, she says, not useful for the circulation and putting into practice of ideas among those outside, or on the margins of, the educated elites, let alone among the illiterate. Here one must think rather of 'an interaction of diverse forms of communication': the spoken as well as the written word, images and pictures, preaching and exemplary action. Sometimes an author is quoted by hearsay without his name being mentioned or even remembered.[56]

Seidel Menchi's work belongs to the movement of the last thirty years towards writing history from the bottom up. Satires in verse for quick comprehension among the common people picked up Erasmus' criticisms of ceremonial religion. Above all, the case records of the Inquisition bring folk from lower social levels into the story. Seidel Menchi is the first to exploit these sources in a study of Erasmus' *fortuna* in a Catholic country. For Bataillon in Spain the Inquisition records were secondary to the literary sources.[57] Seidel Menchi justly makes large claims for these sources; they 'mirror directly religious thought and behaviour,' in fact place the researcher at the point where word passed over into action. The records, she says, not any preference of her own, have set the direction of her research.[58] The truth in this claim is manifest. Yet, one must recognize also that social history, including the use of judicial records to write a history from below, has become a dominant movement within the historical discipline.[59] Obviously, this has had an influence on her work. We are not dealing (to use a legal term) with a wholly uncontaminated encounter with the records.

Seidel Menchi identifies another point in the historiography of the subject. The Erasmus emerging from the Italian sources, Erasmus the heretic, comrade of Luther and the radical Reformers, is very different from the Erasmus presented in most writings about him in the last two generations, especially perhaps in North America, writings to be reviewed in chapter 5 of this book. The latter Erasmus is the exponent of moderate reforms but essentially an orthodox Catholic drawing spiritual sustenance from the Fathers and even Aquinas. Seidel Menchi avoids using the expressions 'Erasmian' and 'Erasmianism' because they have, not least through Bataillon's influence, become identified with an ecumenical Catholicism whose agenda belongs, not to the sixteenth century, but to the twentieth.[60]

The crux methodologically lies in the question which directs Seidel Menchi's whole study: 'How did the sixteenth-century reader read Erasmus?' Seidel Menchi makes contact here with contemporary theory, if not exactly with the death of the author, then at least with the principle that reception is a reciprocal process. The reader is an active element in this interaction; the adjustment ideas undergo when readers apply them to their situations has its own legitimacy. How the reader takes the words is as important as the author's intention in uttering them, for the historian on occasion more important. This is a study in understanding 'Erasmus ex Erasmi lectore' rather than 'Erasmus ex Erasmo.'[61] Readers in Italy, looking for a way through the perplexities of the time, saw, not the distance between Erasmus and the Reformers, but their convergences.

With the appearance of Luther, Seidel Menchi begins, Erasmus, whom Italian readers had until then taken in a traditional sense, his works being bowdlerized even by his admirers, became an 'explosive force' in Italian culture. His critics and enemies gladly linked him with Luther, easing their task by ignoring the main issues of Luther's Reformation, like justification by faith, and concentrating on religious practices, where the two often spoke with a common voice. They accused Erasmus of using his literary skills to promote Luther's ideas and of challenging the Italian preeminence in studies and Rome's authority in religion. In the first half of the sixteenth century, the curia, fearful of alienating the northern humanists at a critical moment, remained unresponsive to calls for his condemnation.[62]

The equation Luther-Erasmus proposed by his enemies was adopted also by Erasmus' admirers. This was especially so within what Seidel Menchi calls the 'generation of 1510,' among those, that is, growing up when the circulation of his books was at its peak, 1520–30. Some later described Erasmus as their stepping-stone to Luther. What is more significant is that Erasmus remained central to the Italian Reformation through its whole history, playing a complex of roles: precursor, surrogate, cover (as with Valdés and others in Spain), sign, and inspiration. Distinctive features of the Italian Reformation, Seidel Menchi says, made and kept Erasmus important for the dissident groups: its intellectual openness and link to humanism, its diversity, the outworking of an intense self-reflection apparent in what even humble people brought themselves to say to the Inquisition.[63]

While the Italian dissidents, like Erasmus' critics, were interested most in what he had to say about religious practices, certain theological ideas drawn from him, or from him and Luther together, were characteristic of the Italian Reformation. The first was Christian freedom.[64] This connected Luther's rejection of works-righteousness and Erasmus' polemic against ceremonialism. Love became the sole imperative, church law lost its binding force and holy places, objects, and times their sanctity, as in the rejection of fasts. The second idea was God's boundless mercy or the openness of heaven. Erasmus' sermon of 1524, *De immensa Dei misericordia*, appeared in three independent translations between 1542 and 1554. At one point in this work, Erasmus was close to Luther's doctrine of justification. That was the point seized on by the Italian Reformers who interpreted Luther's doctrine as assurance of salvation. A practical corollary was the rejection of purgatory and auricular confession.[65] The third was the constructive use of doubt, reservation, and silence (*ars dubitandi*). The dissidents read Erasmus' *Annotations*, with their critical approach to texts and especially texts used traditionally to support dogmatic structures, in a radical way. Doubt expressed itself in the rhetorical question and the hypothesis, but, in the oppressive times after 1559, the Inquisition equated these with heresy anyway.[66]

On the sociology of the movement, Seidel Menchi emphasizes the role of grammar-school teachers, who used Erasmus' books in their classrooms and also, in an age of almost universal illiteracy, for the edification of their neighbours. In both cases, they simplified and radicalized his views, by being selective and by removing nuances and reservations. The movement also depended on couples, households, and families, the more so as persecution heightened the need for security. They found comfort from the enthusiasm Erasmus expressed for marriage and the family in his *Encomium matrimonii*, which Seidel Menchi reads, not as a rhetorical exercise, but as a 'manifesto for moral change,' with its implied rejection of the monks' claim to a more perfect kind of Christian life. Erasmus' didacticism, met in their humanist training, appealed also to Italian notaries and jurists, whose anticlericalism often passed over to religious dissidence.[67]

The late 1550s were a turning-point. The Rome of Paul IV came out against Erasmus. Denunciations of him as heretic and schismatic, friend and furtherer of Luther, the intensity of which had ebbed and flowed since the 1520s, now became uncompromising, unrelenting, and ended, Seidel Menchi concludes, in a 'one-sidedness bordering on the grotesque.' Condemnation was unanimous in the Italian Catholic world. Erasmus' books were demonized, even those which had nothing to do with theology. Yet, the dissidents defended their books with courageous pertinacity. Erasmus, says Seidel Menchi, was unique. No other author, none of the great Italians, Machiavelli, Boccaccio, Aretino, or Valla, became the centre of protest and dissidence as Erasmus did. That was the measure of his success among his readers. But by the end of the century the Inquisitors were masters of the field. The lower orders, once powerfully attracted to him, were now wholly deprived of him, and Italian culture was closed to Erasmus for a century.[68]

V

'A Dutchman by birth, by temper and habit a European, Erasmus has, none the less, very special claims upon the regard of Englishmen.' So a writer in the *Times Literary Supplement* in the anniversary month of July 1936.[69] Yet, strangely, not until the 1960s was there a serious attempt to integrate Erasmus and his English audience with the European religious revolution, as Bataillon had done for Erasmus' Spanish followers. This was despite the persisting authority, at least up to Renaudet's *Erasme et l'Italie* of 1954, of Seebohm's *Oxford Reformers* and the immeasurable debt students of Erasmus everywhere owed to English editing and English publishing, on account of P.S. Allen's *Opus epistolarum* (Clarendon Press, Oxford), finally completed with the index volume in 1958, twenty-five years after Allen's death. Seebohm's narrative stops at Colet's death in 1519, since his interest was in demonstrating a 'fellow-work' between Colet, Erasmus, and their friends, though he gave a distant future, far beyond the sixteenth-century Reformation, to their 'Oxford reformation,' notably in the emergence of liberal Christianity in the nineteenth century. He had nothing to say on the role of 'Erasmians' in the actual Reformation of the 1530s and 1540s. Histories of the English Reformation had concentrated on the acts of state driving the great change or the influences coming from Wittenberg, Zürich, and Geneva. They did not neglect the influence from Basel entirely, acknowledging either its subversion of the old religious order or its ancillary role in bringing in the new.[70] But before 1965 there was no rounded study of Erasmus and his English audience.

The English counterpart to Bataillon, though on a more modest scale in both time-span and content, is James Kelsey McConica's *English Humanists and Reformation Politics under Henry VIII and Edward VI*. McConica begins from Febvre's article of 1929: confessional analysis distorts understanding of the Reformation because it restricts the vision to what led in the end to the Protestant and Tridentine Catholic establishments and ignores the variegated seedbed from which the reforming movements sprang. McConica makes the link immediately with Bataillon and the idea of 'pre-reform.' He accepts, with Febvre and Bataillon, that the national interpretation of the Reformation is as limiting as the confessional. Like Bataillon on the solidarity of the Spanish Erasmians with the European religious revolution, McConica insists on the openness of England to continental influences and the exchange of ideas within what he calls 'humanistic evangelism.'[71]

The name could as easily have been 'Erasmianism,' for Erasmus' understanding of Christianity, his *philosophia Christi*, with its laicism, inwardness and practical moralism – not renouncing dogma and sacrament but displacing them from the central position in favour of the words of Christ and the Pauline admonitions as recorded in scripture – was the best-known definition of the movement. 'He was,' says McConica, 'pre-eminently the movement's propagandist, by far its most prolific proponent. It is for this reason that his name is chosen to describe the common cause in which they were engaged.'[72] McConica sees Erasmianism as a social movement, ranging from the aristocracy to a 'popular fringe' and held together by Erasmus' correspondence, especially with the 'groups of laymen of prestige and influence who proclaimed the gospel of reform.' England had a special place in the movement, above all through Erasmus' bond with Thomas More, *Utopia* being, in McConica's view, 'a fuller exposition of the Erasmian programme than any set forth in a single work by Erasmus himself.' The English Erasmians found patrons in the City, among the lawyers, at the court of Henry VIII, especially with the royal ladies, among the bishops and the noble families. Despite differences of status, position, and outlook, these people constituted, says McConica, a broad reforming movement, not shy altogether of radical thinking but, in the 1520s, accepted as orthodox.[73] In the first decades of the century, humanism, with reforming associations and continental connections, was advancing also in the universities. There is evidence by 1520 of Erasmus' emergence there as a best-seller.[74]

The pivot of McConica's argument is in his fifth chapter, 'Erasmians and Policy: The Crisis from 1529 to 1534.' With the fall of Wolsey in 1529, the Erasmian humanists saw the opportunity to implement their program and threw themselves into publication. The activities of the government – from the king's divorce, through the Submission of the Clergy (1532), to the royal supremacy – sometimes went in parallel to, sometimes ran ahead of the Erasmian consensus which yet remains the best clue to what was going on. Under Thomas Cromwell government policy placed 'Erasmian thought in the fore as the positive doctrine of the Henrician settlement,' especially through a program of translation and publication, notably of Erasmus' works, with the *Enchiridion* (Wynkin de Worde, 1533), as it had often been in Europe, at the head.[75] The break with Rome undermined the Erasmian consensus, as the executions of More and Fisher tragically indicated, but a substantial centre, royalist and doctrinally orthodox, remained, and on this Cromwell built in shoring up the Henrician settlement. This was, McConica concludes, 'an Erasmian polity, and a capacious mansion which could contain most opinions except the extremes of Protestantism and a rooted attachment to Rome.' Continuity held after Cromwell's fall and, indeed, to the end of the reign. The pietism of Henry's last queen, Catherine Parr, and the new generation of writers she encouraged linked back to the 'pre-reform' generation of Erasmus and his friends. The centre held, supported, it would seem, by the king himself. Even in the frankly Protestant regime of Edward VI, when the religious divisions became irreconcilable and the humanist camp itself split over the meaning of the Henrician settlement, Erasmian preoccupations persisted, as is demonstrated, on the official side, by the translation of Erasmus' New Testament *Paraphrases* and their placement in the churches for the people to read.[76]

McConica presents us with a synthetic picture. Erasmian humanism is a frame holding diverse, even contradictory, elements. The method is appropriate for tracing spiritual and intellectual continuities beneath a surface of rapid or violent change. As a way of interpreting those changes themselves, it is less effective. In the last thirty years, McConica's synthesis has been squeezed from two sides. His ample depiction of humanism has been challenged by a narrower, at times minimalist, definition of the movement, and a much-vaunted revisionism has questioned the case for reforming movements, pre-reform, and, not least, the English Reformation itself.

McConica and his contemporaries, says Alistair Fox, have overstated the unity and coherence of English humanism to the point of defying credibility. Fox's prescription is to define humanism strictly (as Paul Kristeller had done earlier) as commitment to classical education and learning, but also to recognize it, in its applications, as a 'multifarious phenomenon.' Further, its application to reform and politics in the Henrician age cannot be described as 'Erasmian.' The humanism which influenced policy then was not Erasmian; the humanists in Thomas Cromwell's circle were not like Erasmus. Thus, Thomas Starkey in his *Dialogue between Lupset and Pole* 'replaces the old medieval *contemptus mundi*, still forcefully present in Erasmus, with an Italianate sense of the dignity of man and a secular excitement.'[77]

As can be seen, these judgments rest on a certain interpretation of Erasmus. The bias of his mind, says Fox, was towards the Platonic and the transcendental, even the otherworldly. In balancing the classical and the Christian, the secular and the spiritual, it inclined always towards the latter pair. Confronted with the world's hard and imperfect realities, Erasmus' instinct was to withdraw and to leave politics to the good and absolute prince, the 'logical exemplar' of his political theory turning out to be, incredibly, James I. We know, from the present study, that there are ways, quite different from this, of seeing Erasmus' attitude to the secular world and to politics. Richard M. Douglas finds in his idea of vocation, for example, precisely an Italianate sense of the dignity of man and a secular excitement, in contrast with Luther's and Calvin's providentialism.[78] Fox's spiritualized and affrighted Erasmus could not be further from the Erasmus of the *Flugschriften* studied by Holeczek or the Erasmus received by Seidel Menchi's Italian readers, an Erasmus right at the centre of the world's affairs in a time of religious revolution and cultural shift. Fox does not ask in Seidel Menchi's vein how Erasmus was read by contemporaries. He has chosen texts, above all from the *Enchiridion*, which confirm the picture of Erasmus as Platonizing and otherworldly, whereas a reader approaching him through other texts, say the *Epystle in laude and prayse of matrimony* (English, 1531), would find a worldly Erasmus with a distinctive attitude to the natural and active life. The methodology is unsatisfactory, since the crux in Erasmus interpretation is to moderate tensions in his thought, not remove them by privileging one stage of his life and one kind of writing.[79]

As for humanism and the broad sweep of reform, Fox is right to insist on its multifariousness. Maria Dowling's survey *Humanism in the Age of Henry VIII* has humanists associated with each twist and turn of the regime's religious policy, though oddly dismissing the Erasmian phase (Colet, Erasmus, and More) as 'naïve in the extreme.' Recent writings emphasizing the essentially rhetorical character of humanism, the rhetorical conventions governing its discourse, and, above all, the play of irony within that discourse have taken a further step away from the venerable image of a progressive humanism in this generation overcoming, in the universities and intellectual life generally, the old learning and scholasticism.[80]

The 'revisionist strategy' on the English Reformation posits the continuing vitality and popularity of English Catholicism in the first half of the sixteenth century, the weakness of Protestant ideology and the minority status of its adherents until well into the second half of the century, and the piecemeal introduction of religious change as a side-effect of factional struggles at the court. Although his review of the recent historiography of the English Reformation does not mention McConica's book, Christopher Haigh's arguments there leave little room for a Bataillon-like Erasmianism, giving expression to the intellectuals' and the people's demands for reform, reshaping piety towards the more personal and intimate, inducing a shift from a clerical, institutionalized religious culture to one according equal status to the lay people and their spiritual aspirations. For McConica, 'the secret streams of learning and evangelism which drew their vigour from the writings of Erasmus and his friends, and which coursed through England as through the rest of Western Europe,' affected every stage of England's religious history in the six-teenth century and helped determine the shape of 'a religious settlement unique in the annals of the Reformation.' The claim for continuity and consistency over a long epoch of changing politi-cal and religious fortunes is too large, but it at least, revisionism notwithstanding, respects the authenticity of the religious objec-tives of English reformers of different stamps and affirms their openness to continental influences, indeed a certain level of mutuality between the English and European movements.[81]

VI

In the middle decades of the twentieth century, the model drawn by Febvre and Bataillon dominated interpretations of the reli-gious movements of the early sixteenth century ('Préréforme' and the beginnings of the Reformation) and, in particular, of the significance of Erasmus and his relation to his audiences. McCon-ica's opening paragraphs are testimony to its place and prestige in the 1960s. On this model, Erasmus spoke to and for a literate audience, Europe-wide, avid less for classical wisdom than for a reconstituted Christianity, a religion not primarily ceremonial, dogmatic, and institutional but personal, sociable, and ethical. The institutional changes that eventually followed, through the Reformation and Catholic Reformation, were the residue of these aspirations, not their essence or explanation. In the last decades of the twentieth century, this model has been weakened, first, by the criticism (Seidel Menchi on Italy) that it etherealized or over-spiritualized Erasmus and his audience and undervalued his readers' more down-to-earth understanding of what he wrote, and, secondly, by the argument (revisionist writings on the English Reformation) that religious change was a contingent thing, more a consequence of day-to-day politics and factional compromises than of broad ideological and spiritual movements. Yet, the Bataillon model is set to survive. In its taking with the utmost seriousness the Erasmus received by his Italian readers, Seidel Menchi's work is less a break from, than an immense vari-ation on, Bataillon's theme, and mere reliance on the contingent and pragmatic falls before Febvre's original strictures against explaining big effects by little causes and can hardly endure.

Erasmus had readers, correspondents, and admirers also in Eastern Europe. In its apparent (but only apparent) marginality, this represents a final test-case. Essays on the theme appeared in the quincentenary publications of 1967–70. The narratives familiar from Western Europe, the reception of humanism, the coming of the Reformation, and the division of loyalties that followed within the elite ran their course here, too, and various parties invoked the name and friendship of Erasmus.

Erasmus' influence in Poland, Maria Cytowska has said, was 'superficial enough but broad.'[82] From the essays of 1970 and thereafter emerges the following pattern. Pedagogical and religious writings of Erasmus were known in Poland before he had any Polish correspondents, and some were printed there. His pedagogy was influencing Polish schools from the 1520s. A humanist circle at the University of Cracow, stimulated by contacts with German humanists, promoted his ideas; it depended, however, on a small group of leaders, including the itinerant Englishman Leonard Cox, and with their dispersal quickly disbanded.[83] Members of this circle spoke of Erasmus with enthusiasm and wrote to him with devotion. So did his other correspondents who came from the elites of church and state, government and economy, including King Sigismund I himself, to whom Erasmus wrote a famous letter in 1527 which was quickly published. His correspondents drew Erasmus into the perplexities of East European politics, factions at the Polish court splitting over the country's relations with the Habsburgs following the dynasty's contested acquisition of the Hungarian crown on Hungary's defeat by the Turks in 1526. How one reads Erasmus' response to this debate depends on how one estimates his loyalty to the dynasty and the imperial idea.[84]

Erasmianism as an ideology, a religious sentiment or set of ideas, the Erasmianism of Bataillon, was not a quick growth in Poland. There was no equivalent to the generations of 1510 in Italy and Spain. In a searching quincentenary essay, 'La fortune d'Erasme en Pologne,' Claude Backvis finds 'something precarious ... and to a degree deceptive' in the Polish elite's adoration of Erasmus. They came to him from an acquaintance with the more sceptical, even neo-pagan, humanism of Italy. He and they were not on the same wavelength.[85] Even so, these leaders of the Catholic church and state in Poland welcomed his break with Luther and looked to him as defender of the old faith. His Catholic enemies, dominant in the Sorbonne and at Louvain by the 1520s and among the Spanish monks soon after, made little headway in Poland before 1570. By mid-century, indeed, the many-sided nature of his spiritual inheritance had become apparent. Claude Backvis speaks of a 'generation of 1543,' men from the middle and lower gentry who understood Erasmus' reform program more deeply than his brilliant correspondents and who were drawn, by 'at least a sympathetic curiosity,' towards the Reformation. They were irenicist and sought religious reconciliation.[86] He was claimed as master or forerunner by some who became Protestant leaders, notably Jan Laski, organizer of the influential reformed church at Emden in Friesland and, later, of Polish Calvinism, by the first serious proponents of Catholic reformation in Poland, like Stanislaus Hosius, and, eventually, even by the Polish antitrinitarians.[87]

There were quincentenary essays also on Erasmus in Hungary. They suggest a sequence of developments lke the Polish: humanist literary enthusiasms, the attraction to Erasmus, often superficial and contradictory, of an elite, the use of the *Praise of Folly* as a vehicle of social criticism, the moment of pre-reform, when Erasmus was understood more fully and penetrated the society and culture more deeply, the incoming of the Reformation and the splitting of the Erasmian inheritance. But these occurred in Hungary against the backdrop of a nation in profound crisis, invasion, war and civil war, and, in particular, the scattering of the elite after the disastrous defeat by the Turks at Mohács (1526). Mary of Habsburg, the widow of the fallen Hungarian king, Louis II, became in 1531 regent of the Netherlands for her brother Charles V, so that Hungarian Erasmianism under her patronage passed, as it were, through a Belgian phase. Already at the Diet of Augsburg in 1530 she and her humanist secretary Nicolaus Olahus appealed in the Erasmian spirit for religious accommodation to strengthen Europe before the Turkish onslaught which had overwhelmed Hungary. In that moment, Hungarian Erasmianism had European significance.[88]

In his essay Claude Backvis puts two methodological points raised by the Polish case, but applicable to other situations. First, what sounds like Erasmus may be less the result of his influence than a practical necessity, as was mutual toleration between the religions in Poland. Nevertheless, practical necessity requires formulation, and by the second and third decades of the sixteenth century Erasmus' words were ready to hand and known to a broad educated public. The same words may have rival sources. Pacifism, for example, may have come from a number of quarters, from medieval heresy, fifteenth-century Czech radicalism, or Anabaptism, as well as from Erasmus. We have noted the difficulties in disentangling the intellectual and spiritual strands elsewhere, in Spain and the Netherlands, for example. The second point gives proper definition to the problem of 'Erasmus and his audiences.' Reception is active. Backvis anticipated what Seidel Menchi was to say about Erasmus' Italian readers. In the end, the receivers take what they are already looking for, what in a sense they already have.[89] These points are necessary controls on any discussion of Erasmus and his audiences.

FOUR

Interlude:
Quincentenary (1967–70)

꽃

I

In 1969 students at a Dutch university shouted down a faculty member intending in an address to commemorate the five hundredth anniversary of Erasmus' birth.[1] For the Festival of Holland in June of that year Hugo Claus and Harry Mulisch wrote the opera *Reconstructie*, where Erasmus appears as the low-life acolyte, not only of Don Juan, but also of capitalism and colonialism. 'Erasmus,' exclaims Cornelis Reedijk incredulously, 'as Leporello, the abject valet of imperialist powers!'[2] The quincentenary of 1967–70 coincided with the student rebellion and generational conflicts in Western societies and with various 'culture wars,' as they later came to be known. The quatercentenary of Erasmus' death in 1936 had been overshadowed by the rise and rampaging of the dictators. There was behind the celebrations an anxiety about the fate of Western civilization, of which Erasmus was a bright star, and a wish to assert its durability and continuity. That made Stefan Zweig's biography of Erasmus, though marginal to scholarship, a representative book of the time. By 1970 the fashionable word was not continuity but discontinuity. In North American universities, the Western civilization courses, which had been a staple of the undergraduate curriculum since World War 2, were under attack. Those who taught them, often refugees from the dictators, expounding a tradition they had fled Europe to preserve, were giving way to others graduated in post-war America and now, in a time of student protest over the Vietnam war or race relations, sceptical about the 'Western tradition.'[3] In the minds of some, Erasmus and the Christian humanism he represented were casualties of these distempers. When humanism was condemned as a cover for the crimes and hypocrisies of bourgeois civilization, and the very notion of the human was under question, it might well seem that Erasmus had nothing worthwhile to say to us any more.[4]

Yet, evidence for public interest in, and sympathy for, Erasmus was overwhelming. An open-air exhibition in the public square by the theatre in Rotterdam, 'Meeting with Erasmus' in the setting of a sixteenth-century village, attracted hundreds of thousands of visitors in the summer of 1969. There were in the 1960s 'intelligent experiments' at presenting him through mass media. Still in Rotterdam in the main anniversary year of 1969, the 'Maastad Players' revived the scenes from Erasmus' life devised by Garmt Stuiveling and first presented in July 1936, with Bob van Dulken again playing the part of Erasmus after thirty-three years. Towards the end of the year students of the Gymnasium Erasmianum, Rotterdam's Latin school, which had carried Erasmus' name since 1636, offered a 'collage' of pieces, with some dramatizations, from his letters and writings, 'Erasmus sprekend.' Both the Belgian and Dutch Post Offices issued stamps.[5]

Above all, there was music. Its prominence indicates how, since 1936, concert-going and other kinds of listening had come to rival reading as a pastime of the educated class. Music from his time, choral and on the organ, accompanied the opening events of Rotterdam's 'Erasmus Year' in St Lawrence's Church on 12 April 1969. In September at Louvain in the Festival of Flanders a lutanist, organist, and three vocal groups illustrated a lecture by J.-C. Margolin on 'Erasmus and Music'; one of the groups, Quator Vocal of Brussels, had performed a similar service for a lecture by R.B. Lenaerts on the same theme at the Brussels commemoration of Erasmus at the end of April. The choir 'A coeur joie' performed sixteenth-century polyphonic music during the scholarly meetings on Erasmus at Tours in the summer of 1969. The high-point of the 'Erasmus Year' at Rotterdam, 27–9 October, concluded with a concert of early modern instrumental and choral music in the Reformed church at Maastricht. Two nights before, in the new concert hall 'De Doelen,' the Rotterdam Philharmonic under Jean Fournet had given the premiere performance of a work by the Swiss composer Frank Martin, commissioned by the Rotterdamse Kunstichting and entitled 'Erasmi Monumentum,' a work for full orchestra in which the organ, riding over the orchestra but never playing solo, represents Erasmus' voice.[6]

There are ironies in all of this. As writings of Margolin and others on 'Erasmus and Music' make clear, he was ambivalent about the art as practised in his time. He was technically aware and musically sensitive, acquainted with works of the leading composers of the time, as his poem on the death of Johannes Ockeghem, set as a motet by Johannes Lupi (Antwerp 1547) and given a modern performance by the Schola Cantorum Basiliensis in November 1966, demonstrates. But he had decided preferences determined by his aesthetic sobriety and sense of decorum, by the priority he accorded word, text, and sense over complexities of sound. He was not partial to the organ or brass instruments. The evangelical message should not be clouded by musical performance too profane, too assertive, too human. Plainchant met the need better than polyphony.[7]

That the libraries of Europe (Western and Eastern), Britain, North America, and beyond should exhibit their Erasmian treasures in the years of commemoration, and especially in 1969, was to be expected. The connection between Erasmus and the book was a staple of Erasmus studies, and there were many related questions: Erasmus' dealings with his printers and the insight these gave into his relations with places and regions, his influence on the schoolbook of his time, and his role in the publication of the classics, the Fathers, and the scriptures. The commemoration occurred at a time of more radical inquiry into the relation between author, text, and reader, and of more acute awareness of the equivocal character of the word. These found, as we shall see, early expression in the commemorative papers and addresses. Some exhibitions, and notably the greatest, that in the Museum Boymans-van Beuningen in Rotterdam, 'Erasmus and His Time,' broke the dominance of the book and the word characteristic of such exhibitions and gave fresh prominence to the visual.[8] Nearly six hundred exhibits, gathered from over a dozen countries, recreated the life of Erasmus in continuous sequence through eleven rooms and attracted fifty thousand visitors.[9] In political and economic circumstances quite different from those of 1936, the wooden figure of Erasmus found its way once again from Tokyo to Rotterdam.

The word had its triumphs. By the time of this commemoration, massive literary monuments to Erasmus were in preparation or coming to fruition. On the morning of 27 October 1969, Queen Juliana of the Netherlands and the burgomaster of Rotterdam received, in a ceremony in St Lawrence's Church, the first two copies of volume 1 of a new critical edition of Erasmus' works. The idea for such an edition had been conceived in Rotterdam at the beginning of the decade and nurtured in the Netherlands; by 1963 the scheme was under the guidance of the leaders of Erasmus scholarship internationally. The first volume of a French translation, by Marie Delcourt and others, of Erasmus' correspondence in Allen's edition appeared in Brussels in 1967 and in Paris in 1968. In August 1968, R.M. Schoeffel initiated discussions within the University of Toronto Press which were to lead, by the mid-1970s, to the publication of the first volumes in a, by now, projected series of around ninety volumes of Erasmus' works and letters in English translation, with the aim of reaching 'the widest possible audience with the finest texts and apparatus that modern scholarship can provide.'[10]

Only the massive expansion of the academic profession and of universities in Europe and North America since World War 2, the parallel development of foundations and grant-making bodies, the patronage of the state or the corporate sector could sustain publishing enterprises on this scale. Erasmus has not been unique. The collected works of his friend Thomas More and of his sympathizers of the eighteenth and nineteenth centuries Samuel Johnson and S.T. Coleridge – merely to pluck cases from English history and literature – have appeared in the post-war era. James McConica has asked, even so, why Erasmus came to be singled out for so many big and expensive commitments in the troubled 1960s. A corresponding question might be asked about the quincentenary celebrations of 1967–70: why in a time apparently unpropitious did Erasmus arouse a broad public interest? McConica attributes the Erasmus editions, and especially the Amsterdam edition of the *Opera omnia*, to the generation of scholars who, as young people, had suffered in the European conflicts of the 1940s and now presented Erasmus and the editions as a witness to European community.[11] Do both the celebrations and the editions belong also to the uneasy debate about Western culture, its vitality and unity, in the last quarter of the twentieth century? The celebrations passed. The editions, begun in the 1960s and 1970s when the claim to cultural unity and vitality still stood, though not unchallenged, continued at century's end amid cultural fragmentation under the sign of postmodernism; they will end in the twenty-first century in cultural conditions unknown and unpredictable.

Meanwhile scholarship about Erasmus went its way largely, but not entirely, unscathed by the culture wars. It was self-generating and self-sustaining, in itself an indication of the expansion of the academic profession, especially in the humanities, between 1945 and 1970. Some were already speaking unkindly of an 'Erasmus industry.' The main purpose of this 'Interlude' is, from a perusal of the major commemorative volumes, all deriving from conferences and seminars, to seek a pattern in Erasmus scholarship, to try to sum up its interests and emphases, at the time of the quincentenary.

II

Whereas in 1936 Basel, where he died, and Rotterdam shared centre stage, in 1969 – to be precise, on 27–9 October 1969, which was then taken by most to be the actual quincentenary – pride of place went to Erasmus' birthplace, and the *Actes* of the Congress organized by the municipality and held under the auspices of the Royal Netherlands Academy of Sciences and Letters followed in 1971. On the same dates two years earlier, the newly created University Centre at Mons, the nucleus of a planned University of Hainaut, successor of an abortive attempt in Erasmus' lifetime to establish a university in the region, had organized a colloquium, whose own *Actes* (1968) became the first in the quincentenary series. The founders of the Centre were seeking to meet the needs of a depressed region, above all by introducing technological studies, but they seized the opportunity of Erasmus' quincentenary to assert their commitment also to humane studies. In this, Mons might be thought to represent the new generation of Western universities of the 1960s. The Belgian Interuniversity Centre for the History of Humanism adopted 'Erasmus and Belgium' as the theme of a national commemoration under the patronage of King Baudoin, a conference meting on successive days in early June 1969 in three Belgian cities known to Erasmus, Brussels, Ghent, and Antwerp, and a fourth city, Liège, where Erasmus studies flourished in the generation of the quincentenary. 'The decisive role played by Erasmus,' said Aloïs Gerlo at the opening in Brussels, 'in the cultural life of the southern Netherlands ... can hardly be overestimated.' Louvain, the scene of friendships and enmities, of triumphs and defeats, for Erasmus, raised its own distinctive monument in 1969, *Scrinium Erasmianum*, a large two-volume collection of essays edited by Jozef Coppens, professor at the university. In the summers there gathered in the Centre d'Etudes Supérieures de la Renaissance at Tours mature scholars and postgraduate students for lectures and discussions on a chosen theme. In July 1969 the theme was Erasmus at his quincentenary. Observers commented on the courteous intensity of the encounters and exchanges during this *stage* and, above all, in an era of student rebellion, on the atmosphere 'of great harmony between the generations and under the shadow of Erasmus.' The subsequent publication, a compilation of almost all the lectures delivered during the three weeks of the *stage*, rivalled, without outdoing, *Scrinium Erasmianum* in scale and substance: *Colloquia Erasmiana Turonensia*.[12] We will take the dozens of essays from these commemorative volumes as a more than adequate sample of tendencies in Erasmus scholarship at the time of the quincentenary, while not neglecting what other commemorative events produced or, indeed, other contemporaneous publications.

The quincentenary aroused interest once again in the vexed question of Erasmus' year of birth, a matter clouded by his own equivocations and never resolved by later scholarship. The uncertainty allowed celebration over the range 1966 to 1969. The case for 1969, which won majority and, to an extent, official support, had been put by R.R. Post in a study of 1953, strategically translated into French and republished in 1964. Post's naïve hope was that his paper might produce 'a simultaneous and unanimous celebration of Erasmus' birth in 1969.' It rests on datings for the main events of Erasmus' early life and education. In 1966 E.-W. Kohls supported the case for a birth-year of 1466 from Erasmus' own assertions, those made when he had no reason for equivocation. A recent exhaustive study by Harry Vredeveld has endorsed the argument for 1466 from Erasmus' plain statements about his age. At the very end of the anniversary period, A.C.F. Koch, archivist and city librarian at Deventer, in a monograph *The Year of Erasmus' Birth*, while revisiting, from the Deventer archives, questions about Erasmus' early life and schooling, also sought an explanation for a phenomenon observed by others, his tendency in later life to inflate his age. Koch found it in his superstitious fear of the climacteric or seventh year which, from his forty-ninth year, he judiciously skipped. The whole case led Koch to a birth-year of 1467. It made a strong impression at the time but its influence faded, above all because it depended on an out-of-character level of superstition in Erasmus. On balance, Post, veteran scholar of humanism and the *Devotio moderna*, who died on Erasmus' birthday a year before his chosen date for the quincentenary (27 October 1968), won the argument in the anniversary years themselves, but later work has led scholars back to 1466.[13]

It is not surprising that, in the atmosphere of 1967–70, the opening and closing words at commemorative conferences should be about the up-to-dateness of Erasmus and the present relevance of his message. Both the weight of scholarship, which threatened to smother the man and the message, and the state of the culture, wherein the humanist tradition was under scrutiny, or even attack, pressed the question. It is also not surprising that the veteran Erasmians Marcel Bataillon and Léon-E. Halkin, who in 1962 succeeded to the chair in the history of humanism at the University of Liège occupied since 1929 by Marie Delcourt and, like his predecessor, gathered there a company of distinguished students and collaborators, should receive the commission to answer it. They appealed to the community of Erasmus scholars, the *Sodalitas Erasmiana*, sole vestige of the *Respublica literaria* of which Erasmus had dreamed. P.S. Allen had made the same appeal nearly half a century earlier, after the terrible catastrophe of the Great War. There was reference, as one would expect in times of Cold War and, for that matter, of real war in Southeast Asia, to Erasmus' passionate plea for peace among governments and peoples. In its contemporary *aggiornamento* through Vatican 2, the Catholic Church was, so it was said, at last catching up with Erasmus, a quip which subsequent events have justified only in part. Most compelling is what Bataillon has to say about Erasmus and the written and published word, his role as a public intellectual, living free, his ready understanding of what the multiplication of words through printing meant for the shaping of public opinion. Erasmians must accept, Bataillon concludes, that Erasmus' actuality in the present can be only in and through translation. His very playing with ambiguities, so offensive to his right-minded critics, makes him congenial to a contemporary audience.[14]

III

How, on the evidence of the major commemorative volumes, did scholarship stand at the quincentenary on the main questions about Erasmus' life, thought, and influence? Biographical questions should fairly come first. Erasmus' beginnings, his intellectual formation, the origins of his distinctive understanding of Christianity had had a preeminence in Erasmus studies up to the celebrations of 1936. The legacy of Seebohm, Mestwerdt, Hyma, and Schottenloher was not a consensus but at least a common understanding of where the interesting issues lay: Erasmus' debt to the *Devotio moderna* and the Brethren, his response to Italian humanism, his encounter with John Colet. In biographies of the generation between the end of World War 2 and the quincentenary, this understanding persists. In her brief and affectionate study of 1949, Margaret Mann Phillips, like Hyma, sees the Erasmus of the *Antibarbari*, of the 1490s, as 'a rationalist only' and ambitious above all for literary fame, though a residue of the *Devotio moderna* remained; with Seebohm and Mestwerdt, she attributes to his English friends 'the honour of resolving his inner conflict' and identifying his vocation: 'the setting of the wisdom of the ancients at the service of the interpretation of Christianity and the betterment of man.' He was to take a middle way between the man-centred and the God-centred, sure 'that human wisdom is inspired and finally crowned by the revelation of the Divine.'[15] The second edition of Karl Meissinger's biography *Erasmus von Rotterdam*, first published in Zürich in the depths of the war, had appeared in the previous year. Unlike Phillips, who found in Erasmus one source of the 'erudite piety' of the Anglican church 'which she loved, content to live out her life in its fellowship and liturgy,' Meissinger did not see himself as an 'Erasmian.' After a classical schooling, he studied Protestant theology at Giessen (1902–6) and became a co-worker on the Weimar edition of Luther's works. Yet, in the war years under the Nazi regime, he formed in Munich an Institute for Reformation Research, which had as complement a similarly underground *Societas Erasmiana*. His *Erasmus* of 1948 was the Institute's first publication; its most ambitious project was a critical edition of Erasmus' works, which did not eventuate.[16] For Meissinger, the *Devotio moderna*, like humanism, was an expression of the urban, bourgeois culture of the Netherlands. Erasmus was unsympathetic to the conservative strains still to be found in it, but its drive for a simple, active, biblical Christianity ran through his life and work like a bass ground in a musical composition. Meissinger's treatment of other claimed influences on Erasmus' mind is subdued; Colet appears here as a largely unknown figure, whose primary significance lay in providing Erasmus with a link to Italy.[17] He notes the paucity of studies on late scholasticism, a lack which began to be made up only in the quincentenary decade, and, consequently, the uncertainty of Erasmus' relation to scholasticism.[18] As early as the *Antibarbari* of the 1490s, says Meissinger, Erasmus had, with fine philosophical perception, in a way anticipating Kant, seen the danger of self-assertive rationalism in humanism's legitimate claim to autonomy and had sketched out a characteristic solution: learning is one thing, goodness is another.[19]

The biography of the quincentenary was Roland Bainton's *Erasmus of Christendom*. Bainton himself sensed the fitness of his coming to Erasmus in old age after a career of writing and teaching about the Reformations, magisterial and radical. His account of what attracted and held him to Erasmus touched on elements in his own personal and intellectual make-up set in early life: the glow of piety seen first in his pastor father and rediscovered in Erasmus; what he calls a 'wistful scepticism,' actually a robust critical temper, stimulated by his father's experience of the modernist-fundamentalist controversy and honed by his own teachers at Yale; his pacifism, again shaped in dialogue with his father and tested by non-combatant service in the Great War; his sense of humour; his respect for the classical tradition, and his love of language: 'Words are tools to be carefully selected and dextrously handled.'[20] The prose of *Erasmus of Christendom* is clipped rather than flowing. It precipitates the reader forward. The sense of humour turns on noticing, almost in passing, unrecognized contradictions, like the discrepancy between the injunctions of the *Enchiridion* and the character of him to whom they were addressed. Bainton was himself capable of that gentle, undemonstrative deflation he recognized in Erasmus.[21]

On the shaping of Erasmus' mind, Bainton integrates the work of his predecessors while softening claims that are too exclusive, angular, or assertive. Erasmus associated himself with one of two strands in the *Devotio moderna*, that which valued classical learning and was represented in his early days by Rudolf Agricola and

Alexander Hegius. He had read the scholastics, as Christian Dolfen had seen in the 1930s, but was out of sympathy with the dominant teachers at Paris in his time. Colet gave him a 'new impetus' but was not alone in that, and the debt was more personal than intellectual. Within the Neoplatonism which came to him through Colet and his friends, he was highly selective. The Brethren's emphasis on inner religion remained, and Colet reinforced it. In this account, Seebohm is left far behind. Erasmus' purposes were already settled before his English visit: 'From the beginning to the end of his career he was dedicated to the dissemination of the classical Christian heritage.' Those purposes made him 'the mouthpiece of the liberal Catholic reform.'[22]

To these great themes, which had occupied scholarship for over a century, the commemorative studies of 1967–70 had little to add. It was as though a scholarly trail had run out. A sceptical voice asked how it was that the *Devotio moderna*, which left no trace on the documentation of Erasmus' formative years themselves, could reappear in his writings of fifteen or thirty years later. In reply the positive interpretation was put in a metaphor: 'Erasmus bathed in this atmosphere from his childhood and breathed it all his life.' That was about the sum of it. The one essay on Erasmus and Colet, by Germain Marc'hadour, draws out, not the coalescences, but the contrasts between the two friends, as in their debate of 1499 over Christ's agony in the garden, thus recalling Eugene Rice's essay of 1952, with its striking title 'John Colet and the Annihilation of the Natural,' and anticipating John B. Gleason's full revisionist study of 1989, *John Colet*. Otherwise, the word in 1970 seemed to be: the outstanding questions must remain unresolved; on them a certain defeatism was acceptable.[23] In recompense, questions largely neglected, or neglected until recently, came into prominence and set a new course for scholarship. These were Erasmus' relations to the Fathers and to the scholastics.

Already the Mons colloquium, the first main event of the scholarly quincentenary, signalled a big expansion of studies on Erasmus' relation to the Fathers. His attraction to Jerome, his labours devoted to the works of that Father, had long been recognized and would continue to be studied in depth.[24] The Mons signals were to less familiar connections, Augustine and Origen, and to rivalry between them in influencing Erasmus. The arguments for the priority of Augustine and Origen were pressed by, respectively, Charles Béné and André Godin, though each hesitated to make an exclusive claim. Jean Hadot moderated between the rival views with the formula: 'Erasmus is at the meeting of two currents; with him there is neither a pure Origenism nor a pure Augustinianism.'[25]

In his paper at Mons, Béné demonstrates how both sides used Augustine's *De Doctrina Christiana* in the controversy at Louvain in 1518–19 over the role of languages and humanist culture in theological education. From the 1490s Erasmus himself, Béné says, used the *De Doctrina Christiana*, which he had discovered at Groenendal in 1494, with ever greater fidelity to Augustine's teaching. At Mons, Béné was foreshadowing his great thesis *Erasme et Saint Augustin*, which was to appear in 1969, still within the quincentenary period. In the first stage of Erasmus' life, he begins there, he used the Fathers to justify his essentially profane enthusiasm for classical literature, Jerome especially but also, after 1494, Augustine, who was a more unusual and, consequently, a more cogent witness. During his studies at Paris in the second half of the 1490s, there was a shift in his perception of culture and a deepening of his piety, under the influence of his associations and friendships of that time; through them had come a more authentic understanding of Augustine. Colet but confirmed his resolution to give priority to sacred letters. What was fresh and original in the *Enchiridion* (first published in 1503) had its source in Augustine's *De Doctrina*; Jerome and Origen were of secondary importance, and the appeal to Plato, which seems so prominent on the surface of the work, was under the authority of Augustine. The Erasmus of the *Enchiridion*, unlike the Erasmus of the *Antibarbari* of a decade before, which used the Father for Erasmus' own purposes, followed Augustine faithfully, in now according profane culture a subordinate place and in searching for the spiritual sense behind the literal text of scripture. The *De Doctrina* was the principal patristic reference for the famous prefaces to Erasmus' New Testament edition and, by the time of the *Ecclesiastes* (1535), he had appropriated Augustine's thought on the relation between culture and Christian piety and made it his own: human studies must be pursued only in moderation, with concentration on what was indispensable for piety alone.[26]

'When Erasmus listens to the reasons of his heart,' says Béné, 'he exalts Jerome without hesitation; but when he will expound his most original and newest views on culture, piety and exegesis, we witness the "marriage of reason," which makes of Augustine the most fruitful source of Erasmian thought.' Béné admits a 'curious discordance' in Erasmus' appreciation of Augustine. He was reserved towards him, even critical of him as theologian and, in that sphere, always preferred Jerome, Origen, and Chrysostom. Yet, he quoted him more and more as the years passed and always with fuller understanding. Jean-Claude Margolin remarked, at the Rotterdam celebration, that Béné's study was 'entirely convincing.' It has, we may conclude, demonstrated that Augustine had a prime part in the shaping of Erasmus' mind. Nevertheless, there are strains in the argument. The claim to priority borders on exclusiveness, crowding out other influences. It is said that only the inner logic of Augustine's thought and his authority could persuade Erasmus to subordinate the humane culture he held dear. But arguments from inner logic or authority do not clinch the case for a near-exclusive influence. Why might not the *Devotio moderna* have had an effect on Erasmus' eventual 'antihumanism,' his limited enthusiasm, at the end, for classical culture? One must, Béné says, refer this to Augustine, but precise citations are lacking and the argument can, he concedes, only be hypothetical. This has the weakness of all arguments from silence.[27]

To Origen Erasmus' pointer was Jean Vitrier, warden of a Franciscan house at Saint-Omer, pastor, preacher, and Paulinist, whom Erasmus had met there in 1501. Biographers had noted the association; Erasmus himself had celebrated it in the same letter of June 1521, which provided Justus Jonas with the pen-portrait of Colet for which he had asked.[28] In one paper at Mons and two at Tours, André Godin, in confirming the accuracy of Erasmus' portrait of Vitrier, also verified the closeness of Vitrier and Origen in Erasmus' mind and indeed in reality; from his discovery at Saint-Omer of twenty MS homilies of Vitrier, Godin was able to demonstrate Vitrier's devotion to and dependence on Origen. Thus he opened fresh possibilities in the study of the 'mysterious alchemy' of Erasmus' formation: that beside the *Devotio moderna* and Colet must be placed Origen as presented to him initially by Vitrier and a Franciscan tradition of affective spirituality, which Vitrier also represented. There was a double influence, Vitrier and Origen. In Vitrier we find features characteristic of Erasmus' religion: the primacy of the preached word derived from scripture, the refusal of reliance on ritual acts, the spiritualizing of the present life. In *Ecclesiastes*,

Godin concludes, the quantitative superiority of references to Augustine's *De Doctrina*, with its guarantee of orthodoxy, is outweighed by a qualitative preference for Origen's emphasis 'on spiritual understanding of the mystery of the incarnate Word, unveiled by scriptural allegory.' The counterclaim (for Origen) may be as strained as the claim (for Augustine), but Godin properly remarks that the aim is not to settle the issue of precedence among Erasmus' favourite Fathers – Jerome, Augustine, Origen – but, more fundamentally, 'to measure the patristic impregnation in the work, thought, and, possibly, the very being of Erasmus,' a reminiscence of Jean Hadot's warning at Mons against exclusive claims. At the same time in *Scrinium* John B. Payne argues for an 'uneasy balance' in Erasmus' hermeneutics between the philological and historical tradition of Jerome and the Platonizing and spiritualistic one of Origen.[29]

Godin rounded off his work on this theme many years later with his *Erasme lecteur d'Origène* (1982), a massive demonstration of the importance of Origen for Erasmus' work and a case study of the role of patristics in his evangelical project. The book contributed to the debate, alive in the 1980s, on the character of Erasmus' theology, and to that aspect we will return in the next chapter. Godin's search is for both explicit borrowings from Origen, identified by historical semantics, and a more diffuse cultural impregnation traced by traditional methods of the history of ideas. Erasmus' originality and boldness derive, not from his Augustinianism, commonplace in the sixteenth century, but from his Origenism, the source of a new religious culture capable of confronting the existing theological order and scholasticism. In the anthropology of the *Enchiridion*, the tripartite division of the human being, Erasmus, fresh from his meeting with Vitrier, showed the 'ardente et naïve ferveur de néophyte origénien.' Origen occupied a strategic place in the *Enchiridion*, not by literary design, but by a kind of inner necessity, both intellectual and existential, since Erasmus was seeking to reconcile in a reasoned way learning and piety and to justify to himself his change of direction, from the cloister to the life of a free intellectual in the world. In the exegetical sphere, 'whether it be to establish "critically" the sacred text or – more frequently – to make it intelligible to the reader, Erasmus' first reflex is to consult [Origen] to determine his own line of conduct.' This is so, despite the resistance of a philologist, interested above all in the application of scripture to

moral and spiritual life, to philosophical speculation and excessive allegorizing. Even in relation to his preferred Father, the
master of the spiritual sense, Erasmus took a distinctive stance
and was *homo pro se*. Yet, his more astute critics rightly saw the
significance of Origen for the challenge Erasmus' exegetical
method posed to the speculative type of theological culture; Erasmus' Origenism was a 'Trojan horse' in the theologians' citadel.
He was not, as some scholars have claimed, a defender of the
established four-sense pattern of scriptural interpretation; he preferred the patristic double sense, the grammatical or historical
and the spiritual, and found an essential harmony between the
classical-rhetorical and the patristic inheritances. In the *Paraphrases*, the heart, says Godin, of the Erasmian project, there was
both selectivity in the use of Origen, apparent in the moderate
use of allegory, and a dependence on him at all levels, semantic,
stylistic, exegetical, and thematic. Erasmus' Origenism was 'a
tranquil possession, a recovered confidence in a man and a work
Erasmus holds for fundamentally orthodox and perfectly admis-
sible by Christians.'[30]

The lead Christian Dolfen had given in 1936 in the study of
Erasmus' relation with the scholastics was followed at last at the
quincentenary. Important papers explored his relation to Thomas
Aquinas in particular, but discussions were, naturally, more
exploratory than conclusive. At Mons the Protestant theologian
Ernst-Wilhelm Kohls showed that Erasmus shared with Thomas
his far from Pelagian view of free will and grace, by which the
freedom of the will operates only within an economy of grace.
His *De libero arbitrio* against Luther stated a theological position
held consistently from his first writings, which separated him
from humanist theologies like Pico's and put him in solidarity
with the high scholastics. In discussion on Kohls' paper, the veteran Erasmian Pierre Mesnard, while accepting that his thought
had, especially on the cooperation of nature and grace, Thomist
foundations, even so asked whether Erasmus, despite his caustic
comments on his Scotist teachers at Paris, did not owe a debt to
Scotus, notably in his stress on the absolute initiative of divine
grace in human salvation. At Tours, Jean-Pierre Massaut of Liège
questioned the claim that Erasmus had a preference for Thomas.
Over all, he did not distinguish Thomas from the scholastics
he criticized for mixing human philosophy with revelation; indeed, Erasmus said, Thomas bore the heaviest responsibility for

enthroning Aristotle within theology. The praises of Thomas in Erasmus' correspondence and writings, Massaut says, diminished when read in context; they were sometimes tactical, a cover for or diversion from his more fundamental criticisms in an age when Thomas' disciples around the seats of power defended their master 'with intemperate, fanatical and excessive zeal.'[31]

The issues were, it is plain, far from resolved in these quincentenary essays. The comparison of texts could not be decisive in itself, especially if they were divorced from their whole contexts and historical settings. At the same time, tactical interpretations, psychological and, in a sense, political interpretations were, beyond a certain point, speculative. Why might not Erasmus have intended a balance of praises and criticisms of his predecessors? The inconclusiveness of the discussion at this stage is confirmed by reference to the major works of the time on Erasmus' theology, pioneers in the opening up of that subject, Kohls' *Die Theologie des Erasmus* (1966) and Payne's *Erasmus: His Theology of the Sacraments* (1970). Kohls concentrates on three early works, *De contemptu mundi*, the *Antibarbari*, and the *Enchiridion*, arguing that already in these the recurring, fundamental themes of Erasmus' theology had appeared. These themes were: the role of the classical authors (Cicero, Plato) in preparing for Christanity, since Christ draws all things to himself; the authority, sufficiency, and contemporaneity of the scriptural record, which extends and continues the incarnation; the priority of grace in human salvation and restoration, Christians claiming victory in their spiritual warfare only through Christ's victory on the Cross, which is the heart of the gospel, though folly and an offence to the world (1 Corinthians 1). Central is not what Christ might be in general, philosophically and theologically speaking, but what he is to us; this theology is driven by its doctrine of salvation, its soteriology. Its trinitarian character is confirmed by its high doctrine of the Spirit: the outward, visible, and material have Christian meaning only when informed by the inner, invisible, and spiritual. This is true for interpreting scripture, where the literal and spiritual senses must be held in an unbreakable dialectic, and for understanding the church, which is not essentially an authority or institution, but a community of love formed by the Spirit. Erasmus, says Kohls, used in effect the ancient scheme of *Exitus-reditus*: the saving power of love flows out from God through the members of the church and returns to him.[32]

Kohls' interpretation of Erasmus' theology breaks with all rationalistic and moralizing interpretations. This was an orthodox theology, from Paul through the Fathers and the early and high scholastics. In important respects, it was not remote from the mainline Reformers. Among immediate influences Kohls accepts both the *Devotio moderna* and Thomas Aquinas, the former above all for its efforts to reform monasticism, not by increasing exclusiveness, but by infusing the love ethic applicable to all Christians, the latter for his dialectic of divine sovereignty and human responsibility and for his understanding of the relation between spirit, love, and law.[33]

John Payne also finds in Erasmus an accepting as well as a critical stance towards the scholastics. In an explicit break with Kohls, however, he considers Erasmus' dependence on Thomas formal rather than substantive and his acquaintance more with Thomas' exegetical than theological works. Both recognize in Erasmus an admiration for Jean Gerson, but, for Payne, Gerson was not a high road to Thomas Aquinas but rather a link to the late-medieval nominalists to whom, on matters of substance, Erasmus was closer than to Thomas. Among such matters was especially the soteriological question, on which Erasmus accepted the place nominalist theology gave to human effort, to that doing what was in one's power, which God's promised grace would further and complete. Similarly, the sacraments bestow grace because God has bound himself by a promise. On this theme Payne is able to draw on Oberman's revaluation of late-medieval scholasticism. He also links the nominalists' scepticism about high speculation in theology to Erasmus' 'reverence before the divine majesty.'[34]

Payne betrays a gentle impatience with Erasmus' uncertainty on questions that exercised the minds of scholastic theologians. He recognizes that that vagueness was studied, that Erasmus' avoidance of scholastic terms and his lack of reference to the scholastics' names were deliberate. Nevertheless, both Payne and Kohls, while doing great service to Erasmus scholarship by taking him seriously as theologian and demonstrating that his thought was not merely discursive and circumstantial but to a degree systematic, can be accused of over-systematizing him, of straining to bring him within frameworks that were not natural to him. While Kohls stresses throughout the primacy of grace, Payne brings Erasmus closer to the Platonist tradition by making the dichotomy of flesh and spirit central to his thought, indeed its 'fundamental principle.' He begins his systematic presentation of Erasmus' theology with an anthropology based, above all, on the *Enchiridion*, a starting-point Kohls explicitly rejects.[35] Though, like Kohls, Payne highlights the authority of scripture for Erasmus, what he says about the struggles of flesh and spirit ties him still to those who have seen Erasmus' theology as essentially moralistic. While Erasmus recognized the objective ground of salvation in divine action, he nevertheless, says Payne, put 'much more emphasis upon the imperative than the indicative of Christian existence.'[36] This was a practical theology. But does such a theology, or a biblical theology for that matter, have a 'fundamental principle'?

This discussion of Payne's book has taken us away from our starting-point, Erasmus' intellectual and spiritual formation and the treatment of that issue in the writings of the quincentenary. Payne was a participant in the debate, to which Kohls and Massaut also contributed in those years, about Erasmus' dependence on the scholastics. There was no resolution. Erasmus' relation to Thomas and to the late-medieval nominalists was a question posed rather than settled at the quincentenary. Much of the evidence had been gathered and alternative solutions stated unambiguously. Similarly, Erasmus' claims to a special relationship with Augustine and with Origen had been put by, respectively, Charles Béné and André Godin. That debate, too, awaited further development in 1970. In summary, we may say: on the old questions of Erasmus' dependence on the *Devotio moderna* and Colet the quincentenary, while casting an eye more sceptical than that of previous generations, largely left the scene unchanged; on the new questions of his relations to the Fathers and the scholastics, it could report the opening up of bright prospects for study and research.

It is possible that interest in Erasmus' beginnings, in the idea of origins generally, was waning. Was the shift in interest from the 'young Luther,' who had dominated Luther scholarship in the first half of the century, to the mature and embattled Reformer of his last years replicated in Erasmus' case?[37] A generation before the quincentenary Richard Newald's biography *Erasmus Roterodamus* (1947) had promised more attention than was then usual to Erasmus' last years. The promise is not fulfilled in an arithmetical sense, but Newald does demonstrate that the old Erasmus, far

from weltering in self-pity and recrimination, exercised a constructive intellectual and pastoral influence on a younger generation of leaders, especially in the Upper Rhineland, a sphere of
special interest to Newald. In his late educational works, Erasmus offered the fruits of his reading and experience over a lifetime. His devotional writings of that time, his Psalms
commentaries, for example, both reiterate his long-held convictions and address contemporary dilemmas, like the division of
the church. Above all, his work on preaching, *Ecclesiastes*, shot
through, says Newald, with evening light, completed what he
had begun in the *Antibarbari* and the *Enchiridion* and expressed
the faith of the Upper Rhine humanists in preaching as the most
effective way to church reform.[38] Even so, in 1961 Karl Heinz Oelrich, in his important monograph on the late Erasmus and the
Reformation, to which we will return in the next chapter, still
regrets scholarship's neglect of Erasmus' last decade. Students of
the Reformation, he says, have concentrated on the years 1517–25
and Erasmus' relations with Luther.[39]

Quincentenary essays present the old Erasmus as both a sharp,
even bitter, controversialist and a constructive irenicist.[40] At
Tours M.P. Gilmore called for a closer study of Erasmus' controversies and himself argued that, while Erasmus found many of
his critics intolerable, he never abandoned his faith in dialogue as
the way to recover the lost unity of the church.[41] One paper above
all fulfils Newald's hope of a more sympathetic and penetrating
presentation of the old Erasmus, Cornelis Reedijk's 'Erasmus'
Final Modesty.' Why, between 1527 and 1533, Reedijk asks, did
Erasmus give up plans for a posthumous edition of his collected
works financed from his estate? Was this an admission of defeat?
The evidence rather suggests that, through all his disappointments, he remained true to his aim of the unity and purification
of the church. But he asked himself: could he, in a time of deepening religious division with its evil consequences, not least in
Basel, for the studies he valued, 'expect to leave to posterity a
spiritual heritage in which his thoughts and intentions would
appear as a whole, as one efficacious instrument, deriving its
strength from the inner harmony of its component parts?' Might
not his work, after his death, be distorted or dismembered, for
reasons of profit or propaganda, by enemies on both sides of the
religious divide? Would it not be better, in a 'fine gesture, well
thought out and made in an ecumenical spirit,' to leave his for-

tune to the poor, and especially to poor students of Protestant Basel, and so contribute to the revival of studies where he had most feared their destruction? Producing his collected works could be left to the courage and discretion of his friends.[42] Reedijk proclaims Erasmus' spirited defence, right to the end, of his spiritual independence, as he had done ten years before in a famous article on Erasmus' death.[43]

IV

From the biographical we turn to contextual questions, the environments within which Erasmus had an influence, the networks he created, the powers of attraction and repulsion he exercised over friends and enemies in their various locations. Places associated with the quincentenary events and, consequently, with the provenance of commemorative volumes, which had in 1936 been concentrated in Basel and Rotterdam, prompted local and regional studies.

Naturally, Basel and Rotterdam were not neglected. The indefatigable and erudite Nicolaas van der Blom, master at the Gymnasium Erasmianum in Rotterdam, wrote, as he was to do at other times of commemoration, and especially for his fellow-citizens, about Erasmus' relation to his natal place.[44] One could speak of an Erasmian culture in Rotterdam, as in Basel. Peter Bietenholz added nuances to the latter theme by a study in *Scrinium* of the Basel book trade and its relations with France. By the mid-1520s, when Erasmus was well settled in Basel, that trade was predominantly under his influence. In the next generation, his younger associates and disciples sustained his spiritual heritage; by the second half of the sixteenth century, under the pressure of religious war, the inheritance was broken up, though, despite their differences, Catholic irenicists and radical Protestants pleading for toleration still both bore the mark of Erasmus.[45]

Louvain was a problematical place for Erasmus, and it is natural that *Scrinium Erasmianum*, the university's quincentenary tribute, should include essays on their troubled, if at times constructive, relationship. A chronicle of his sojourn there in 1517–21 exposes both friendships and enmities. As early as 1518–19, Louvain theologians associated Erasmus and Luther in a common condemnation. Against dangerous criticisms made of his *Collo-*

quia by one theologian, he both defended himself and refined his text. The last word went to his enemies. R. Crahay shows how the posthumous *Opera* of one prominent theologian, Jacques Masson (Latomus), provided arguments for the first prohibition (1558) of a book by Erasmus in the Netherlands, his tract on Christian reconciliation *De sarcienda ecclesiae concordia* (in French and Flemish translation). Members of the faculty were active in preparing materials for Erasmus' condemnation, not so much for his particular dogmatic denials as for undermining dogmatic structures as such and ecclesiastical authority.[46]

When extended from Louvain to the Netherlands generally, the picture brightens. Quincentenary studies of the fate of his books in his homeland demonstrate their continuing presence in libraries and private collections and their continuing influence, though, thanks in part to the work of the censors, Erasmus the 'master of Latin style and classical culture' survived better than Erasmus the theologian. The Commémoration Nationale of June 1969 celebrated Erasmus' relations with Belgian cities. Antwerp, cosmopolitan metropolis, offered friendships beyond the circle of humanists in the narrower sense. Erasmus had many friends and disciples in Ghent, first city of Flanders, as his bitter enemy Aleander saw, and he wrote studied praises of the city.[47]

In Erasmus' praise of cities the balance between rhetorical form and personal observation is not easily struck. His most famous encomium is of Strasbourg: 'the rule of one man without tyranny, aristocracy without faction, democracy without civil strife, wealth without self-indulgence, success without insolence.' The Strasbourg quincentenary celebrations produced their own distingushed publication. Two essays there deal in fact with complications in Erasmus' relationship with the city. Otto Herding shows that a gulf existed between Erasmus and Jakob Wimpfeling, to whom the encomium of Strasbourg had been addressed, partly because of Wimpfeling's theological conservatism and attachment to scholasticism, partly because of his devotion to the institutions of the city and the empire, Erasmus by contrast remaining detached from institutions. Jean Lebeau treats the *contretemps* between Erasmus and the religious radical Sebastian Franck when Franck in 1531 – a year of shortage and difficulty in Strasbourg – published his *Geschichtsbibel* and associated Erasmus with his revolutionary denunciations of papacy and empire. This incident represents a late and depressed stage in Erasmus' relations with Strasbourg, no longer in his eyes a city of classical balance and moderation but 'a nest of hungry tricksters.'[48]

There is not, in the quincentenary essays, an obvious response to the challenge of Bernd Moeller's monograph of 1962, *Reichstadt und Reformation*, which had made a link between the high civic self-consciousness of the imperial free cities and the Zwinglian Reformation, with its Erasmian roots, a challenge Reformation historians were already taking up.[49] Paris, whose Erasmian resonances Margaret Mann had evoked in a 1936 essay, was, as a royal capital, not in the category of cities studied by Bernd Moeller. In *Scrinium*, Marie-Madeleine de la Garanderie studies the network of friendships woven between Paris and Erasmus in the southern Netherlands during his years of greatest influence and reputation (1517–21); there were dark shades, 'a kind of cold war, under the name of friendship,' existing between Erasmus and the great French humanist Guillaume Budé, and his relations with the Parisian intellectuals deteriorating badly long before he left Louvain in 1521.[50]

The move is an easy and necessary one from the Erasmian networks of the great humanist's lifetime to Erasmianism, though, still at the quincentenary, the concept remained elusive. A generation had passed since the publication of Bataillon's book, but the critical assessments had still to be assimilated into the Erasmus literature. At Tours in 1969 Bataillon himself asked again what content could be given to the term 'érasmisme' for establishing the religious influence of Erasmus on his time. Bataillon recognized that 'spiritualisme' and 'évangélisme' had other sources beside Erasmus, differing from location to location, but almost everywhere pre-existent, like illuminism in Spain. Definitions of Erasmianism must, he concludes, take account of these contingencies and avoid abstraction. At Rotterdam he added a large footnote to *Erasme et l'Espagne* by reconsidering the influence in Spain of the *Praise of Folly*, which had not been translated by the Spanish Erasmians, Bataillon therefore concluding in 1937 that Erasmianism had advanced in Spain without the help of that paradoxical masterpiece. He could now report, in 1969, that an adaptation, admittedly with the paradoxes blunted, appeared there as early as 1521. An influence can be discerned through the century and ultimately on the second part of *Don Quixote*.[51]

The most substantial contribution of the quincentenary to the topic 'Erasmianism' was the Rotterdam essay by Craig Thompson, editor of Erasmus' *Colloquia*, who looked forward to the appearance one day of an English equivalent of *Erasme et l'Espagne*, a hope now, in the current mood of scholarship as described in the previous chapter, perhaps forlorn. The author of the projected book would need, Thompson says, to distinguish between the popularity and the influence of Erasmus and between formal or conventional acknowledgments, even royal commands, and the reality. Thompson himself deals with Erasmus' early appearance as a best-seller in England, the adaptation and propagation of his ideas under Thomas Cromwell and the publication of the *Paraphrases* in translation under Catherine Parr's patronage and their obligatory use in chrches in the reign of Edward VI. This is material familiar from McConica's book but given by Thompson a distinctive circumstantial texture. Fresh is the incorporation of Erasmus into the English Protestant traditions taking shape in the second half of the sixteenth century: for John Foxe he was a Christian hero, for John Jewel 'a man of singular learning and judgment.'[52]

Quincentenary essays also demonstrate Erasmus' long-term influence on his homeland. 'Among different currents characteristic of the social, religious, political and literary life of the Netherlands in its golden age,' writes J.-C. Margolin in his contribution to the Belgian commemorative volume, 'an Erasmian tradition revives and expands in a large number of works.' This is an essay on Erasmianism in the work of the homely, yet learned, Dutch poet Jacob Cats (1578–1660), notably in his long poem on marriage and in another on children's games. The young Cats, growing up in the last decade of the sixteenth century, received the tradition through the literary productions of the ancient chambers of rhetoric and through a popular culture of proverbs and wise sayings, illustrated in the works of Pieter Bruegel the elder, which themselves carry marks of Erasmus' influence. His Calvinist religion and the exuberance of the baroque style are also apparent in Cats' work, but, despite the changes worked by a century of turbulent events, the Erasmus of the book on Christian marriage and the *Colloquia*, the sober, practical moralist of everyday life and *homo ludens*, remained for Cats an avowed master. Margolin uses the concept of national psychology ('psychologie des peuples') to bridge the two epochs. Cats was a representative figure in that, like him, most of Erasmus' many admirers among the scholars and writers of the golden age saw him from one main angle, the didactic. The greatest poet of the age, Joost van Vondel, was, says Gilbert Degroote in *Scrinium*, an exception: he came close to Erasmus' many-sidedness.[53]

It is not clear that Erasmus' connection to his great French successors, Rabelais and Montaigne, can be safely put under the head of 'Erasmianism.' Essays by M.A. Screech and Margaret Mann Phillips in the Tours collection suggest caution. Screech makes a distinction, which could be applied to other connections of Erasmus, his dependence on Colet, for example, between personal and intellectual influences. Erasmus profoundly affected Rabelais the man, but speaking of literary and intellectual influences requires careful discriminations. Rabelaisian folly had its source as much in Erasmus' biblical writings as in the *Praise of Folly* but, even so, the two men understood the Christian foolishness of St Paul differently. Phillips recalls the voices hostile to Erasmus, the anti-Ciceronian and theologically suspect, in Montaigne's environment. His connection to Erasmus was, not surprisingly, largely unavowed; between them there was not so much direct influence as a kind of family resemblance, above all in their appeals to classical wisdom. Montaigne, and Rabelais, too, used Erasmus' *Adagia* as a quarry.[54]

In studies of influences upon Erasmus, the quincentenary of 1967–70 came at a watershed. A balance had been struck in assessing the place in his formation of the *Devotio moderna*, Italian humanism and Neoplatonism, and John Colet. Extravagant claims in any direction had been discounted. New questions were being put, about Erasmus' relation to the Fathers, in particular, but also to the scholastics, and some would soon attract massive works of scholarship like those devoted earlier to his more immediate antecedents. The issue of the influence of Erasmus had not by 1970 come so clearly to a watershed. Bataillon's great book both attracted and overshadowed, and there were many calls, up to then unheeded, to emulate its scale and vision for other parts of Europe. Discussions of the methodological problems in establishing intellectual influences and of the concept of Erasmianism continued sporadically through the quincentenary, perhaps even picked up pace, not least in connection with Eastern Europe, as we have seen in the previous chapter.[55] It was, however, only with Seidel Menchi's work of the 1970s and 1980s, especially with her emphasis on the relationship between

Erasmus and his readers, that the history of Erasmianism crossed its watershed and entered a new phase.

The subject of Erasmus' character and personality, to which Mangan had applied his crude psychological colourings and Huizinga his refined ones, was not much laboured in the quin-centenary volumes. There was some sense of a fresh start but no watershed. At Mons, the veteran Erasmian Pierre Mesnard, whose death two years later was to overshadow the meeting at Tours, attempted briefly to characterize Erasmus by the mysteri-ous science of *caractérologie*. Under this scheme, character is deter-mined above all by the interaction of three factors: *émotivité*, *activité*, and *vitesse de réaction*. Erasmus' capacity to surmount, without psychopathology, the peculiar circumstances of his early life, his illegitimate birth and his escape from the monastery, proves that he was of the sanguine type, non-emotive and egoist. He was active and capable of a quick response. A characteriza-tion more in line with contemporary preoccupations opened the Rotterdam congress, S. Dresden's 'Présence d'Erasme.' Dresden sets out to explain the apparent contradiction of mobility and constancy in Erasmus. The resolution lay, he says, in his special relation to books, to writing, and to words. Erasmus recreated, indeed he created, himself in writing and was in a sense both present and absent. A written presence might even, in his view, be more real than a bodily presence, as his remarkable statement in the *Paraclesis* suggests: Christ is present to us in scripture more clearly than if we saw him with our very eyes. Hence, Dresden concludes, Erasmus' sharp distinction between the spiritual and the mundane, Christ and the world, and his absolute preference for the first over the second. A critic might, however, respond that, when Erasmus asks himself in the *Enchiridion*, the most Pla-tonizing and spiritualizing of his works, what following Christ actually means, he answers: the social virtues. That scruple aside, this is a profound essay which points forward to a major preoccu-pation of Erasmus scholarship in the next generation, the central-ity of words, language, grammar, and rhetoric in his life, work, and personality.[56]

Erasmus' constancy and mobility in a more concrete sense were recalled at Mons in a paper on his travels, which presents him in the, to some, surprising character of horseman and horse fancier, and in another, by Franz Bierlaire, summarizing his monograph based on studies at Liège and Tours and soon to be published (1968), on the *familia* of Erasmus, the young men he gathered around him as secretaries, messengers, and servants. In this study of Erasmus as master and patron, his character, its generosities and littlenesses, appears from a fresh angle. Bierlaire's book is also a contribution to the history of Erasmianism, since many from Erasmus' *familia* became influential figures in their generation.[57]

V

If one of the major topics of Erasmus scholarship in the last third of the twentieth century, Erasmus and language, can be discovered at the quincentenary only in small springs and rivulets, another, Erasmus as theologian, appears then in full flood, as the commemorative volumes demonstrate. His claim to the title had already been made in Kohls' book. A reviewer appreciated Kohls' demonstration of the essential unity of Erasmus' theological thought, but considered that his too systematic, even scholastic, presentation of it needed to be mitigated by a more careful distinguishing of what was explicit and what implicit.[58] Theological presentations were, in fact, prone to over-systematization. On the main question, a kind of consensus had emerged by the quincentenary: in *Scrinium* Jozef Coppens and at Rotterdam Robert Stupperich, one Catholic, the other Protestant, accepted that Erasmus was authentically theologian.

Coppens has no doubt of the seriousness of Erasmus' ambition to be a theologian and indeed to set the foundations of a new theology. This was a biblical theology, but Erasmus was not a strict biblicist. Scripture is indispensable because it points to Christ. In more technical language, Erasmus' was a positive theology of the sources of Christianity. Had he also a positive theology of the teaching authority of the church? Yes, answers Coppens, but primarily by placing that authority in context, by relating it to the sources of which it is the interpreter and to the common belief of the faithful. On this last, Coppens says, Erasmus anticipated the Vatican 2 document 'Lumen Gentium,' with its 'Utopian vision' of the Christian people. Coppens sees Erasmus, if not as a sure guide, yet as one worthy of reflection by Catholics caught up in a great *aggiornamento*.[59]

Stupperich asks a question reminiscent of those asked about the young Luther: where do we first find the distinctive theological program of Erasmus? Not, he believes, in the *Enchiridion* (1503), which remained a program of moral reform, but rather in the introductory writings to his edition of the New Testament (1516–18). In the preparatory work he moved ever deeper into the New Testament world of thought and in the introductory writings he broke through to the biblical principle and to Christocentrism. Anyone coming to Erasmus from the Reformers, Stupperich says, is surprised to find how far he anticipated principles customarily described as Protestant. Stupperich's is a modern Protestant standpoint. Erasmus is seen in relation to his Protestant successors and the Reformation breakthrough. The formulation recalls, in its forward-looking character, the liberal language of progress. Yet the appraisal of Erasmus as theologian is very positive. Kohls himself in a *Scrinium* essay argues for a seamless conjuncture between the Erasmian and early Reformation movements, and for a sense of solidarity with Erasmus in the minds of many of the early Protestants. The argument is against those Protestant observers who have distinguished sharply between Erasmus and Zwingli, characterizing the one as 'rational' and 'anthropocentric' and the other as 'existential' and 'theocentric.' Such judgments appear in this collection in G.W. Locher's commemorative lecture 'Zwingli und Erasmus' at Zürich University in January 1969, which overstates the rational and subjective in Erasmus' thought and underestimates his sense for the social realities of his time.[60]

On the Catholic side, the greatest concentration of work in support of a positive view of Erasmus as theologian, 'enfant terrible, mais enfant fidèle de l'Eglise,' was at the University of Liège. At the end of his Rotterdam lecture on the theme of pilgrimage in the *Colloquia*, Léon-E. Halkin remarks that Erasmus' criticism of pilgrimages and his going on pilgrimages were like two panels of a diptych, different but not contradictory, indeed complementary. Erasmus prayed to the saints in the childlike spirit that faith requires, but he insisted, as he believed the church should insist, that there is but one Saviour, Jesus Christ. Although it would be a travesty to expect members of the 'school' of Liège to have a common view of Erasmus' Catholicism, Halkin's image of the diptych represents strikingly a picture of Erasmus' religion and theology to which other quincentenary studies from 'liègois' can be linked. We have seen how R. Crahay and Jean-Pierre Massaut, in their studies, respectively, of Erasmus and the Louvain censors and

Erasmus and Thomas Aquinas, demonstrate the defensive rigidities of scholastic theologians against Erasmus' biblical, undogmatic, and irenic theology. At Mons, Massaut dealt with Erasmus' conception of the church, as revealed especially in his controversies with the Sorbonne. On the church both visible and invisible, on the place of sinners in the church, Erasmus held positions consonant with the main Catholic tradition coming through the Fathers and the high scholastics, against the exclusive emphasis on the visible, authoritative institution increasingly apparent in his time and enshrined at the Counter-Reformation. His was an ecclesiology in struggle like that of the nineteenth- and twentieth-century theologians whose work has led to the formulations of Vatican 2, a return to the main tradition to which Erasmus belonged. Thus, Massaut concludes, in his doctrine of the church one finds both *nova et vetera*, 'past and future, tradition and the present moment, the classical and the modern.'[61]

On Erasmus' relation to Catholic church and dogma, the quincentenary presented less an established consensus than an arena of competing views. In *Scrinium*, C.J. de Vogel argued that, while he adopted the philologico-historical method come from Italy rather than the scholastic and dialectical, his essential position was 'an integral acceptance of Church dogma,' which should penetrate the life and being of the believer, and that his importance for modern Christianity attaches as much to his 'attitude of firmly and unwaveringly sticking to the *fundamenta ecclesiae*,' scripture and tradition, as to his call for spiritual freedom. In the immediately succeeding essay, C. Augustijn contends, on the contrary, for Erasmus' essential detachment from the ecclesiastical institution: 'the Church as such does not mean anything to him.' Augustijn uses Erasmus' famous statement on putting up with the church – 'I shall therefore tolerate this Church until I see a better one; and it will be obliged to tolerate me till I myself have become a better man' – to argue, as Renaudet had done, for Erasmus' belief in another kind of church, the Christian 'fellowship of love.' But, a critic might object, this remark was about mutual sufferance of human weakness, not ecclesiology; the parallelism or mutuality is instructive. Erasmus' aversion to the institutional church, Augustijn goes on, came from his fundamental distinction between flesh and spirit, visible and invisible. His wish was not, as Renaudet thought, for a 'third church,' but for the spiritualizing of the universal church he knew.[62]

De Vogel and Augustijn take extreme positions, at opposite ends of the spectrum. Each has awkward elements to accommodate, the one Erasmus' substantial independence and freedom in handling institution and dogma, the other his uncontestable loyalty to the Roman church. Massaut's more developmental approach, with its sense for differing traditions, treats the nuances more comfortably. At the time of the quincentenary, it was easier to write with balance and discrimination about Erasmus' understanding of the whole Christian society than of his ecclesiology in the strict sense, his view of the ecclesiastical institution. The latter issue remained clouded by the still-uncertain outcome of Vatican 2 and the ecumenical movement. In his 'Erasmus and the Grammar of Consent' in *Scrinium*, James McConica analyses the meaning of Erasmus' favoured terms, *consensus* and *concordia*. What lay behind his description of the church as 'the consensus of the whole Christian people' or his famous declaration: 'Summa nostrae religionis pax est et unanimitas'? There were, says McConica, Stoic-Platonic elements. Erasmus had caught from the Fathers the 'Platonic vision of the intelligible harmony of all creation,' but not of Reality as immutable behind the meaningless flux of events in time and history. Christ, at once unchanging and ever-changing, constantly addresses people within this flux. They have assurance that they are hearing him rightly only through the agreement of trustworthy witnesses. The activity of the Holy Spirit in creating such bonds is essentially social. The classical idea of the harmony of the created universe is taken up into the Christian doctrine of the Holy Spirit.[63]

Similarly, Otto Schottenloher, one of the veterans of the quincentenary, shows how the *lex naturae* and the *lex Christi* are related in Erasmus' thought. Christ's work is the restitution of nature well created but fallen. Natural law is normative but only as reconstituted by Christ through faith and love. Erasmus' Christianity, the idea of *restitutio christianismi*, is both a fulfilling and an overcoming of the classical tradition. The restitution, Schottenloher continues, is social as well as individual, and here again there is a tension between fulfilling and overcoming. How is Christ's law of love related to the laws of society? Erasmus is aware of the difficulties. Nevertheless, the former must be brought to bear on, without ever replacing, the latter.[64] Both this essay and McConica's question the oft-repeated assertion that Erasmus had a poor sense for the institutional, or even for the social and communal, and for the dilemmas of law and love in the common life.[65]

VI

If at the quincentenary Erasmus' ecclesiology remained a contested issue while his sense of community in a broader sense attracted more serene and comprehensive discussion, a further issue, already mentioned, was opening up new ground. This was 'Erasmus and language,' a broadening and intensively worked field from the quincentenary on. We have already seen how, at Rotterdam, Sem Dresden defined Erasmus' character by his relation to words and to books; through that relationship his personality was both vividly realized and forever elusive and out of reach. At Tours, Dresden addressed the question of *festivitas* in Erasmus (and also in Rabelais), a kind of serious play ('jeu sérieux'), which, as the *Moria* makes clear, had for Erasmus a theatrical quality, 'making an illusion of reality and representing as real, in a literary manner, what is without doubt illusory.' His way of talking was a kind of 'esthétisation' of reality, as when he spoke of the Lutheran tragedy or drama ('fabula'), and this was for him a way of keeping his distance from that unwelcome reality. His interventions seem ambiguous because they are purely literary. Of course, keeping one's distance had a deeper meaning for Erasmus: the Christian keeps his distance from the world and everything worldly and will hold to higher realities. It is at the last the Platonizing Erasmus who reappears in Dresden's pages. In *Scrinium*, writing on Erasmus' notion of *humanitas*, Dresden says that the struggle of the writer to realize his thought typified for Erasmus the restlessness of the truly human life. *Humanitas* is not something already possessed; it is rather 'a good to be acquired which will never be finally conquered.' Erasmus connected *humanitas* with the Christian ideal of *humilitas*. Here Dresden separates him from the high-flying speculations of the Neoplatonists.[66]

The precipitation and improvisation, which Erasmus himself saw as characteristic of his writing style, was for Dresden a sign of the human condition. For Margaret Mann Phillips, writing also in *Scrinium*, his 'free and personal style, with its wide vocabulary and swift ranging from the sonorous to the colloquial, its love of diminutives and puns and echoes, its sense of fun and drama' was creating a pathway from classicism to modernity. This way was to be followed by writers, not of Latin, but of the vernaculars. Like Phillips, J.-C. Margolin, in an essay on 'Erasme et la verbe: De la rhétorique à l'herméneutique' published first in the Strasbourg commemorative volume, begins with the *De Copia verborum ac rerum*, which posed the central problem of humanism, the relation of words and things. For Erasmus *res* came before *verbum*, content before form; the word must faithfully represent the thing, and Erasmus' own language, 'instrumental, contingent, créateur,' authentically represented his personality. Since Erasmus was expressing Christian ideas in classical language, subtle transmutations and a cleansing of associations were required, part and parcel of Phillips' pathway to modernity. Ultimately, words have sacred, not to say sacramental, use; they incarnate the person in relation to other persons and to God; through them indeed the divine Word is spoken. At Mons, Margolin spoke on 'Erasmus and the Truth,' beginning again with his sense of authenticity and the characteristic oppositions in his thought – letter and spirit, reality and appearance, things and words. The unveiling of truth, of the authentic, happens in dialogue between persons; dialogue was a form natural to Erasmus. Truth cannot be imposed on the other; it requires respect for his liberty; a fanatic defence, even of truth, is destructive. Truth thus becomes a bond among all. Finally, in any philosophical sense, truth is bound to Christian revelation.[67]

It is perhaps not fanciful to think of Dresden and Margolin as the leading voices of the quincentenary. Margolin was in a French tradition of lucidly presenting Erasmus as writer and moralist.[68] Early in the commemoration (22 November 1966), he had delivered for the university and the Andreas-Silvius-Stiftung in Basel a luminous lecture on Erasmus' idea of nature, an idea which embraced the determinism universally accepted in antiquity and the Middle Ages, yet attributed to humans a self-determining character susceptible to education but also needful of grace, the grace which restores, renovates, and fulfils. For Erasmus, Margolin concludes, the world is, as Michel Foucault has said of thinkers of his age in general, not so much a spectacle to be observed as a language to be read.[69] At this point Margolin links up with Dresden's intricate and elusive writings rich in nuances and qualifications on any too simple statement about Erasmus as writer and thinker. Both pioneered studies on Erasmus and words, Erasmus and language, a wave of the future in Erasmus scholarship. Both accepted that for Erasmus himself the crucial relationship was that between words and the Word.

VII

The quincentenary was of its time. Public presentations gave Erasmus star quality and, in reaction, the counter-culture offered a reverse image. For cultural organizations such commemorations are an opportunity, and galleries, libraries, and music groups seized the moment. In scholarship the quincentenary put on display what had been accomplished since the celebrations of 1936, which had virtually coincided with the appearance of Bataillon's *Erasme et l'Espagne*. The literature included many works inspired by that masterpiece, but they had not exhausted the discussion of the methodological issues it had raised. The problems about Erasmus' intellectual formation identified with the names of Seebohm, Mestwerdt, Hyma, and Schottenloher were treated now in muted fashion, if not finally laid to rest. That Erasmus was to be taken seriously as a religious writer was, one might guess, universally accepted, though there might still be discussion in some quarters about the designation 'theologian.' The strongest claim to him now was that of Catholic Christianity, which, marvellously, found him among the antecedents of its modernized form in Vatican 2. His own antecedents had been enormously extended, to the Fathers – Augustine and Origen, as well as Jerome – and to the scholastics. The Enlightenment claim to him had been countermanded, though, in the deeply pietist atmosphere now surrounding him, there were still voices reminding us of Erasmus the critic, the spokesman for the natural life of the family and the child, the keen observer of the tangible world, the 'man on his own.'[70] His relation to the Reformers was also freshly up for discussion; the simple image of confrontation across an impassable divide could no longer suffice. That recognition aroused an interest in the older Erasmus. For one thing, his commitment to the primacy of scripture made a link to Reformers of all stamps. On all this, there was much work to do, as there was on the Erasmus, not only of the Word, but also of words. A culture at all levels obsessed with words would impose that as the task of the future for Erasmus scholarship.

FIVE

Erasmus Theologian:
In the Penumbra of Vatican 2

꽃

I

'Erasmus believes he is Christian; he wishes to be Christian. He is Christian in his own way.' So, a monograph of the 1920s, J.-B. Pineau's *Erasme: Sa pensée religieuse*. But, says Pineau in another place, to wish to be Catholic is not to be Catholic. Erasmus' religion, as Pineau depicts it, is, by medieval standards and by Roman standards, a much-reduced thing. It is hard to know what of traditional theology he would maintain; for him scholasticism, with its tyrannical formulas, was 'useless, dangerous, or ridiculous speculation.' His preference in every sphere, in his attitude to monasticism, in his philosophy of education, was for the human, natural, and utilitarian over the transcendent, authoritative, and heroic. 'For enthusiasm he prefers sobriety and for inspiration he substitutes inquiry.' On the church itself, he was more than irenic, he was universalist: 'Humanity forms but one church inspired by one unique and multiform Spirit.'[1]

Pineau's is the classic statement of an orthodoxy about Erasmus. Actually, he feels Erasmus' charm: the latter's picture of Christ, like Renan's, was joyous, not sombre as in late-medieval devotion; his own piety was serene and verdant. From the ancient philosophers and Christianity he extracted 'an essence of wisdom.' But, like many Catholic writers since the Counter-Reformation, Pineau runs a doctrinal plumb-line through Erasmus' thought. He may be charmed by Erasmus, but those committed to absolutes, the mystics and the simple believers whom Erasmus scorned, also attract him. There is a paradox about the theological reductionism Pineau attributes to Erasmus. For the heirs of both the Counter-Reformation and the Enlightenment, it defines the significance of Erasmus in the history of theological thought. In its extreme form this definition makes Erasmus a direct precursor of the Enlightenment: he reduced Christianity to a small stock of common truths, agreeable to all Christians and to many even beyond the borders of Christianity; with him Christianity sank back into classical wisdom; he made Catholic structures, dogmatic, institutional, and liturgical, matters of mere convenience and utility; he dissipated Christianity into a morality or a spirit of goodwill and tolerance, volatilizing it, as P. Godet remarked in a striking phrase.[2]

There had always been another view of Erasmus among Catholics, just as many Protestants did not accept Luther's condemnation of Erasmus' religion, even in the Reformation era itself. At the end of the nineteenth century, in the aftermath of the *Kulturkampf* and the battles over clericalism and anticlericalism, the loudest voices on the Catholic side were those of Erasmus' judges and critics, but the alternative voice was not silent. This was the balance of interpretations that the inter-war period inherited. Pineau's book and Mangan's biography and, in a spirit different from both, Renaudet's writing in those years seemed set to make that balance permanent. The other view, that Erasmus was essentially a Catholic thinker, had, however, its representatives then, and the drift, not truly discernible until the 1950s, was towards them.

In the Netherlands an authoritative figure was among them. Jan de Jong, from 1936 Archbishop of Utrecht, had, when professor of ecclesiastical history at and then rector of the seminary at Rijsenburg, written on Erasmus. In 1936 other Catholic professors assessed him theologically, as we have seen. De Jong and his colleagues were not exactly enthusiasts for Erasmus, but they corrected Pineau. Erasmus was, they said, by temperament and inclination, sceptical and independent. Yet, his aim was not the undermining, let alone the destruction, of Catholic structures, but the purification of the church by reference to scripture and the early church. If he had difficulty with the idea of authority, he nevertheless distinguished between dogma, which was indisputable, and the opinions of the theologians. If he had too little appreciation of how the church, under the leadership of the Holy Spirit, developed beyond its scriptural and patristic origins, he yet wrote plainly about following the judgment of the church. Even before Luther's appearance, he had stated the principle of submitting one's exegetical practice to that judgment. He did not reject even scholasticism completely, though he thought the theologians of his own time were running amok. He was, says de Jong, 'a Catholic with great gaps.' It would be hard, he remarks in passing, even if the facts require it, which they do not, to abandon Erasmus and thirty years of the intellectual life of Thomas More to the Protestants or freethinkers. De Jong had spotted that Pineau's judgment of Erasmus' religious thought was identical with that of liberal Protestants like Paul Wernle and Ernst Troeltsch and began the Catholic reclaiming of him, laying the first stone in what was to become, in two generations, a new orthodoxy about him.[3]

In the 1930s Rudolf Pfeiffer led the case for seeing Erasmus' thought as all of a piece and in essence Catholic and Christian. For Pfeiffer, there was no substantial break between the younger and older Erasmus, though the latter was less of a cultural critic and more oriented to the church. The liberty central to his thought was not spiritual autonomy but a sense of moral responsibility grounded in the doctrine of free will. Christianity was not for him reduced to culture-religion or moralism; all were directed towards Christ. In its commitment to unity his thought was medieval, though he insisted most on the continuity between the ancient cultural ideal of *humanitas*, uniting antique wisdom and form (*sapientia* and *eloquentia*), and Christianity.[4]

Humanitas or *Menschenbildung* had been the subject of Pfeiffer's lecture to the Warburg Institute, 'Humanitas Erasmiana,' published in the ominous year for Germany of 1931. Pfeiffer concluded that lecture, which can hardly be read apart from the circumstances of the time, with the remark that the human spirit can resist the barbarism present in every age only under the standard of *humanitas*, the idea for which Erasmus stood. The barbarians he resisted denied the continuity between the ancient and Christian cultures, dealt frivolously with the Christian sources, and neglected the languages in which they were written. For Erasmus, Pfeiffer says, the gospel was not the cancelling but the crowning of *humanitas*, the ancient ideal of human formation at once cultural and moral. All came together in Catholic Christianity. Erasmus' true tragedy, Pfeiffer concluded in 1937 and again in 1955 when he returned to the theme, was not his break with Luther, which was inevitable, but his rejection by high-minded Catholic opinion down to writers of the recent past.[5]

II

In the 1950s, the rival view, that Erasmus was, not the custodian, but the betrayer and destroyer of Catholic Christianity, had still vigorous and influential exponents. The two interpretations stood in unreconciled confrontation, as they had done nearly a century before in the time of Janssen and Schlottmann and, indeed, as they had done since his lifetime. Amid the ecumenical calming down, when historians on both sides were taking a fresh and reconciling look at the religious history of the sixteenth century, there were Catholic writers offering an inversion of the argument put by Gibbon and the heirs of the Enlightenment that real and deep religious reform had come, not from the Protestant Reformers, but from Erasmus and the humanists: Erasmus and his associates were the true destroyers of medieval Christendom. 'That the papacy, neglecting Aleander's advice ... made the mistake of fulminating first of all against Luther, when Erasmus was the more dangerous enemy, was a tactical and capital error which has cost Western civilization dear, by throwing it into a spiritual disarray from which it has barely recovered.'[6]

This quotation belongs to the argument, which Emile V. Telle developed on a great scale, that Erasmus was a root-and-branch critic of monasticism, its true enemy and would-be destroyer. Luther, by contrast, was more reluctant and, at least for a time, more reserved. Joseph Lortz, the famed Catholic church historian, made a similar contrast between Luther and Erasmus. Lortz's history of the German Reformation, first published at Freiburg in 1939, was a landmark in the ecumenical appreciation of Luther. While Luther arrived at a one-sided position theologically, it was, Lortz says, a one-sidedness of surpassing earnestness and inner force; he was, for the church, a lost leader who might have worked great reforms. In the same work Lortz makes sharp criticisms of Erasmus and precisely for lacking those qualities he valued in Luther. Meissinger called these judgments 'shockingly retrograde' in light of the then state of Erasmus studies, and Lortz defended them in a long essay of 1950, 'Erasmus-kirchengeschichtlich.'[7]

Although their starting-points are different, Lortz and Telle take similar views of Erasmus' historical setting and significance. For both, Catholic piety in the late Middle Ages was in danger of losing its objective content, becoming centred, not on outward revelation, but on inward experience, the subjective. Lortz attributes this to understandable reaction against excessive externalism in religious practice, to the decline of scholasticism and to the rise of humanism which, while not necessarily pagan, introduced, through its enthusiasm for ancient culture, a moral and religious relativism. He depicts a long secular decline from the scholastic heights of the thirteenth century to the swamps and shallows of the eighteenth-century Enlightenment. Telle uses more colourful language, but the model is essentially the same. There was at the end of the Middle Ages a vogue of impiety and a wave of unbelief, especially among academics and intellectuals, but the wave spilled over to the people, not least through Erasmus' own notoriety, conjured up in part by the fulminations of his orthodox enemies against him. The church, paralysed by lukewarmness and indifference, was ill equipped to resist Renaissance hedonism.[8]

Lortz asks: did Erasmus increase or diminish the danger in which the church stood from the fateful weakening in the authority of revealed truth? For him the church historian has two tasks. One is to attend to the cultural context, for 'the church never occupies a vacuum.' The other is to make a theological judgment. Without that the church historian is caught in a relativism for which 'every historical phenomenon carries "absolute" worth simply because it exists.' To refer to the Christian element in any historical agent is to speak of an absolute and binding demand. So, of Erasmus one must ask: does he take Christian revelation as a whole without picking and choosing within it, and does he accept its absolute primacy? Within this framework Lortz sees indecisiveness as his predominant characteristic. Erasmus stood in a perpetual twilight; he would say both yea and nay. He was misled by an inordinate intellectualism into believing that he could be the great reformer of the age. 'Erasmus represents the height of the Socratic fallacy – so fatal when the mastery of life is at stake – that the learned man is the good man, that education ensures moral improvement.' He looked for light to culture rather than to revelation and reduced Christianity to moralism, to a noble humanity and a few simple truths. He had an imperfect awareness of the teaching church. He remained within it as a 'half-Catholic.' For him the Bible, as interpreted by scholars, was the true norm of Christian belief. He did not attack the Catholic idea of the church but in practice deprived it of its force. In his claim to be, as it were, the judge of the church, he became the father of modern individualism. 'With Erasmus – not with Luther – the destructive domination of the purely individual conscience appeared upon the scene of modern history.'[9]

Like Pineau, Lortz feels the charm of Erasmus, of his call to refresh Christianity by a return to its sources, of his wish to save studies from paganism and return them to Christ. Yet, in dealing with Erasmus we are, he concludes, following a line which is still actually Christian but along which Christianity will in the end be struck to its very heart. A historical methodology and a confidence in the comprehensive clarity of Catholic doctrine underlie this judgment. In Lortz's view, a movement or idea cannot be given its full character if its 'here and now' at any given moment is alone described. Its inner tendency, the directions in which it is moving, what it will become if its inner character is allowed to work itself out must be taken into account. Seen in this way, Erasmus is, according to Lortz, truly a forerunner of the Enlightenment and of the weakening of Catholic Christianity and its place in Western culture. This methodology has some force, but its dangers, of anachronism and of making false conjunctures and unwarranted continuities, are immense. Lortz makes a still more questionable move. He undermines even Erasmus' correct and appealing expressions by asking: 'has Erasmus really encountered the Master?' Is such a question permitted to the historian?[10]

For Telle the key to Erasmus is his implacable, obsessive hatred of the monks and monasticism, fuelled in large part by his desire to escape a monastic obedience burdensome to his touchy, delicate, and solitary nature. His struggle against monasticism was apparent in his first writings but, by the time of the new edition of the *Enchiridion* in 1518 and his introductory letter to Paul Volz, he had declared a total war on the monastic institution, even if a war engaged more by stratagems, flanking movements, and constant sapping than by open assault. His quarry was not bad monks; the success of efforts at monastic reform would have been a frustration to him. His enemy was the monastic ideal itself and its best representatives. It was to him legalism and pharisaism.[11]

Telle calls his book a diptych. The two sides of the subject are Erasmus on monasticism and Erasmus on marriage. They are better seen as Siamese twins, for the one bloodstream circulates through both, hatred of the monks and rejection of celibacy by profession. Erasmus' positive view of marriage, set forth in many writings, beginning with the *Encomium matrimonii* (first published in 1518 but written much earlier), was driven by a negative. Telle cannot ignore other possibilities, Erasmus' acceptance of the natural life in marriage and the family or the value he put on lay life in the church, for they are there in the texts, but the driving force does not come from them. Erasmus' true enemy, according to Telle, was the vow, the monastic vow above all, but Telle uses his radicalism on divorce, as expressed in his note on 1 Corinthians 7:39, to demonstrate his hostility to all lifelong vows. So Telle, like Lortz, makes Erasmus the progenitor of the moral relativism which has, in their view, eroded the substance of Christendom over the last four centuries. His exegesis of the relevant New Testament texts undermined the orthodox privileging of virginity over marriage. His treatment of marriage began the dismantling of the Catholic sacramental system which the Protestant Reformers furthered after 1520. Erasmus and Luther arrived at the same position on the sacrament of marriage, though beginning at opposite ends, the one from an inordinate Augustinianism, the other from an 'Epicurean Pelagianism.' The latter found expression in the *Colloquies*, through which Erasmus popularized his ideas among the men and women of his time. In later chapters Telle deals with the orthodox controversialists who nailed Erasmus as a heretic *primae classis* for his works on marriage, independently of any collusion between him and Luther. Despite this, Erasmus, in his *Institutio matrimonii christiani* (1526), like 'an insect attracted to the flame,' reiterated, if with more caution, his essential positions.[12]

Telle's is an offensively polemical book. The character of Erasmus which emerges is bad – fearful and cowardly, but obstinate and garrulous; he was a liar and deceiver who betrayed Catholic orthodoxy and Christian civilization. The pity is that Telle had important points to make and evidence to support them: that Erasmus did have doubts about the monastic institution, and that he put a high value on marriage and the lay life. But Telle chose, as he avows, to concentrate on the negatives and put positive features aside for another time.[13]

The writings of Eugene Rice, the Renaissance historian, also of the 1950s, offer another version of the Lortz-Telle view. Naturally, they lack Telle's inquisitorial tone and the strict dogmatic standards Lortz requires in the writing of church history. Nevertheless, Rice defines Erasmus' positions much as they do. Erasmus was naturally secularist. In the transitional years of the 1490s he retained the traditional frameworks, in theology, monasticism, and personal piety, but he emptied them of meaning or, at least, bound them to another body of thought, classical, secularist, and naturalist, which was essentially inimical to them. He evaded the contradiction by not pressing the issues – his well-known moderation – and by transforming religion into an ethic. He was linked to the Florentine humanists of the early fifteenth century, who sought a wisdom 'whose meaning is ethical rather than metaphysical and active rather than contemplative.' Rice divides sixteenth-century thinkers about wisdom into two camps, those like Colet, Luther, and Lefèvre, who were still in the medieval mould and saw wisdom as revelational, receptive, and otherworldly, and the secularizers and moralizers like Erasmus who turned Christian revelation 'into a naturally acquired moral virtue,' draining away its theological substance until 'only ethical meanings are left.'[14]

Hans Baron criticized Rice for identifying Christianity with particular medieval cultural and theological forms and treating any alternative or deviation as secularist. One can extend this critique to the whole view, represented in different ways by Lortz, Telle, and Rice, that Erasmus' world-affirming outlook was in itself anti-Christian or, at least, a threat to Christianity and a pathfinder for modern secularism and naturalism. There is a critical difference between accepting the secular world as the sphere of Christian duty and activity and an antireligious secularism. The incarnation can provide a Christological and theological foundation for the acceptance of the secular. Lortz, Telle, and Rice rightly recognize Erasmus' resistance to world-denying elements in medieval culture; they mistakenly associate this with moves to escape the Christian framework altogether.[15]

The contrary view, that Erasmus stood for an integral Catholicism, was put with equal force in the 1950s. There were exaggerations on this side, too, just as there were in Rudolf Pfeiffer's romantic integralism, making of Erasmus' thought a seamless web of antique culture and late-medieval Catholicism. Louis Bouyer's *Autour d'Erasme* presents Erasmus as the high-point of Catholic Christianity's attempt to come to terms with the Renaissance. The fifteenth-century church's attitude to humane studies was, it argues, benign. Fears of neo-paganism evoked, not a merely defensive or tactical response, but the development of a case that traditional Christianity and the new studies, the whole recognition of the place of the human and the natural, were compatible. In this struggle, Erasmus followed Nicholas of Cusa and Pico della Mirandola. Bouyer directs his critique mainly against Renaudet's association of Erasmus with 'modernism,' but he is also conducting an unavowed debate with Lortz. To the contention that Erasmus replaced the body of dogma with a pale spirituality and an all too human moralism, Bouyer replies, on the basis of an analysis of the *Ratio verae theologiae*, that he well knew how to distinguish between dogmas enunciated by the church and opinions debated in the theological schools. His distaste for scholastic disputation was not heretical. His own service was to positive theology, the study and exposition of the Bible. To argue from the sparseness of his formal references to certain traditional doctrines that he rejected them is an abuse of the argument *e silentio*. But, one might say in response to Bouyer, silence is impartial; it proves neither Erasmus' heterodoxy nor his orthodoxy. Either way, it is clear that his interest was not in metaphysics or systematic theology.[16]

In one of the most important monographs of the 1950s, *Die vollkommene Frömmigkeit des Christen: Nach dem Enchiridion militis Christiani des Erasmus von Rotterdam*, Alfons Auer took up the questions that interested Bouyer about Erasmus' Catholicity and gave, by and large, Bouyer's answers, while sharing some ground with Lortz. Erasmus' awareness of ambiguity, says Auer, corresponded to the theological uncertainties of the time, as Lortz depicts them; yet, he was not so much indifferent to dogma as hostile to dogmatism. Truth was not relative, but the forms expressing it were. To the charge of moralism, pressed by Pineau and Lortz, Auer returns a firm answer. Erasmus was no Pelagian; on sin and its origin, 'he thought as a Catholic through and through.' Christ is for him, not only teacher and example, but also grace and power; moral achievement can be built only on a religious reality.[17]

The starting-point of Auer's interest in Erasmus' *Enchiridion* is his search for a Catholic lay piety. His book belongs to that time in church history before Vatican 2 when Catholic faith was finding fresh expressions, but the ethos of the institution inherited from Trent and the nineteenth-century controversies over clericalism and anticlericalism remained unchanged. Auer believes that the *Enchiridion* is an important source-book for Catholic lay piety. It was not systematic theology, for its aim was right living in the world; it was, nevertheless, more than his popular, ironical works like *Folly* and the *Colloquies*, the key to Erasmus' thought: 'Who knows the *Enchiridion* knows Erasmus.'[18]

Although Erasmus was no systematist, his thought, Auer says, had systematic foundations, especially an anthropology influenced, if not wholly determined, by Platonism. In human nature there is a balance and a tension between body and spirit; the balance has been disturbed and the tension heightened by sin. A spiritualizing tendency is present in Erasmus' thought without being dominant. The earlier study, by Jacques Etienne, of Erasmus in confrontation with Luther and the Louvain theologians, *Spiritualisme érasmien et théologiens louvanistes*, had made his theology predominantly spiritualizing and 'personalist.'[19] Auer accepts that for Erasmus the fundamental law of Christian piety is to move through visible things to th invisible; visible things are not in themselves evil, however, but neutral. This is, he says, not a world-denying piety like Thomas à Kempis,' for the visible world remains a metaphor or parable of the other world. Besides, the spiritual is not to be understood in an idealist way; it is centred on a living, helping, saving Person, Jesus Christ. Auer concludes: a powerful passion, like that of the Old Testament prophets, informs Erasmus' Christocentrism. Christ encompasses the world, in which he works his redemption and through which human faith and piety can be expressed.[20]

Auer's common ground with Lortz is over Erasmus' conception of the church. He said many fine things about the church and the sacraments; he always expressed himself correctly about them. Yet he undervalued the church. The crux theologically was in his understanding of the incarnation. He did not give enough value to its extension, the *incarnatio continua* in dogma, sacrament, and institution. His call for Christians to pass from visible to invisible, from outward to inward things, could weaken the devout traditions of the church, and the exclusiveness of his interest in the Bible could destroy the idea of tradition itself. He did not solve, perhaps he was not fully aware of, the problem of Bible and church.[21]

In his book on Erasmus' theology (1966), E.-W. Kohls takes Auer to task on this very point. The difference is partly between Catholic and Protestant views of the church. Perhaps, while

Kohls was writing, Vatican 2 was changing the terms of the discussion for Catholics, too. Auer's view of the incarnation and its extension is concentrated, Kohls says, on the institutional church, whereas Erasmus' understanding of the incarnation was centred on Christ and his saving work; it was soteriological and Christocentric, and the church appeared there as the body of Christ and the community of believers, a community of love (*Liebesgemeinschaft*). Kohls' challenge goes further: Auer is mistaken, he says, in making Erasmus' anthropology the foundation of his thought; rather, that thought moved around two poles, epistemologically around the primacy of scripture, existentially around his doctrine of God and his Christology. What Auer misses, he goes on, is the centrality, in the gospel and in Erasmus' thought, of a theology of salvation. All springs from the folly of the Cross, as Paul said in 1 Corinthians 1:23–4.[22]

Auer and Kohls have in common recognition of Erasmus' seriousness as a theologian. They both reject the depiction of him as a secularist, by intent or tendency. Kohls rightly questions an approach which builds his thought up from a theoretical or doctrinal base. He also recognizes the inappropriateness of an institutional or ecclesiastical measure for Erasmus' thought. Yet, he himself shapes that thought to the Reformation pattern, with its poles of scripture and salvation. Are there not many markers in Erasmus' theology, touching all the Christian essentials, sometimes identifiable with medieval Catholicism, sometimes approaching or anticipating the Reformation? The point, as Margolin remarks in one of his quincentenary essays, was always practical: for Erasmus, truth was 'non pas un concept théorique, mais une valeur pratique.'[23] Auer ends his search for a lay piety in Erasmus' *Enchiridion* by recognizing that for Erasmus the life of the religious was not the sole or standard way of Christian perfection; in every way of life Christians must aim at perfection by taking Christ as their only target ('unicus scopus').[24] In his little essay 'The Erasmian Idea,' posthumously published in 1950, the young scholar Wilhelm Shenk put the point strikingly, if paradoxically: 'In his life [though not himself a layman] he embodied a new social type: the lay scholar writing for educated laymen. ... It was a genuine secularization of the *homo religiosus*, combining old elements with new ones, attempting to transmit to the "world" the message of Christ in a way which had not been tried before.'[25]

III

In the early 1960s, a number of books took up the issue of Erasmus' relation to the Reformation. One of them, Jean Boisset's *Erasme et Luther: Libre ou serf arbitre?*, itself of limited interest to Erasmus scholarship, began a new line of substantial works on the theme 'Erasmus and Luther.' Two others, Karl Heinz Oelrich's *Der späte Erasmus und die Reformation* and Cornelis Augustijn's *Erasmus en de Reformatie: Een onderzoek naar de houding die Erasmus ten opzichte van de Reformatie heeft aangenomen*, narratives of Erasmus' actual experience of the Reformation, had no successors, certainly no successors of a weight equal to their own. The explanation of the difference lies partly in the special place Luther occupies in the theological history of the twentieth century, partly in the interest in ecumenical dialogue in the age of Vatican 2, to which Luther was a critical figure. For some Erasmus has been marginal to that dialogue, for others central.

To Boisset, Erasmus and Luther represent, historically, two anxieties ('inquiétudes') besetting the sixteenth century, one over the reform of human society, the other over alienation from the divine. Erasmus appears as rationalist, opportunist, and probabilist. For him, truth was to be won from the biblical text by the historical, philological, and exegetical methods of the scholar. For Luther, truth in the highest sense was the gift of grace, not a tranquil possession, but the outcome of an anguished confrontation with the Absolute, not historical and textual but personal and of the here and now. Boisset's Luther was the predecessor of Kierkegaard. He shades Luther's expressions into those of existentialist philosophy. Though Maurice Blondel (1861–1949), early French Catholic existentialist (*L'Action*, 1893), was distant from Luther in time and philosophy, he wrote, says the Protestant Boisset, about the will and about grace in terms very close to Luther's.[26] The weakness of Boisset's treatment of Erasmus is epitomized in his image of the living scholar wringing truth out of a dead text. But for Erasmus the text was not dead; he wrote that the one and only aim of the scholar was to be changed, to be seized, to be inspired and transformed by what he read.[27]

Harry McSorley's *Luther: Right or Wrong? An Ecumenical-Theological Study of Luther's Major Work 'The Bondage of the Will'* belongs to Lutheran-Catholic dialogue. Erasmus, McSorley says, though not lacking in genuine Christian conviction, as Luther and his imitators asserted, must remain tangential to contemporary Catholic-Protestant dialogue, even after Vatican 2. This is because he admitted as possible 'neosemipelagian' views current among late-medieval theologians, especially the view that man can in some sense prepare himself for justification. The main Catholic tradition, from the New Testament through Augustine and Thomas, held on the contrary that such preparation is itself a work of grace. Personally Erasmus adhered to that tradition but, in allowing the possibility of the alternative and in his own unguarded definition of free will, he made, says McSorley, a 'tragic example' of that theological uncertainty Lortz had found characteristic of the late-medieval church. Luther is the prime subject of ecumenical dialogue because he held to the main Catholic tradition, though he introduced a distortion by over-extending his argument about necessity and God's foreknowledge, so threatening human responsibility and 'free cooperation in saving faith.' McSorley, said to be the first American Catholic priest to go abroad 'precisely for ecumenical studies,' concludes that Luther's doctrine of the will is no bar to Christian unity.[28]

A more direct heir to Boisset's book was E.-W. Kohls' *Luther oder Erasmus*, whose title at once suggests its character: Luther or Erasmus? Its interest lies, not only in its interpretation of Erasmus and Luther, but also in what it says about how the history of theological thought should be written. More than once, Kohls claims Rankean objectivity, but he also presents Luther's thought as a remedy for the present time of revolutionary change, a guide, as his teacher Wilhelm Maurer once said, to the fateful decision civilization has to take between what Erasmus represents and what Luther represents. The core of the latter is the self-activating, self-propagating power of the Word, taught by Luther himself in his famous 'Invocavit' sermons in Wittenberg in 1522, directed against Andreas Karlstadt and the violent student radicals he had incited.[29]

It is important to recognize that Kohls is not contradicting what he had written in his study of Erasmus' theology. If Erasmus and Luther may be taken as representative figures, what Erasmus represented was the best hope of a thorough and thoroughly Christian reform in his time. The best of his contemporaries saw him in that way. The reform would express the Christian law of love; it could be realized only through grace. The elements in Erasmus' theological thought identified by Kohls in his other writings all contributed to the shaping and definition of his reform program: his basic Christology, the trinitarian doctrine of God, a consistently thought out understanding of salvation, and so on. What Erasmus represented in the history of theological thought was the Greek tradition come from Origen and Jerome through Thomas Aquinas. When Luther completely rejected Erasmus, he was not rejecting something second-rate; he was rejecting the best alternative offering to the truths he himself pointed to. Nevertheless, the division between them was deep, if obscured by the apparent common ground, the biblical principle for example. Indeed, they had Augustine in common, though, characteristically, Luther looked to his antipelagian writings, Erasmus to the writings honouring antiquity as a preparation for Christianity, as in Platonism.[30]

What Luther represented, according to Kohls, was not a hermeneutic or a theology, let alone a humanistic one. His message was a pointing to God's own word and action. It carries a 'timeless validity,' independently of the historical figure Martin Luther. This is a theology, not of propositions and aspirations, but in direct relationship to the divine.[31] Kohls comes close to Boisset's contrast between the dry scholar wrestling with texts and the inspired prophet. It is not surprising that Margolin sees Kohls' book as inhabiting a 'transhistorical' world, from which the actual Reformation of the sixteenth century is disengaged.[32] Kohls' ambition to establish how each author saw himself, his *Selbstverständnis*, does not remove the difficulty, since for Kohls Luther's self-understanding rested on an extrahistorical claim to encounter with the divine.[33] Lortz's unacceptable question: 'Has Erasmus really encountered the Master?' haunts such discussions.

A second work entering, in Margolin's view, transhistorical territory is Georges Chantraine's study of 1981, *Erasme et Luther, libre et serf arbitre*. The second half of the book, which began as a doctoral thesis for the Institut Catholique, is an 'Essai théologique.' Early on, Chantraine puts an apparently ecumenical question: what is required to integrate Lutheran thought into universal, that is Catholic, truth? Shortly, however, he establishes limits. Only within a horizon set by the Word of God in association with 'a tradition guided by the Spirit under the vigilance of the apostolic *Magisterium*' is Christian theology possible. Protestant theology cannot then be wholly accommodated. By contrast, in the thought of Erasmus, whose writing on free will and extended reply to Luther, the *Hyperaspistes*, have so far been marginalized in theological discourse, dwells 'the enveloping presence of the living Tradition of the Spirit in the Church.'[34]

For his historical section, Chantraine, like Kohls, sets himself the Rankean ideal of 'telling what happened,' without apologetic or ecumenical intent. Yet, this part can best be seen as an introduction to the theological assessment. Indeed, Chantraine insists, against Renaudet, who called it 'une question psychologique,' that the free-will debate was a theological controversy, bearing on the anthropological foundations of the faith. Crucial, as previous writers had seen, was the relatonship to the Fathers, Luther relying on, even going beyond, the antipelagian writings of Augustine, Erasmus wishing to draw the Greek Fathers, always more generous to 'liberty,' into the discussion and even to build on the scholastic correction of Augustinianism. Two different types of exegesis, two different understandings of the Christian mystery separated Erasmus and Luther, though Erasmus demonstrated his principle of concord by incorporating into writings like his Psalm commentaries what was valuable, and not inimical to tradition, in Luther's theology.[35]

Luther's *De servo arbitrio* has, so the theological section begins, been an embarrassment to some later Protestants, and a certain kind of ecumenism would like to forget about it. Chantraine's aim is to put in confrontation Luther's dialectic, something 'entirely new in Christian theology,' and Erasmus' *philosophia Christi*. He extends his aim to confronting the two types of thought with 'l'idée traditionelle de la révélation,' though, he adds, even the mature observer can bring to a debate where the whole of Christian truth is in play only certain reflections. Thus, to take tradition and hermeneutic as the example: Luther's governing idea was his distinction between law and gospel which, present as it is in both Old and New Testaments, replaces the traditional dialectic of the two Testaments, which Erasmus accepted; so Luther threatened the historicity of revelation. Luther and Erasmus had the same aim, which was to distinguish between the divine Word and human words, but their means and perspectives differed. 'For the one, whatever comes from man must be excluded; for the other, one watches to purify Christian truth of what is too human.' Thus Erasmus distinguished between dogma, which, in church and tradition, affirms the divine Word, and theology, which subjects it to human elaboration.[36]

The controversy touched on issues crucial for both men, the doctrine of justification for Luther, spiritual exegesis for Erasmus. A point, says Chantraine, unrecognized in previous scholarship is the command Erasmus demonstrated, notably in the *Hyperaspistes*, of Luther's thought. The confrontation also brought out the weaknesses of each. Erasmus' thinking on the sacrament was deficient, not through adogmatism, but through a failure to recognize doctrinal evolution within the church and a too natural and social conception of the church. Was Erasmus, Chantraine asks, too absorbed in his polemic against monks and theologians and too fearful of ecclesiastical tyranny to see the full destructive force, for the church, of Luther's doctrine of law and gospel? He quotes Yves Congar, who found in Erasmus a true sense of reform but also the limits of a critical humanism a little too cerebral and a little too narrow. Luther, by denying any natural knowledge of God and detaching the *theologia crucis* from the *theologia gloriae*, was altogether more drastic and destructive.[37] In sum, Luther launched a mortal challenge to tradition and the teaching authority of the church. Any ecumenical salvaging of the relationship would be a testing endeavour. Erasmus, if short of vigour in defending important positions, stood by and for Catholic essentials.

For Boisset, McSorley, and Kohls, Luther is the centre of interest in the Erasmus-Luther affair, in each case, though the cases differ, because his theological message is held to be relevant, urgent, or compelling. Chantraine is more equivocal about Luther than these, but coping with Luther's disturbing presence is somehow the dominant concern, though Chantraine's Catholic appreciation of Erasmus is sympathetic. In the writings which have made Erasmus rather than Luther the centre of interest, a further displacement has occurred. They have tended to find the meaning of the controversy, less in the theological issue itself, than in a clash of methodologies, of rival ways of doing theology or being religious, of patterns that underlie and determine the respective positions on particular issues like the freedom of the will. Representative is John O'Malley's article of 1974, 'Erasmus and Luther, Continuity and Discontinuity as Key to Their Conflict.' In Luther, O'Malley says, the gospel is in an adversary relation to the world, it comes from outside, vertically from above; truth brings disruption and dislocation. Erasmus, by contrast, attached himself to a tradition that was didactic and harmonizing in character, the ancient rhetorical tradition which, with a detour around scholasticism, continued, indeed experienced revival, in Erasmus' own time. It did not contradict the gospel, which itself teaches reconciliation and concord. O'Malley revives Pfeiffer's project of tracing the continuities in Erasmus' thought between the classical and the Catholic Christian. The drive for unity beneath multiplicity, for truths broadly diffused rather than sharply delimited, was Erasmus' essential 'response-pattern.'[38]

B.A. Gerrish, in an essay on Erasmus' *De libero arbitrio* in a collection edited by Richard DeMolen, finds the underlying difference, not in an encompassing, predetermining pattern, but in two distinct understandings of how doing theology relates to piety. Unlike Luther's followers and even ecumenists like McSorley, he does not see Erasmus as neopelagian. Erasmus was closest to Augustine: both beginning and end in justification are works of grace; only in mid-course is human responsiveness possible. 'Not meritorious preparation for grace, but the natural freedom to consent to grace is the minimum of free choice that he will not surrender.' Such a conclusion links Erasmus to the later Lutheran synergists; it even allows, at an intellectual level, much common ground with Luther himself. The gulf appears with the question: what does this theological issue mean for personal religion? 'For Erasmus, the *prime* requirement was for strength to supply what was lacking in the will's best efforts. For Luther, the moment of the will's highest endeavor was the moment of greatest anguish because it marked the end of a tragic mistake.'[39]

The most substantial, and the most elegant, version of the approach which displaces the theological controversy itself from the centre of interest is Marjorie O'Rourke Boyle's *Rhetoric and Reform: Erasmus' Civil Dispute with Luther* of 1983. It belongs to a substantial body of writing by Boyle on the rhetorical elements in Erasmus' theology and in Renaissance theology generally. Received unwillingly by those who resisted the displacement of the theological issue, this book can be seen as an extended, highly literate demonstration of the point made by O'Malley in his article of 1974. Boyle is provocative: the issue of free will was a 'red herring'; Erasmus 'repudiated,' for their polemical style, both Jerome and Augustine, and also his friend Thomas More. Erasmus' aim was to demonstrate a way of going about theology. The key to his intention was the genre to which his writing belonged, the diatribe; in Cicero's classification, it lay within the sphere of 'deliberative rhetoric,' which covered issues of serious moral import but issues, Erasmus added, whose resolution was not required of Christians. For Erasmus and Luther the issue of the will, free or bound, was located on different planes. 'The status of the question is entirely different in their competing texts, and on this second-order distinction hangs their conflict.' Each chose for the discussion of the issue an appropriate genre from among the limited range available, Erasmus the *Diatriba* and Luther the *Assertio*.[40]

Boyle inserts the debate, therefore, into a classical framework. This enables her to explain the significance and limits of Erasmus' attraction to classical Scepticism; he wanted, in matters legitimately open to debate, a weighing of options rather than dogmatism. Two classical epistemologies confronted one another, the Sceptical, satisfied with probabilities, the Stoic, requiring an absolutely firm and clear impression. Her association of Luther with Stoicism was Boyle's most debatable move; it tied him to an essentially propositional kind of discourse; it also contradicted the fashionable existentialist interpretation of him, represented in our discussion by Boisset's book.[41] For Boyle, the *Diatribe* put Erasmus in the tradition of civic humanism. Again, the two men represented two different conceptions of how to serve the commonweal. To Erasmus' deliberative rhetoric, Luther opposed the juridical; he was the 'prosecutor of Christ's lawsuit.' Erasmus counselled prudence, took seriously Paul's distinction between the lawful and the expedient, and, supported by a humanist sense of history, taught accommodation to time and circumstance. Luther, by contrast, demanded the 'unrestricted proclamation of the word of God,' which would do its own work.[42] Boyle is at her most persuasive at this level, and in her setting of classical reference-points for Erasmus. Bending Luther's neck to the yoke of a classical methodology does not carry the same conviction.

We have been following the line for which Boisset's book (1962) was our marker, Erasmus' relation to and controversy with Luther. We must return to 1962 and the two historical and contextualizing studies of Erasmus' experience of the Reformation movements. Oelrich's and Augustijn's books were contemporaneous; they did not influence one another. Oelrich's source is Erasmus' corresponence of the 1520s and 1530s, only patchily used up to his time (the eleventh and last volume of Allen's edition had appeared in 1947, the index in 1958). Erasmus' reaction to the Reformation was, says Oelrich, 'empirisch-induktiv,' and that is a corrective to the doctrinally focused literature on Luther and Erasmus. The latter was an eyewitness to the Reformation in Basel. Occurrences in the city and their threatened outcomes determined his reaction more than any issue of doctrine. Before the appearance of Bernd Moeller's book *Reichstadt und Reformation*, Oelrich identified the importance of the urban setting for the Reformation and Erasmus. He was psychologically and spiritually a *Städter*, a town-dweller. 'For him Reformation is above all an event within city walls.' In the violent events of 1528–9, when the social and religious movements in Basel intermingled, he saw a restless will for change which threatened lawlessness, a decline of piety and morality, division and intolerance, and the dislocation of studies. His relations with the Reformers deteriorated badly from that time, though he continued to hold the tyranny of monks and theologians and the hierarchy's abuse of power responsible for the catastrophe. He is for Oelrich a valuable witness to the events, but his judgments were shot through with subjectivity and at times manifestly unjust.[43] Erasmus' reaction to the Reformation as Oelrich presents it was mostly negative, though, on a doctrinal issue that touched him more deeply than most, he was attracted to Oecolampadius' spiritual doctrine of the eucharist, abandoning it decisively after the crisis of 1528–9, out of respect for church tradition and authority.[44]

What gives drive and shape to the narrative in Augustijn's book *Erasmus en de Reformatie* is the interpretation of Erasmus which runs through it and all Augustijn's writings of the 1960s, including his quincentenary essays. This is the liberal interpretation of Johannes Lindeboom and Johan Huizinga, tempered by an acceptance of the deeper spirituality attributed to Erasmus by Pfeiffer, Meissinger, Etienne, and Auer: he was not a rationalist or mere moralist; the Bible was fundamental for him, especially the gospels and the Sermon on the Mount; he looked, in religion, for purity, clarity, and simplicity and gave the highest value to concord.[45]

Augustijn deals more or less evenly with Erasmus' relations with Luther and with the Swiss and South German Reformers, though the free-will controversy occupies the central chapter of the book. Through this account of all his controversies runs the theme of his wish for independence, driven, Augustijn says, not by care for his personal safety, but by anxiety about the future of his work and movement, which were directed at the bonding of *bonae literae* and *sacrae literae*, the spiritualizing of the church and its liberation from outward and visible things. He must, on the one side, protect them from being crushed by reactionary forces in the old church; on the other, he must keep them separate from new and revolutionary movements with different aims and prospects. He put the blame for the worsening conflict on Luther's enemies, who were also his own, but he thought Luther needlessly provocative. With the appearance in 1521 of Luther's radical book *The Babylonian Captivity of the Church*, he put more of the blame on to him.[46] Both Augustijn and Heinz Holeczek, in a later article (1973) documenting Erasmus' changed attitude towards Luther after the failure of his attempts at mediation in 1520–1, find in a letter of May 1521 to Justus Jonas the best guide to what he was struggling for, the recovery of the gospel without revolutionary uproar and violence. His humanist colleagues must choose between two rival programs for church reform, his own and Luther's.[47]

The *Diatribe* of 1524 came at a point where Erasmus' attempts at mediation were stalled, neither side accepting him as mediator; nevertheless he refused to acknowledge that he was caught in a clash of irreconcilable dogmas. Hence, as Augustijn sees it, the academic character of the subject he chose to debate with Luther, free will, and the cool treatment he gave it. His position on the theological issue was, Augustijn says, 'typically semipelagian.' This is the view challenged by Gerrish, Boyle, Chantraine, and, for that matter, Kohls, and rightly so.[48]

Erasmus' controversies with the Swiss Reformers shunted him into more conservative positions about church authority. For one thing, the Reformers' differences among themselves, especially over the Supper, presented him with a cogent argument against them. Erasmus, says Augustijn, could not find a rebuttal from scripture to the teaching of the Basel Reformer Oecolampadius about the spiritual presence of Christ in the Supper: he fell back on tradition and church authority. In Augustijn's view, this moved him further than he wished to go, away from the spiritual form of religion he espoused, but in the circumstances of the 1520s he had no choice.[49]

Yet, to the end he did not abandon the double objective he had sought through the whole affair: to maintain his independence, for which he left Protestant Basel and went on resisting his Catholic critics; to work, against all odds, for reunion. This he did through his advice to participants in the Diet of Augsburg (1530) and writings like *Liber de sarcienda ecclesiae concordia* (On Mending the Peace of the Church, 1533), though by 1533 the entrenchment of both parties had made the call for mutual concession anachronistic. Against W.A. Visser t'Hooft, who had spoken of 'Erasmian simplification' as a form of ecumenism, Augustijn in his 'Conclusion' insists that Erasmus lived still within the one undivided church, while calling for openness and prudence on issues that God had not yet fully revealed.[50]

When in the mid-1980s Augustijn wrote a biography of Erasmus and returned, a quarter of a century on, to the problem of Erasmus and the Reformation, he was more than ever struck by what Erasmus and Luther had in common. Of course, Erasmus' attempts at mediation failed, and his personal relations with Luther were bad; of course, contemporaries were wrong to attribute to them a common theology. Nevertheless they were at work together in the movement shaking the existing religious culture. The free-will controversy represented rival methodologies, as writers since 1962 had seen, and became an exercise in mutual misunderstanding, but there was to it a common exegetical core. As for the Basel Reformation, Augustijn now, after McConica's 'Grammar of Consent,' accepted that Erasmus' defence against a Protestant doctrine of the Lord's Supper he found convincing was not a mere appeal to authority, but a resting on the deeply based 'consensus of the church.' Here we have reached, Augustijn concludes, 'the heart of Erasmus' religious conviction,' though it did not assure him of intellectual and psychological stability.[51]

To suggest as much common ground as Augustijn does between Erasmus and Luther is to remind readers of Seidel Menchi's studies of the reception of Erasmus in Italy.[52] There he was taken up by reform movements with ideologies sometimes close to, but often distant from, his thought as stated formally in his writings. That is in turn a reminder of how the issue 'Erasmus and the Reformation' can be taken in different ways. Beside Erasmus theologian or exponent of the rhetorical tradition stands Erasmus the sociocultural critic. Narratives of Erasmus' relations with the Reformers and, certainly, studies devoted to his controversy with Luther, which have themselves varied widely according to the observers' starting-points, have not done justice to this Erasmus. Oelrich's description of him as a *Städter* and of the Reformation as an urban phenomenon was a start, and some later biographies have put him in sociocultural contexts.[53] On the whole, however, writings about Erasmus as a religious thinker have not been open to this approach, and Seidel Menchi's influence on the main body of writing about Erasmus is still to come.

IV

By the quincentenary of 1969, it was possible, as we have seen, to link Erasmus to the documens of the Second Vatican Council. In a note to his essay 'Où en est le portrait d'Erasme théologien?' in the *Scrinium* collection he edited, J. Coppens quotes from the twelfth paragraph of the Council's Dogmatic Constitution of the Church 'Lumen Gentium':

> The holy People of God shares also in Christ's prophetic office: it spreads abroad a living witness to him, especially by a life of faith and love and by offering to God a sacrifice of praise, the fruit of lips praising his name. The whole body of the faithful who have an anointing that comes from the holy one cannot err in matters of belief. This characteristic is shown in the supernatural appreciation of the faith (*sensus fidei*) of the whole Christian people, when, 'from the bishops to the last of the faithful,' they manifest a universal consent in matters of faith and morals. By this appreciation of the faith, aroused and sustained by the Spirit of truth, the People of God, guided by the sacred teaching authority (*magisterium*), and obeying it, receives not the mere word of men, but truly the word of God, the faith once for all delivered to the saints. The People unfailingly adheres to this faith, penetrates it more deeply with right judgment, and applies it more fully in daily life.[54]

Coppens finds various 'Erasmian themes' in this passage: faith and love as the true essence of the Christian life; the consensus of Christendom and its infallibility; the importance of a laity capable of Christian perfection realized in daily life. Coppens remarks on the dogmatic safeguards built into the passage quoted from 'Lumen Gentium,' despite its populism. He also contends that

Erasmus' 'minimalisme dogmatique' and spiritualism set limits to his claims to be a theologian of the church.[55] Nevertheless, his linking the embattled humanist to a dogmatic constitution of the Council shows how far Catholic appreciation of him had come since Pineau and even Lortz. We follow the thread of writing about Erasmus' view of the church.

In a work of the 1950s, Karl Schätti demonstrates changes, in Erasmus' relations with Rome, due to time and circumstance, events and personalities, within an essential consistency. In the time of Leo X, he was praised in Rome without being understood; later, there were swings determined by changing policies towards the Protestants, intransigence or concession. He could vary between recognizing the offices as given, like the celestial hierarchy, and emphasizing the integrity of the person more than the dignity of the office. Even so, almost from the beginning, he saw the church as the Christian people, which the hierarchy served rather than commanded.[56] Schätti anticipates the postconciliar mood.

A stronger conception of the church, Catholic in the traditional, Tridentine sense, is attributed to Erasmus in the Frankfurt thesis of Georg Gebhart, *Die Stellung des Erasmus von Rotterdam zur Römische Kirche*. Gebhart's discipline is history, but he is, he says, prepared to make a theological judgment on Erasmus' ecclesiology. He will test it before 'the tribunal of church tradition on orthodoxy and heresy.' This naïve avowal determines the direction of Gebhart's inquiry. His work has, predominantly, a formal systematic character and reaches unequivocal, sometimes startling, conclusions. It can be seen as an over-correction to Pineau, Huizinga, Lortz, and Telle.[57]

Erasmus' writings on ecclesiology after 1514 were, Gebhart asserts, essentially consistent, without serious rupture by the Luther affair. Erasmus insisted that the personal bond between Christ and the believer and the study of the Bible, where Christ is present, must be complemented by obedience to the church, just as tradition stands beside scripture as a source of revelation. This church, though confirmed by consensus, is not merely the gathering of the faithful; it is a visible institution, a *Rechtsgestalt*.[58] There was, before Christ's appearance, a pre-existent church, a *societas sanctorum*, but with the gospel came hierarchy. On this matter, Erasmus actually anticipated post-Tridentine theology. Gebhart contantly leads the evidence towards identifying Erasmus with the traditional and institutional. Reform of the church meant the transformation of individuals; the ecclesiastical institution was to remain untouched.[59] Gebhart has a long discussion of what the dictum 'Outside the church no salvation' might have meant to Erasmus. He recognized an elect beyond the Christian fold, constituted, not as in Thomistic thought, by implicit faith, but by a spiritual and ethical character.[60] As for non-Catholic Christians, he took, Gebhart claims, the position of 'contemporary Catholic theology' as represented by Karl Adam's *Das Wesen des Katholizismus* (1924; thirteenth edition 1957): individual non-Catholics deserve respect but, in upholding the purity of the faith, dogmatic intolerance is a moral obligation. While recognizing the teaching authority, but not the primacy, of Councils, Erasmus adopted a moderate papalism, papal authority itself being essentially pastoral.[61]

Earlier historians, as we have seen, sat in the tribunal and passed judgment on Erasmus' orthodoxy, with very different results from Gebhart's. The differences between them and him mark a trend. The objections to the procedure are the same in both cases. To pass a monitor of orthodoxy, traditional or post-Tridentine, over the thought of Erasmus is to misunderstand its character. More seriously, Gebhart's account lacks any sense of the church as a sociocultural formation embodied in human communities, a sense which Erasmus had and which helped shape his reform program.[62] The quincentenary essays already discussed, James McConica's 'Grammar of Consent' and Otto Schottenloher's 'Lex Naturae und Lex Christi,' while not sociological, treated Erasmus' understanding of the whole Christian society and avoided confining the church to a jurisdiction, hierarchy and *Rechtsinstitution*. Unlike these essays, Gebhart's monograph seems distant from the spirit of Vatican 2.

Schottenloher pursued his theme in an essay of 1970 on Erasmus and the *respublica christiana*. Medieval conceptions of the world order, he says, continued in Erasmus, as the dedication of his New Testament to Pope Leo X as 'prince of the whole world' reveals. At the same time, he sought to reshape the medieval *respublica christiana* as a humanistic cultural and spiritual community ('Bildungsgemeinschaft'). Like Gebhart, Schottenloher recognizes that there was for Erasmus only one visible church, the body of Christ, but, unlike him, he interprets this, not as a legal, but as an educational formation. The church stood in contradiction, not to the temporal order, the 'world' of secular and lay life, which in a sense belongs to the Christian body, but to the world of the vices. Schottenloher interprets Erasmus' image of the three circles of clergy, rulers, and people, centred on Christ, as a spiritual redefinition of the *respublica christiana*, not as an account of its structure.[63] The tasks which for Erasmus justified papal headship were moral, above all the creation or recreation of concord in the Christian world. By contrast, papal power as it had developed in the Middle Ages was political, legal, tyrannical, and corrupt. Hand in hand with legal changes came educational and theological ones (the incorporation of Aristotle, the rise of scholasticism) which restricted Christian perfection to monks and set lower aims for lay people. The recovery of a common end for all Christian people, of Christian unity in that sense, a unity which the eucharist represented and for which it gave empowerment, was both a theological and a cultural task. Thus, as the *Paraclesis* had it, Christ's work was 'the restoration of human nature originally well formed.'[64]

Later writings on the theme 'Erasmus and the church' have held to the main line defined at the quincentenary by McConica's 'Grammar of Consent' and Schottenloher's essays. Erasmus, it is said, valued above all the spiritual bond between Christians and saw as the essential thing the concord among them as a community of love centred on Christ. At the same time, he did not reject the institution or even undervalue it, and he recognized, indeed honoured, hierarchy and authority, provided that their aim was service and their character pastoral. Similarly, Erasmus did not deny the centrality of the sacraments, provided that sincerity of heart accompanied their celebration. In his views on these matters, there was substantial continuity from the *Enchiridion* (1503) to the *Ecclesiastes* (1535). Thus this line amply skirts the anti-institutional interpretation of Augustijn's quincentenary essays, on the one side, and the juridical definitions of Gebhart, on the other.[65] The inquiry has, it would seem, come to its final resting-place beside a devout Erasmus. Yet, dissatisfactions remain. It is as though, in response to Erasmus' call for concord, a harmonizing engine has been passed over his writings. The inner tensions in his thought have been played down, that between its strongly spiritualizing tendency and his acceptance, even celebration, of the institutional church, that between church as ordered hierarchy and church as people of God, as demonstrated by the three circles, where lines are fluid and movement to the centre is possible from every part of the figure. As well, the abrasive Erasmus, the savage critic of popes and bishops, monks and theologians, has virtually disappeared from this literature. The devout Erasmus has become all. Strangely perhaps, Vatican 2 has largely ceased to be a point of reference for Erasmus' ecclesiology, though Germain Marc'hadour has found his teachings on liturgical reform, on the priesthood of the laity, and on peace and justice to be reiterated by the Council. Marc'hadour's essay brings gently into balance Erasmus' essential orthodoxy on priesthood, sacrament, and church and his resistance to clericalism and many manifestations of Catholic devotion in his time.[66] Huizinga and the others may have confined themselves too much to the Erasmus of the *Folly* and the *Colloquies* and neglected his major theological writings.[67] In the new literature, the latter receive their full due. But the Erasmus of the *Folly* and the *Colloquies*, of the radical *Adages*, of the biting letters has also to be drawn into the account.

V

Three books of the 1970s mark the coming of age of the doctrine that Erasmus was first and foremost a theologian. They are Georges Chantraine's *'Mystère' et 'Philosophie du Christ' selon Erasme* (1971), Manfred Hoffmann's *Erkenntnis und Verwirklichung der wahren Theologie nach Erasmus von Rotterdam* (1972), and Marjorie O'Rourke Boyle's *Erasmus on Language and Method in Theology* (1977). There is common ground between these studies but, methodologically, they differ considerably. To a treatment of their themes I will add two codas, discussions of the work of John Olin and of M.A. Screech's provocative book on religious ecstasy and *The Praise of Folly* (1980).[68]

All three books shift interest, among the sources available for the study of Erasmus' religious thought, from the *Enchiridion*, central to Kohls' book of the mid-1960s, to the writings of his maturity, especially those connected to his New Testament edition. Admittedly, Kohls had drawn a mainline orthodox theology from Erasmus' handbook to lay piety of 1503. That achievement in itself had demonstrated his conviction that the fundamentals of Erasmus' theology were to be found there.[69] By contrast, Hoffmann contends that the key to the methodology and form of Erasmus' theological thinking is in the *Ratio verae theologiae* of 1518. His argument runs thus. There was a centre and structure to

Erasmus' world of thought, though he was not a systematist in the scholastic sense. His pragmatism was based in a dogmatic structure; his universalism had a centre. The dogmatic structure was scriptural, and the centre scripture itself. Dogmatics should then be subject to exegesis. Hence, the works ancillary to the New Testament of 1516 are primary. Erasmus' careful revisions of the *Ratio* 1519–25 indicated the importance it had for him.[70]

For Chantraine and Boyle also, concentration on the *Ratio* and other writings from around its time is more than a mere textual preference. It represents a reconception of Erasmus' theology. The journey from *Enchiridion* to *Ratio* traced a progressive realization of Erasmus' vocation as a theologian. The progress, says Chantraine, was coherent, as was Erasmus' thought, but the coherence was a synthesis, not a system. Chantraine continues: in the *Enchiridion*, with its Platonist and Dionysian allure, the spiritual movement is upward; the believer ascends a hierarchy of being. In the *Ratio* and accompanying writings, the movement is not vertical but horizontal; this is movement towards a centre, Christ, who works in the believer a transfiguration. The Christian life is no longer a matter simply of leaving the visible behind in an ascent to the invisible; Christ's action and the work of the Spirit transform the visible itself. Boyle, too, breaks with the Neoplatonist image of Erasmus and finds his distinctive model, not in a ladder of ascent, but in a circle. This model, she says, is 'thoroughly Christian; it is centripetal.'[71]

Erasmus' thought is, for both Chantraine and Boyle, Christocentric. Chantraine concentrates the 'mystery,' which is theology's object for Erasmus, in the 'fabula Christi,' the drama of redemption. The divine love it reveals is, he says, 'at the heart of the Erasmian theology.' This Christocentric theme, to which Erasmus gave the name *philosophia Christi*, can, as Kohls proposed, be shaped to the traditional scheme *exitus-reditus*, love coming from God and returning to him. Boyle has a long and fascinating treatment of the notion of Christ as, for Erasmus, the *scopus* of theology; the appropriate metaphors are astronomical or maritime: Christ is a 'sighting' or 'fix' for the theological navigator. But *scopus* also conveys centrality. Cicero had recommended to the speaker 'a point of reference to which to refer all the lines of argumentation.' For the theologian the rule is: 'Refer everything to Christ'; on him all turns, in him everything is harmonized.[72]

Both Boyle and Chantraine then see the incarnation as central to Erasmus' theology. They link it, however, to different theological methodologies. Chantraine's link is to the idea of mystery, which is his main concern.[73] Thus, Erasmus' criticism of scholasticism is based on a sense of the incomprehensibility of God which demands, not *impia curiositas*, but veneration, 'l'abandon confiant à l'action divine,' associated with the activity of the Holy Spirit. Chantraine's debate is within the discipline of theology itself. Boyle's opening chapter on Erasmus' defence of his notorious translation of *logos* in the prologue to John's gospel by *sermo*, rather than the Vulgate's *verbum*, has different methodological implications. *Sermo* indicates conversation, discourse, utterance, and is therefore the appropriate expression of the Father's self-revelation through the Son. The theologian should value exactness and sensitivity in the use of words and should not despise grammar. Boyle describes her purpose as showing 'how philosophy of language orders theological methodology.' Speech represents the self-revealing of person to person, and of God to man. It makes community possible. The sign of failure in theology is fractured discourse, factionalism and discord. It is on this count that scholasticism stands condemned. Her interest in 'the interplay of language and method in theology' places her inquiry, Boyle says, 'in the historical context of Renaissance studies,' in connection with the Renaissance humanist pursuit of eloquence. The concern is with theology's external relations and, in particular, with its borderlands with language and rhetoric.[74]

Boyle and Chantraine are explicit about the clash of methodologies their work represents. Chantraine, writing, of course, before the appearance of Boyle's work, remarks that, according to the *Ratio*, rhetoric, which she and others would shortly make a key to understanding Erasmus, was but an auxiliary to theology, for awakening the spiritual subject to the mystery of Christ. Boyle's criticism is that Chantraine seeks reference-points for Erasmus only in the Christian theological tradition and neglects the classical element.[75]

Hoffmann sees Erasmus' theology, which for him also is Christocentric, in more philosophical, and consequently more systematic, terms. Does Erasmus work towards his convictions from the observation of outward circumstances, or does he apply preconceived convictions, say from Neoplatonist idealism, to circumstances? What for him is the connection between knowing or believing and doing? What is the relation between how things are and what we should do? In theological terms, the question might be: how is Christ, who is the transcendent aim and end of Christian theology, related to human strivings, how is Christology related to anthropology? The issues can be described more personally and experientially: how should the balance be struck between Erasmus' realism and his spiritualism? As we have seen in other connections, this is a tension which Erasmus himself saw and wished to moderate, between world-denial and world-affirmation.[76]

Hoffmann's answer is broadly this. Erasmus' primary concern is always the ethical outcome, but that does not make his thought wholly unsystematic, outside theory, ontology or dogmatics. In fact, only on the basis of belief about the order of the world can ethical action be realized. Nevertheless, dogmatics do not exist for themselves; they take on meaning only when they issue, on the one hand, in the exegesis of scripture and, on the other, in moral action. Against Kohls, and in line more with Auer, Hoffmann makes anthropology the key to Erasmus' 'system.' When he thinks dualistically about man (spirit and body), the transcendent order claims priority, for spirit's primacy is near to absolute; when he thinks of a trichotomy (spirit, soul, and body), the middle term makes a bridge, for free human action, between lower and higher. Erasmus believed his thought harmonized at this point, but in fact, Hoffmann says, it remains in tension or suspension. He rightly sees in Erasmus an unstable balance between spiritualism and realism. Is he right then to speak of Erasmus' thought as a 'system'? He presses the point over scriptural interpretation, subordinating Erasmus' critical and philological work to his 'Systematik.' Is Erasmus' thought wrested here to a propositional form, necessary perhaps for philosophical consideration, but still uncongenial? However, this approach gives substance to Erasmus' religious thought and resists the temptation to spiritualize it too much, or to vaporize it.[77]

All three writers recognize the importance of the social extension of Erasmus' religious thought. The *Enchiridion*, the *Institutio principis christiani*, and the *Ratio*, Hoffmann says, may be seen as compendia for the three different segments of Christian society, laity, rulers, and theologians. On the model of Erasmus' dualist or trichotomous anthropology, he makes these 'social groups' self-contained; as spirit and body remain forever distinct, so do clerics, rulers, and people. That is to overlook the fluidity suggested by Erasmus' image of the three circles and to tie him too rigidly to medieval, hierarchical patterns. Boyle introduces the image of the three circles as a mnemonic model for focusing theology and ethics on Christ. She suggests analogies astronomical (the heavenly bodies) and urban (the concentric circles of the Renaissance city and, for that matter, of Dutch towns). Though speculative, the latter reinforces Boyle's main, incontestable point, that, for Erasmus, theology is 'oriented towards the practical and common life of the Christian republic.'[78]

Chantraine emphasizes the ecclesial, as well as the social, aim of this theology. It was Catholic, if not always expressed in the forms venerated in Erasmus' time. Erasmus accepted that the sacraments, especially baptism and eucharist, communicated the Christian mystery. He saw, as the ancient writers had seen and 'Lumen Gentium' had now reiterated, that their baptismal vows make all Christians 'ecclesiastics,' a principle which the monastic thinking of Erasmus' time betrayed. So, Chantraine concludes, Erasmus' criticism of the monastic institution derived, not, as Telle claimed, from personal rancour, but from a baptismal theology related to his understanding of mystery. The pneumatology (doctrine of the Spirit) and Christology of the *Ratio* indicated 'a more dogmatic orientation of thought' than in Erasmus' earlier writings. Further, his critique of dialectic did not make him an enemy of all speculative or scholastic theology. Chantraine rejects, as Hoffmann and Boyle do in their own ways, those who have seen Erasmus as adogmatic. That conclusion, he says, treats 'as mutually exclusive history and dogma, philology and theology, scientific objectivity and religious feeling, rationality and faith.'[79]

André Godin, in his book on Erasmus and Origen, challenges Chantraine's attribution to Erasmus of an essential Catholicity, in '*Mystère*' et '*Philosophie du Christ*,' in his later book on the free-will controversy, and in an essay in *Scrinium*, called 'L'Apologia ad Latomum. Deux conceptions de théologie.' The cruder forms of the old controversy, Erasmus Catholic Christian against Erasmus infidel, had been set aside by the second half of the twentieth century, but controversy itself continued, changed, to a degree relocated, and in a subtler form. It was now about where Erasmus was to be located in the order of studies, among the disciplines. To attribute to him a taste for speculative theology, Godin says, is to 'do violence to his intellectual personality.' In the works of

Kohls and Chantraine, he continues, 'the capricious meanders of the Erasmian river, rectified by the theological bulldozers, have given way to a great majestic stream in a straight line, about which all know where it comes from and where it goes.'[80] 'Capricious meanders': the expression seems excessive, even for Godin's own argument, even for one wanting to deny that Erasmus was essentially a systematic theologian.

Erasmus' defence of Origen, in the Parisian controversies about him in the 1520s, is, naturally, part of Godin's case. It was based on 'a certain sense of relativity of dogmatic enunciations, of a historical evolution or development of the truths of faith.' Gladly following Origen, he recognized a plurality of readings, against a monolithic conception of the transmission of sacred texts. Whereas, in the controversy with Latomus, Erasmus' scholastic critic at Louvain, Chantraine sees two rival conceptions of Catholic theology, Godin discerns something more radical, the clash of two *mentalités*, a cultural shift. This was, he says, a debate about the hierarchy of knowledge and the organization of studies in the university. Erasmus' concern was with the signifier properly understood and purified grammatically, Latomus' with the integrity of the signified, the theological and dogmatic content.[81] Godin's Erasmus is in the long run subversive, while Chantraine's is making an accommodation with tradition.[82] Godin's perspective is forward-looking, reminiscent of writers in the liberal tradition. Erasmus was 'a precursor of scientific exegesis.' He and his humanist grammarian colleagues were in at the beginning of a discipline, biblical criticism, that was in the end to escape the dogmatic yoke and achieve autonomy.[83]

Godin sees Erasmus as creating a new Christian culture, centred on exegesis, on grammar and rhetoric, to replace the existing theological order, which was scholastic and centred on dialectic. To this theme we return in the next chapter. But he does not deny Erasmus' orthodoxy; his thought was Christocentric and Trinitarian.[84] Similarly, M.A. Screech, who, startlingly, makes him an exponent of religious ecstasy akin to madness, does not believe that Erasmus 'in anything he wrote, ever put in doubt the credal orthodoxies or the essentials of the Catholic faith,' although the last lines of the *Folly*, with their Montanist suggestion of ecstasy as amnesia, literally being out of one's mind, made it a close-run thing.[85] Here is another, and surprising, version of the notion of Erasmus as serious religious thinker.

Screech's book is a study of that last section of the *Praise of Folly* whose religious character has always been recognized, though often met with bewilderment, ridicule, or disbelief. Screech introduces a control by referring to other writings of Erasmus, notably the *Enchiridion* of eight years before the first appearance of the *Folly* (1511) and the New Testament *Paraphrases* and Psalms commentaries of years, in some cases many years, after. Screech considers concentration on the first edition critical to his argument because later editions, the basis of most modern renderings, significantly changed the balance of the work. The most extensive changes were made to the edition published by Matthias Schürer in Strasbourg in 1514; they include the satirical passages which, above all else, have given the book its reputation across the centuries. Later editions made small prudent changes to the last section, to counter or forestall criticism.[86]

Previous writers on *Folly* in this century have not ignored the last section of the book, which identifies Christ, his disciples, and true Christians with folly. But, by and large, they have counted this the supreme paradox in a work made up of paradoxes.[87] The variety of views has been considerable, and their sophistication, for this has been the most studied, as well as the most popular, of Erasmus' works.[88] For some, the satiric strain has been dominant, a seriousness of purpose, therefore, social, moral, and didactic.[89] Others have revelled in the playfulness, the endless self-correcting and self-undermining, the 'puzzle of Chinese boxes,' though playfulness constantly edged into seriousness.[90] The *Folly* has been related to the classical oration and encomium.[91] Did it not belong also, in important ways, to the medieval world?[92] How firm was its structure and, in particular, how were its three apparent sections to be related?[93] How seriously or how absolutely to take the last section on the Christian fool and religious ecstasy remained contentious.[94] Screech takes it with complete seriousness.

That section, he argues, builds on, extends, the *Enchiridion*'s preference for 'the spiritual rather than the carnal, the invisible rather than the visible, the moral rather than the formal.' There had been, in Erasmus' thought since the *Enchiridion*, and there still was, a syncretism of Paul's foolishness of the Cross (1 Corinthians 1) and the Platonist rejection of the visible wold in favour of the ideal realities of the invisible one. But, according to Screech, Erasmus was not captivated by the Neoplatonist writers of ancient or his own times and saw through the claims made for Pseudo-Dionysius. His preferred guide, as Godin was shortly to demonstrate on a massive scale, was Origen, in this case his doctrine of God's 'emptying himself' in Christ (Philippians 2), a foolishness surpassing all human wisdom, yet far short of God's own wisdom.[95]

Erasmus' syncretism of Jewish, Christian, and Platonist notions came generally from the Fathers, especially the Greek Fathers, but it is recognizable, too, in the mystical writers of the Latin West like Bernard and Bonaventura, though he had no sympathy for the setting they gave it in the religious orders. Ecstasy passes over into ravishment, rapture. Paul's experience of rapture (2 Corinthians 12) and that of the disciples at Jesus' transfiguration are, in different ways, paradigmatic. In Folly's peroration, the link is to madness; the love of the Christian for God, of course prompted by God, is a kind of insanity.[96] Screech's final characterization of Erasmus is as an inspired prophet, 'a prophet in the wake of Christ, Paul, Origen, the fathers and their successrs. He, like they, opened up the *arcana Scripturae*. ... Such an exegete is a prophet whose world is marked by amazement, astonishment, spiritual drunkenness, ecstasy, rapture. He does not mind seeming to be mad: David, Christ and Christ's disciples are mad in that sense, too.'[97]

No larger claim has been made for Erasmus' religion. To those who take the last part of the *Folly* seriously, at face value, without irony, it carries conviction. That there is a difficulty is, however, demonstrated by Screech's pages on the madness or lunacy of Christ. The reference is to Christ's encounter with kinsfolk who thought him mad, 'beside himself' (Mark 3:19–21), and to Erasmus' comments thereon, as in his *Paraphrases*. Screech is particularly scornful of the alternative view of Jesus, 'meek and mild.' Erasmus' Jesus is, Screech says, ecstatically insane. But the *Paraphrase* of this passage is less about ecstasy than about ethical choices: 'He who pours out his inheritance for the poor is mad (*insanit*) in the opinion of the man who places the defence of his life in riches. ... He who spurns the honours of princes and of the people to obtain glory with God, is mad (*insanit*) for those who really are mad (*insaniunt*).'[98] And not far away in the *Paraphrase* is the alternative Jesus, the Jesus who, as a Vatican 2 document put it, observed the laws of his country, led the life of an ordinary craftsman of his time and place, and sanctified human ties, espe-

cially family ties.[99] Jesus, says Erasmus' *Paraphrase* of Mark 1:9,
'came from a small humble village ... [and] went forth, a humble
man without retinue, like one of the people ... he put John's
authority into the shade by his innocence, his meekness [*mansue-
tudine*], and his kindness towards all. ... He did many things, not
to satisfy his own needs, but to give us in himself a pattern of
life.'[100] Erasmus the sober moralist, looking in Jesus for a pattern
of life, must be put beside Erasmus the inspired prophet emulat-
ing the rapture of his Master.

The writings of John Olin offer a sober portrait of Erasmus,
though one not confined by the expression 'moralist.' His own
review of Erasmus interpretations leads to the image 'of a profoundly Christian Erasmus fully orthodox and Catholic.'[101] This is
the end-point of the trends we have been following in this chapter.
Olin has argued his case from both sides, Erasmus' bond to the
Fathers, his influence on the Catholic Reformation. He accepts, as
explanation of Erasmus' life's work, his wish to reorient theology
on scripture and the Fathers, as Denys Gorce had already done in
a landmark essay of the 1950s, 'La patristique dans la réforme
d'Erasme.' Gorce wrote in a *Festschrift* for Joseph Lortz. The association is piquant, for Gorce, contrary to Lortz's model of a long
decline into secularism and infidelity, sees the humanist effort in
patristics as a healthy reaction against a decadent scholasticism
and a return to the reverent respect Thomas and his contemporaries accorded the Fathers. Erasmus' crushing labours in this field,
Gorce says, find their explanation in 'l'amour profond d'Erasme
pour sa matière.'[102] More than once Gorce quotes Imbart de la
Tour, and, indeed, both Gorce and Olin are in the line of Imbart's
great book *L'Evangélisme* (1914) in asserting Erasmus' essential
Catholicity.[103] Olin recognizes that the bond with Jerome, which
he explores in essays of a learning ample but lightly worn, identifies Erasmus with theologies of a certain kind, focused on scripture and affirming of the union between religion and culture. The
implication must be that these theologies, too, are Catholic and
that scholasticism is not Catholicism's only theological form.[104]

Henri de Lubac, coming to Erasmus towards the end of his
magisterial study of medieval exegesis, also makes his relation to
the Fathers the critical indicator of his theology and hermeneutic.
Overlooking this has, from his lifetime on, from the Sorbonne
censures to twentieth-century critics, produced bad misunderstandings, fruits of tradition being taken as dangerous heterodox-

ies. Erasmus did not reject scholasticism completely; his criticism was of a theology that obscured scripture and the Fathers. He continued the patristic tradition but, de Lubac concludes, could not altogether recapture its vitality.[105]

Olin, in looking forward from Erasmus, thinks especially of his relation to the early Jesuits, whose heirs were among Olin's own teachers. On the vexed question of Loyola and Erasmus, he draws, against a long tradition and the older literature, a positive conclusion: if Loyola was not an Erasmian 'in the usual sense of that term,' there was no 'wall of separation' between them. That conclusion coincides with Bataillon's.[106] The Society's educational apostolate, Olin says, was 'one of the great extensions and consolidations of Renaissance humanism.' The hard judgments on Erasmus in the Jesuit literature after Loyola's death were more expressions of an increasingly intransigent Counter-Reformation spirit than of his original impulse. For Olin the humanism, whose leading figure Erasmus was, was infused with Catholic Christianity, aimed at reform and led into the creative movements of the Catholic Reformation.[107] Henri de Lubac, too, distinguishes between Catholic Reformation, sought and prepared for by Erasmus, and Counter-Reformation, the Roman church's reaction against Protestantism. Attitudes to Erasmus divided and his influence was diffused. The Jesuits were both Erasmian and anti-Erasmian.[108] This conclusion is more equivocal than Olin's, but the tendency is the same.

In these writings, and in John Olin's essays in particular, the tendency reached its peak. Humanism, as represented by Erasmus, had a religious and theological purpose, defined by the study of scripture and the Fathers. Learning and piety blended; from the blend came programs of both educational and church reform, different from the scholastic, but Catholic none the less. In the 1980s, views alternative to these were present, views distinct also from the old liberal tradition, to which Huizinga and Renaudet were heirs. Seidel Menchi was arguing that Erasmus' historical associations were essentially subversive. It was also being argued that the bond between learning and piety in Erasmian humanism was not a seamless web but a bit of rough stitching, and that 'the welding of profane learning to lay piety requires a certain amount of intellectual sleight-of-hand.'[109] This challenge came from a particular quarter, the history of education, and to it we will return in the next chapter.

VI

The pattern established in this chapter, the trends and, to a degree, the debates reappear in the studies, flourishing in the 1970s and 1980s, of Erasmus' work on the New Testament. They present that work as confiming his claim to be a theologian, though a sensitive frontier remained between the theologian and the grammarian. Above all, it reinforced his reform program for church and society. Thence arose, these writings of the period aver, the furious controversies enveloping it.

It is nevertheless noteworthy, and indeed curious, that two articles of 1984, appearing in journals not of first resort for Erasmus specialists, should revolutionize our understanding of Erasmus' priorities in his New Testament work. Pride of place had always been given to his Greek text, the first ever published. H.J. de Jonge in the *Journal of Theological Studies* argued that, for Erasmus and his contemporaries, his Latin translation, corrected from the Greek text, which was itself included for validation, was primary. Critics, de Jonge says, saw correction of proof-texts from the Vulgate as threatening both church and society. Erasmus indeed saw his Latin text as heralding reform: 'Real influence could only be exercised by a Latin text.'[110]

More drastically, Andrew J. Brown, in *Transactions of the Cambridge Bibliographical Society,* successfully challenged the whole accepted chronology of Erasmus' labours on the New Testament and, furthermore, verified Erasmus' own overlooked account. He demonstrates that the manuscripts, by the renowned Flemish scribe Pieter Meghen, used to prove a very early start by Erasmus on his Latin translation had in fact been written in two stages, possibly twenty years apart. Parallel columns carrying the Vulgate and Erasmus' translation, in the more radical version prepared for his second edition of 1519, were in significantly different scripts, Meghen's earlier and later scripts. This, and evidence that the translation relied on Greek manuscripts which Erasmus could not have seen before his arrival in Basel in 1514, confirm what his correspondence suggests, that the idea of a new Latin translation first arose in that year, and, consequently, that the decision for a tripartite publication, Greek text, Latin translation, and notes, came late.[111]

The effect of these exquisite demonstrations is to weaken, but not to destroy, de Jonge's case for the importance of the Latin translation, which, in any case, has to contend with the difficulty that the revisions to the Vulgate in the first edition of 1516 were limited and conservative. A further effect is to give prominence to Erasmus' *Annotations*. They came first in time, and in Erasmus' scheme, and were, as Erika Rummel was to say later, 'the nucleus of the project.'[112] As late as 1978, Catherine A.L. Jarrott could describe the *Annotations* as uncharted, if surprisingly fruitful, terrain.[113] She herself had already used them to examine themes of significance for the Reformation in Erasmus' theology: repentance, justification, papal power, law, and liberty; she concluded that, over successive editions, Erasmus used his notes to advance his own reform program, making criticisms and suggestions now voiced again, for the twentieth century, in the debates of Vatican 2 'and in some modern moralists' rejection of legalism in favor of that love that is the fulfillment of the law.'[114] From the mid-1970s the *Annotations* attracted concentrated research for the first time, culminating in Erika Rummel's monograph of 1987, *Erasmus' 'Annotations' on the New Testament.*[115]

In parallel ran studies on Erasmus' hermeneutic. Substantial areas of agreement appeared: his preference for the literal, historical-grammatical sense, his turning scripture to a moral purpose (in traditional terms, the tropological sense) and to purposes of reform, his looking to predecessors, distant (the Fathers) and recent (above all, Lorenzo Valla), his anticipation of modern biblical scholarship. We can also notice some distinctive emphases and interests among the authors. The whole body of writing confirms the point emerging in the later twentieth century, that Erasmus was, if not for all today a professional theologian, a serious writer on theological themes.

His studies from around 1505 committed Erasmus more and more to the literal sense of scripture and moderated the spiritualizing and allegorizing passionately recommended in his *Enchiridion* (1503). Even so, he always acknowledged the presence of mystery and, with Origen, accepted the need for allegory, although he came to reject the latter's 'wild allegorizing' (as John Payne puts it). Especially suspect to him was the defence of mistranslations or misunderstandings because dogmatic structures or liturgical practices depended on them, a position ferociously attacked by his conservative critics. This much is agreed.[116] Recognized also is his readiness to apply the text to the moral formation of the believer, the castigation of the failings of contemporary society and making the case for reform.[117]

Consistently with the position argued in his book on Erasmus and the sacraments, John Payne grounds this moralizing in an essentially Platonist anthropology, the dichotomy of flesh and spirit. This applies, he says, to the issue, critical in Erasmus' time, of faith and works: the works rejected in the Pauline literature were for Erasmus the ceremonial requirements of the law. Yet, Payne admits evidence of a broader interpretation of 'works' in the annotations added to later editions. In any case, one might ask: does not rejecton of trust in ceremonies imply the need for saving grace, what Payne calls 'the soteriological ground of Christian existence,' whose acceptance by Erasmus Payne (surprisingly) finds 'somewhat surprising'?[118] In a further essay, he asks whether the later changes were due to Lutheran influences and suggests rather that Erasmus and Melanchthon shared an 'ecumenical exegesis' for promoting Christian unity. Albert Rabil also takes that line and scouts the suggestion of Lutheranizing. Jerry Bentley thinks it enough that the experiences of the old Erasmus gave him a deeper appreciation of Paul.[119]

The first full-length study of the *Paraphrases*, Friedhelm Krüger's *Humanistische Evangelienauslegung: Desiderius Erasmus von Rotterdam als Ausleger der Evangelien in seinen Paraphrasen* (1986), shares Payne's view that a Platonist ontology stands behind Erasmus' biblical interpretation. Man, nature, the incarnation, scripture must, in their different ways, be interpreted by the key distinctions flesh/spirit, sensible/intelligible, inner/outer, visible/invisible. Scripture must be read spiritually. Allegory is, therefore, indispensable and really the heart of biblical interpretation, although Krüger recognizes that Erasmus was a sober allegorizer. The allegorical passes naturally into the tropological or moral sense, since the meanings relate to Christian life in the present and to the contemporary church and society.[120] In pioneering extended study of the *Paraphrases*, Krüger has substantially confirmed the consensus on Erasmus as biblical interpreter that we have seen emerging in the 1970s and 1980s. He has, however, not escaped the trap of oversystematization that seems to await those who attempt full-length studies of Erasmus' religious thought.

Despite earlier debates, a fair consensus has also emerged on Erasmus' debt to the Fathers, so that Rummel could in her monograph provide a balanced overview.[121] Differences, at least nuances, have appeared over his relation to his more immediate predecessor Lorenzo Valla, whose own *Annotationes* he discovered in 1504 and published in 1505. Conventionally, a distinction had been made between Valla's predominantly philological interests and Erasmus' work oriented to theology, or at least piety. Bentley, while acknowledging Erasmus' debt to Valla, marks their differences, Erasmus' wider critical scope and, above all, his adapting 'his scholarly observations to the needs of religious reform.' Jacques Chomarat, on the other hand, attacks the tradition. Valla's theological observations may have been drier or more cautious but, on the essentials, Valla and Erasmus were as one. Both were theologians, but this was a theology grounded in grammar and rhetoric, not dealing, like the scholastic theology, in abstractions, but addressing, as Paul and the Roman orator had done, people of a particular time and place.[122]

Chomarat's essay, like Godin's book on Erasmus and Origen, emphasizes the cultural shift implicit in Erasmus' biblical work. Valla and Erasmus accomplished an intellectual revolution, shifting the frontier between the divine and the human, the sacred and the profane, between what depends on authority and what is open to discussion. They desacralized the Vulgate. While scripture is, for them, divinely inspired, it also has the human component of language, a humanist argument recognized earlier by Heinz Holeczek in his book *Humanistische Bibelphilologie* (1975) and, earlier still, by Werner Schwarz in his pioneering work of 1955 on these themes, *Principles and Problems of Biblical Translation*.[123] For Chomarat, the biblical work of Valla and Erasmus opened up a revolutionary future. A further shift in the frontier between the divine and the human would produce the theologies of the Enlightenment, however shocking that outcome might have been to the two great humanists themselves.[124] Other commentators have rightly been more prudent. Holeczek recognizes an ideological and polemical edge to Erasmus' work and sees it directed by a strongly biblicist theology. Erasmus' Latin translation was the most ideologicaly charged element. Nevertheless, he, like Valla, was careful in diverging from the Vulgate, deferred to the church on theological exegesis, and in principle eschewed the idea of replacing theology by grammar.[125] Some have judged modest his work on the manuscripts, but the more considered commentaries – by Holeczek, Bentley, Rummel –

have pointed to its extent and the difficult and discouraging circumstances in which, by modern standards, it was carried on. It was highly creative and productive and, even on the less generous view, stood at the beginning of critical history.[126] He anticipated modern critical practice by his use of inference from the works of the Fathers and, most notably, by his adoption of the principle of the harder reading.[127] The main stream we have been following, disturbed here and there by substantial crosscurrents, is best described by the subtitle of Rummel's book: from philologist to theologian.

VII

By 1988, when CWE published its first volume on Erasmus' *Spiritualia*, the tendencies followed in this chapter had reached, not, of course, completion, but fruition. J.W. O'Malley's 'Introduction' to that volume (CWE 66) may be taken as the summation of the new consensus on Erasmus' religious thought, replacing that of Huizinga, Smith, and Pineau of sixty years before. Already in 1971, in commenting on the quincentenary volumes, François Wendel had written: 'In spite of all the nuances of interpretation which naturally come to light, there is now forming a sort of consensus among the majority of Erasmus specialists.'[128] There had been nuances – substantial enough – between Huizinga, Smith, and Pineau, but also a 'sort of consensus': that Erasmus was best understood as a pre-Enlightenment figure. In the new consensus, beautifully epitomized by O'Malley's essay, piety 'envelops' the whole of Erasmus' work, not a diffused spirituality, but a piety with sinewy ties to theology and the practice of ministry. The theology was not scholastic; Erasmus saw the scholastic exercise, in its high intellectualism, as fundamentally wrong-headed. His own theology, O'Malley concludes, was balanced and orthodox. As piety needed the backbone of a theology, so theology could be saved from dryness only by a piety that had also within it 'a strong moralizing strain.' Above all, both piety and theology must issue in pastoring.[129]

It could be prudent to place the word 'consensus' in quotation marks. Nuances continued to come to light, as this chapter has shown. How comfortably, for example, do Christian theology and classical thought, piety and profane learning, ministry and secular eloquence sit together in Erasmus' mind? The issue arises over his relation to the rhetorical tradition, the subject of the hour in Erasmus studies, as the next chapter should show. O'Malley, like Pfeiffer, finds correlation, 'almost compelling compatibility.'[130] Other interpretations are possible, including the one already mentioned, that Erasmus' welding of profane learning to lay piety required 'a certain amount of intellectual sleight-of-hand.'[131]

Twice in the twentieth century there was talk of an 'Erasmus Renaissance.' On both occasions, the reference was to the rediscovery of Erasmus in theological circles. The first came originally with liberal Protestantism, in the essays of Dilthey, Wernle, and Troeltsch: Erasmus, more than Luther and the Reformers, broke with medieval supernaturalism, stood for Jesus' religion of the Sermon on the Mount, and prepared the way for rational theology. The position was soon attacked but remained firm into the 1920s.[132] It had an extended existence in Renaudet's depiction of Erasmus as advocate of a 'third church.'[133] The revival of interest in Erasmus in Germany after World War 2 was interpreted at the time as a 'search for a new humanism.'[134] Lortz's unfriendly portrait, heightened in his 'Erasmus-kirchengeschichtlich' of 1950, was the reverse image of this new humanist Erasmus. H.R. Trevor-Roper, in a famous and eloquent essay of 1955, repeated Renaudet's themes: the third church, Erasmus preacher of a religion of simple and sincere faith, of toleration and a rational theology. Beyond Renaudet, Trevor-Roper returned to Gibbon's idea of an 'Erasmianism after Erasmus, a secret stream which meandered to and fro' across the Catholic/Protestant divide, 'creating oases of rational thought impartially on either side.'[135] In 1961, Enno van Gelder, without reference to Gibbon, reiterated and elaborated his case: Luther's and Calvin's Reformation was a minor affair compared with the major Reformation of Erasmus and the humanists which propelled Christianity further than it could do, away from medieval Catholicism and towards the modern world.[136] Meantime, the foundations of the new consensus were being laid by Bouyer and Auer and Rudolf Padberg's work of 1956 on Erasmus' catechetics. The last named was the first work to present Erasmus as a kind of systematic theologian (the biblically and historically based kind). Naturally, the nature of the two catechetical works Padberg studied made systematic presentation easier, just as a study drawing on the *Colloquies* might find in Erasmus a mind of a different stamp.[137]

The second 'Erasmus Renaissance' has belonged to the penumbra of Vatican 2, though it has not been denominationally exclusive: Erasmus has also been called 'a teacher of Protestants.'[138] 'Lumen gentium,' O'Malley writes, 'reads at times like Erasmus himself.'[139] This is a striking formulation of the new orthodoxy about our subject: Erasmus sincere Christian, orthodox Catholic on all essential points, and candid ecumenist. The new orthodoxy flourishes and is assured of a long life, but a promise of permanence is another matter. That is because there is no way the argument can be finally clinched. Orthodox expressions on church and sacraments can be accumulated and given their face value. Or they can be read as defensive or preventive actions or as a kind of insurance policy against charges that Erasmus was subverting the existing religious order. There is agreement that he was an orthodox Christian in a broad sense, his thought incarnational, Christocentric, and Trinitarian. The argument is about how he stood to medieval Catholicism and its dominant cultural forms, scholasticism, monasticism, a religious practice highly sacramental and objectivist, and a literalist and proof-text approach to scripture. His relation to later forms of Catholicism, the Tridentine or those associated with Vatican 1 and Vatican 2, is an interesting and important question in itself, especially for understanding how he was interpreted in the eras concerned. This chapter has shown how the last became a reference-point for Erasmus interpretation in the twentieth century. But pursuing this question may cloud as easily as it illuminates the main issue Erasmus' stance in his own time. That much of his thought and writing was theological, that he made a distinctive contribution to theology, is also part of the consensus, but that leaves open what priority he gave theology in comparison with other disciplines. Some at least of those who have written on Erasmus' interest in grammar and rhetoric have put his priorities there, as we shall now see.

SIX

Rhetoric and Reality

※

I

Jacques Chomarat's *Grammaire et rhétorique chez Erasme* occupies a place, for the last two decades of the twentieth century, analogous to that of Bataillon's *Erasme et l'Espagne* from the 1930s to the 1960s. Each was an endorsement of trends already apparent in Erasmus scholarship, a massive crystallization of interests, to then diffused and fragmented but demanding full articulation and justification. The first interest was in Erasmus' audiences throughout Europe and their response to him, the second in Erasmus' relation to language, summed up in the double expression 'grammar and rhetoric,' owed above all to his classical masters. Both in turn stimulated other work, though, in Chomarat's case as in that of the other great book of the 1980s, Seidel Menchi's on Erasmus in Italy, an uneasy feeling remains that there has been more reference than real confrontation or assimilation.

Beyond their specific subjects, Bataillon's book and Chomarat's offer both a portrait of Erasmus and a view of his place in Western culture. That this is so in Chomarat's case needs emphasizing, since, at first glance, his topic might seem technical or highly specific. Rhetoric is, for him, central to the understanding of Erasmus, but his Erasmus is not a rhetorical construction. He seeks, through the accepted conventions of historical inquiry, the real Erasmus. The result is a challenge to the new orthodoxy about Erasmus, the emergence of which we have traced in the last chapter. He shares that finishing point with Seidel Menchi, though they have taken different routes. She began from the contemporary interest in reading as a creative act; what his readers made of Erasmus was, historically, as important as what he said or intended, and perhaps revealed intentions too easily obscured. Chomarat's position is that, if Erasmus' interest in language, in grammar and rhetoric, is given its due, then the dominant image of 'Erasmus theologian' falls to the ground.

We have seen how, in and around the quincentenary, writers like Dresden, Margolin, and Phillips were highlighting the importance of language, in its variety and versatility, for inter-preting Erasmus' thought and personality. Studies of the 1970s were to pursue this interest in various ways. Their significance went, of course, beyond Erasmus scholarship. They reflected a broad shift in scholarship and in the culture. Around the time of publication of Chomarat's book, collaborative works appeared on Renaissance rhetoric, at once celebrating the importance of the subject and bemoaning its neglect hitherto. That combination is the sign of a burgeoning field in scholarship, as is the holding of conferences on the theme. In April 1979, the Newberry Library was host to a conference from which came a collection of essays on Renaissance rhetoric edited by James J. Murphy; 'one of the most-mentioned and least-studied subjects in modern scholar-ship,' he called it.[1] His contributors paint a more favourable pic-ture. Rhetoric, says John Ward, was central to the urban culture of the Renaissance and the pursuit of eloquence 'the identifying characteristic' of Renaissance humanism, a position he demon-strates from contemporary commentaries on Cicero's rhetorical works. In fact, there was a 'tremendous diversification' in the publication of both classical and new rhetorical works. In Renais-sance education, adds W. Keith Percival, rhetoric 'dramatically enhanced its standing' over against the other two branches of the *trivium*, grammar and dialectic, though the former remained the 'foundation of the whole educational edifice.' In fact, the state of affairs suggested by remarks of this kind had long been recog-nized. Hanna Gray's essay of 1963, 'Renaissance Humanism: The Pursuit of Eloquence,' was widely influential, and Paul Oskar Kristeller's magisterial reorienting of thinking on humanism, towards its origins in the rhetorical tradition, went back to the late war years.[2]

At the same time, in the early 1980s, there were calls for the history discipline to redirect itself towards current cultural preoc-cupations with language, whose irreducible multiplicity makes radical difficulties for the reading and interpreting of texts and other cultural artefacts. Where does history stand, what, further-more, is to be made of traditions, classical or rhetorical, when texts are seen as an unresolved mixing of cultural references, in last resort 'untraceable,' if 'already read'?[3] Those who speak of a 'linguistic turn' in historical studies around 1980 are thinking of something less drastic than this. The hope was to resolve dilem-mas for the discipline by exploring language as a guide to cultural formations. Thus, in his presidential address to the American Historical Association in 1978, William J. Bouwsma sought to restore meaning to the concept (or myth) of the Renais-sance, after the breakdown of the traditional structure of Middle Ages–Renaissance–modern times, by looking for the origins of 'the skeptical, relativistic, and pragmatic strains in contemporary culture.' A promising place to search was the Renaissance aware-ness of the mutability, and the creativity, of language and, conse-quently, of the variety of cultures. Further, any discovery could be caught only in language as part of that 'vast rhetorical produc-tion' that makes up the human world.[4]

A reviewer of works on the linguistic turn in intellectual histo-ryin the 1980s sees the trend as away from the reductionism that takes historical experience as a reflection, or effect, of psychologi-cal or sociological realities and 'toward theories that recognize language in all its density and opacity as the place where mean-ing is constituted.' From the literature he surveys, beginning with Bouwsma's essays, this reviewer elicits three points: the changed relation between the producer of texts and the receiver, the reader being also an active participant in the exchange (as Seidel Menchi was arguing at this very time); the changed understanding of context, itself to be read now as a text rather than used as causal explanation; the concept of discourse as a way of linking or grouping texts. From such considerations there emerged in this literature the idea of a dialogic relationship between the historian and the texts of the past.[5]

Two tendencies then prepared the way, or made the time right, for the appearance of a major work on how Erasmus understood and used language, grammar, and rhetoric. The first was a strengthening scholarly interest in the rhetorical tradition come down from antiquity through the Middle Ages and reshaped and freshly empowered in Renaissance humanism.[6] The second was the turn towards language in historical studies as a way out of the impasses and apparent dead-ends that a relativist, postmod-

ern culture created for the study of texts. How far these tendencies were in harmony with one another, or otherwise, how far the
one's refined sense of decorum was in contradiction with the
other's acceptance of the infinite malleability of language may
remain a question. Another question was whether, in various
ways, rhetoric had replaced reality. Had history arrived at a new
form of reductionism, the 'reduction of experience to the meanings that shape it'?[7] By the end of the next decade, at century's
end, the case was being put that a humanism largely identified
with the rhetorical tradition was too narrowly conceived and that
its history now required a 'cognitive turn,' to recognize its affective elements, its sociability and grasp of a real past.[8]

II

Since World War 2, there had, of course, been many works on
Erasmus' commitment to language, on his interest in the different
genres and literary forms, and on the classical sources of his style.
Such studies ran in parallel to the more vigorous and assertive
ones on Erasmus as theologian. We will make a selection, especially among those that were, in some sense, antecedent to
Chomarat's work, constituting its prehistory.[9] Erasmus' writings
covered include his pedagogical works, the *Adagia*, the *Colloquies*,
his works on history and biography, letter-writing and preaching.

That Erasmus had first place in the defence and maintenance
of the classical tradition there has been no disputing. To purify
and correct Latin usage had a public significance; it was not an
exercise merely for the study or the classroom. He wanted, says
M.M. Phillips, to make Latin a flexible, contemporary language
for everyday use among educated people. He was then a popu-
larizer, hostile to pedants like the Ciceronians, but also out of
sympathy with the vernaculars. Hence his favourite forms were
the adage, the dialogue, and the paradoxical declamation. The
purpose was ethical, even devout: hence also the recovery of
Greek and the favour for moralists like Plutarch. For him, Rudolf
Pfeiffer adds, there was an intimate connection between the dete-
rioration of language and moral corruption. Erasmus' *philosophia
Christi* took up 'the Socratic theory that knowledge is the necessary condition of acting well and that ignorance leads to evil. ...
And so it was with language that spiritual and moral renaissance
must begin.'[10] In all this, there are intimations of Chomarat,

though not the direct challenge to the predominant image of Erasmus as theologian which he was to make.

That challenge had been anticipated by a work whose timing and larger purpose carried a certain poignancy, Walter Rüegg's *Cicero und der Humanismus: Formale Untersuchungen über Petrarca und Erasmus*. Published in Zürich in 1946, that study began with the problem posed, for German cultural history, by Theodore Mommsen's judgment on Cicero as a shallow time-server. Rüegg links that condemnation to the rejection of Ciceronian humanism in nineteenth-century Germany, following the emergence of a *Neuhumanismus* connected above all with the name of J.J. Winckelmann. It was in substantive terms a rivalry between the Roman rhetorical and the Greek poetic traditions, but Rüegg's concern is with what he considers a rationalizing, absolutizing, and objectifying tendency in the new humanism. Personality was set aside for abstract ideas and objective categories, or subsumed in extrahuman forces of nature or history. The older humanism was subjective, centred on the person (the author or speaker), interested, above all, in the three-way relationship between speaker, hearer, and topic. Language and rhetoric were then basic to it. The many layers of reality, as distinct from ideal types, were mirrored in the variety of styles. This, says Rüegg, in a somewhat circular argument, alone deserves the name of humanism.[11]

Of Ciceronian humanism, Erasmus, along with Petrarch and Valla, was standard-bearer. He did not follow Cicero slavishly, or even closely; his was a free kind of imitation, as recommended by Cicero himself and Quintilian, as well as Petrarch and Valla. That corresponded to the conversational character of Ciceronian humanism, its responsiveness to changes in time, place, and circumstance, and, above all, to human variation. Erasmus, in the *Antibarbari*, for example, was not anti-Christian, but each of the disciplines, rhetoric, poetry, philosophy, had, in his view, a valid autonomy.[12] The purpose of reading, he said in the preface to his edition of Cicero's *De officiis* in 1501, is not to learn rules or facts, but to come to know the author, to enter into dialogue with him and be influenced by him in one's own subjectivity.[13] Correspondingly, writing, as was apparent from his own *Enchiridion*, should be personal, composed in a morally and stylistically appropriate form, associative and suggestive, not making a logical progression, but circling its themes as it deepens and enriches them. In all this, Rüegg argues, Erasmus broke from medieval

culture with its insistence on objective truth and absolute standards. Scripture was not to be treated as an external authority
and read by scholastic methods; Christ was to be seen, not as
'ontological ground,' or even as Redeemer, but as the pattern and
goal of human possibilities. In the 1520s Erasmus fought a three-
way battle against the prehumanist scholastics and two parties
which had objectified elements in the humanist program itself,
the Reformers and the Ciceronians, who represented a 'classisis-
tic ossification of humanism.' Rüegg rejects the idea of a shift in
Erasmus, away from Ciceronian humanism, towards a predominantly theological position; it was precisely on the humanist
ground that he fought.[14]

In bringing out the personalist and relational elements in Erasmus' thought and in emphasizing its empiricism against generalizing, abstract, and absolutist systems, as well as in recognizing
how fundamental language and form were for him, Rüegg anticipates Chomarat's thesis of thirty-five years later. From the recognition of the centrality of language and rhetoric rather than
theology derives an alternative line of interpretation to that of
'Erasmus theologian.' Unlike Chomarat, Rüegg strays too far
towards an undoctrinal Erasmus who does not even recognize
Christ as Redeemer; there, he meets up with Lortz, coming from
another direction altogether: 'Objective dogmas of the church are
given up and a Christianity proclaimed which rests wholly on
subjective behaviour.'[15] The Erasmus of Wilhelm Dilthey and liberal theology is close by. Nevertheless, in its sense for the broader
cultural issues, Rüegg's study is of profound importance.

Rüegg recognized what Chomarat was to demonstrate much
later, that even the textbooks of Erasmian humanism represented
cultural shifts of broad significance. Similarly, in an essay of 1958,
'Erasmus and the Apologetic Textbook,' J. Kelley Sowards
showed that the maturation, between 1499 and 1512, when it was
first published, of Erasmus' guide to the abundant style, *De
Copia*, went hand in hand with the development of his reform
program. There was a bond between the reform of language and
the reform of men, as there was (at least there was no insoluble
paradox) between the classical and Christian traditions.[16] Eleven
years later at Tours, Guilio Vallese of the University of Naples
made the same point: the student learns first to appreciate beau-
ties of expression but, since 'le style est l'habit de la pensée,' a
moral understanding must follow. For Erasmus, that could only

be preparatory to and integral with the Christian ethic.[17] Chomarat was to give the *De Copia* a more radical significance. *Copia*
brings variety; indeed, language itself is in constant movement.[18]
One of Erasmus' deepest commitments, he argues, was to the
particular, the singular, the personal, and the individual (once
again, against the abstraction and generalizing of the scholastics).
Mastering the rules is a first indispensable step, but then life and
art depend on being free with them.[19]

A book on the *Adagia*, Margaret Mann Phillips' *Adages of
Erasmus* (1964), rapidly became a classic of Erasmian learning.
Chomarat was to find in the *Adagia* a tension which, for him, was
characteristic of Erasmus. What value have the proverbs of the
common people? If Christ's incarnation dignifies them and the
whole common life, nevertheless culture remains aristocratic and
the adages used to form style must be sought elsewhere.[20] Phillips, too, accepts that the origins of Erasmus' adages were literary
and erudite, but she is interested also in their destiny: they
became part of the common culture, the stock of everyday
speech.[21]

The affection Phillips' book has inspired is due in part to the
warmth and grace of her depiction of Erasmus' circumstances
and connections when he was working on the successive and
ever-expanding editions of his book, the Oxford and Paris of
1499–1500 for the slim first edition (*Adagiorum collectanea*, 1500)
and the Venetian circle of Aldus Manutius for its more robust
successor (*Adagiorum chiliades*, 1508); in part also to her picture of
the inclusive character of Erasmus' mind, the depth of his classical culture, whose treasures he was opening to the educated
reader, as well as to the student, and his ambition to knit together
the classical and the Christian. However, the peak of her presentation is the chapter on the *Chiliades* of 1515, with the latter's
incorporation of the great essays on government and war and the
condition of the church. We are reminded that her book belongs
to the time when McConica was applying Bataillon's approach to
English humanism, and J.H. Hexter and Edward Surtz were preparing the Yale edition of Thomas More's *Utopia* and placing that
work, which followed on Erasmus' 1515 edition, in its broad
social and cultural setting. Phillips calls that 'the Utopian edition'
of the *Adagia*: 'all the main topics which excite More's indignation
[in *Utopia*] had been touched upon in the long essays of the
Adages,' though the two works differ in character as 'an experi-

mental dream' from a reflective essay. Both recall the conversations between the two friends, from the time of Erasmus' arrival in More's house in 1509, and make of their humanism an engine of social and church reform. What links Phillips' study of the *Adagia* to McConica and Bataillon and the editors of *Utopia* is that she presents him as, momentarily at least, a social reformer on a world scale.[22] Historiographically, that study belongs as much to the era opened by Bataillon as to that centring on Chomarat.

As with the *Adagia*, so with Erasmus' pedagogical works, notably his *De pueris statim ac liberaliter instituendis*; Chomarat could refer to a complete work of scholarship from the 1960s, in this case Jean-Claude Margolin's study and text published by Droz (1966). Chomarat himself makes two more or less extended references to the *De pueris*. The first, early in his book, deals with the high vocation of the teacher of grammar, the *grammaticus*, a theme touching two deep preoccupations of Erasmus: grammar as the foundation for all studies, and the need for the teacher to accommodate to the nature of the child, to exemplify, in relations with the child, the humanity being taught. The second places *De pueris* among the declamations of Erasmus; in this declamation, unlike others, he drew on personal experience and observation and so gave life and verisimilitude to his remarks.[23]

For Margolin, the nature of the child determines the Erasmian pedagogy. The *De pueris* was, after all, directed at the education of very young children; the boy was not merely 'a man in miniature.' Its psychological foundations, Margolin says, give this pedagogy relevance: its pragmatism, its naturalist awareness of the body, its empiricism (a simplified Aristotelianism), anticipating Locke. It can fairly be called 'liberal,' because it aimed at producing an individual (the individualism was conscious) capable of liberal discernment, of a free judgment between right and wrong.[24] Margolin poses the problem of how to relate recognition of the distinctive, constitutive nature of each individual and a liberal faith in education as a formative power. The resolution, he says, was in the place of reason as common to all humans and the primary mark of humanity. That gave education its opening and opportunity for drawing out from the unformed child the good person and the good citizen. Margolin is not incommoded in demonstrating, against Pineau in particular, the Christian character of Erasmus' thinking at that point. For Erasmus, the mind of Christ is best expressed by Paul, champion of evangelical freedom.[25]

Margolin's uneasiness about a possible contradiction between the individual nature of the child and the humanist scheme of formation comes close to the point where Grafton and Jardine introduce the more radical scepticism referred to in the last chapter. They see a contradiction in humanist education from the beginning, between its high-sounding moral claims and the deadly drills and rote learning that actually made it up, as evidenced by the teaching materials used. Possibly, the contradiction is resolved by the purpose which humanist education served, preparation for working in the bureaucratic Renaissance state, where both the moral claims and the discipline had their uses, if not exactly those extolled by the moralists. By the time of Erasmus, educational programs had become more methodical, catering for a broader, less dedicated and less gifted group. Rhetoric was the core of these programs. Erasmus 'marketed' the claims of his predecessors, like Rudolf Agricola, for that discipline as a 'spiritually enlightening *educatio.*' In the view of these authors, the case was not proved, although they allow the possibility of a convincing connection between the pedagogical programs and the Erasmian reform agenda. Erasmus insists on an 'intimate and vital relationship' between the moral and the rhetorical, the Christian and the classical, the philological and the theological, but, say Grafton and Jardine, the arguments are in the end vague and unsatisfactory.[26] The value of this intervention is that the relationships it questions deserve reinvestigation, especially in the pedagogical field, where Grafton and Jardine give a lead by going beyond the manifestoes, into what actually happened in class. One might none the less respond that perceptions are also realities. Erasmus' commitment to the unities he celebrates was more than a propagandist exercise; it was an act of faith that carried its own conviction.

Margolin attributes to Erasmus a genuine, but limited, sense of history, limited, for example, by his imperfect awareness of large historical, sociopolitical constructions like the nation-states with their emergent vernaculars. He looked, not for linear development in history, but for return to an authoritative and sanctified past, pagan and Christian antiquity.[27] That Erasmus' view of history was essentially negative is the argument of the one substantial monograph on the subject before the appearance of Chomarat's *Grammaire et rhétorique*, Peter Bietenholz's *History and Biography in the Work of Erasmus of Rotterdam*, also published by Droz in 1966.

There is a balance in Bietenholz's argument, but it is obscured by the greater space and attention given the negative colourings. Thus, Erasmus did not share the enthusiasm of his humanist predecessors for the study of history; he was sceptical about historical truth. He wrote no histories. The rhetorical use of exempla of moral integrity or civic virtue, which, Bietenholz recognizes, was a primary interest for him, did not counteract his historical scepticism. Again, Erasmus had no real idea of historical development or progress: there were no discernible stages in human history or patterns of any kind. History was a perpetual flux, mostly destructive. If the study of history had a use, it lay in revealing the moral or spiritual truth hidden in events, as the god appeared in the Silenus figure. In such imagery, says Bietenholz, Erasmus anticipated Sebastian Franck and the radical spiritualists. Only direct divine intervention from time to time gave meaning to the flux. These 'flashes of light from above,' 'the flashlike illumination of world history by consecutive men of the spirit' constituted the *kairoi*, revelatory moments in the darkness of historical time.[28] Erasmus' predecessors in this cataclysmic view of history were some of the Fathers, not Augustine, but Origen and the Origenists.[29]

Nevertheless, embedded in Bietenholz's discussion, but only fleetingly lit up, is his acknowledgment of Erasmus' sense of history; his very scepticism about historical knowledge, Bietenholz confesses, 'forecast many facets of the complex historical thought of the modern age.' The moral exempla should, Erasmus said, be used prudently, with decorum, that is with a sense of historical context and awareness of the absurdities of anachronism. In Bietenholz's view, biography was, for Erasmus, the working out of a set image of the character, a 'static vision,' therefore, and 'monocentric.' Erasmus' Christocentrism itself was antihistorical, primarily, it would seem, because of Christ's Protean and historically undefinable character, which his followers are called to emulate.[30] Yet, Erasmus' life of Jerome, which must be the prime exhibit in any examination of his sense for history, contains a vigorous defence of historical criticism against pious frauds and a circumstantial depiction of its subject. Similarly, his lives of contemporaries (Colet, Vitrier, and More) 'strike the reader as the perfect presentations of three thoroughly different characters.' Bietenholz is aware that with these reflections he is balancing out the predominantly negative conclusions of his previous discussion.[31]

Myron Gilmore, in an essay of 1954 republished in 1963, had struck a more deliberate balance and, far from denying Erasmus any sense for historical development, attributed to him a linear interpretation which, Gilmore admitted, sat uneasily, indeed was incompatible, with his other view that 'the chief function of history was to furnish examples of virtue and vice ... timeless truths.' 'Like many great historians before and since, what he said *about* history was often singularly unrelated to what he did when he actually wrote history.'[32] In an essay of 1972, two critics directly questioned Bietenholz's view that Erasmus had an aversion to the historical genre. They agreed that he was no historian; even the life of Jerome belonged to the oratorical, rather than the historiographical, tradition from antiquity. That said, the evidence makes clear that Erasmus loved and admired the ancient historians and the genre. His properly critical assessment of their work – their judgments differed and were often dubious – did not lead to wholly negative conclusions, and even his shift towards theology did not change this. The passage from Erasmus' commentary on Psalm 33, on which Bietenholz relied, demonstrated the uniqueness of the biblical record, not the worthlessness of profane histories.[33]

Study of the *Ciceronianus*, Erasmus' satirical dialogue against those requiring an exact replication of Cicero's language and discourse, produces a more positive impression still. A contradiction remains, but at a deep level. G.W. Pigman's study of the reception of the *Ciceronianus* shows that the historical criticism, which was central to Erasmus' case against the Ciceronians, was scarcely understood by contemporaries: it was a changed world, he had said, socially, politically, and religiously, and language and usage must register the fact. This case rested on the rhetorical principle of decorum, fitness to person, time, and place. One or two responses to the *Ciceronianus* cut deeply. Might not fitness to time and place now require dispensing with Latin altogether and the use of the vernacular? Might not the historical argument subvert the humanist faith in history as moral teaching by example? 'If everything has changed since antiquity, what relevance does it have for the present? What becomes of the exemplarity of the past?' The historical and the transhistorical are in contradiction.[34]

Chomarat recognizes a mix of the historical and the transhistorical in Erasmus' approach to the past and, in particular, to the writers and orators of the past. The persona of each is a combination of the role demanded by the conditions of the time and the writer's or orator's own nature or native genius. Further, there is something beyond nature ('surnaturel') in the 'singular, unique, irreplaceable and untransformable personality of each human being.' Thus, Erasmus' sense of history, which Chomarat rates highly, rests ultimately on the notion, central in Erasmus' work, of personal subjectivity; but the latter also transcends history.[35]

All these writers, then, from Bietenholz to Chomarat, recognize that, alongside Erasmus' sense of history, his appreciation of concrete circumstances, his sensitivity to anachronism, went notions that broke out from the historical frame: the extrahistorical character of the biblical record, the use of the past for philosophy teaching by example, the individual's transcendence beyond time and circumstance. Does not this conclusion support those who resist claims that historicism, the view that everything human is temporal, contingent, subject to change and development, had its beginnings, not in the late eighteenth and early nineteenth centuries, but with the humanists and jurists of the sixteenth century?[36] Yet, the final taste in the mouth is positive. Erasmus' awareness of historical change, from which there is no return, must ultimately be subversive of the other ways of seeing the past, which are still present and apparent in his own work.

For Erasmus' sense of time and place, most readers would turn first to his *Colloquies*, which catch his contemporaries in their various avocations and relationships, especially the amatory and marital, with concreteness and conviction. Chomarat, in treating the colloquy as the first of the four rhetorical genres (the others being the declamation, the letter, and the sermon), remarks that, of the three functions of rhetoric – to teach, to delight and to inspire (*docere, delectare, movere*) – the second, to delight, is its function.[37] As with Phillips on the *Adagia* and Margolin on *De pueris*, he is able to refer to predecessors on the *Colloquies* and limit his own discussion in light of their achievement. He is thinking, above all, of the two books by Franz Bierlaire, *Erasme et ses Colloques: le livre d'une vie* (1977) and *Les Colloques d'Erasme: réforme des études, réforme des moeurs et réforme de l'Eglise au XVIe siècle* (1978).[38] The first is a history of the book, from its beginnings as a guide to speaking Latin in daily life, *Familiarum collo-*

quiorum formulae, sketched out for a circle of students and friends in Paris in the late 1490s, through various stages, to a portly final edition of eight hundred pages (1533), rounding off with the colloquy 'Epicureus,' whose serene Christian 'hedonism' Bierlaire conveys beautifully. The crucial turn in the history of the book came in March 1522, when the *Formulae,* first published without Erasmus' initiative in 1518, were superseded by an edition which, after putting those models of conversation virtually in final form, brought forth dialogues of another kind, touching, through their various personages, on the moral, social, and religious issues of the hour.[39] The student's manual had become a *Comédie humaine,* a book for adults, where Erasmus 'exploited his satirical verve and narrative talents to influence opinion or, at any rate, open eyes.'[40]

Bierlaire's second book reflects further on this transition and, in particular, on the dramatic character of the new colloquies. He notices, for example, how many encounters occur in public places, in the street or on the road, how prominent young people are and the laity generally. There is great mobility, apposite for a text which presents, in extempore and everyday language, a reality taken from life. Bierlaire shows how widely the *Colloquies* appeared in school syllabuses, especially in Britain and Lutheran Germany, but he recognizes, without being able to overcome, the difficulty in that kind of investigation: mention of a book in a syllabus does not demonstrate how it was used or, indeed, whether it was used effectively at all.[41] His chapter 'The Battle of the *Colloquies*' exposes another difficulty. In defending himself against the savage criticisms of the Louvain and Paris theologians and the Spanish monks, Erasmus pointed to the variety of personages engaged in his dialogues. Should he be saddled with the views of these characters? For that matter, why do the critics attribute to him only the heretical and doubtful views of his personages and not the orthodox ones? Bierlaire's method is to interpret Erasmus by Erasmus, identifying him with views he expresses elsewhere or generally. He understands the disquietude of the theologians, whose method was to isolate problematical propositions and then ask about their effect on readers. Bierlaire's conclusion is neatly summed up in his remark on Erasmus' attitude to devotions paid to relics: 'What he denounces is not kissing the relics in itself but the superstition and deception.' Erasmus does not reject the institutions, monasticism, ceremonies, sacraments, but the misuse of them.[42] If anything, Bierlaire identifies him with 'the more serious and less compromising arguments' in these dialogues, and leaves him, therefore, on essentially orthodox ground.[43]

In his chapter on 'The *Colloquies*, Guide to the Christian Life' Bierlaire makes a composite portrait of the Christian from what is said by Erasmus' characters. It is possible, he says, to see a sequence in, to represent as one life, the devout adolescent of 'The Whole Duty of Youth' (*Confabulatio pia*), the modest and learned host of 'The Godly Feast' (*Convivium religiosum*), the sober ancient of 'The Old Man's Chat' (*Gerontologia*), and the one making a good death in 'The Funeral' (*Funus*). Erasmus, he concludes, may not have been a saint, 'but the Christian whose portrait appears in filigree in the *Colloquies* is not far from being one.'[44] In rhetorical terms, this conclusion is too neat; there is not enough allowance for changes in level or multiple ironies.[45] On these last, Terence Cave, in his book *The Cornucopian Text* (contemporary with Bierlaire's books), uses the image of the host's garden in the colloquy *Convivium religiosum*, its different levels and perspectives, to illustrate the multiplicity of significations in any text: 'the house of dialogue has an intrinsic elusiveness which is never fully dispelled.'[46] Bierlaire recognizes the critical tendency in Erasmus' thought, his reserve about monasticism and preference for chaste marriage, his conviction that Christian perfection is possible in every way of life, his universalism, but, in the end, the institution survives intact. Recalling a title of Halkin's, he calls Erasmus 'enfant difficile mais fidèle de l'Eglise.'[47]

Chomarat comes to a different conclusion. He shares Bierlaire's admiration for the *Colloquies* as observations of daily life; the ensembles are 'naturel, vif, plaisant.' Both recognize also Erasmus' appreciation of the lay life and, as they appear by and large in the *Colloquies*, his respect for women. But Chomarat takes a further step. For him the Erasmus of the *Colloquies* rejected the traditional hierarchy among ways of life; virginity was not inherently superior to marriage; if anything, Erasmus reversed the order between the married and monastic states. He denounced the monastic institution as such. All will be judged by their conformity to the gospel law, each on individual merit. The *Colloquies* demonstrate abundantly the respect for individuality apparent in Erasmus' pedagogy. Chomarat turns the ambiguity of the dialogue form, with its different and conflicting voices, to the advantage of his argument; promoting Erasmus' spiritualizing reform of Christendom required a 'pious ruse.' The flexibility, denounced by his enemies and critics and captured in the image of the cuttle-fish, was a necessity and, in its way, a mark of honour.[48]

Variety and flexibility are supremely the qualities of that other genre of which Erasmus was master, the letter. On this, Chomarat and his predecessors speak with one voice. In both his prescriptions in the *Opus de conscribendis epistolis* (1522) and his practice as a correspondent, Erasmus demonstrated 'marvellous variety and truth to life.'[49] Indeed, the word 'prescription' is misleading because he wished the letter to take as versatile a form as possible. In this he distinguished himself from the medieval *ars dictaminis*, which, while honouring the letter as a literary form, was formulaic and prescriptive and mostly assumed an official setting. Even more, he resisted 'Ciceronian legalism.'[50] He did not expect untrammelled spontaneity. He grouped letters according to ancient rhetorical tradition. Over all, he applied the rhetorical principle of aptness, but there, in itself, was the source of almost infinite variety. His own published collections, defying chronology and logic, seemed set to illustrate the richness of the genre. For Erasmus, the best letters were familiar, personal, conversational. A particular view of human nature, its variety and mutability, and the idea of Christian freedom were at the basis of this. Letter-writers need cultivation and taste, but culture is a fund on which they draw for a personal purpose, which may also, on occasion, be a public concern. The letter is the self-expression of a personality, aware of itself. In Erasmus, following Petrarch, there is here a significant cultural shift from medieval norms.[51]

Of the oratorical genres, there is, finally, the sermon. Preaching is the subject of Erasmus' last great work, *Ecclesiastes sive de ratione concionandi* (1535). The paucity of scholarship on the *Ecclesiastes* to Chomarat's time matched Erasmus' own reluctance to complete the work, projected since 1519. Chomarat explains the latter by Erasmus' lack of natural sympathy for vernacular preaching to the multitude, adding one of those startling images that enliven his long book: imagine Anatole France or André Gide preparing a manual for speakers at trade-union meetings.[52] Two essays in English on the *Ecclesiastes* represent the two broad views of Erasmus' thought and work that have emerged in this part of our study: Robert G. Kleinhans' essay in De Molen's collection on the works of Erasmus from 1978 and an article by

James Weiss of four years earlier.[53] For Kleinhans, the work can be used as 'an interpretive tool' for elucidating Erasmus' other theological writings, especially in light of its long maturation. In contrast to contemporary theologies which centred on justification (Luther) or church and sacraments (the Council of Trent), Erasmus' theology 'stressed the acquisition of peace through virtue attainable by union with Christ through meditation upon the documents of the early church's witness to him.' Preaching was as important for his doctrine as for the others, and this made *Ecclesiastes* a reform document, since the state of preaching was, in many places, dismal, and the bishops' supervision lax.[54]

By contrast, Weiss begins with rhetoric, though it soon becomes apparent that there is no clear, let alone hard and fast, boundary between rhetoric and other concerns and disciplines: 'the technical categories and issues of humanist rhetoric, transmuted by Erasmus, became the categories and issues which informed his assumptions, goals, and procedures.' The rhetorical problem of nature and art, as exemplified in the skills and performance of the orator, illustrates this transmutation and the regular shift from rhetorical to other, including theological, issues. Oratorical power is from nature, a gift, but it must be nurtured by the disciplined exercise of mind and will. Here is a parallel to what he had to say about free grace and the human will in his controversy with Luther. Similarly, where, in book 4 of *Ecclesiastes*, Erasmus deals with the topics of preaching, he avoids the philosophical and dialectical and concentrates on that 'primary category of rhetorical invention,' the practical and the ethical. Weiss adopts Jacques Etienne's term 'personalism' in defining the place Erasmus gives to the spiritual subject and the relation he recognizes between knowledge and affectivity, in exegesis for example.[55] The rhetorical, one might say, serves the pastoral, which is the heart of Erasmus' thinking about the church and Christian community. Yet, the exact force that rhetoric exercises over other disciplines remains, in Weiss's account, uncertain; his expressions range from the relatively weak ('affected') to the pretty strong ('molded') or even startling: Erasmus 'envisioned rhetoric's relation to the other disciplines as one of domination and coordination.'[56] The case poses nicely the question of who is handmaiden to whom: rhetoric to theology or theology to rhetoric?

Kleinhans remarks on the distance from Weiss to Kohls and Payne.[57] Naturally, Chomarat, in his study of the *Ecclesiastes*, follows Weiss. Nevertheless, the ease with which theological issues slip into centre stage is noteworthy. As well, the real world is very close. In the sermon, Chomarat quotes Erasmus as saying, rhetoric rests less on rules, which are useful only if they have become second nature, than on practice and experience.[58] A long digression indicates, from Chomarat's study of the sermons of a famous mendicant preacher of the early sixteenth century, that Erasmus' satirical picture of the preaching of his time was no caricature.[59] The essential thing for Erasmus was that faith and salvation come from preaching. There his enthusiasm lay; his orthodox expressions on the sacraments were, by contrast, precautionary. And preaching, to be effectual, must be governed by the rhetorical principle of decorum (Quintilian's 'apte dicere'), by which what is said is accommodated to circumstances and, above all, to the spiritual needs of the listeners, without subtracting anything from truth. So, rhetoric and theology are intertwined. Here, at the end of his long book, Chomarat reiterates the matters that separated Erasmus from medieval culture: his rejection of dialectic and dogmatism, which he equates with violence, his limited conception of heresy, his confrontation with the orders, whose tyranny Chomarat, in a daring anachronism, compares with the totalitarian parties of the twentieth century.[60]

Before attempting a summation of Chomarat's book and its significance, we should, in ending this review of its predecessors, recall that Marjorie Boyle had put the case for the bond, in Erasmus' thought, between rhetoric and theology, the classical and the Christian, in her *Erasmus on Language and Method in Theology* of 1977.[61] She reiterated it in a graceful and richly allusive study of 1981 called *Christening Pagan Mysteries: Erasmus in Pursuit of Wisdom*. He went, she says, beyond a call for Christians to appropriate the wisdom of the ancients, the christening of pagan mysteries. His contention was for a profound concordance between classical wisdom and Christian revelation. That was because both came from Christ, the centre and source of all things. That classical culture was founded on grammar and rhetoric was not incidental, for Christ acted as *Logos*, the spoken word of God, his 'eloquent revelation.' This is the argument of the *Antibarbari*, the subject of the first of the three essays that make up this book.[62] To the second essay, the expression 'christening pagan mysteries' belongs more literally, for it relates *Folly* to the mystery religions of the ancient world. Her own image of the vernal greening of the world at

Moria's coming reveals 'that Moria is a mystery goddess and that her oration will disclose secrets of immortality.' Boyle, like Screech contemporaneously, affirms the ecstatic, near-to-madness conclusions of the *Moria* and their eschatological component: death is both satire on human pretensions and release for the initiates. But here, a critical reader may observe, classical wisdom (or folly) and Christian wisdom (or folly) appear as rivals rather than as integral with one another, as in the *Antibarbari*. Contrary to Chomarat, who finds the unifying force elsewhere, Boyle considers Erasmus' work a 'radical unity' in and because of its theology.[63] Nevertheless, the reader senses a disjuncture between the pictures in these two chapters, between the Erasmus who looked to the ancient world for practical wisdom and the Erasmus who extolled its quest for religious ecstasy, a quest finally to be outclassed by Christianity. The third essay deals with Luther's charge that Erasmus was an Epicurean and the humanist's response, the colloquy 'Epicureus,' Erasmus enfolding 'into the divine economy the very pagan philosophy' which his fellow-Christians most detested and defending the idea of common grace, at work even among the ancient pagans.[64]

On the very eve then of the appearance of Chomarat's book, Boyle reasserted Erasmus' claim to be, primarily, a theologian and posed once again the issue of the unity of his thought.

III

It is time to attempt a summation of Chomarat's book. References already made to the work give, even to those who did not know him, intimations of the character of the author, confirmed by the obituaries which appeared on his death, after debilitating illness, on 9 June 1998: an acute awareness of individual personality and a sense of community centring on personal friendships rather than institutions, a great erudition and capacity for work, devotion to humanist traditions about words as the authentic expression of self-aware human beings, against the submergence of the author (in contemporary discourse) in the unconscious or the impersonal.[65] Only those who knew him could speak of more personal qualities: courage, diffidence, sensitivity, even touchiness.[66] The whole sketch suggests affinity with Erasmus.

'Fundamentally, Erasmus is not a theologian.' Thus Chomarat sums up his garnering of the humanist's remarks and comments over the years about his vocation and his relation to the theological discipline. By contrast, he was above all a lover of language and literature. His services to religion lay in applying his studies to the demands of piety. He was 'pieux philologue.' Grammar and rhetoric must be the foundation of studies for the theologian himself, the preacher, the sacred orator. Only ancient classical culture can provide the necessary richness of sources for educating all, including the theologians. So it is fundamentally misguided to make of him, as Charles Béné attempted to do, a single-minded disciple of Augustine. Could there be temperaments more discordant than those of Augustine and Horace, deeply admired by Erasmus from his monastic years? Might he not be called 'the Christian Horace'?[67]

Erasmus' way of approaching language and literature shaped his thinking about religion. The movement was in that direction. Chomarat sums it up thus: 'grammar and rhetoric involve a conception of man; the practice of "eloquence" is linked to a certain idea of the other and of oneself; piety comes to confirm, to complete, to crown what is born of a certain way of practising letters and reflecting on them.' The matter goes deeper still; Chomarat, like Boyle, begins with the Johannine prologue and the *Logos*. Further, language, not reason, is the distinguishing mark of humanity, for evil as well as good, since words are the source of discord, the heart of evil, as Erasmus' *Lingua* of 1525 showed. Thus, language sets the direction of his ethical and religious thought. For that reason, Chomarat thinks, it would be as appropriate to speak of a humanist Christianity as of Christian humanism, the conventional name for Erasmus' amalgam of the classical and the Christian. The cultural ideas structure the religious. It is true that Erasmus read the pagans of antiquity in the light of Christianity, but, says Chomarat, his Christianity was already informed by his reading of the pagans. Here the rhetorical principle of accommodation had a decisive part in shaping his idea of *humanitas*.[68]

Chomarat, like most commentators before him, emphasizes the essentially dualist character of Erasmus' thought. For Erasmus spirit stands in contradiction to the flesh and the world. There was nevertheless a change, in his conception of sin, between the *Enchiridion* of 1503 and the *Lingua* of 1525, as we have seen: its root is no longer sensuality, but the fomenting of discord. A certain fastidiousness is apparent in Erasmus. In him mistrust of the body arises, not because of sex, as with the ascetics, but because of decomposition. Hence the doctrine of the soul was important to him. His Platonism was not complete; he did not condemn absolutely the natural passions, for they can be spiritualized. The distinction between flesh and spirit applied to institutions and ceremonies; worship must be in spirit and in truth.[69] If anything, Chomarat overstates Erasmus' indifference to institutions; the state does not for him, I believe, belong wholly to a world outside and beyond the spirit.[70] While speaking, especially late in life, correctly of the sacraments, he qualified their absolute centrality. Above all, he mistrusted and condemned a clergy preoccupied with ritual and carnal ceremonies and possessed by worldly ambitions.[71]

There is then, in Erasmus' view, a marked hierarchy between the spiritual and the carnal. At times, if not always, it seems total, absolute. To this there corresponds a hierarchy in the sphere of language. Though a main theme of Chomarat's book is that Erasmus broke with absolutism, abstraction, systematizing, in favour of the experiential, practical, and singular, he has to accept that there is an absolutist element in Erasmus' thinking about language. The classical languages have absolute priority. By contrast, the vernaculars belong to the carnal world, no longer informed by spirit; they are a corrupted, degenerate form of the ideal; they represent the triumph of the vulgar and barbarous. Erasmus sensed the contradiction between this prejudice, which was moral as well as aesthetic, and the Christian love at the heart of his ethic.[72] He made amends by pleading for vernacular translation of the scriptures; he recognized, too, that the apostles' simple and artless language was God's chosen way of addressing mankind, a point with which even Chomarat's classicism seems faintly embarrassed.[73] Erasmus' stand in the Ciceronian controversy qualified his elitism and absolutism in a certain sense, but Chomarat draws out the deeper issues. There were, he says, two humanist attitudes to language. The Italian humanists wanted to preserve and purify Latin as a high language; they also used the vernacular. Erasmus and his colleagues in the north aimed at restoring Latin to everyday use, at least among the educated. It meant qualifying its purity and producing a composite kind of Latin. This was, says Chomarat, an admirable, audacious undertaking, but doomed. Meantime, Erasmus' critique of Ciceronian claims was not primarily religious, let alone national, but rhetorical; the ambition to recover Cicero's language in its entirety was an affront to the principle of decorum.[74]

It also broke the principle that discourse should express the personality of the speaker in its uniqueness. This touches, however it might cohabit with Erasmus' own linguistic absolutism, the element in him that is fundamental for Chomarat. 'Erasmus,' he says, 'is one of those thinkers for whom every system is only a false trail and the more ambitious it is, the more it loses the particular, which alone exists, in its complexity and richness.'[75] His *Annotations* illustrate his sense for the concrete; they abound in observed detail, anecdotes, personal recollections, and satirical comment on morals and manners. Before Montaigne, Erasmus discovered subjectivity. He made the discovery, says Chomarat, not with, but against, the medieval church, a social institution preoccupied with power. The source of his discovery was the notion of decorum, the orator's attention to particularities. Luther also discovered subjectivity, but on a supernatural plane, whereas Erasmus, beginning with words, locates it in the world. Chomarat does not draw out the point, but surely this conclusion must qualify the view of Erasmus as, simply, devotee of the spiritual and eternal, enemy of the flesh and the world. He condemned the monks, along with the Ciceronians, for their taste for uniformity; he must also reject their otherworldliness, equally enemy of the individual subject living in the world and striving there to express Christ's spirit.[76] Chomarat identifies the paradox of a rhetorical system that produces temperaments resistant to system and valuing individuality. The pupils learned routines, not creativity, but the outcome was a singular, personal style. It was precisely about this 'mystery' that Grafton and Jardine were sceptical. For Chomarat, the resolution must lie in reading, the reading and discerning imitation of the best authors.[77]

This deep preference in Erasmus, for the singular, personal, subjective, expressed itself in language and literature and also in religion. In grammar, the foundation of all, he always preferred the practical to the abstract and systematic. Quintilian and Valla taught him that usage, the usage of real people (admittedly, educated people), not rules and logic, was the norm. For him, usage was to logic as piety to scholastic theology, the human against the system.[78] Along this line, Chomarat argues against Sem Dresden's contention in the quincentenary *Actes* that Erasmus realized himself above all in writing. For Chomarat conversation is fundamental. The power for good and evil portrayed in *Lingua* belongs to the 'living word.' This line is, in fact, difficult to sustain. Chomarat admits that Erasmus himself was not an orator but a writer. Was writing a substitute for a spoken word which some inhibition, 'quelque disposition secrète de la sensibilité,' prevented him from expressing? But to take that course is to return to Dresden. The act of writing best united for him, as Dresden sees, 'spontaneity, communication and yet distance.'[79]

As for religion, all that has been said in this section and the last indicates the assessment that Chomarat gives of Erasmus' Christianity. He opposed scholasticism and dogmatism. Dogmas are necessary, but few are essential and they are simple; to complicate or multiply them damages the piety they are intended to nourish. Similarly, he rejected as 'Judaizing' the authoritarian, legalist elements in sixteenth-century Catholicism. Piety must be relieved of the ceremonial burdens the centuries have imposed. This s a piety founded, not on fear, but on love, as his work on confession, the *Exomologesis*, shows. The work of the gospel is the restoration of a human nature damaged but not destroyed by sin. There is no great abyss between the pre-Christian and Christian worlds, so that the ancient writers, too, can serve piety. Such reflections make clear, Chomarat concludes, that, while Aquinas and Erasmus may use the same theological formulas, these express different experiences and reflect different cultural settings.[80] In the scriptural field, he accepted the fallibility of texts, rejected literalism, and reduced, without denying, the traditional claims for inspiration. Rhetoric was essential here, too; Erasmus sought explications, not vertically, as it were, in direct inspiration, but horizontally, in the context, the connection of ideas and the intention of the author. To a degree, he desacralized the text. Nevertheless, the fecundity of scripture and the very nature of language, the necessity of tropes, required different levels of interpretation, although Erasmus (Chomarat, with Godin, asserts) did not apply the traditional four senses.[81]

What then are the lineaments of the Erasmus emerging from this long text? He was (all precautions taken against anachronism) an 'Enlightenment' Christian, who broke, in almost every respect, from medieval Catholic culture, without fomenting, or wishing to foment, revolution and uproar. This conclusion depends on catching expressions that drop from him unguardedly or interpreting

his silences.[82] At one point, drawing an essentially spiritual understanding of the sacraments from the *Paraphrases*, Chomarat asks
himself: has he, in reaction against the dominant picture of his subject as a straight-line Catholic, radicalized Erasmus? The *Paraphrases* themselves, with their consistent preference for spiritual
over 'carnal,' ceremonial or ritual, forms, give, he claims, the
answer. Erasmus was no Voltairean. He was a sincere believer in
Christ as Word of God and Redeemer. He also believed in the
church, as the invisible community of those bound together in
love, to Christ and to one another.[83]

Chomarat extends his conclusion to Erasmus' personality. He
was, above all, 'd'esprit latin.' He admired the Romans' sense for
the individual, as exemplified in their sculpture, against the
Greek bent for abstraction and Jewish transcendence. Chomarat
picks up Rüegg's post-war recovery of Ciceronian humanism.
The rhetorical tradition was crucial for Erasmus' personality, as
for his thought. Chomarat speculates a little further: does Erasmus' religion of Jesus, his devotion to the Son, leaving the Father
in the shadows, stem from the circumstances of his birth and
upbringing? Does this silent rejection carry over to all authority
figures and authoritative institutions?[84] Perhaps the strains
already noted in the rhetorical tradition itself, between a strict
hierarchy of value, with its many discriminations, and an acceptance of individuality, also showed up in these traits of Erasmus.
Chomarat hints at the possibility.[85]

This great work makes its case for the importance and, to a
degree, for the primacy of language, rhetoric, and grammar, for
Erasmus. It destroys the notion that his interest in these things
was purely for the service of theology. The debate over whether
Erasmus was a theologian, or primarily a theologian, is unresolvable and, in any case, smacks of the scholastic controversies over
names and parties which he himself detested. What Chomarat
demonstrates is that his rhetorical commitments helped determine the whole cast of his mind. He cannot be linked exclusively
to theological traditions. A return to Renaudet is to strain the
point too far, but the correction is salutary.[86]

IV

Bataillon's great book of 1937 was recognized immediately as
magisterial. It was constantly referred to, but substantial critical

assessments appeared only gradually, or in later years, as we have seen.[87] The history of Chomarat's great book of 1981 could be seen as following the same course, although its strongly personal judgments here and there and its anachronistic flourishes may have inhibited the use of 'magisterial' and in fact provoked some assertive rejoinders in early reviews.[88] In the early 1990s two studies broadly in Chomarat's sphere of interest made reference to it critically, though also appreciatively. They were Walter M. Gordon's *Humanist Play and Belief: The Seriocomic Art of Desiderius Erasmus* and Manfred Hoffmann's *Rhetoric and Theology: The Hermeneutic of Erasmus*. They both sought, if along different lines, to restore the claims of 'Erasmus theologian.'

Gordon criticizes Chomarat for denying Erasmus the name of theologian because he was no systematist. He rightly emphasizes that there are different kinds of theology, the 'biblical' and 'rhetorical' as well as the 'scholastic' and 'dogmatic,' but he is mistaken in suggesting that Chomarat's position is determined by an exclusively systematic view of theology; Chomarat's interest is rather in where the primary impulse in Erasmus' thought comes from, and he answers: from his interest in language and rhetoric.[89] Nevertheless, Gordon argues tellingly against a too unitary view of medieval culture, against which Erasmus might be set. He points to an alternative theological tradition to the highly metaphysical and propositional one, essentially literary in character and centring on image, symbol, and metaphor.

The centrality of the movement from the visible to the invisible, from the shell to the kernel, from the lower to the higher, generally recognized as a feature of Erasmus' thought, had, Gordon suggests, medieval antecedents, above all in the symbolist mentality of the twelfth century. Hugh of Saint-Victor said: 'The entire sense-perceptible world is like a sort of book written by the finger of God.'[90] The historian of the symbolist mentality speaks of 'the unlimited playing of symbolism across the limits of nature, of sacred history, and of the sacraments and sacramentals.'[91] In such language, one senses already the presence of the ludic, Gordon's concern. The latter suggests a tradition coming from the Fathers and Pseudo-Dionysius, through the symbolist thinkers of the twelfth century and even John Colet. Aquinas is not excluded. Gordon also associates Erasmus' name with that of Urs von Balthasar, twentieth-century theologian, already introduced in Chantraine's *'Mystère' et 'Philosophie du Christ,'* who, at the start of his massive study in theological aesthetics, confronts scientific, expository, and polemical theology with another, more rhapsodical and 'enthusiast' kind that may even appear 'dilettantish.'[92] When the discussion moves to the liturgy, Gordon can bring in a figure closer to Erasmus, Johan Huizinga, who, in his *Homo Ludens*, writes of the formal play-element in ritual.[93]

There is a danger in Gordon's methodology. It arises from the accumulating of witnesses to a point of view across the centuries, among whom Erasmus is noticed without his becoming the primary focus. He may take on the views of the witnesses by attribution, even become part of a 'tradition,' in a kind of halo effect. In a few pages at one stage Gordon refers to the modern theologians Hugo Rahner, Romano Guardini, Alexander Schmemann, and Cornelius Ernst, the painter Hieronymus Bosch, and the poet Wallace Stevens, as well as the Venerable Bede, Colet, and Huizinga.[94]

Gordon's concern is with the relation between the ludic and the sacred. The ludic links to the rhetorical, because of the importance of word-play in a persuasive reasoning which respects the identity of the other participants in a conversation and eschews violence. Erasmus accepted that the propositional and the dogmatic had a place but, for himself, was most at home in the more playful atmosphere of what he called the *schola declamatoria*. He could 'toy' with ideas he took seriously.[95]

Gordon identifies the tension we have already encountered: between Erasmus the sober moralist, reformer, critic, and satirist, the author of the *Antibarbari*, with its serious dialectic of work and play, and the Erasmus who let himself go in both comedy and religion, heading towards 'ethical anarchy' in the one and mystic ecstasy in the other. (An example of ethical anarchy is the colloquy 'Exorcism' where 'Erasmus the entertainer wins out over Erasmus the teacher.') The paradox is that the two are linked: uncontrollable laughter and contemplation of the absolute have much in common. Here we are approaching the Erasmus of M.A. Screech.[96]

Gordon draws the strands together in a final substantial section on the *Moria*. Here, not so much the declamation as the drama becomes the dominant form. We are reminded of Erasmus' liking for the dialogue and for the image *theatrum mundi*, the world as theatre. Again, there is a dialectic or, at least, a balancing, between a Platonist view of the unreality of human affairs and the Christian doctrine of the incarnation: God cared enough to assume human form. The incarnation is a drama, Chantraine's *fabula Christi*.[97] The *Folly* is not only a declamation to be analysed rhetorically, as by Walter Kaiser and Chomarat himself, but also a dramatic conflict.[98]

A key moment for Gordon is the arrival on stage of an intruder from heaven exposing the illusions of Folly's disciples. The incident reveals the double character of folly, benign illusion on the one side and wilful or vicious blindness on the other.[99] The distinction between the two kinds of folly takes on its ultimate form in the last part, with the celebration of divine foolishness, as we know. A link must be made between that divine foolishness and the illusions of the first part, between carnival joy and religious ecstasy, demonstrating the 'cohesion of the ridiculous with the sublime.' Once again, the Silenus figure gives a clue, for under a shameful exterior the divine may be hiding. Reckless, even amoral, action may be a metaphor for the divine, as with drunkenness, carnal and spiritual. An exegetical tradition, of which Pseudo-Dionysius was representative, handled unedifying biblical stories in this way.[100] Carnival, to which Mikhail Bakhtin and, later, Donald Gwynn Watson had linked the *Folly*, involved self-forgetfulness, as well as the setting aside of normal conventions and controls.[101] Religious ecstasy requires self-emptying, for which the self-emptying, the *kenosis*, of Christ (Philippians 2:5–11) is the model. Here, in a 'strongly felt extroversion,' is, Gordon concludes, the bond between the first and last sections of the *Moria*, the ludic and the sacred.[102]

Gordon finds a similar complementarity in Erasmus' sayings on marriage, natural and mystical. The comic marriage *Colloquies*, with their optimism about the human condition, including bodily life, are, he adds, a safeguard against too spiritualizing an interpretation of his views on this subject or of his thought generally. Marriage is the model for the incarnation, for the relationship between Christ and the church, as Paul taught, and even for relations within the Trinity itself. Or, as complementarity demands, the association may be put – is perhaps, from a theological standpoint, better put – the other way round. True understanding of human marriage derives from the mystic and eschatological bond between Christ and the church. However that may be, as the spiritual does not annihilate the bodily, so the theological does not dismiss the ludic; the two are held inextricably together as complementary, dialectical.[103]

Gordon's merit has been to see the possibilities, for the understanding of Erasmus, in the works of Huizinga and the modern
theologians on play and the ludic. He has done justice to the play
element in Erasmus' humanism and felt for the connections
between the ludic and the sacred. He has found them in the being
beside oneself that accompanies both ungovernable laughter
and religious ecstasy; as for the latter, he agrees with Michael
Screech's conclusions. At the same time, he has resisted attributing to Erasmus a complete dualism, too absolute a disinction
between spirit and body.[104] One has with Gordon, as with all
those wanting to find unity or harmony in Erasmus' thought, a
sense of issues being forced. At least, an act of faith is required.
Might it not carry more conviction in a postmodern culture to
recognize that there are different impulses in his ideas leading to
different ends which go together, sometimes comfortably, sometimes uneasily, sometimes jarringly? Similarly, the theological tradition to which he is said to belong is a somewhat artificial
creation, as we have seen.

While Gordon criticizes Chomarat for closing theology off
from the literary and the ludic, Manfred Hoffmann puts Chomarat's book, and other work affected by the linguistic turn, 'on an
independent track,' somewhat aside from the emerging consensus in Erasmus scholarship.[105] Already, in a review article of 1985,
Hoffmann gave reasons for this judgment, reasons consistent
with the argument of his earlier work *Erkenntnis und Verwirklichung*: for all their importance, language and rhetoric operate
within a systematic framework provided by philosophy (epistemology, ethics, anthropology, and ontology) and theology. 'Language, grammar and rhetoric function ... as means to an end
rather than constituting an end in themselves.'[106] One could say
that Hoffmann's new book relates to Chomarat's in the following
way. Chomarat's work is full of theological comments and reflections, but the theology hangs loosely there, its place in the last
resort contingent and circumstantial; in the age of Erasmus, rhetorical principles, his main concern, found expression above all in
the religious sphere. Hoffmann's aim is to search out the integrat-
ing elements in Erasmus' theological and rhetorical ideas, on the
assumption that they must form a system, though one utterly different from the scholastic.[107]

One can see Hoffmann's interpretation of Erasmus' thought
as proceeding in three stages. The foundation is the humanist

appreciation of language. Hoffmann begins, that is, from the point scholarship had reached by the 1990s: 'Erasmus was one of the key figures in the cultural shift from the medieval prominence of visual images to the humanist preference for letters.' Language had a metaphysical as well as a human and social significance. It 'was not only a means of communication but also a mirror of the transcendent world.' This was the common ground of Renaissance scholarship. Hoffmann's aim was to move on to a second level: 'Now that linguistic studies have opened the way, it is time for us to turn to his theological language and draw attention to the systematic implications of its use.'[108] Hidden in that sentence is the third stage to which we will quickly come.

The key to understanding the second stage is the idea of language as mediation. Through Hoffmann's whole study the words 'middle' and 'mediator' and related terms like 'moderation' and 'accommodation' constantly recur. Since language is a means of making contact, of mediation, theology, in a religion for which words spoken by God and recorded in scriptures are fundamental, must respect grammar and rhetoric. That was Erasmus' way of doing theology; biblical interpretation was central to the activity. 'My method,' Hoffmann says, 'aims at deriving from a conglomerate of representative references a sense of Erasmus' understanding of the synthesis between rhetoric and theology.' Already again, the word 'synthesis' points to the third stage. There is a kind of interpretative circle: the general rules of grammar and rhetoric apply to the interpretation of scripture, but theological topoi drawn from scripture help determine the real meaning of the words. In the whole scheme, the place of allegory is indicative. Thus, allegory provides, in hermeneutic, a middle between letter and spirit, 'throws a bridge over the chasm.'[109] It overcomes dichotomy, qualifies dualism. 'The biblical humanist was in the final analysis not a dualist. He saw his vocation in building bridges.'[110] Over these bridges runs a two-way traffic: the higher accommodates itself to the lower, the lower is lifted by the promise of transformation. Incarnation is the Christian doctrine encompassing these things: 'Christ's presence in the sacred word signifies that the word medium now actually embodies the divine mediator between God and humankind.'[111]

At the third stage, Hoffmann argues that there is system to Erasmus' thought in its various parts. The rhetorical tradition in its Ciceronian form was practical, civic-minded, probabilist, consensual; yet it 'was structured into a system.' Further, Erasmus took in elements of Platonist philosophy – cosmology, anthropology, and epistemology – perhaps, 'as if by osmosis,' from the Renaissance Platonists but, more directly, from his favourite Fathers. Above all, reality in the philosophical sense, the order of the world, is determining. Hoffmann is always listening for 'ontological overtones.' Apparently empirical text-critical work on the scriptures 'served a given ontological and theological order elicited by means of the rhetorical structure of divine speech.' The course of interpretation is not set by human experience, historical or inward and subjective; it occurs 'in the context of the universal orders of nature, culture, and salvation,' which are all centred on Christ and must be understood Christologically.[112]

In quoting, as the last words of his book, Erasmus' contemptuous dismissal of those who accused him of teaching 'nothing but rhetoric,' Hoffmann has pinpointed his own achievement.[113] He has – to use a word of his own – demonstrated the intertwining of rhetoric and theology. He has, to that extent, brought the trend we have been following in this chapter to fulfilment. The question remains: in a field where sensitivity to language is paramount, is there not something distorting about the words Hoffmann uses to give shape to Erasmus' thought, words like 'system,' 'schema,' ontological order? Is it not instructive that the closest Erasmus comes, on Hoffmann's account, to 'a systematic blueprint of his thinking' is at the end of his last book at the very end of his life?[114] Erasmus uses his chosen image of the circle in various, sometimes inconsistent, ways, but more to light up our moral and spiritual choices than to define the ontological order of the world.[115] The reader of Erasmus' religious writings rarely feels that he is being presented with a schema; he is being persuaded to faith and Christian life.

In the 1990s there were two further moves in this realm of rhetoric and reality. The first was to make of Erasmus himself a rhetorical construction. Lisa Jardine's *Erasmus, Man of Letters* is a challenge to all the conventional views of the great humanist. Nevertheless, it extends the theme of this chapter, Erasmus' relation to the rhetorical tradition, and is continuous with it. That is because it studies, not simply Erasmus' self-portraiture, which is familiar enough from his biographers, but what is more revealing, his conscious self-production and self-projection, things to which late twentieth-century minds, aware of self-promotion as a feature of their own culture, have been sensitive. Erasmus, Jardine argues, used the means available to him – actual portraits, where he sat for the distinguished artists who were his friends, and his books, especially his published correspondence – to fashion a picture of himself as the quintessential European man of letters, the central figure, not only of networks of scholars, friends, and disciples, but also of a whole culture, named in retrospect 'northern humanism.'[116] It is important to say that Jardine presents this, not as an exercise in self-aggrandisement, but as the advancing of an agenda, a 'cluster of exemplary sacred/secular activities.' These she understands as modern scholarship understands them; their aim was to replace the formal, technical, prescriptive studies of the universities, which in any case held Erasmus and his friends at arm's length, with 'a training in persuasive and affective discourse more appropriate to the civic and forensic context of sixteenth-century education.'[117] But Jardine's interest is not there, in the issues of the debate; it is rather in the image-making through which the issues were canvassed and the cause promoted on Erasmus' side. They appeared initially in a local or regional setting, in or around the University of Louvain, but their promotion gave them a Europe-wide, a universal significance.[118]

Personal connections and associations were a part of this image-making. Erasmus relied on the readers, editors, correctors, usually younger than he, who saw his work through the presses; the print-shops were his base, the source of his influence, rivals to the classrooms of the university teachers. He could laud his collaborators, or distance himself from them, as the moment, or the needs of the cause, required. More importantly, he linked himself to a tradition. In the case of his immediate predecessors, he created, even contrived, a tradition. Jardine demonstrates how tenuous was Erasmus' claim to have as his master Rudolf Agricola, seen conventionally as the pioneer of Italian humanism in the north. The two scarcely met, but 'the *story* of the affective bond' was crucial in Erasmus' self-fashioning and the fashioning of his movement, 'part of a *purposive* narrative, emanating from Erasmus himself.' All this was about creating an intellectual lineage for himself, while enhancing Agricola's importance and endorsing him as rival to the champions of the dominant studies in Louvain.[119] Above all, in editing Jerome's letters and writing his biography, Erasmus presented Jerome as a 'culturally exemplary figure' for his own time and place, the model for the northern humanist program; more, he was working a subtle shift of the aura from the austere saint to the charismatic man of letters, in short to himself.[120] This meant a realigning of the balance between the sacred and the secular in studies.

Jardine's use of the letters best illustrates her methodology, which marks an important step in Erasmus scholarship. She reads them as Erasmus collected them, in 'remarkably diverse volumes,' in specific situations and in relation to other contemporaneous publications of his. L.-E. Halkin had studied these collections in his *Erasmus ex Erasmo* of 1983 and brought out elements of calculation in the selection and presentation of the letters.[121] Jardine subjects them to radical scrutiny as exercises in self-fashioning and stage-management. 'We have begun to accept,' she concludes, 'that each volume of letters issued served some specific publishing purpose.'[122] The narrative, documentary way of presenting the letters, as in Allen's 'formidable edition' and CWE, obscures this intentional element and creates an illusory continuity. The 'quarrel' with Martin Dorp in 1515–16 over the *Praise of Folly* and humanist exegesis, for example, turns out to be stage-managed, Dorp remaining a member of Erasmus' circle throughout. Such contrivings, Jardine says, give a distinct meaning to 'context' or 'intellectual milieu' as conventionally understood in intellectual history.[123] Similarly, the works must be related to the circumstances revealed by their prefaces, dedications, and other ancillary materials which a conventional reading of the text, aimed at establishing its place in intellectual history, often overlooks.[124]

This way of reading his texts assumes a high degree of calculation and of career planning (as we might say) on Erasmus' part, a 'virtuoso command' (as Jardine puts it) over his own writings, and especially his letters.[125] Erasmus is never not in control. Was his 'life' (in deference to Jardine's scepticism about the possibilities for biography we use inverted commas) really like that? What of the contingencies that were part and parcel of any sixteenth-century life? Cannot the letters be used to construct a narrative, however contrived their original assembling might have been? Jardine's book raises acutely the problem of rhetoric and reality. Must history maintain so astringent a regime that it cannot detach a historical reality from rhetorical constructions? Jardine herself confesses to being 'lured' occasionally into treating Erasmus' letters as evidence for a real life. On her own showing, they are reliable enough to provide exemplary stories.[126] That said, one must add with emphasis that Jardine's study is an illumination at a time when pietism dominates the Erasmus literature.

The second move has been to associate Erasmus and contemporary critical thinking in the humanities, which goes under the name of postmodernism, with its scepticism about recovering authors' intentions or finding in texts a univocal meaning or coherence of thought. It is fitting that James D. Tracy, who has otherwise contributed notably to Erasmus studies, should make this move in a long essay, 'Erasmus among the Postmodernists: *Dissimulatio, Bonae Literae*, and *Docta Pietas* Revisited.'[127] He asks two main questions. The first is: in face of radical scepticism about attributing a coherent meaning to a text, or discerning the presence – the mind and personality – of an author behind the text, how are we to approach the writings of Erasmus? Tracy recognizes that, in the case of Erasmus, it is essential to give ground to the sceptics, for there is something deliberately elusive about Erasmus' writings. He enunciated a doctrine of *dissimulatio*.[128]

Tracy's general guide is Hans-Georg Gadamer's *Truth and Method*, which limits scepticism by allowing the possibility of locating a text within a world or 'horizon' of thought and of moving from preconceptions, provided perhaps by the tradition, to a 'more suitable' understanding.[129] Tracy's test-case is, once again, Erasmus' publication of his correspondence. He investigates in particular the letters that Erasmus chose not to publish and, by juxtaposing these and the published ones, expects them to throw light on one another. Halkin had already commented on the changes the unpublished letters make to the self-portrait Erasmus composed in his successive editions.[130] Tracy remarks: 'I hope ... to have shown that Erasmus' unpublished letters can plausibly be used as a guide or baseline for reading published texts.'[131] Success requires the assumption that unpublished letters expose Erasmus' intentions more clearly, though those on public record have their own 'meanings.' As well, each kind has its own *dissimulatio*.

Tracy's second question concerns the unity of Erasmus' thought or, rather, the consistency between its parts, classical and Christian, aesthetic and moral or even spiritual. This is the issue Grafton and Jardine posed in their book of 1986. Tracy is hard on their dismissive conclusions. How could one ever test the assertion that the moral claims of a classical education were a fraud?[132] Even so, he accepts that tensions underlay the cultural ideals of *bonae literae* and *docta pietas*, which were Erasmus' way of describing the ultimate compatibility of the Christian and classical cultural systems. He says: 'Both *bonae literae* and *docta pietas* had meaning for contemporaries precisely because each of these ideals sought to resolve tensions that readers would have felt in themselves, between cherished and yet seemingly incompatible values.'[133] Tracy finds the resolution for the tension between the aesthetic and the moral in humanist/classical education (*bonae literae*) in the idea of civility, whose emergence between the sixteenth and eighteenth centuries the sociologist Norbert Elias (in a book first published in 1939 and famous later) saw as a major cultural shift, 'an advancement of the shame frontier.' Of its beginnings Erasmus' little handbook on juvenile manners, *De civilitate morum puerilium*, was a marker.[134] Both Elias and Tracy understand Erasmus' views on this subject historically; they 'made sense' in the sociocultural circumstances of the epoch.

Similarly, *docta pietas* was a way of combining a classical ethic of self-esteem and the Christian ethic of selfless regard for others. Theologically, the combination depended, as Erasmus' *De pueris* showed, on an optimistic view of uncorrupted human nature and on reducing, if not removing, the importance, in Christian teaching, of the doctrine of original sin. Historically speaking, it meant rejection of the ascetic, punitive, guilt-ridden culture of the later Middle Ages.[135]

What is driving Tracy in this long essay is respect for Erasmus' project, and he rightly rejects Grafton and Jardine's throwaway expressions, like 'sleight of hand.' Nevertheless, it may be both more convincing and more salutary to accept that the tensions remain unresolved than to take humanist claims of harmony at face value. Indeed, it may do more honour to Erasmus to see him struggling to the end with incompatible goods, correcting his own too exuberant moves in one direction or the other.[136] As for the postmodernists, it is surprising that, until the 1990s, Erasmus' work, preoccupied with issues of language and meaning, rich in ironies and ambiguities, textual through and through, had not attracted much attention of the contemporary critical kind.[137] Studies in the areas of language and rhetoric had, naturally, concentrated on Erasmus' relation to the rhetorical tradition and were, to that extent, conservative, at times regretful, even nostalgic, about humanist values. Tracy's initiative was pioneering, but properly cautious. In this domain, there is more to be said.[138]

SEVEN

Epilogue:
Sesquiquatercentenary (1986)
and After

꽃

I

On 13 November 1986 at a ceremony in the Great or St Lawrence's Church in Rotterdam, in the presence of Queen Beatrix, Václav Havel, Czech playwright and dissident, received the Erasmus Prize. The blitzkrieg of May 1940, with which these studies virtually began, had left standing only the walls of the late Gothic church; they were, in the war and post-war years, the chief relic of old Rotterdam. Restoration of St Lawrence's in the centre of the modern city was complete less than twenty years before the ceremony of November 1986. Prince Bernhard of the Netherlands had founded the Praemium Erasmianum Foundation in 1958 to award money prizes in honour of persons and institutions 'that have made an exceptionally important contribution to European culture, society or social science.' The award to Havel, who had in his plays depicted the predicaments of human beings in modern societies, especially totalitarian ones, and who had, with his colleagues, given hope to his compatriots with the Charter 77 movement, recognized his commitment to individual identity and responsibility, his fidelity to conscience and his courage. Also mentioned was the demonstration, through his ideas, 'that his country's culture is rooted in a European tradition which goes back for centuries and which must not be allowed to die.'[1]

Václav Havel was not present on 13 November 1986. The risks of being away from his country were too great. His representative, Professor František Janouch, received the prize on his behalf. It is enticing to seek linkages between the ideas expressed in this occasion's three main speeches, Prince Bernhard's citation for the award, the occasional address by Sem Dresden, Professor Emeritus of Leiden University, and Havel's acceptance speech, delivered by his friend, the actor Jan Tríska, who had snce 1977 been living in the United States. There are three such linkages. The first is about living and acting authentically. Dresden, as he had done on other occasions, wrestled with the enigma of a personality (Erasmus') which realized itself only or supremely in words, writings, and books. Havel, too, was a writer, of whose message in 'his intelligent and powerful plays' Prince Bernhard said: 'Havel has made it clear that in principle every human being needs an area of personal privacy in which he or she can be authentic.' His award, Havel himself said, was 'a sign of recognition of all those who, in that part of Europe in which I happen to live, and in the face of all the difficulties they have to contend with, endeavour to live in truth.' The second was the curious dialectic between vision, illusion, and reality (or truth). Naturally, there was reference to the *Praise of Folly*; for Dresden, Dame Folly was the clear-eyed observer of the world's vain spectacle; for Havel, she was a goad to action against the odds. Yet, at a deeper level they were of one mind. Havel was asking: who or which would prove illusory in the end, those 'demanding that the unchangeable be changed' or 'the gigantic power of the state bureaucracy and police with their puny typewriters'? 'Havel believes,' Prince Bernhard said, 'that ideals and the world of illusion are all too often improperly separated from the real.'[2] At the time of the ceremony, the Bristol Old Vic was playing in Rotterdam Havel's *Largo Desolato*, which he had written in four days in 1984, the year after he came out of prison. Writing it was 'an act of self-preservation, an escape from despair,' but it was also a 'human parable,' examining 'what happens when the personification of resistance finds himself at the end of his tether.'[3]

The third idea was tolerance. Dresden showed how Erasmus' search for peace and unity inspired in countrymen of his, especially William of Orange, the idea of tolerance as 'a necessary part of intelligent statesmanship' in an age of religious war. Havel spoke of European consciousness, to be realized only through state administrations accessible to popular pressure. He found in Jan Patocka's idea of the 'community of the shaken' a contemporary variant of Erasmus' old notion of the supranational brotherhood of the learned.[4]

The ceremony for Václav Havel took place four months after

the 450th anniversary of Erasmus' death. The quatercentenary of 1936 had been overshadowed by the rise of Hitler and the threat of war. That was a time of foreboding. The quincentenary of the great humanist's birth, 1966–70, had been contemporary with the student rebellions in Europe and North America and their accompanying manifestations. It might seem that, since 1936, tragedy had given way to farce. In fact, the experience then of cultural and moral shift introduced uncertainties and ambiguities which had their effects even on interpretations of Erasmus, as we have seen. The award to Havel during the 1986 commemorations unknowingly anticipated the end of the morally bankrupt Communist regimes in Eastern Europe. As with every other change through the long history of European culture since Erasmus' death, this last great resounding event of the twentieth century was accompanied by fresh appreciations of Erasmus. Havel himself suggested that, through his many-layered talk about folly, the 'community of the shaken' could find an empowering voice.

The event in St Lawrence's Church came in the midst of an international seminar commemorating the sesquiquatercentenary with public manifestations and scholarly workshops. Activities centred on two institutions. The first was the Erasmus Universiteit Rotterdam, formed, thirteen years before the celebrations of 1986, from the amalgamation of the Netherlands Economics University, established early in the century, and the Rotterdam Medical Faculty, founded in the post-war years. Though concentrated on modern studies, in economic and social sciences and the clinical subjects, it took, in a demonstration of cultural continuity, Erasmus' name. It drew most of its thirteen thousand students from the Rotterdam region and southwest Holland and directed much of its research to the needs of the region, though, as befits its name, it had strong international connections.[5] The second was the Gymnasium Erasmianum, the Latin school which had carried Erasmus' name since the seventeenth century and which still offered its students a broad humanistic education based on the classical languages.[6] The gathering had a public face – lectures, concerts, exhibitions – and a closed, more intimate side – 'workshops' and scholarly exchanges. Concerts and exhibitions raised afresh the questions, discussed at the quincentenary, of Erasmus' attitude to music and the visual arts. Towards the former, it was concluded, he showed as much reserve as enthusiasm.[7] Inevitably, performers presented, not music of personal significance to Erasmus, but rather music of his time. There was a frank admission that the 'piquant' French *chansons* and German *Lieder* of the third concert in the series 'Erasmus en de muziek' would not have had his approval.[8] The Museum Boymans–van Beuningen did not attempt to replicate the great exhibition of 1969; it gathered in its print room a more modest collection of pieces under the title 'Erasmus: View of a Scholar in His Time.' The accompanying publication by A.M. Koldeweij noted, as Erwin Panofsky had done in a famous quincentenary essay, the paucity of Erasmus' references to the visual arts. As, in musical composition, the text had priority, so in this sphere Erasmus looked first to the literary component, 'with a strongly moralizing undertone.' Panofsky had said that his interest in the written word pushed the world accessible to the eye into second place.[9] A remark in the catalogue anticipated Jardine's *Erasmus: Man of Letters*: in his relations with his portraitists, Erasmus remained in control, though he looked in their portrayals, not so much for Jardine's leader of a movement, as for 'the modest, circumspect scholar, looking to the front or working.'[10] The exhibition also featured Erasmus' comparison of his editorial efforts to the labours of Hercules, as Jardine was to do.[11]

The public lectures of the time stand at the points where scholarship and the wider interest in Erasmus intersected: Erasmus and power (by W.P. Blockmans, professor of social history at Erasmus Universiteit Rotterdam and a specialist on institutional forms and practices in the Netherlands of Erasmus' time) and Erasmus on education (by Jan Sperna Weiland, professor of philosophical anthropology there, and, between 1979 and 1983, *rector magnificus*). Blockmans emphasizes that Erasmus rejected arbitrary power and its counterpart, the passive subject. He looked for popular participation, but he had not worked out the institutional forms this would require. He fell behind much Netherlands opinion in not accepting active resistance. The 'topicality' of his thought was apparent most in his 'startlingly progressive' social opinions.[12] At first sight, Sperna Weiland says, Erasmus' topicality for education in an industrial and technological age is nugatory; for him, wisdom is won, not from observation, but from books; his world and Galileo's were poles apart. But, on a second glance, there is relevance, even for a contemporary university, in what he said about reading and writing and, above all, about teaching as a distinct value, separate from a mere transfer of information, and not a poor relation of research.[13]

From the scholarly workshops at Rotterdam came a volume of essays edited by Sperna Weiland and Willem Frijhoff, *Erasmus of Rotterdam: The Man and the Scholar*. Other conferences of the sesquiquatercentenary, also in great Erasmian centres, Liège and Tours, produced their volumes, Liège the *Colloque Erasmien de Liège* and Tours the *Actes du Colloque International Erasme (Tours 1986)*. Conscious of the place of Erasmus studies at Liège, the Institute for the History of the Renaissance and the Reformation there, whose director was Jean-Pierre Massaut, organized a 'Journée Erasme' on 23 April 1986, under the patronage of a 'Committee of Honour' representing the university, the Amsterdam project for Erasmus' *Opera omnia* (ASD), and the international scholarly federations. The program for the day replicated in miniature the pattern of all Erasmus commemorations: the opening of an exhibition, a dramatic presentation of three of Erasmus' colloquies, and musical interludes. Above all, there was a celebration of the eightieth birthday of the noble Erasmian L.-E. Halkin.[14] The three main lecturers represented a span of generations in Erasmus scholarship: Margaret Mann Phillips, Sem Dresden, and Silvana Seidel Menchi. To these the consequent publication added fifteen studies on a variety of themes. Members of the Institute imposed on themselves a self-denying ordinance and offered no papers, so that the volume derived from Liège but did not exhibit it.[15] At Tours, memories remained vivid of the splendid gathering in the summer of 1969, which produced the two massive volumes *Colloquia Erasmiana Turonensia*: three weeks of conference, forty participants, fifty presentations. For 1986 the Centre d'Etudes Supérieures de la Renaissance planned something more modest. Yet, Jean-Claude Margolin's 'schéma directeur' mapped a very broad front: Erasmus and classical culture, Erasmus and Christianity, the language and style of Erasmus, Erasmus in the world of his time and in the surrounding world, Erasmus' subsequent destiny ('fortune d'Erasme'). The eventual book remained close to this plan, though, interestingly, the third theme was the thinnest and was, in effect, amalgamated with the first.[16] The exhibition in this case included Erasmus editions from the legacy to the Municipal Library of Tours of another Erasmian, Raymond Marcel, of which, as it happens, Margolin gave an account in the volume from Liège.[17]

By 1986 the Erasmus of Rotterdam Society was providing through its *Yearbook* a new outlet for Erasmus studies. It had been founded in 1980, single-handed, by Richard DeMolen, who had himself written essays on Erasmus' piety. It aimed to produce the *Yearbook* and to organize public occasions, at once commemorative and scholarly. Thus, Clarence Miller delivered the first Erasmus Birthday Lecture at the Folger Shakespeare Library on 27 October 1980 ('The Epigrams of Erasmus and More: A Literary Diptych'). In his 'Preface' to the first number, DeMolen promised to draw in both 'seasoned scholars' and 'promising neophytes.' In fact, the numbers to 1986 exposed, as the commemorative volumes of that year themselves were to do, the passing of the generations in Erasmus scholarship. Early numbers included tributes to the great biographers of the post-war years, Margaret Mann Phillips and Roland Bainton, and in time the annual program was to include lectures bearing their names. The new generation of leaders was represented in those early numbers (to 1986) by pieces from Chomarat, Godin, Hoffmann, Holeczek, O'Malley, and Tracy.

By 1986 also, the Amsterdam edition of Erasmus' *Opera omnia* (ASD) was already well advanced and the *Collected Works* in English (CWE) had published six volumes of letters and somewhat more of Erasmus' other writings. The success of these enterprises produced a change in the balance of Erasmus scholarship. Historical and biographical notes and commentaries had accompanied earlier publications of the Erasmus sources. Jean Le Clerc at the beginning of the eighteenth century had built a substantial biography on the writings, and especially the letters, gathered in his edition of the *Opera omnia* (LB).[18] Allen's notes, introductions, and appendices, in company, of course, with the correspondence itself, provided resources for biographers and commentators from Renaudet to Jardine. But ASD and CWE brought a new abundance of interpretative material for the student of Erasmus' writings; it stimulated, but also overshadowed, work of the essayistic and monographic kind. The essays, articles, and monographs which have been the base for this study over the four-and-a-half centuries it has covered are no longer the exclusive, or even the dominant, matter for Erasmus interpretations. Nineteen-eighty-six is an appropriate moment for bringing it to an end.

Was the commemoration of that year more muted than its predecessors? Perhaps that befitted a fractional commemoration (*sesqui*quatercentenary). Were there other reasons? There was a renewal of the sense that, despite the massive accumulation of studies since 1936, Erasmus remained elusive. Margolin, in his

'Avant-propos' to the Tours volume, remarks that the perennial interest in Erasmus does not mean that his traits are now fixed. In his preface, Massaut asks: do we commemorate a failure? He answers 'Yes and no'; historians are still evaluating the balance of success and failure. He adds, in a remark that justifies our historiographical studies: Erasmus dominates the centuries but, for that very reason, his reputation is subject to the 'choc de leur métamorphose.' Most telling is Halkin's comment on the evening of his celebration: 'all questions are open, all interpretations remain open provided that they are seriously documented and honestly argued.'[19] A consensus in Erasmus interpretations was rather confidently claimed after the quincentenary. It, too, has remained elusive.

There was, as we have seen, a sense at this time of the generations passing. The Tours volume includes a tribute by Aloïs Gerlo to the doyenne of humanist studies at Liège, Marie Delcourt, who had died there in February 1979 in her eighty-eighth year and whose first course in that field had opened fifty years before. He recalls, above all, the lively commentary her correspondence made on the preparation of the French edition of Erasmus' letters, whose first volume appeared at Brussels in 1967.[20] In an article for the Liège collection, on Erasmus' autobiography, the *Compendium vitae*, André Godin refers to the provocative and spirited piece on the same subject published by Roland Crahay in 1939. He finds anachronistic its teasing of the bourgeois, always appealing to young minds and especially perhaps young minds of the 1930s, Crahay's target being the bourgeois of Leiden who had first published the *Compendium* in the early seventeenth century.[21] Here was one way for the 1980s to recall the 1930s.

In one of the main lectures at Liège, Margaret Phillips included affectionate recollections of her own mentors and teachers, figures already established by World War 1 or emerging in the interwar years: Allen, whose kindly interest she met as a young graduate at Oxford in 1927, Bataillon, with 'the courtesy and dignity of a grandee of Spain,' and, above all, Renaudet, 'un professeur d'une intégrité parfaite, d'une sévérité sans relâche,' who put before students, not his own views, but the ideal of objectivity and honest work.[22] In reflecting on the late twentieth-century vision of Erasmus as a religious, even a mystical, thinker and, in particular, on the dazzling work of Michael Screech on the *Praise of Folly*, Phillips came through to a generation beyond her own.[23]

Many who had taken up Erasmus scholarship just before or soon after World War 2 were active still at the 1986 commemorations: Phillips herself, Cornelis Reedijk, L.-E. Halkin, Roland Crahay, Rudolf Padberg, Aloïs Gerlo. ... Many of those who had joined them in the greater celebrations of 1966–70 and produced or helped fill the commemorative volumes from those years accompanied them again in 1986: Dresden, Augustijn, Chantraine, Margolin, Béné, Kohls, Herding, Bietenholz, Screech. ... One cannot help feeling that those volumes from 1966–70 marked the true moment of flowering of Erasmus scholarship in the twentieth century. Yet, in the mid-1980s there were masterpieces just produced or just around the corner: Chomarat's, Godin's, and Seidel Menchi's, and notable biographies, as we shall see. And there was North American scholarship, imperfectly represented in the commemorative volumes of 1986, and names fresh to the 1970s and 1980s: Boyle, Tracy, Rummel.[24] In the Fourth Annual Birthday Lecture of the Erasmus of Rotterdam Society, 'Three American Erasmians,' Craig Thompson recalled, as Phillips had done in her case, teachers and mentors: Hoyt Hudson, translator of the *Praise of Folly* and restorer (along with others) of rhetorical studies at Cornell and Princeton, and the two prodigiously productive historians and biographers, the rationalist Preserved Smith and the liberal Christian Roland Bainton.[25]

II

What do the commemorative volumes tell us about the preoccupations of Erasmus scholarship as the twentieth century drew to an end? In the first place, there were signs of renewed interest in Erasmus' personality. Romanticism had first distinguished the personality from the historical figure as a subject of study. In the twentieth century, Huizinga and Mangan, in their different ways, had made his character traits keys to their interpretations of Erasmus. In essays written just after World War 2, V.W.D. Shenk applied psychological categories to Erasmus' character and found in him a dualism of active or aggressive and passive traits, linked to narcissism and latent homosexuality.[26]

A more elaborate attempt 'to resolve the seeming contradictions of Erasmus' character and arrive at a psychoanalytically intelligible configuration consistent with the historical data' was made in an essay written jointly by a historian, Nelson H. Minnich, and a psychiatrist, W.W. Meissner, 'The Character of Erasmus' (1978). The double promise of psychoanalytical intelligibility (on the basis of evidence written in another age, in other terms and for other purposes) and positivist history (based on 'data' often equivocal and hard to interpret) was ambitious from the start. The key to Erasmus' personality, the authors say, and also to much in his work and ideas, was his loss of his father. The *Compendium vitae* presents an idealized and romantic version of his family, typical of one in Erasmus' position. In his growing up, classicism became a father-substitute. Narcissism, the sense of himself as something special, arose from deep embarrassment at his illegitimacy. There was symmetry between his psychological needs and elements of classicism, between his ambivalent feelings towards his mother ('probably' too doting) and rhetorical ambiguity, for example, or between his wish for a secure family life in his past and his idealizing of antiquity. Victimhood followed, apparent in what he said about his experience of school and monastery. His rejection of the call by his superior, Servatius Rogerus, to whom for a time in their youth he had been passionately attached (latent homosexuality reappears), to return to the monastery was 'a manifestation of the hidden and repressed anger at the abandoning father of his childhood.' Even more adventurous than this are attempts here to associate Erasmus' psychology and his publicly stated moral and intellectual positions. Thus, beneath the famous Erasmian moderation lay a desire 'to play the part of a silent victim' and 'paranoid tendencies.' His controversies exposed 'a narcissistically vulnerable character structure.'[27]

John Olin has made telling points against this effort in an appendix to his essay 'Interpreting Erasmus.' It is, he says, insufficiently grounded and lacks the sheer accumulation of data necessary for any judgment on Erasmus' personality. Its categories are unnecessary for explaining Erasmus' most characteristic and enduring productions. There is, in other words, a needless resort to the personal and the clinical. Intellectual choices may be just that, intellectual choices. But Olin enters on more treacherous ground when he calls these interpretations unworthy of Erasmus.[28] Further, to make of Erasmus a settled personality devoted, without crosscurrents, to scholarship and the universal church is no less a construction than to find him, through his associations and experiences however described, psychologically disturbed and on edge.

One turns to a work well grounded in the sources, using the historical method, avoiding clinical pretensions and all 'jargonized nonsense,' Yvonne Charlier's substantial study of Erasmus' friendships, *Erasme et l'amitié*. What emerges is the picture of a man who thinks nobly (and classically) about friendship and pursues it, but whose relations with his friends often betray a personality disturbed, preoccupied, even driven. Against his own conviction, taken from antiquity, that one should have few, but highly valued, friendships, he delighted, Charlier says, in counting up his friends. She asks: 'Does he need constantly to reassure himself by the number of those who support and value him?'[29] Erasmus had sincere and straightforward friendships: with Cornelius Gerard, who helped his studies in the monastic years, with Mountjoy, his first English patron, with Andrea Ammonio, who, as an Italian settled in England, more easily shared his confidences over money matters and health problems than the better-off Englishmen.[30] Then there were the deep and creative friendships, with John Colet and, above all, with Thomas More. The latter was clouded only in the years when More was occupied with state affairs; their different approaches to the Reformation controversies had, Charlier believes, less effect.[31] Erasmus' egocentrism checked other friendships full of promise, with Batt, whom he used to cultivate patrons, or with Vives, whose work he underrated. Towards Guillaume Budé, his equal in humanistic renown, he showed a near-incredible insensitivity.[32] Over the problematic relationship with Servatius Rogerus, Charlier accepts D.F.S. Thomson's demonstration that Erasmus' effusive letters to his youthful companion had a literary and rhetorical character, drawn from a monastic or quasi-monastic tradition.[33] Yet, she rightly accepts the sincerity of their content; they betray a badly controlled emotionalism. Charlier believes that Erasmus came to regret his excess; his letter of refusal to Servatius, now (1514) his superior, distilled a calculated malice.[34] As for Aleander, once an intimate friend, as papal legate in Germany in the Reformation years his bitter enemy, he became for Erasmus an obsession, bordering on the paranoiac.[35]

This last relationship is the subject of an essay by André Godin in the Tours collection. The course of events carried the two men ever further away from the intimacy of their months in Venice in 1508, Erasmus becoming a public intellectual and critic of the establishment, Aleander a willing servant of that establishment, papal legate and archbishop. The cultural associations of Christianity were, Godin adds, different for each: Erasmus' outlook was Hellenizing; Aleander, otherwise traditionalist in his religious outlook, appreciated the Judaic context of Christianity. In the Luther affair, Erasmus looked for mediation, Aleander for suppression. All that is explicable, comprehensible, even rational.[36] What is mysterious, requiring but evading explanation, is the depth of the bitterness, the utter sense of alienation, especially on Erasmus' part. Even Charlier's account is, for Godin, too moralizing. Was Erasmus, Charlier asks of his attempt at reconciliation in 1524, sincere?[37] For Godin, the fires are stoked psychologically at a deeper level. Aleander's exposure of Erasmus' ignorance of Hebrew threatened the self-esteem of one who, through his work and reputation as *grammaticus*, had made his way to eminence from beginnings obscure and contemptible.[38] He unjustly saw Aleander's hand behind all the controversialists of his last years, behind J.-C. Scaliger, for example, who, in his *Oratio* of 1531, mentioned the touchiest point of all, the circumstances of Erasmus' birth.[39] In Erasmus, there was a profound sense of friendship betrayed, which he caught in the image of a royal betrayal, Absalom's of David.[40]

A number of essays from the 1986 celebrations make the circumstances of his birth a continuing anxiety for Erasmus. It does not require Freudian categories to recognize this claim. Nevertheless, André Godin uses those categories in a second paper, this one for the Liège collection, 'Une biographie en quête d'auteur: le *Compendium vitae Erasmi.*' He fairly remarks that traditional historical explanations rely on psychological and sociological understandings, no less debatable than the Freudian ones.[41] Godin's starting-point is G. Avarucci's demonstration that Erasmus' father was in Italy as a very young man in the mid-1450s (with others he rejects Avarucci's hypothesis that Erasmus must then have been born ten years earlier than is usually thought). Godin accepts, for good reasons, Erasmus' authorship of the *Compendium vitae*. The question then is: why did Erasmus compose the romantic fable found there about his parents' relationship? Godin's answer relates partly to the threats in Erasmus' life in April 1524, when he wrote the strange little autobiography, and the fears they aroused in him. Pressure was on him from above, as from a father, to change his stance in the Luther affair and write openly against Luther. He was caught in an oedipal dilemma. His way out was to compose 'une fiction des origines,' as in Freud's *Familienroman der Neurotiker*. He produced an ideal portrait of his father to which the man's actual achievements, as scribe and scholar in Italy, could lend plausibility.[42]

Jacques Chomarat also considers his illegitimacy an obsession for Erasmus and finds the reason in both canon and civil law. Only by becoming a monk could he escape the handicaps it imposed; he could not inherit, he could not become a priest.[43] Escape came through a way of life, itself increasingly burdensome to him. The two misfortunes of his life, his illegitimate birth and his monastic state, were associated. Further, Chomarat recognizes a link between this predicament and certain attitudes of Erasmus: his questioning of 'human constitutions,' his exalting of baptism, the common rite of all Christians, over against distinctive vows and hierarchies.[44]

For both Godin and Chomarat, Erasmus was driven by the dread of exposure of the circumstances of his birth. The latter prudently avoids psychoanalytical language, yet finds a psychological meaning in Erasmus' studied silence about his origins: 'this silence is eloquent.'[45] On this small point, there is a revealing contrast with J.K. Sowards' later reading of the same silence: evidence is lacking that his illegitimacy was ever a source of anxiety for Erasmus.[46] It neatly indicates the difference between those who press psychological explanations and those who eschew them. The dangers for the former are apparent; they have been highlighted by Olin. Chomarat himself asks: why does the psychoanalytical approach always produce pejorative results?[47] The dangers for the latter are that biography becomes simply intellectual history, literary convention explains away the personal and emotional, and the idylls of the subject are accepted at face value. For Sowards' picture of 'a close and loving family fondly remembered' the evidence is as cloudy as for Chomarat's of an intense brooding over the burden of illegitimacy.[48] The fact is nevertheless that the crucial documents, the *Compendium vitae* and the letters to Servatius (1514) and to Grunnius (1516), betray serious tensions. Of Erasmus' hateful account of his brother Pieter in the letter to Grunnius, Richard DeMolen reasonably remarks that 'the excessiveness of the language betrays an inward, emotional conflict.'[49]

One feels that there is more at stake in these differences than meets the eye. The personalities of the authors are somehow engaged. There are those drawn to, looking for, and finding a poised, balanced, and settled personality. By 1500, at just over thirty, Erasmus was, Kelley Sowards says, 'secure in his own identity,' in his profession, his vocation, his beliefs. Struggle, the threat of fragmentation, inner insecurities attract others. Jacques Chomarat finds in the letter to Grunnius, sixteen years later than the Erasmus depicted by Sowards, a tone 'of rancour, of resentment, but also of indignation and anguish.'[50] Hovering in the background is Erasmus the exemplary figure. All accept his prodigious learning and scholarly output, the variety of his intellectual gifts and accomplishments, his signiicance in cultural history, his power as a polemicist and public intellectual. Would such things be possible, one side asks, for a man handicapped by inner conflict, self-doubt, and repining? Does not the dynamic come, others reply, is not the very character of the performance set by the fierce inner struggle to hold together, to keep in balance what does not easily or naturally go together? To this observer at least the second alternative rings true. Contributing to the tension, but also to the creativity, were his physical weaknesses, about which J.-P. Vanden Branden of the Maison d'Erasme at Anderlecht writes in the Tours volume.[51]

III

In the sphere of Erasmus' theology and religious thought, 1986 gathered up the tendencies since the quincentenary and rehearsed continuing debates. Thus John Olin and J. den Boeft recalled at Rotterdam the recent recovery of Erasmus' patristic scholarship, largely ignored in the age of Smith and Huizinga.[52] How the preparation of the editions stimulated scholarship in this sphere was illustrated by works on Erasmus' Psalms commentaries. Screech had remarked that, unconstrained by the Greek scholarship integral to his New Testament work, Erasmus could here give free rein to his emotions and imagination in exposing the Christian mysteries.[53] C.S.M. Rademaker, who edited the commentary on Psalm 86 for ASD, agrees that there was a freedom and personal expression in these commentaries which make them good indicators to Erasmus' religious thought and deserving of 'more attention than they have received up to now.'[54] Charles Béné, general editor of the Psalms volumes in ASD, wrote on Erasmus' last commentary (1536), on Psalm 15, *De*

puritate Tabernaculi sive Ecclesiae christianae: Erasmus' religious
thought remained consistent with itself over the years since the
Enchiridion; it was spiritual, Christocentric, unclerical – and
essentially orthodox.[55]

The consistency of Erasmus' religious thought remained an
issue in 1986. From the commemorative papers two differing
interpretations can be teased out. One view accepts its essential
unity over time. Richard DeMolen argues that the substance of
his *philosophia Christi* was settled by 1489–90, while Erasmus was
still in the monastery. From that time, adds E.-W. Kohls, his life
was the working out of an established mission. The unity was
also across cultures: *bonae literae* and Christian piety were compatible. In this, says Kohls, Erasmus represented the best in late-
medieval culture.[56] The difficulty, at least with Kohls' argument,
is that it puts the evidence in a straitjacket. At one point he
remarks that, if we are not to miss the wood for the trees of biographical detail, we must see Erasmus' life as the fulfilment of the
theological life's mission ('Lebensaufgabe') just mentioned.[57] But
the biographical static cannot simply be screened out, the tensions betrayed in the letter to Servatius, for example. Similarly, in
an article of 1976, DeMolen has Erasmus' wish for personal freedom, his piety, with its roots in late-medieval spirituality, and his
commitment to his order (the Augustinian canons) cohabiting too
easily.[58]

The alternative view, that Erasmus' thought was not a total
design, long settled, was put by Cornelis Augustijn in the Liège
volume and is more convincing. This was, Augustijn says, two-
track thought: there is a finality about the gospel, but development is also necessary. How are we to distinguish between what
is settled, beyond dispute, and what is subject to change and
development? Christ is the test. Erasmus sought to connect theology and culture. Christ is the connection, the realization of all
goodness, wisdom, and beauty. So to see things requires an open,
receptive, and responsive theology. Erasmus', Augustijn concludes, was 'eine dialogische Theologie,' something Luther could
not understand.[59] For assessing the laws of the church, humanity,
meeting human needs, is the norm. In two essays, respectively in
the Liège and Tours volumes, Marie-Madeleine de la Garanderie
uses a literary analysis on passages from his *Paraphrases* of the
Johannine books to demonstrate Erasmus' unease with the numi-
nous and transcendent and, by contrast, his ease with human-

divine exchanges, as in Jesus' encounters with Nicodemus and the Samaritan woman at the well. This is a very human piety, a piety, not of stupefaction, but of 'extreme sobriety.'[60]

The case for seeing Erasmus' thought as changing and developing throughout his life, even to its last decade, had been made years before, in the wake of the quincentenary, in James Tracy's first full-length study on Erasmus, *Erasmus: The Growth of a Mind.* It appears here, out of chronological order, because it had been, to 1986, the fullest statement of the developmental approach. Tracy's aim is 'a full chronological account of Erasmus' intellectual development throughout his life.' He is wanting to steer between two errors of interpretation (as he sees them), one that Erasmus' thought can be defined by its sources, the other that it was 'the product of circumstance and conflict,' determined by its context. Erasmus' was an independent mind which approached its sources, even revered ones, 'with a certain critical reserve'; he was a distinctive personality, who put a peculiar stamp on both his reading and his experience and was not, as some have said, inordinately malleable.[61] Tracy defends the personal reference in intellectual history; Erasmus drew intellectual conclusions from personal experiences.

Admittedly, Tracy sets out, in an initial orientation of the reader, 'the fundamental thought structures of Erasmus' reform program'; in other words, he puts Erasmus' thought, to an extent, in systematic form.[62] These fundamental principles were *humanitas, libertas,* and *simplicitas. Humanitas* produced peace, the absence of *libertas* produced its opposite (anger over trivialities – rules, ceremonies, and dogmatic definitions), *simplicitas* produced sincerity and authenticity.[63] But, Tracy argues, these principles bear an intimate relation to Erasmus' life experiences and psychological make-up. For example, out of the conflict between his temperament and the monastic life came his conviction that the monks and theologians were the enemies of his cherished values.[64] He developed this line into a massive critique of late-medieval culture, Tracy, at this point, explicitly approving Hans Treinen's earlier and neglected study.[65] There are dangers of reductionism in explanations from temperament and experience, but Tracy's general point stands: personal experience, predisposition, and moral reflection and decision determined the course of Erasmus' intellectual development more than philosophical emulation or systematic thought. 'Erasmus was never anxious about the underpinning of his thought.' Tracy rightly approves Rudolf Padberg's remark that 'Erasmus used Platonic categories mainly as metaphors for the moral and psychological categories that really interested him.'[66]

At the end, Tracy radicalizes Erasmus' thought too much. He attributes to him 'ethical optimism' and 'cerebral moralism,' so recalling the views of liberal Protestant commentators of the early twentieth century, of whom the most notable was Johannes Lindeboom.[67] This is to underestimate Erasmus' moral and social realism and, in his theology and personal religion, his centring on Christ, Redeemer and helper. He began moving, Tracy says, towards a doctrine of justification by faith as soon as he encountered Luther. On this point, it is generally agreed that, at least in later editions of his New Testament *Paraphrases*, Erasmus drew closer to Luther, but, as we have seen, opinion differs on what lay behind this.[68] In any case, the change itself confirms Tracy's argument that Erasmus' mind was in constant movement, that he never ceased developing and 'continued all his life to grow.'[69] It is a conclusion relevant to the debates of 1986.

Putting the matter in the simplest terms, one might say that these debates, and all modern debates about Erasmus' thought, come down to this: how radical was he? How comprehensive was his rejection of late-medieval culture? In what sense did he remain within Catholic tradition? Did he criticize monastic abuses, merely, or reject monasticism? How drastically did he wish to change the status of the clergy? The problem has been to marry expressions of loyalty whose sincerity cannot be doubted, since they appear in documents of a very personal character like the Psalms commentaries, and criticisms that seem to go, not merely to the corruptions in institutions, but to their foundations. How should orthodoxy be defined – in relation to the dominant religious culture of the time or by the standards of, say, Vatican 2? In an article on 'Erasmus and Religious Toleration' in an early number of the *Yearbook*, Manfred Hoffmann argues for the essential unity and orthodoxy of Erasmus' thought but, at the end, accepts that, on the specific issue of toleration, he took a position, based on the parable of the wheat and the tares, denounced by the defenders of orthodoxy in his time.[70]

There was also the less controversial, and perhaps less simplistic, question of how the classical and the Christian, the rhetorical and the theological, cohered in Erasmus' thought. In a lecture of

1984, John O'Malley drew on his formidable erudition in the history of 'sacred rhetoric' to argue that, despite its place as a 'major monument' in that history, Erasmus' *Ecclesiastes* left questions of this kind unresolved. The difficulties were, he believes, endemic 'to any attempt to adapt classical rhetoric to the Christian pulpit': how are the classical prescriptions to be wedded to a theology of the divine Word and Spirit? How can the text of scripture, central to Christian preaching, be integrated with classical oratory? How do preaching and the liturgy relate to one another? How can sober moral wisdom be imparted without neglecting the spiritual and affective elements?[71]

The papers of 1986 were, by and large, agreed that Erasmus' social and political thought was radical. Shortly, Brendan Bradshaw would link him to liberation theology.[72] In the Liège collection, Rudolf Padberg praises Erasmus' consistent pacifism, comparing it favourably with Augustine's arguments for armed defence of the faith. He recognizes, of course, that the historical situations were different, for Augustine stood at the beginning of the Constantinian settlement, with Christians anxious to prove their loyalty, and Erasmus, by contrast, at the moment when the connection between power and religion began to dissolve. The latter returned, says Padberg, to the gospel pacifism of the early Fathers. Writing in what turned out to be the last decade of the Cold War, he thought this a good guide for Christians in a time of balance of terror. In fact, he overstates the unequivocal character of Erasmus' pacifism.[73] In later writings especially, we find Erasmus accepting armed action for preserving the Christian peace as a rude necessity, a lesser evil, if nothing to do with the gospel.[74] This was his way of resolving the tension between a gospel that was wholly spiritual and the inescapable demands of the human situation. Power was suspect to him, especially power with universalist ambitions, but he knew that it was indispensable.[75] He struck this balance exactly in his writings on the Turkish war, as essays by A.G. Weiler in both the Liège and Tours volumes demonstrate: armed resistance to the Turkish invasion was justified but there must be no crusade, and the people must amend their own lives and keep a watch lest the princes twist the emergency to bring in tyrannies.[76] There was also, as Margherita Isnardi-Parente showed at Rotterdam, a kind of balancing act in Erasmus' views on socioeconomic questions and, in particular, on the Platonic (and apostolic) ideal of community of goods. At his most idealist and most radical, as in the adage *Dulce bellum inexpertis* (1515), he held to the principle, while recognizing, without accepting the moral superiority of, present realities. Shocked by the social disorders of the 1520s and 1530s, he abandoned the principle.[77]

It is perhaps instructive that, of the three commemorative volumes of 1986, only the one deriving from the symposium centred on the Erasmus Universiteit and the Gymnasium Erasmianum of Rotterdam grouped papers under a heading on 'Education.' The relevant essays put Erasmus' views on education in a context of substantial change: urbanization and laicization, especially in Erasmus' own country, altered conceptions of time, space, and cosmology, deriving from the archaeological, geographical, and astronomical discoveries of the age, and also altered conceptions of the person and the self. The Erasmus represented as responding to these changes seems surprisingly conventional, 'moderate' through and through. His refusal of the vernaculars exemplified the limits to his response.[78] His originality, his distinctiveness lay in the realm of relationships – in the humanizing of the pupil-teacher relationship in pedagogy itself.[79]

This review has indicated the markers (and the pitfalls) between which reflection on Erasmus as a religious thinker was steering by 1986. The field had narrowed even since Tracy's book of 1972. Presenting him as, in essence, a cerebral moralist would not now do. If not in the eyes of all his contemporaries a professional theologian, he yet thought theologically, and there were strong affective, spiritual, and near-mystical strains. But within the narrower compass, options presented themselves. Or, were, as has been suggested here more than once, tendencies in tension, or even in contradiction, within Erasmus himself? We may set the boundaries thus: how unitary or divided was his thought? How far was he traditionalist or an innovator?

We should ask, since they were much preoccupied with Erasmus' thought, how two biographies of the 1980s (let us call them biographies of the sesquiquatercentenary) steered between these poles. They are by masters in the Erasmian craft, though of different generations, Cornelis Augustijn (born 1928) and Léon-E. Halkin (born 1906). For Augustijn, the drive for unity, for a synthesis, was the main dynamic of Erasmus' thought and in his life. The synthesis was to be between Christianity and classical learning: 'how can one, with a good conscience, be both a man of culture and a Christian?'[80] The possibilities were greatest where the faith documents of Christianity, the scriptures, intersected with the grammatical and rhetorical studies of the classicists. The meeting-ground was, in short, language. Erasmus is fairly described as a theologian, but one working with a grammarian's tools. Augustijn thus integrates the two main preoccupations of Erasmus scholarship in the second half of the twentieth century: Erasmus and theology, Erasmus and language. He adds that the best description of him remains Lindeboom's from the beginning of the century: 'biblical humanist.' By and large, Augustijn believes, Erasmus achieved his ambition.[81]

The picture on the other dichotomies (radical or conservative, traditionalist or innovator?) is more complicated. Augustijn makes this perceptive remark: 'Erasmus was subjectively a conservative *par excellence*, and thus not very aware of the objectively revolutionary character of his life's achievement.'[82] He was 'objectively revolutionary' because he opposed or criticized characteristic forms of organized Christianity in his time in ways that led contemporaries to question them fundamentally. Monasticism was but one way of Christian life, 'no better or worse' than others. From the *Enchiridion*'s hierarchy of spirit/flesh and invisible/visible came the downgrading of rule and ceremony, including the 'whole external ritual of the mass.' Scholasticism produced a sterile kind of religion, its 'confusing and useless complexity' condemned by a contrast with apostolic clarity and simplicity.[83] Augustijn agrees with Renaudet that this reform program was different from any that had gone before. It was not a restoration, a revival of medieval forms. It was meeting the spiritual needs of contemporaries, which Luther and Zwingli also were to address, even before they were heard of.[84]

Erasmus' sense of community expressed both his conservatism and his radicalism. It was turned towards the past, if a more distant past than that honoured by contemporary theologians. But it was not embodied in hierarchy or constituted by power or force. Centred on Christ, it belonged to those liberated by him in their inner dispositions.[85]

One senses, from what is said and from the whole tenor of the discussion, that Augustijn is in dialogue over Erasmus with his great compatriot Johan Huizinga. There is, for all the achievements of the intervening scholarship, including Augustijn's own, a similarity in their appreciations of Erasmus' mind, his freedom from institutional and dogmatic constraints, for example. But Augustijn wants also to correct Huizinga's picture of Erasmus' personality. There delicate, fastidious, even somewhat faded traits predominate. Augustijn's Erasmus is a more robust character. He speaks of Erasmus' toughness.[86] He sees him as a force among his contemporaries, as the late nineteenth-century historians and Bataillon had done.

The title of Halkin's biography is *Erasme parmi nous* (Erasmus among us).[87] Who are the 'us' with whom Erasmus is associated? The book is addressed to the general educated reader – that is plain. The question is rather: among whom, from a reading of Halkin's book, is Erasmus at home, among which of our contemporaries? The answer must be: among Christians. The whole cast of the book, the balance of treatment suggests the seriousness of Erasmus' piety, a piety centred on Christ.[88] To continue: among Catholics in particular, though there is no spirit of contention here with the Reformers or their heirs. Erasmus was loyal to the church, the Roman church.[89] From this point on, it is necessary to make distinctions. Erasmus is at home among Catholics who make no break between faith and culture; in his own case, of course, the continuity was between Catholic faith and classical culture. The synthesis which, for Augustijn, is the object of Erasmus' striving is, for Halkin, a given.[90] Erasmus' association is with Catholics who have got free of scholasticism, with its 'impious curiosity,' who have rejected superstitions and the excesses of popular piety, who have rejected also 'a moralizing, juridical, military and bureaucratic conception of the Church,' while wanting to keep the institution intact and respecting the devotions of others, no matter how uncongenial.[91] It is with lay Catholics whose asceticism is 'not an accumulation of hagiographic performances, but the courageous acceptance of daily trials,' with Catholics devoted to peace and social justice (as a man of the Resistance, Halkin himself had suffered in that cause during World War 2). One might say: Erasmus is at home among Catholics, not of Trent, but of Vatican 2. His is a theology of liberation, if not of secularization.[92]

On Erasmus' personality, Halkin captures the elusiveness of the man by somehow replicating it. There is a shimmering complexity to his portrait. The many-sidedness of Erasmus comes out, even to elements of contradiction. Halkin's conclusions themselves do not escape contradictions. His Erasmus is elusive, secretive, evasive about his inner life. Yet, Halkin's judgments about that inner life are confident: Erasmus achieved an assured spiritual equilibrium, his inner orthodoxy was secure, he had no longing for marriage. Even on Halkin's own account, one could make more space here for inner tensions.[93]

These two biographies have much in common. For both, Erasmus was a strong character. In this they break with a long, unfavourable tradition about his character which Huizinga had continued in his own way. They both accept the results of twentieth-century scholarship: Erasmus was Christian and, some allowances made, theologian; he sought to integrate the classical, rhetorical tradition with Christianity. Yet the differences are not insignificant. There is a harder edge to Augustijn's study; Halkin's is more suffused in enthusiasm. Unity was a harder struggle for Augustijn's Erasmus, an easier acquisition for Halkin's. The radical elements in the latter are always balanced out; in the former they retain full force. A small but revealing point is their difference over the long-standing issue of the nature of the *Devotio moderna* and its influence on Erasmus. Augustijn is negative on both counts: it was by now 'pedestrian, unworldly, legalistic,' incapable of inspiring Erasmus. Halkin speaks still of its 'spiritual vigour' and has Erasmus reading its earlier classic, Thomas à Kempis' *Imitation of Christ*.[94] In question here is the vitality of the whole late-medieval Catholic culture.

IV

It is not surprising that the volume from Tours should devote its first section, under the heading 'Humanae litterae,' to the issues that had come on to centre stage between the quincentenary and 1986, Erasmus and the word, Erasmus and rhetoric, Erasmus and dialogue, Erasmus and the literary tradition. Once again, the issue of unity and contradiction is prominent.

Thus, a study of Erasmus' aesthetic (by Alain Michel), which must needs be about his literary style, finds its heart in a harmonizing of contraries. The latter were surmounted (one dares to make the comparison) in a Hegel-like synthesis. They were *copia* or abundance, of which Erasmus was the master, and *brevitas* or conciseness, expressed in his abiding love of proverbs and, therefore, in the *Adagia*, his masterpiece. As well, there were grandeur, which Erasmus thought both necessary and dangerous, and adopted in the more sober form of *dignitas*, and irony. This synthesis between contraries made for a complex aesthetic, matching the complexity of Erasmus' thought, as revealed in the *Folly*, a thought associating intellectual modesty, laughter, and Christian love. Michel argues that, in the history of rhetoric and style, unlike the history of thought, where the breaks were substantial, the transmission from antiquity through the Middle Ages to Erasmus was continuous.[95]

Two other essays, Daniel Kinney's on 'Erasmus and the Latin Comedians' and Jorge Alves Osorio's on the speaking subject in the *Colloquies* ('Enoncé et dialogue dans les *Colloques* d'Erasme'), establish Erasmus' preference for debate and dialogue over enunciation by a single authoritative voice. In both cases this leads to an appreciation of his religion as based, not on pronouncement and definition, but on mutual exploration and understanding. Colloquy, exchange, and communication belong for him, Osorio says, to 'le cadre spirituel chrétien.' In Ciceronian dialogue, the author is always present; in Erasmus' *Colloquies*, he effaces himself, so that the characters may occupy the whole space. It says much for his character, and his faith, that he elaborated his *Colloquies* on the comic model in years when he was most under pressure, 1522–6.[96] Kinney finds, between the *Enchiridion* and the *Folly*, which Erasmus himself explicitly linked together, 'an unresolved dialectic,' which recalls the multiple voices of comedy. The progress through the three parts of *Folly* to 'a daring exposition of the purposeful folly of Christ' is comparable. It is a 'sort of conversion by trial-and-error ... anything but a definitive, unequivocal call to an orthodox creed.'[97]

In a main lecture at Liège, Sem Dresden, who at the quincentenary had opened up the whole subject of Erasmus and words, returns to the theme of Erasmus and texts, in his view the preeminent theme about Erasmus. On the Renaissance understanding, literary texts did not have autonomous value; literature was to serve truth, culturally and morally, if in a pleasant, or even a playful, manner. Dresden argues for continuity through the whole of Erasmus' intellectual career, even to seeing his devotion to letters as a kind of separation from the world; Erasmus remained 'cloistered in a certain sense,' a 'monk after his own fashion.'[98] Is this Erasmus too ethereal? Any who think so may find an antidote in Betty Knott's down-to-earth treatment at Rotterdam of 'Erasmus' Working Methods in "De Copia."'[99] He was most at ease when dealing with real, demonstrative examples of what to do and how to live. Later, T.O. Sloane reinforced the point by arguing that those who had concentrated on the first part of the *Copia*, with its guide to 'linguistic bountifulness,' had missed the point. Erasmus' concern was more with substance than with style, with *inventio*, as treated in the second part of the book. There he recognized the place of contraries, of *pro* and *contra*, in argumentation, as with copiousness and brevity.[100] Every matter calls up its opposite. This reminds us of the emphasis in the Tours papers on transcending contraries. Erasmus' advice to students was: do not take anything uncritically. Sloane's conclusion is worth quoting: 'Erasmian copiousness is the sign of a versatile and complex mind whose rich resources of language and skill in such argumentative procedures as *in utramque partem* were the surest safeguards against the educated man's gravest pitfall, that narrowness of mind which, in Erasmus's lexicon, as well as in ours, is called dogmatism.'[101]

What emerges – to put it in a broad-brush way – is that, while those who begin with the question about Erasmus and theology tend to finish with an orthodox and devout Erasmus, those who begin with the question about Erasmus and rhetoric tend to finish with an Erasmus of dialogue and openness. The difference resides, not only in the evidence marshalled, but also in the structures of two traditions with distinctive orientations. This account is too broad-brush because there have been, as we know, various attempts at meshing the two traditions in Erasmus' case. Silvana Seidel Menchi's work requires a reorientation beyond both traditions, a reversal of perspective, as her lecture at Liège on Erasmus and his readers demonstrates. She adduces evidence of what possessing Erasmus' books meant to Italian readers in the sixteenth century, the sacrifices they were prepared to make for them and the risks they were willing to run. Contemporary markings in his books held in Italian libraries and the Inquisition records suggest a selective, even tendentious, reading, drawing out Erasmus' more radical expressions. He was radicalized by being separated from his own context and linked to reformist activity in Italy. This, Seidel Menchi insists, was not a falsification; it was what happened to genuine elements in his thought when applied to action in a critical historical situation. She even says: these readers understood those elements better than the old, more calculating Erasmus himself.[102] Here, as we recognized earlier when considering Seidel Menchi's book, is a major methodological shift, away from the preoccupation of the vast bulk of the Erasmian literature in the twentieth century with Erasmus' intention and meaning. What his readers made of him in their various environments was as important historically as his intention and meaning. Other essays of 1986, if in different ways, picked up the theme of 'Erasmus and his audiences.'[103]

V

Over fifty years after P.S. Allen's death, the papers of 1986 demonstrated once again how his edition of Erasmus' letters remains the foundation of all study of the man and his audiences. This will continue to be so, even after the considerations pressed by Lisa Jardine in her *Erasmus, Man of Letters* have properly been taken into account.

At Rotterdam, L. Voet presented what could in the circumstances be no more than a sketch of Erasmus' correspondents as a body, 'Erasmus and His Correspondents,' but the initiative was important. They belonged above all to the republic of letters, and scholarly matters predominated, though the high number of correspondents in power and office gave Erasmus at least the opportunity of influencing public affairs. Their geographical spread indicated where the cultural centres of the time were: in Germany, for example, 'correspondents from the Northern provinces remain far under the average.' Voet himself recognizes the difficulties in analysing a body like Erasmus' correspondents: the fluid sense of nationality then, the very uncertainty of boundaries, the anachronistic traps in defining 'social positions and functions.' A chronological grid must be laid across the pattern. How did it change after the eruption of the Luther affair?[104]

There is also, even in so apparently voluminous a correspondence, the historian's chronic problem of balance. The silence of the sources makes our accounts unbalanced inevitably. For some parts of Erasmus' life and activity, the evidence is thin or absent.[105] This is the case for his two or three years' service in the 1490s with Henry of Bergen, bishop of Cambrai and man of influence and power in the Netherlands church and the Burgundian state. Richard Schoeck rightly presses the evidence and speculates on Erasmus in the unlikely role of official secretary. He puts in doubt the standard picture of the humanist as naïve and ignorant about affairs of state.[106] The contrast between Thomas More, man of state, and Erasmus, remote intellectual, is an accepted part of the standard image. Both Germain Marc'hadour (at Rotterdam) and Hubertus Schulte Herbrüggen (in another sesquiquatercentenary volume, from Wolfenbüttel, to which we will return) cast doubt on the cliché. Far from wringing his hands over More's entry to royal service, Erasmus presented it to humanist colleagues as a model.[107]

More is a player in another presentation by Marc'hadour, on Erasmus and Tyndale in the Tours volume, More appearing, of course, as Tyndale's orthodox critic. This is one of a number of essays from 1986 on Erasmus' relations with Reformers.[108] Tyndale, who was a generation behind Erasmus, graduating when the older man was at his apogee, set himself to fulfil for England the promise of the *Paraclesis*, the scriptures in the vernacular. For More, Tyndale's *New Testament* was a 'Trojan horse' and, indeed, the first edition carried many of Luther's glosses. Yet, as Marc'hadour admits, Tyndale remained, consciously and avowedly, indebted to Erasmus, even when he was passing into Luther's orbit and beyond, indebted, for example, for his preference for verbal over ceremonial expression of the faith.[109] Melanchthon's debt was greater still and the connection closer. At Tours again, J.M. Weiss demonstrated how Melanchthon maintained the connection, even in Luther's circle and among the Lutherans after the great Reformer's death. He deals with two orations prepared by Melanchthon, one of 1536 and the other, about Erasmus by name, of 1557. Naturally, he emphasizes their rhetorical features, especially those of the second, delivered by Bartholomaeus Kalkreuter at an academic promotion. Historical and biographical material was subject to the purpose of 'instruction and persuasion to good example.'[110] On both occasions, Melanchthon's concern was with concord. It was explicit in 1536, just after Erasmus' death, when there was still hope for the reconciliation of Protestants and Catholics in Germany, and tacit in 1557, when the prospects for peace on all sides were gloomier. Then, Melanchthon, through Kalkreuter, addressed another controversial question of the time, the place of humanistic studies in the curriculum. He used Erasmus for making his case and made of him Luther's forerunner and of humanism the first step to Reformation.[111]

Two essays, one in the Tours and the other in the Rotterdam volume, treat Erasmus' last years and the darkening atmosphere on the Catholic side. The first concerns a relatively unknown figure, the second one of the great princes of the age. Cassander of Col-mars-les-Alpes in Provence was a humanist and gifted teacher who had a brief correspondence with Erasmus in 1530–1.[112] This was a time and place wherein to be a friend of Erasmus was to have dangerous enemies, as Erasmus himself saw.[113] Jan Pender-grass's fascinating vignette is a study of Erasmians under pressure, with the lines between them and Lutherans not sharply drawn, at least in the eyes of their enemies.[114] Ferdinand of Habsburg was the pupil and patron of Erasmus. At Rotterdam, Jean-Claude Margolin presented two unpublished letters from him to the humanist, located (in draft) in the State Archives in Vienna and first made public in an exhibition there in 1974 and later included in an important thesis (Graz 1977) by Eberdorfer Heinz: 'Ferdinand I und Erasmus von Rotterdam: Ein Beitrag zur Geschichte des Humanismus in Osterreich.' They, too, belong to 1531 and to Erasmus' time in Freiburg. Above all, they reflect the menacing atmosphere of the 1530s, with the aging humanist entangled in religious controversy and under personal attack and the prince promising protection.[115]

We thus come to Erasmus, subject of controversy and contro-versialist. A group of papers at Rotterdam took up the theme. Nelson Minnich, in a study of his attitude to the Fifth Lateran Council (1512–17), called initially by Pope Julius II and main-tained by his successor Leo X, raised again the issue of con-ciliarism and papalism.[116] Resistant to ideologies, Erasmus was neither a confirmed conciliarist nor an unqualified papalist. In the end, he accepted submission to the pope as necessary to faith, but he always retained a reserved, if not absolute, conciliarism.[117] What strikes a reader of this piece is how Erasmus' attitude to the Council was determined, not by ideology, but by the personali-ties concerned. Under Julius II, whom he condemned, it had no authority; under Leo X, whom he trusted, it deserved respect, though its decrees lacked the final authority of general accep-tance.[118] Personality bulked large in the savage controversy between Erasmus and Alberto Pio. Why, asks Chris Heesakkers, was Erasmus so bitter, scornful, and unrelenting in that contro-versy? Why did he show no regret, as he had done over Ulrich von Hutten, for pursuing the attack after his adversary's death? Heesakkers' answer is: he saw Pio as the pawn of a murderous conspiracy against him led by Aleander and the Franciscans. We see, as we have seen before, that, though the attacks on him were real and threatening, his own anxieties heightened and darkened the perception he had of them.[119]

Erasmus' relations with the Louvain theologians, which had bulked large at the quincentenary, when Louvain was a centre of commemoration, are represented here by a paper of M. Gielis, concerning the controversy between Erasmus and Latomus (Jacques Masson), occasioned in part by the deaths of the first Protestant martyrs in the Netherlands. That controversy was representative. Latomus stood, against his opponent's reductive approach to dogma, for an integral dogmatism; the whole body of dogma, received through tradition, must be accepted; even opinions held in common by the scholastic theologians belong to the deposit of faith.[120] For Erika Rummel, writing on Masson in her *Erasmus and His Catholic Critics*, the crux was the relative authority of scripture and the Fathers on one side and the scholastics on the other.[121] Her paper on Erasmus' Spanish critics was the most important in this group at Rotterdam, partly because it presaged that major work. His controversy with the Spanish monks passed through three stages. It is possible, Rummel remarked at Rotterdam, to trace these stages in other controversies.[122] First, there was the time of rumour and uncertainty. Then Erasmus' anxieties and obsessions, even his paranoia, in this case with the role in the affair of his English opponent Edward Lee, had free rein.[123] At the second stage, matters came to a head with formal investigations into his orthodoxy; in Spain it cast monks and theologians into 'frenetic activity' in preparation for an official conference at Valladolid, where his friends and enemies were in direct confrntation. In the third stage, Erasmus, often against the advice of his friends, took the offensive with his rebuttals and apologies. His forensic skills were formidable and his spirit staunch; he made few concessions of any substance to his critics.[124] Here is the clearest evidence of the kind of man he was.

Rummel's larger work (1989) is finely textured, with quotations from the controversial works, and especially the correspondence, neatly deployed and Erasmus' wit often on display. There is a reminder, if we needed reminding, of how ungracious sixteenth-century controversy was. Erasmus himself was not behindhand in needless sarcasm, accusations of bad faith, and arguments in bad faith of his own, and what Chris Heesakkers

aptly calls playing the man and not the ball.[125] Broadly, he had
the best of the argument – in his own terms (in rebuttal of a common charge, he was not a Lutheran and avowed submission to
the teaching authority of the church) and in modern terms
(against literalism and a dogmatism that closed issues off prematurely, he let the scriptural evidence lead and kept options
open).[126] Above all, we see again how he held to his positions and
gave little ground to his critics. The many writers since the
Enlightenment who have found him as a character weak, malleable, susceptible to pressure have not come to terms with the
documents of these debates.

A further conclusion can be drawn from the essays and other
works reported in this section. Despite his broad allegiance to the
Roman church, Erasmus had unrelenting enemies on the Catholic
side, many of them belonging to powerful orders and organizations used to getting their way. At the same time, despite his own
bitter controversies with the Reformers (Luther, above all, and
the Strasbourg Reformers), he had friends and supporters on the
Protestant side who continued to avow their loyalty, even, as in
Melanchthon's case, in circumstances difficult and testing for
them. This complex result derives, not just from the essays of
1986, but from Erasmus scholarship generally in our time. When
stumps are drawn on Erasmus interpretation in the twentieth
century, this must be entered in the final score.

A clutch of essays in the Liège volume demonstrates how the
complexity continued in the generations after Erasmus' death,
especially in Counter-Reformation circles. If the Counter-Reformation was, over all, hostile to Erasmus, there were shades of
opinion as, for example, between the Jesuits Antonio Possevino
(uniformly hostile) and Peter Canisius (more poised).[127] With his
own name and writings suppressed, some authors could still
refer to him, even to his most contentious works like the *Annotations* and the *Folly*, their own 'silences and discretions' drawing
attention silently to him.[128] Charles Béné, in indicating how
François de Sales built on Erasmian positions, like a piety
addressed to the laity, the acceptance of mental prayer, and the
valuing of pagan wisdom, points to a burgeoning field of
research, Erasmus' influence on the *spirituels* of the late sixteenth
and the seventeenth centuries.[129]

We are here already broaching the subject of the next and last
section of our review of the sesquiquatercentenary, studies on

Erasmus' posthumous reputation. Before entering on that, we should note the broadest treatment of the theme 'Erasmus and his audiences' in 1986, a collection of essays (already referred to a number of times) from a conference (3–5 November 1986) at the Wolfenbüttel Renaissance centre, *Erasmus und Europa*. It shows how the question of nationality, which preoccupied nineteenth-century historians, remains of interest, even to our contemporaries.[130] Even so, there is an uncertainty embedded in this collection. August Buck, in his Introduction, makes no clear affirmation of the theme 'Erasmus and the nationalities.' He begins with Erasmus' cosmopolitanism, his sense of a Europe-wide 'respublica literaria,' but he also notes the importance, for the spread of his ideas, of vernacular translations.[131] Full studies of Erasmus' national audiences here concern the Netherlands, France, Spain, and Hungary.

We have seen how, in this volume, Léon Halkin links Erasmus to his homeland through the ambience of the *Devotio moderna* (one must add his connections with friends, especially Jean Vitrier, who inspired in him a kind of conversion, and patrons).[132] J.-C. Margolin, as we have also seen, in seeking an explanation for the *contretemps* between Erasmus and Lefèvre d'Etaples, speaks, 'a little schematically, even cavalierly,' of a Christian humanism *à la française* and a Christian humanism *à la néerlandaise*, the one more mystical and Spirit-filled, in debt to Platonists and Neoplatonists, the other more human and down-to-earth, in debt to the *Devotio moderna* and the Brethren of the Common Life. Thus, despite the more sceptical mood about the *Devotio moderna*, especially in the Netherlands, it retained still, in 1986, a place and a residual explanatory power in Erasmian historiography. Margolin's broader interest is in Erasmus' understanding of the common life and culture of France in its concrete reality and his relations with sociocultural circles there. May one find in Erasmus' ideas, he asks, consonances with the outlook of the Gallican church and the policies of Francis I? He finds, running through French culture, an Erasmian stream, putting, in thought, the concrete before the abstract, the ethical before the speculative.[133]

It is instructive that, in *Erasmus und Europa*, Erasmus' relations with England come down to his friendship with one man, Thomas More,[134] and the German world is represented by an essay on Erasmus and the Reformation, by the distinguished Lutheran theologian Bengt Hägglund. It is as though we had returned full circle to Seebohm's preoccupation with Erasmus' English friends and to the many early twentieth-century works on Erasmus and Luther. For, though Hägglund recognizes that scholarship has broadened its understanding of Erasmus' relation with the Reformation beyond the polemics between him and Luther, this is essentially a study of their two theologies. Hägglund follows Manfred Hoffmann in attributing to Erasmus a dualist Christology (rather than a fully incarnational one, like Luther's), which had its foundation in philosophic idealism and bordered on the docetic. Would a study of the *Paraphrases*, especially the *Paraphrase* of John 1, confirm this judgment?[135] The tendency to make of him a systematist and its perils persist in studies of Erasmus and the Reformation.

Dietrich Briesemeister traces, through a correspondence that was limited in time and scope but intense, the trajectory of Erasmus' relation with Spain, from early distaste or distrust through enthusiastic affirmation and unreal hopes to a disenchanted silence. The initiative was not his; he was responding to moves in Spain by his admirers, translators, and commentators. In noting that, Briesemeister recognizes his essay as a late gloss on Bataillon's 'Meisterwerk.'[136] Correspondence with Hungary was, it would seem, equally intense, but the connections were on a narrower front. This was, as yet, a land without universities and printing shops. The first enthusiasts for Erasmus in Hungary, in the time when his theological works were becoming known there, formed an elite, courtly circle, without secure institutional footing. Even so, he assisted in the emergence of a new kind of public consciousness among these people, combining a sense of the self and an awareness of civic duty. This elite was dispersed by the catastrophe at Mohács in 1526, the defeat by the Turks and the destruction of the Hungarian 'Renaissance state.'[137]

Agnes Rotoók-Szalay, in an essay extending for non-Hungarians what the quincentenary essays offered on this subject, makes that the first stage of a three-stage process. The Erasmism of the next generation of Hungarian literati (the second stage) struck deeper roots in the community, especially by heeding Erasmus' call for the vernacular Bible, for which there was a demand, notably from educated women. A characteristic figure, as well in his Erasmian self-awareness and sense of vocation as in his work, was Gábor Pesti, who translated the gospels and promoted other parts of the Erasmian program by his philological work and translation of Aesop. In the third stage, the hard lines drawn by Trent, the influx of Reformation ideas, and divisions among the Reformers themselves broke up what groupings there were and finally put an end to Erasmus' influence.[138]

The topic of 'Erasmus and the nations or nationalities' is perennially appealing but somehow, in the end, unsatisfying. It has a will-o'-the-wisp quality. That tells us something about Erasmus and about nationality and nation-building in his time. Briesemeister shrewdly observes that the trajectory of Erasmus' feelings about Spain is replicated in his relations with other countries, if not so sharply defined. 'He should never have left Italy; he should have stayed in England; would that he had gone to France; would that he had never seen Germany.'[139] But these – here is one side of the problem, the counterpart to his own changing moods and interests – are, in his time, not comparable political systems or cultural formations: Italy, England, France, Germany, not to mention Spain or Hungary.[140]

VI

In each of the great commemorations from which we have taken soundings in the contemporary interpretations of Erasmus (1936, 1967–70, 1986), there have been essays on his posthumous reputation, image-making about him and the clash of interpretations.[141] J. Sperna Weiland's remark that, by contrast with the collections of essays on his theology, politics, and views on education, this was the most modest section at Rotterdam in 1986, could be applied to all the commemorations. Nevertheless, from scanning the whole array of that year, it is possible to conjecture an increasing interest in this theme.

At Liège, as we have seen, Roland Crahay, Charles Béné, and Michael Screech recalled contrasting appreciations in the age of Catholic (or Counter-) Reformation.[142] Along with her touching recollections of her teachers and mentors (Allen, Bataillon, and Renaudet), Margaret Phillips reviewed the change over a century from the agnostic Erasmus of Emile Amiel's *Erasme: Un libre-penseur du XVIe siècle* (1889) to Michael Screech's mystic.[143] At Rotterdam, Cornelis Augustijn recognized, in Hutten's and Luther's polemics against Erasmus in his lifetime, the origins of a prevailing hostile image in Germany, which Joseph Lortz reiterated in the mid-twentieth century.[144] To his studies over the years on the appreciation of Erasmus in his home-town, Nicolaas van der Blom added 'some remarks,' especially on the vicissitudes of his statue there. He mentions great names in the history of Erasmus interpretation (Hollanders or based in Holland), including Bayle (with a legend about a threatened sale of the statue to Basel in 1672) and J.B. Kan, Rector of the Gymnasium Erasmianum in the late nineteenth century, whose scepticism about it began the modern study of Erasmus' autobiographical fragment, the *Compendium vitae.*[145]

It is noticeable that the moment in the history of Erasmus interpretations which has most attracted attention across all three commemorations is that between the early Enlightenment and the revolutionary epoch at the end of the eighteenth century.[146] Werner Kaegi offered a classic essay in the genre at Basel in 1936 in his 'Erasmus im achtzehnten Jahrhundert.' It traces the journey of Erasmus' reputation from a time in the seventeenth century when he was seen as but a master of Latin style to his recovery in the eighteenth century of a central position in cultural, and even theological, history. At least until the emergence of other possibilities in the *Sturm und Drang* and Romanticism, the image was favourable and belonged to the Enlightenment.[147] Three papers of 1969 touched on elements in the prehistory of this recovery in Erasmus' reputation, one on the devotion to the great humanist of the free-thinking doctor Guy Patin, another on his rehabilitation as essentially orthodox by a writer who had Jansenist connections and irenic sympathies. This was an orthodoxy not incompatible with his attacks on contemporary legalism and superstition, on the tyranny of the monks and theologians and the embroilment of the hierarchy in worldly affairs.[148] The third concerned a French translation of the *Enchiridion* from the early eighteenth century, which likewise, and with the help of bowdlerizing touches, affirmed Erasmus' Catholic orthodoxy.[149] These rehabilitations were not purely Catholic events; they were part of a broad cultural shift, presenting an Erasmus, as the translator of the *Enchiridion* put it, appropriate 'for an age as enlightened as ours.'[150] It is not enough to make a contrast between such devout writers and, say, Pierre Bayle, seen as precursor of the full Enlightenment. In many quarters, there was a sense of enlightenment and the dawning of a new age. This shift made possible the first great recovery in the reputation of Erasmus after its disastrous plunge in the era of religious wars. So this study of the history of Erasmus' reputation, begun in the 1960s, comes full circle to the main themes of my *Phoenix of His Age* (1979).

For 1986, Jean-Claude Margolin wrote a characteristically long and rich essay on two eighteenth-century translations of the *De Contemptu mundi*. It continues an interest Margolin had already shown in Erasmus as seen in the Enlightenment.[151] The first translation was by the same translator as that of the *Enchiridion*.[152] The second was of the late eighteenth century, by another *parlementaire*, issue of the *noblesse de robe* of Burgundy, Claude-Charles Devoyo, born at Dijon in 1745 and dying, as an *émigré*, at Constance in 1797.[153] The point of interest for us is the contrast between two translators seventy years apart, the one, if enlightened in his own way, still protective of, even defensive (to the point of bowdlerizing) about, Erasmus' Catholicism, the other addressing his fellow-Masons of Dijon in the spirit of Bayle. Devoyo's frankness is more faithful to Erasmus, especially in the translation of the last chapter of the *De Contemptu*, which is critical of monasticism.[154] Here, in this contrast between two translations of a minor work, is a small measure of the intellectual transformations of the century.

In an equally rich essay in *Erasmus und Europa*, Cornelis Reedijk recalls the earlier stages of that transformation and of Erasmus' rehabilitation (in this case on the Protestant side), with a study of Jean Le Clerc, the indefatigable editor of his *Opera omnia* (1703–7). 'Earlier stages' may be misleading, for Le Clerc had predecessors in being well disposed towards Erasmus, especially among the Arminians and liberals of Holland.[155] Reedijk finds a certain 'ecumenical innocence' in Le Clerc's wish to present an Erasmus attractive to all parties. But he also notes the absence of Le Clerc's name from the title-pages of the edition, witness to his and his publisher's prudence in light of the affront his critical studies had given the Calvinist ministers.[156] It is not anachronistic to see Le Clerc as forerunner of the Protestant Enlightenment and liberal theology.[157]

There have been two times of recovery in Erasmus' reputation, one in the eighteenth and the other in the twentieth century. The first was in reaction against the rigidities of the confessional age and its sometimes murderous party spirit; the second surmounted the mixed press Erasmus had received in the nineteenth century and the sharp contradictions then over his character and religion. The tendency in modern thinking, especially among those emphasizing his Catholic orthodoxy, is to widen the gap between these two experiences of rehabilitation, the first producing a rational, tolerant, and free-thinking Erasmus, the second a spiritual, loyal, and devout one. The content of the two experiences may well be different; yet, their respective dynamics may bear comparison. Let us conclude these studies on the interpretation of Erasmus by reviewing in summary three English-language biographies of around 1990 and test the issue by comparing them with the eighteenth-century biographies at the peak of the first great Erasmus revival.

VII

It would be too much to claim that these three works (Richard Schoeck's *Erasmus of Europe*, James McConica's *Erasmus*, and James Tracy's *Erasmus of the Low Countries*) represent three main positions in Erasmus interpretation. Nevertheless, one is able to trace a movement from (in the first) an Erasmus essentially comfortable in the tradition, or traditions, to (in the third) an Erasmus by and large in confrontation with the culture.

Schoeck's two volumes are the most ambitious Erasmus biography of their generation. They build on Schoeck's studies on Renaissance humanism and jurisprudence, Thomas More, and, of course, Erasmus.[158] From the last, Schoeck had already gathered a number of his previous papers and essays in *Erasmus Grandescens* (1988), which affords a larger view than the biography allows of his methodology and intellectual or historical assumptions. In that respect, the latter's notes also repay careful reading.

Late in his second volume, Schoeck finds Erasmus' concept of himself caught in W.S. Heckscher's words about the Holbein portrait of 1525, which speaks 'of the humanist's self-denying suffering ... reveals his constancy and tranquillity amidst tribulations, and ... proclaims the ultimate triumph of man's dignity in spite of all the vagaries of Fortune.' Schoeck accepts Erasmus' concept of himself so defined: a Stoic *tranquillitas*, in harmony with self and the world. Schoeck's biography of Erasmus is a study in equilibrium.[159]

That sense of self could be arrived at only, as we would expect, after struggle and growth. This is for Schoeck, as for Sowards, a balanced personality, but for Schoeck it took longer, and a larger zone of edginess remained. From an unstable and unhappy childhood, with its aura of shame, Erasmus won through to psychic wholeness, of which the *Adagia* were a symbol. That book grew from slender beginnings to rounded fullness, comparable to the tower Carl Jung 'built in sections.' The task of an intellectual biography of Erasmus, Schoeck says, is to 'study the grand maturing of Erasmus.' He uses a theory of 'liminality,' of thresholds or stages of life. Liminality has two aspects, mental (bringing over the threshold of consciousness, as in Erasmus' articulating in the 1490s his humanist ambitions) and sociocultural (as in the move from monastery to bishop's court). Schoeck takes the traditional view that an important threshold came around 1500, with Erasmus thereafter turning his humanist skills to scriptural study under the influence of 'two holy and learned men,' John Colet and Jean Vitrier. They were models of that combination of holiness and learning which became Erasmus' own ideal. This characterization discloses a difficulty with Schoeck's harmonizing narrative, with biography as 'growth by stages.' Colet and Vitrier, the recent literature suggests, were not only holy and learned, but root-and-branch men, profoundly radical and confrontational, at odds with the civility, the attuning of the classical and Christian, the human and divine, which was part of Erasmus' ideal. Did he perhaps learn from his disjunctures from them as much as from his conjunctures with them? In any case, was not his maturing sense of vocation mostly his own work?[160]

The emergence of a personal vocation is the main theme of Schoeck's biography. Throughout his account, independence and commitment are in counterpoint. Erasmus showed independence of mind from the beginning. His monastic profession, Schoeck says, was sincere, but for him it was a false vocation. Here Schoeck's is again a mollifying, harmonizing narrative. Following Richard DeMolen, he has the mature Erasmus living as a canon regular but in another setting than the monastery (the world) and engaged in other work (his writings). It is possible to give a harder reading than this to his exchanges with his prior. I find (the dangers of anachronism admitted) his vocation closer to that of the modern public intellectual than to Schoeck's 'independent cleric living in but not of the world,' though the latter's expressions, 'not openly defying canon law, but circumventing it; not openly defying his prior, but not agreeing with him,' seem just. Erasmus' common feeling with, indeed his exaltation of, the laity helps justify the harder reading.[161]

Schoeck relates Erasmus' intellectual and spiritual maturing to the tradition or traditions. In line with Halkin and against Post (and Augustijn), he considers the *Devotio moderna* a creative force in late-medieval culture and a constructive influence on Erasmus. Spiritual debts are not always avowed, he rightly says. This may well be what he means by Erasmus' 'received medievalism.' In general, the humanist was faithful to tradition, though his relation to it was free: 'Living tradition is process, not product.' This freedom distinguished Erasmus sharply from the Thomas More of the Reformation controversies, for whom tradition had become a fixed deposit. As for the classical tradition, Schoeck is with those who make words, language, and Ciceronian rhetoric central to Erasmus' purposes. 'The fusion of the classical and the Christian' was for him an achievable objective, and Schoeck agrees with him, in the line of Rudolf Pfeiffer's great essays of the inter-war years. He adds a distinctive and heartening touch. The *philosophia Christi*, based on this conflation, was strongly moralistic, but not puritanical. There was in Erasmus, along with awareness of the complexities of life, joy and exuberance and 'a sense of felt life.' The question remains: does not this fusion require, in last resort, an act of faith? Might the last generations of the twentieth century, which stood outside or beyond the culture it produced, be more aware of that than those who took it as a given?[162]

Schoeck warns then against taking Erasmus too bookishly, but texts remain, of course, fundamental for him. In approaching Erasmus' texts and the texts for his life, like the letters, Schoeck applies two principles, first, the historical imperative of placing the text in context and, secondly, the principle of intertextuality. The latter means at its simplest linkage between texts, cross-referencing, which works by evocation. It shows how a text operates at different levels and with different points of reference. It can disclose the interweaving of the classical and the Christian, for example, and demonstrate Erasmus' historical significance as a bridge-builder.[163]

I am wanting to suggest that Richard Schoeck's Erasmus, critical, reformist, in some ways contradictory, still had a positive, fruitful relationship with his environment. He was imbued with the late-medieval spirituality of Thomas à Kempis; he remained committed to the medieval religious culture represented by the Augustinian canons regular; he found in the classical or patristic devotion to words or the Word the source of good order and civility; he was, at least up to his last subdued years, confident of the civilizing effect of an education incorporating the classical-Christian amalgam.[164]

James McConica's extended essay of 1991 presents a more radical Erasmus. It, too, links him to tradition, in the historical sense, since his theological position was in a line running back to Augustine's *De doctrina*, through Jerome, Lactantius, Ambrose, Hilary, Bede, and Gregory the Great, and also in a philosophical sense. That is because education in the *bonae litterae* 'derives its regenerative power finally from the Word, to the degree that it is vested in traditions stemming from authentic wisdom.' Already in the 1490s the *Antibarbari* taught a *Logos* theology which unites primordial wisdom (as in proverbs) and the incarnation of the Word. Erasmus' thinking for McConica, as for Schoeck, is strongly unitary, 'a single fabric, woven in many hues and from more than one fibre, but it is the fabric of Christian culture.'[165]

Nevertheless, when McConica turns to Erasmus' theological writings, the radical edge of his enterprise appears more sharply. The whole Erasmus is in the *Paraclesis* with its 'proclamation of lay authority.' Compared with the *Devotio moderna*, which was backward-looking, an adaptation of the monastic tradition (this is a fair judgment on the long-discussed issue), the *Enchiridion* expressed a fresh and contemporary vision. It was a practical wisdom accessible to lay people freed of clerical direction and domination, not unlike, one senses, the civic humanism of the Italians. The image of the three circles in the letter to Paul Volz depicts a Christendom where the true relationships are set, not by order or status, but by interior disposition and, above all, by love. There were deficiencies (in understanding scholastic theology, for example) and confusions (between Platonist and Pauline doctrines of the body) and also, of course, conservative counterweights, above all in Erasmus' teaching on Christian community and consensus. This last, however, was no defence of church structures and hierarchies. On that front, he showed a subversive, iconoclastic face.[166]

The title of James Tracy's *Erasmus and the Low Countries* might be misleading if it were taken to promise essentially a study of his relation with a region of Europe. Its interest is both broader and narrower than that. This is a general biography, but it confronts Erasmus with, in particular, the contemporary culture and society of his homeland. For Schoeck, the urban, bourgeois culture of

the Netherlands appears as background to Erasmus' beginnings.[167] In Tracy's narrative, it has a more active, confrontational
role in the humanist's development. The radicalism identified by
McConica is here given specific point. The culture and society of
his time were strongly corporative, and against that Erasmus
struck out towards a kind of individualism. The members of
Christian society were individual human beings, not corporate
entities, as the social organizations of the time assumed. Erasmus' critique hit the ecclesiastical institution, too, for the church
hallowed the corporate society at all levels, from kinship connections through the town and village communities to the religious
orders themselves. The mendicant orders displayed corporatism
in its worst form. The battle for what was dearest to Erasmus –
the *bonae litterae* and reform in the church – was a battle against
the 'mendicant tyrants.' If he wanted to empower the laity, he
also wanted to enhance the status, socially and spiritually, of the
secular, parish clergy. In Tracy's eyes, reform for Erasmus meant
freeing the gospel of Christ (in the two senses of his teaching and
his centrality as object of faith) from the clutter of ages, from ceremonialism with its attendant distortion of theology and misuse of
ecclesiastical authority. These two, more than ever apparent in his
own time, served the greed and ambition of the powerful. If what
happened in the 1520s was a 'Reformation gone wrong,' his controversies with the Reformers never drove him back into the arms
of old enemies, the scholastic theologians, the papal apologists
and 'mendicant tyrants.' If Tracy accepts the view (by far the
majority view now) that Erasmus intended to remain loyal to the
Catholic church, he is still picturing somebody who was at odds
with much in inherited Catholic culture and in no way a forerunner of Counter-Reformation or of confessionalization. Against
both militants on his own side and the more strident Protestant
Reformers, he offered a quest for mutual accommodation, his
fundamental principle of concord, not (what was barely conceiv-
able) 'toleration as a principle of civil law.' On this last point,
Tracy follows the article of 1991 by Mario Turchetti, 'Une question mal posée: Erasme et la tolérance. L'idée de sygkatabasis.'
Yet, if no herald of toleration in the modern sense, he was deeply
antipathetic to forcing consciences.[168]

These three writings (the last in our study) have much in common in their interpretation of Erasmus: the humanist foundations
in grammar and rhetoric; the fusion of Christian and classical cul-

tures (differences remain still about how complete and successful th fusion could be); a broadly Catholic spirituality, one strand within the 'multilayered' structure of Catholicism (the expression is Tracy's);[169] a social activism on behalf, above all, of peace and concord. In all this, they are heirs of sixty years of Erasmus scholarship. The picture of Erasmus' personality is also recognizable from one to the other: on the down side, his hypersensitivity and unexpected (for a pacifist) bellicosity in controversy, on the up, his charm and capacity for friendship and, less predictably, his profound light-heartedness, Schoeck's 'exuberance,' Tracy's 'moral optimism,' and McConica's 'mercurial intelligence.'[170] Yet, there is a significant range from Schoeck to Tracy. In a broadbrush way, it can be put as the difference between one coming to Erasmus from the side of literary and religious traditions and one coming from the side of sociocultural formations. I find the difference epitomized in their respective views on Erasmus' anti-Semitism, a disputed and still unresolved issue. Schoeck considers the charge not proved; for him, Erasmus' expressions against the Jews are aimed, metaphorically, at Christian failings, 'Judaizing' or excessive legalism or ceremonialism in religion. Tracy approves the charge, for he sees anti-Semitism as a hateful expression of Erasmus' suspicion of those who, behind the scenes, manipulate influence and opinion for nefarious ends, as with the converted Jew Pfefferkorn in the Reuchlin affair. On the issue itself, one can accept the theological metaphor demonstrated by Schoeck, without denying the racist edge to Erasmus' language.[171]

The recovery of his reputation as a religious thinker and the recovery of his connection with the rhetorical tradition are the two great achievements of Erasmus scholarship in the second half of the twentieth century. Within the first, a fair range of opinion remains, from the Roman Catholic Erasmus to the 'protoliberal,'[172] but the broad judgment is universally accepted. On the second, scholarly work continues, but the fact is again incontestable. The three biographies just considered make these things plain. The biographies of John Jortin and Jean Lévesque de Burigny, landmarks in the first major recovery of Erasmus' reputation in the mid-eighteenth century, naturally cover similar ground. Jortin, for example, said: 'This worthy man spent a long and laborious life in an uniform pursuit of two points; in opposing barbarous ignorance and blind superstition; and in promoting useful literature and true piety.'[173] But demonstrating to a twentieth-century reading public Erasmus' connection to the classical rhetorical tradition requires specific academic preparation and unusual scholarly skills in a high degree. In Jortin's and Burigny's time, if the humanist age itself could be said to have come to an end a century before,[174] a Latinate 'republic of letters' still persisted. On the religious question, both Jortin (on the Protestant side) and Burigny (on the Catholic side) had escaped the narrows of confessionalism. Yet, they lived still within a recognizably Christian civilization, if not exactly Christendom. If, in the second half of the twentieth century, that civilization has finally petered out, a new challenge is posed to the reputation of (and the public's interest in) the great Christian scholar, whose image as 'pious Erasmus' has just now been secured.[175]

Conclusion:
Erasmus in 2001

What has been accomplished in Erasmus interpretation in the twentieth century is plain. The last paragraph of the last chapter summed up the two main considerations. He has emerged, finally, as an important religious thinker and contributor to the Christian tradition, many would say as a theologian. He has been related to the classical rhetorical tradition, which determined his methodologies, his literary and scholarly assumptions and expectations. These two considerations come together in his preoccupation with texts, central to both the Christian and rhetorical traditions. A third matter, dealt with here in chapter 2, deserves mention, his social and political thought. That was radical enough for some to link him with liberation theology, but realist enough to save him from the charge (still occasionally heard) of shallow moralizing.

Within the broad consensus, there are differences of a fairly specific kind. There are differing opinions over his personal vocation and what he meant by his liberty. There are those who find him a settled personality, settled by his intellectual and spiritual commitments. There are others who, with or without the benefit of psychohistory, find his a tense personality, under strains imposed especially by the unhappy circumstances of his early life. Such differences are not great gulfs, but they are not insignificant either. The two views of his personality are not mutually exclusive, necessarily, but, if the issue were pressed, I would consider the case for the second more plausible.

Differences of interpretation over his thought are summed up in the questions about Erasmus' attitude to institutions. Did he have a weak understanding of structures? Was his appreciation of power too spiritualized, too sentimental? As for the church, in what sense was he anticlerical? What did his claims for the laity amount to? In the literature, there remain differences over these questions. The conclusion of this book is that, in his political thought, he was less anti-institutional and ignorant of political realities than has often been supposed, but that, in his ecclesiology, he was profoundly suspicious of institutional, bureaucratic, authoritarian understandings of the church. In all spheres, his outlook was essentially pastoral. From here leads out another range of questions. Was his outlook world-affirming or world-denying? Nearby are questions about his attitude to natural life, to marriage, to women and children; thus we circle back to monasticism and celibacy and church questions of that kind. It is not clear to me that the differences of interpretation on these matters right down to the present moment can be resolved. There are well-founded arguments that he distinguished sharply between spirit and flesh and was in a kind of inner retreat from the world. There are equally well grounded views that he exalted natural gifts and natural powers and cherished the ordinary lives of men and women in the world. The differences are no doubt related to the different writings on which the respective interpretations are based. In that respect, the rhetorical turn, the recognition that different works serve distinct rhetorical purposes, deserves to be pursued ever more vigorously.[1] Even so, I would not think it a scholarly defeat to end by recognizing that on this matter an unresolved tension remained with Erasmus all through, to the very end. In the circumstances of early modern times, a time of social change and cultural shift, that tension does him credit. It is a mark of his greatness.

If, as seems certain, 'Erasmus theologian' remains a dominant way of seeing him, there will be a continuing flow of monographs on his attitude to particular doctrines and books of the Bible, on his theological connections and on his own theological writings. These will correspond to the monographic studies now common on the other major figures of the Reformation era. His pastoral writings, relatively neglected so far, will be prominent, because the pastoral motif may well prove to be the thread linking his various endeavours as scholar and religious thinker. The *Ecclesiastes*, edited for ASD by Jacques Chomarat, is a candidate for more attention. Hilmar Pabel's book on his writings on prayer is exemplary in drawing out the pastoral theme. Pabel remarks also on the irenic significance of those writings; Erasmus was party to the 'considerable measure of devotional cross-fertilization' between Protestants and Catholics in the sixteenth century.[2] Just as works on Erasmus' rhetoric tend to bring out the open-ended elements in his thought, because of the place of debate in the rhetorical tradition, studies of his pastoral writings have an ecumenical tone, because that is how pastoral theology is now and, to an extent, has been in the past.[3]

Future studies will produce fresh, in some cases unpredicted, results on Erasmus and his audiences. That is the nature of archival research, on which progress in this area depends, as Seidel Menchi has demonstrated. Attached is the somewhat disembodied notion of 'Erasmianism.' As Erasmus himself has taken on more substance, achieved a firmer outline, that notion has become more wraithlike or, at least, more problematic and lacking in definition.[4] This is at any rate the impression left by the colloquium on the subject at Amsterdam in 1996. Perhaps analysis is jinxed by the use of the '-ism.' M.E.H.N. Mout suggests simply more work on the reception of Erasmus' writings (in her case, in the Netherlands), for which Seidel Menchi's paper for the colloquium (incorporating an inventory of Italian editions of Erasmus in the sixteenth century) provides one model.[5] But even then the issues are not easily resolved, as a little controversy earlier between Jan van Dorsten and Richard Schoeck demonstrates. Van Dorsten questioned whether Erasmus' influence in England and the Netherlands in the later sixteenth century corresponded to his fame. Influence came from being read, and being read from being published. The Dutch presses showed a reduced interest and, in England, translations of Erasmus virtually disappeared. In Protestant Europe, Erasmus had become a man of yesterday. Schoeck counted the evidence not decisive and spoke of influence through secondary sources. That is slippery ground, as van Dorsten's reply declared.[6] Even so, such inquiries and debates are the only way forward on the subject of Erasmus and his audiences, whether the '-ism' is used or not.

On how things stand for Erasmus in 2001, it is necessary to distinguish between Erasmus the scholarly project and Erasmus the figure, symbol, or image in the general culture The editing of his works is producing results in detail which scholarship will assimilate over time. In the nature of the case, this will reinforce the picture of Erasmus as scholar, as deployer of the resources of the ancient literatures and cultures, pagan and Christian, as heir to the traditions of Christian thought through the Middle Ages. Such work is, of course, indispensable. It clears away misconceptions and achieves a fuller understanding of his intellectual debts. It can also be subtly distorting by reducing his originality and diminishing the actuality of his thought. Notice André Godin's remark: by seeking to trace the smallest influence received by an author, does one not run the risk of reducing his literary creation to a laborious exercise in patchwork, of reducing to nothing the originality of his discourse, if not of his person?[7] How engaged was Erasmus, whatever intellectual resources he deployed? This is the issue of his personality in another form.

Another kind of distortion (some would think) is possible, but there will be profit in it as well as danger. Their common interest in texts cries out for a connection to be made between contemporary literary and cultural theory and Erasmus' life's work. Schoeck (on intertextuality), Tracy (on postmodernism), Kathy Eden (on hermeneutics), Gérard Defaux (on Derrida and writing) have been pioneers, and in the 1990s a flow of work has belatedly begun. There have been essays on the proverb as a discursive practice and its connection with friendship, community-building, and tradition; on the emergence of subjectivity in Erasmus, against the view that subjectivity in anything like the modern sense belongs only to a later period; on Erasmus' articulation of the boundary between the scriptural text and its readers, with reference to the New Criticism and Gadamer's hermeneutic circle; on Erasmus' use of commentary, not as subservient to the text, but as vehicle for his own persona.[8] The flow will quicken substantially. It is inconceivable that ways of thinking that have changed profoundly the study and teaching of literature, by, for example, questioning the established or assumed relationship between writer, text, and reader, will not affect writing on Erasmus. By this route, a new posthumanist generation of scholars may come into Erasmus studies.

If one relates this possibility to the second question, about Erasmus and the general culture, a paradox emerges. The bonding of Erasmus more closely than ever to the humanist tradition, one of the achievements of twentieth-century scholarship, has located him in an enclave to which diminishing numbers, even among the educated, have access. But an Erasmus taken up by critical theory is likely to appear in a linguistic and conceptual garb even more specialized and esoteric than the humanist. In short, whether the methodology is humanist or posthumanist, a continuing work of popularization (including translation) will be necessary, to which notable writers of the second half of the twentieth century, like Phillips, Bainton, Thompson, Halkin, Augustijn, and McConica, have shown the way.

Any reflection on Erasmus as a figure in the general culture must be speculative. Towards the end of *Phoenix of His Age*, I remarked that around 1700 Erasmus became 'again a figure of the cultural majority.'[9] I meant that, after the confessional age, so uncongenial to his reputation, the eighteenth century, not only the more strictly Enlightenment figures, but across a broad spectrum, found admirable the traits commonly ascribed to Erasmus, moderation, tolerance, religious syncretism (of a certain kind), a critical intellectual temper. To ask about his relation to 'the cultural majority' in 2001 is probably unhelpful and perhaps meaningless. But an exploration or two may be made. If the main achievement of Erasmus scholarship in the twentieth century is read as identifying him as, pure and simple, an orthodox Roman Catholic, then we have a figure of denominational, but not of general, interest. Only the Erasmus whose relation to late-medieval culture was a mix of alienation and commitment, whose sense of self was caught somewhere between the individualist and the communitarian, who – devout, practising Christian – yet had (whether one defines it as tolerance or condescension) a radical kind of openness, can arouse interest in this time. By influencing individuals and helping to create (through his writings and the literature about him) a climate of opinion, he may have contributed to the renewal of Catholicism in the twentieth century (Vatican 2) and the growth of ecumenism. May his conception of *humanitas* contribute, in the twenty-first century, to what G.W. Locher in a quincentenary lecture called a task 'still unfulfilled,' the dialogue of Christians and non-Christians, interfaith dialogue?[10]

That touches the problem of peace which Marcel Bataillon, in his 'Actualité d'Erasme' of 1969, put at the head of the list of Erasmian themes closest to our present preoccupations.[11] It was not easy to apply his writings on peace to the Cold War, where peace was maintained by a balance of terror. The wars of the twenty-first century will be more like the wars he knew, savage encounters along ill-defined frontiers, the depredations of warlords and ethnic supremos in volatile and unstable political systems. Even the mercenary, his ultimate *bête-noir*, has reappeared. Perhaps, as happened in America and Europe in the Napoleonic era and after 1914, little, popular editions of the *Bellum* and *Querela pacis* will appear in the capitals of Africa or Asia or the Middle East.

Finally, we must return to Erasmus' personality and ask about its continuing attraction to us. Some may find consoling the picture of him as a settled and composed personality. Others, as we have seen, find in his personality fissures, repressions, ambiguities. They (and I number myself among them) find this the more attractive Erasmus. His composure was bought at a cost. His wit can be gentle; it can break out into bitterness. In controversy, resentments and anxieties can get loose, countermanding the Christian imperative of love to which he was devoted and which runs as a *leitmotiv* through all his writings. These strains make him a figure of never-dying interest and still a man for our anxious and fragmented times.

Abbreviations

BIBLIOGRAPHIES

Quartorze années   Jean-Claude Margolin *Quartorze années de bibliographie érasmienne (1936–1949)* Paris 1969

Douze années   Margolin *Douze années de bibliographie érasmienne (1950–1961)* Paris 1963

Neuf années   Margolin *Neuf années de bibliographie érasmienne (1962–1970)* Paris and Toronto 1977

Quinze années   Margolin 'Quinze années de travaux érasmiens (1970–1985)' BHR 48 (1986): 585–619

COMMEMORATIVE VOLUMES

1936

Gedenkschrift   *Gedenkschrift zum 400. Todestage des Erasmus von Rotterdam* Basel 1936

1967–70

Actes   *Actes du Congrès Erasme Rotterdam 27–29 octobre 1969* Amsterdam 1971

Coll Eras: Mons   *Colloquium Erasmianum: Actes du Colloque International réuni à Mons du 26 au 29 octobre 1967* Mons 1968

Coll Tur   *Colloquia Erasmiana Turonensia* 2 vols, Paris 1972

Commém Nat   *Commémoration Nationale d'Erasme: Actes* Brussels 1970

Scrinium   J. Coppens (ed) *Scrinium Erasmianum* 2 vols, Leiden 1969

1986

Actes du Colloque International	Jacques Chomarat, André Godin, and Jean-Claude Margolin (eds) *Actes du Colloque International Erasme (Tours 1986)* Geneva 1990
Coll Eras: Liège	Jean-Pierre Massaut (ed) *Colloque Erasmien de Liège: Commémoration du 450e anniversaire de la mort d'Erasme* Paris 1987
Erasmus of Rotterdam	J. Sperna Weiland and W.Th.M. Frijhoff (eds) *Erasmus of Rotterdam: The Man and the Scholar* Leiden 1988
Erasmus und Europa	August Buck (ed) *Erasmus und Europa* Wiesbaden 1988

ERASMUS' WORKS

Allen	P.S. and H.M. Allen (eds) *Opus epistolarum Des. Erasmi Roterodami* 12 vols, Oxford 1906–58
ASD	*Opera Omnia Desiderii Erasmi Roterodami* Amsterdam 1969–
CWE	*The Collected Works of Erasmus* Toronto 1974–
Holborn	Hajo Holborn (ed) *Desiderius Erasmus Roterodamus: Ausgewählte Werke* Munich 1964
LB	Erasmus *Opera omnia*, ed J. Le Clerc, 10 vols, Leiden 1703–6
Olin *Christian Humanism*	John C. Olin (ed) *Christian Humanism and the Reformation: Selected Writings of Erasmus* 3rd edn, New York 1987
Reeve	Anne Reeve (ed) *Erasmus' Annotations on the New Testament: The Gospels* London 1986
Reeve and Screech	Anne Reeve and M.A. Screech (eds) *Erasmus' Annotations on the New Testament: Acts – Romans – I and II Corinthians* Leiden 1990
Thompson *Colloquies*	Craig R. Thompson *The Colloquies of Erasmus* Chicago and London 1965

GENERAL

AHR	*American Historical Review*
ARG	*Archiv für Reformationsgeschichte*
BHR	*Bibliothèque d'Humanisme et Renaissance*
Contemporaries	Peter G. Bietenholz (ed) *Contemporaries of Erasmus: A Biographical Register of the Renaissance and Reformation* 3 vols, Toronto 1985–7
DTC	*Dictionnaire de théologie catholique* 15 vols, 1903–50
ERSY	*Erasmus of Rotterdam Society Yearbook*

New Cath Enc	*New Catholic Encyclopedia* 15 vols, New York 1967
RQ	*Renaissance Quarterly*
SCJ	*Sixteenth Century Journal*
TRE	*Theologische Realenzyklopädie* Berlin/New York 1976–
Man On His Own	Bruce Mansfield *Interpretations of Erasmus c1750– 1920: Man On His Own* Toronto 1992
Phoenix of His Age	Mansfield *Phoenix of His Age: Interpretations of Erasmus c1550–1750* Toronto 1979

Notes

CHAPTER ONE

1 *Quartorze années* nos 66, 79, 157, 213, 336, 350, 391, 395, 397. Margolin's comprehensive bibliography, which includes journalism and ephemera, is an indispensable record of the 1936 celebrations. On the statuette, cf Nicolaas van der Blom 'The Erasmus Statues in Rotterdam' 8 n7.

2 On Erasmus, Rotterdam and the quatercentenary, *Quartorze années* nos 106, 128, 151, 371, 422; on Stuiveling, ibid nos 280–3, Anton van Duinkerken 'Nieuwe Erasmiana' 237–9. The papers of the conference on 10–11 July were published in *Bijdragen voor vaderlandsche geschiedenis en oudheidkunde* and separately as *Voordrachten gehouden ter herdenking van der sterfdag van Erasmus*.

3 *Quartorze années* nos 372, 393, 344

4 See ch 2.

5 J.N. van der Heijden 'Erasmus als pacifist' (cf *Quartorze années* no. 119)

6 *Quartorze années* no. 337

7 On Zeeland, P.J. Meertens 'Erasmus en Zeeland'; on popular beliefs and customs, Paul Hermant 'Le folklore dans les écrits d'Erasme'; Oene Noordenbos 'Erasmus en de Nederlanden.' Cf *Man On His Own* 274–80.

8 *Quartorze années* nos 65, 67; Daniel van Damme *Une heure à la maison d'Erasme et au vieux béguinage d'Anderlecht* 20–2

9 On Brabant, *Quartorze années* nos 201, 262; on Antwerp, ibid nos 369, 418 and Maurits Sabbe 'Erasmus en zijn Antwerpsche Vrienden'; on Louvain, *Quartorze années* no. 304

10 Paul Roth 'Die Wohnstätten des Erasmus in Basel,' in *Gedenkschrift* 270–81; Carl Roth 'Das Legatum Erasmianum,' in ibid 282–98; Emil Major 'Die Grabstätte des Erasmus,' in ibid 299–315; *Quartorze années* nos 180, 182, 184, 254, 272

11 On Paris, Margaret Mann 'Autour du Paris d'Erasme'; on Spain, *Quartorze années* nos 48, 261; on Seebohm, *Man On His Own* 338–41 and my 'Erasmus and Frederic Seebohm: The "Oxford Reformers," Down but Not Out?'; on England, Henry J. Cowell 'Erasmus' Personal and Literary Associations with England,' *Quartorze années* nos 360, 365; on Cambridge, ibid no. 107; on friendships, not lacking in tensions and ambiguities, Gertrud Jung 'Erasmus und Vives' and Ernst Staehelin 'Erasmus und Ökolampad in ihrem Ringen um die Kirche Jesu Christi,' in *Gedenkschrift* 130–43, 166–82

12 *Quartorze années* nos 133–4

13 John Joseph Mangan *Life, Character and Influence of Desiderius Erasmus of Rotterdam* 1:vii–viii, 282–3, 312, 2:15, 87. Mangan accepts the tradition that Erasmus' father was a priest at the time of his conception (2:62).

14 Ibid 1:viii, 176 (*Enchiridion*), 2:118–19, 157 ('latitudinarianism'), 287, 349, 381. A reviewer described Mangan's argument as a 'psycho-Catholic thesis' (*American Historical Review* 33 [1927]: 110).

15 Bart de Ligt 'Erasmiana' 657, 663–4 (criticism of Mangan), 667 (on Bart de Ligt, Herman Noordegraaf 'The Anarchopacifism of Bart de Ligt,' in Peter Brock and Thomas P. Socknat (eds) *Challenge to Mars: Essays on Pacifism from 1918 to 1945* 89–100, esp 98); G.A. Lindeboom 'Erasmus in zorgen'; *Quartorze années* nos 62, 70, 80, 218; on Lavater, *Man On His Own* 102–4

16 Huizinga 'In Commemoration of Erasmus'

17 *Quartorze années* nos 69, 77, 263

18 R. Casimir 'Erasmus' opvoedkunde en de opvoeder van nu' (report in *Nieuwe Rotterdamsche Courant*, summarized *Quartorze années* no. 380); J.H. Gunning 'Desiderius Erasmus, 27 October 1466(?)–12 Juli 1536' 140–1; Otto Kluge *Erasmus damals und heute* 10–11

19 Zweig's wife Friderike suggested he read Huizinga (D.A. Prater *European of Yesterday: A Biography of Stefan Zweig* 210).

20 *Quartorze années* nos 319–20, 529, 594, 879. On the book as a publishing success, despite Zweig's sincere indifference on that question, see Margolin *Erasme, précepteur de l'Europe* 356.

21 Zweig *Triumph und Tragik* (references to standard English translation in parenthesis) 23 (12), 57–8 (40–1) [Lavater], 62 (44), 67 (47), 84 (60) ['Nazarene purity'], 117–21 (85–8); on early twentieth-century theologians, *Man On His Own* 290–1

22 Zweig *Triumph und Tragik* 35 (22), 98–101 (71–3), 145 (107), 227–8 (169–70); Zweig *The World of Yesterday* 324; Prater *European of Yesterday* 8, 38

23 Zweig *Triumph und Tragik* 25 (14); *World of Yesterday* 229, 254; Mann to Zweig 8 November 1933 *Briefe* 1 (*1889–1936*) 338 (trans Prater *European of Yesterday* 216).

24 Zweig *Triumph und Tragik* 124 (90), 136 (100), 153–9 (113–18), 166 (124), 207 (155), 214 (160)
25 Zweig to Hesse 9 December 1933, in Sabine Kinder and Ellen Presser (eds) *Die Zeit gibt die Bilder, ich spreche nur die Worte dazu: Stefan Zweig 1881–1942* 127; Zweig to Schikele 27 August 1934, q. Prater *European of Yesterday* 229–30; Thomas Mann, q. Klaus Zelewitz 'Raconter l'histoire – est-ce un risque? Les biographies de Stefan Zweig' 23; Zweig to Klaus Mann 15 May 1933, in Kinder and Presser (eds) 127 (cf Margolin *Erasme, précepteur de l'Europe* 352–3); Zweig to Alfred Wolfenstein 15 October 1938, q. Prater 270
26 Critical judgments in 1936, *Quartorze années* nos 41, 102, 179, 204, 324; favourable judgments, W.M. van de Pas 'De onbekende Erasmus,' *Quartorze années* no. 310; for assessments of the rival views of B.H. Molkenboer *Erasmus* (critical) and H.J.J. Wachters *Erasmus von Rotterdam: Zijn leven en zijn werken* (favourable), see A. van Duinkerken 'Nieuwe Erasmiana' 228–32; see also H. Reijnen 'R.K. beoordeeling van Erasmus.' See further ch 5 below.
27 Dolfen *Die Stellung* 11–12, 30–3 (Gerson), 46–9 (Jerome), 84–8 (Scotus, Aquinas), 110–11; on Dolfen, ibid 114
28 Kenneth A. Strand (ed) *The Dawn of Modern Civilization: Studies in Renaissance, Reformation and Other Topics to Honor Albert Hyma* 5–10
29 Hyma 'Erasmus and the Oxford Reformers (1493–1503)' 212, 226–31, 239, 245–8. The publication history of this essay is complex; for convenience, the references are to the version in *Renaissance to Reformation*.
30 Hyma *The Christian Renaissance: A History of the 'Devotio Moderna'* 227, 229; *Youth of Erasmus* 41–2, 125, 127, 142, 168, 187, 204
31 Hyma *Youth of Erasmus* 164–5, 180; Strand *Dawn of Modern Civilization* 10
32 On Mestwerdt, *Man On His Own* 341–7
33 H.A. van Bakel 'Erasmus en Luther,' H. Reijnen 'Erasmus en Luther'; liberal Protestant views, *Quartorze années* nos 108, 174, 286, 307; Barthian response, ibid no. 169
34 *Quartorze années* nos 160, 171, 176; Walter Köhler 'Erasmus von Rotterdam als religiöse Persönlichkeit' 218–23; Erasmus and mission, *Quartorze années* nos 54, 139 (cf *Ecclesiastes* I ASD V-4 148 lines 314–17, 320–1, 325).
35 Eg, Rudolf Pfeiffer's 'Die Wandlung der "Antibarbari,"' in *Gedenkschrift* 50–67, which follows the complicated history of Erasmus' *Antibarbarorum liber* in a way which remained authoritative when K. Kumaniecki edited the work for ASD.
36 Moore 'The Search for Erasmus' 523; Werner Kaegi 'Erasmus im achtzehnten Jahrhundert,' in *Gedenkschrift* 205–27; J. Lindeboom 'Erasmus in de Waardeering van het Nageslacht'

CHAPTER TWO

1 Brendan Bradshaw 'Transalpine Humanism,' in J.H. Burns (ed.), with the assistance of Mark Goldie, *The Cambridge History of Political Thought 1450–1700* 127–8

2 R.B. Drummond *Erasmus: His Life and Character As Shown in His Correspondence and Works* 1:260

3 Quentin Skinner 'Meaning and Understanding in the History of Ideas,' in James Tully (ed) *Meaning and Context: Quentin Skinner and His Critics* 54; Skinner *The Foundations of Modern Political Thought* 1:xi

4 A poignant case in my 'Anguish of an Erasmian: P.S. Allen and the Great War'

5 L.K. Born 'Erasmus on Political Ethics: The *Institutio Principis Christiani*' 540, 543; *Education of a Christian Prince* 99–100

6 Isocrates (Loeb edition) 1:41, quoted Born *Education* 43; *Education* 98

7 Born 'Some Notes on the Political Theories of Erasmus' 226; 'Erasmus on Political Ethics' 543; *Education* 24n

8 Bainton 'The *Complaint of Peace* of Erasmus, Classical and Christian Sources' 219, 232–3

9 Isocrates 1:46–7

10 Otto Herding 'Isokrates, Erasmus und die Institutio principis christiani' 103, 110–14

11 Ibid 121, 124–5, 128, 132, 135–7; *aliter possidet*, ASD IV-1 166 line 985, CWE 27:236

12 Adams *The Better Part of Valor: More, Erasmus, Colet, and Vives on Humanism, War, and Peace, 1496–1535* chs 2, 5; James D. Tracy *The Politics of Erasmus: A Pacifist Intellectual and His Political Milieu* ch 3

13 Adams 78, 82, 108–9, 113, 165, 211

14 Ibid 3, 112. Cf W.K. Ferguson's review in *American Historical Review* 68 (1963): 720–1.

15 Tracy *Politics* 107; *Holland under Habsburg Rule 1506–1566* 65–73

16 Maurice Keen *Chivalry* 228–34, 243, 247

17 J.R. Hale *War and Society in Renaissance Europe 1450–1620* 91–7; J.H. Hexter 'The Education of the Aristocracy in the Renaissance'; D. Potter *A History of France 1460–1560* ch 6; H.F.K. van Nierop *The Nobility of Holland: From Knights to Regents 1500–1650* 220–1. On nobility in general, see Jonathan Dewald *The European Nobility 1400–1800*.

18 J.R. Hale *War and Society* 34; Adams *Better Part of Valor* 55–9; J. Scarisbrick *Henry VIII* 40–7; Steven Gunn 'The French Wars of Henry VIII,' in Jeremy Black (ed) *The Origins of War in Early Modern Europe* 28–51, esp 47. One would now need to take account of current work demonstrating that personal honour and prestige were central issues in international relations in the early modern period. See, eg, Susan Doran *England and Europe in the Sixteenth Century* ch 2; Glenn Richardson 'The Privy Chamber of Henry VIII and Anglo-French Rela-

tions, 1515–1520,' and now his *Renaissance Monarchy: The Reigns of Henry VIII, Francis I and Charles V* esp 36–8.

19 One thinks of J.N. Figgis' famous but implausible aphorism: 'Had there been no Luther there could never have been a Louis XIV.' Cf J.W. Allen *History of Political Thought* 29.

20 W. Maurer *Das Verhältnis des Staates zur Kirche nach humanistischer Anschauung, vornehmlich bei Erasmus* 13–14, 16–17, 19, 23, 25

21 James M. Estes '*Officium principis christiani*: Erasmus and the Origins of the Protestant State Church' 52

22 Estes '*Officium* '61. Cf my 'The Social Realism of Erasmus: Some Puzzles and Reflections' 10–16 and sources there cited.

23 Estes '*Officium*' 63–72. Cf Estes 'Erasmus, Melanchthon and the Office of Christian Magistrate,' in ERSY 18 (1998): 21–39.

24 C.R. Thompson 'Erasmus as Internationalist and Cosmopolitan' 167–8, 183–4, 190

25 Hans Treinen *Studien zur Idee der Gemeinschaft bei Erasmus von Rotterdam and zu ihrer Stellung in der Entwicklung des humanistischen Universalismus* 31–2, 38, 42, 56, 60, 75, 82, 89, 108. The relative thinness of Treinen's sources, his reliance on the *Colloquies*, has been noted (R.W. Scribner 'The Social Thought of Erasmus' 3n).

26 Treinen *Studien* ch 6; on Maurer 181–2n, 183–4

27 A. Renaudet *Etudes érasmiennes (1521–1529)* 92, 95–7; Pierre Mesnard 'L'expérience politique de Charles-Quint et les enseignements d'Erasme'; John M. Headley 'Gattinara, Erasmus, and the Imperial Configurations of Humanism,' esp 83; Frances A. Yates *Astraea: The Imperial Theme in the Sixteenth Century* 19–20; Suetonius, Erasmus to dukes of Saxony, 5 June 1517, Ep. 586 Allen 2:578–86, CWE 4:373–83. I have not seen Rafael Maria de Hornedo 'Carlos V y Erasmo' *Miscelánea Comillas* 30 (1957): 201–47 (summary in *Douze années* 116).

28 Elise Constantinescu Bagdat *La 'Querela Pacis' d'Erasme (1517)* ix; Margolin *Guerre et paix dans la pensée d'Erasme* 9; Pierre Brachin 'Vox clamantis in deserto: Réflexions sur le pacifisme d'Erasme,' in *Coll Tur* 1:257–9, 264–6

29 Georges Chantraine 'Mysterium et sacramentum dans le "Dulce bellum inexpertis,"' in *Coll Eras: Mons* 33–45; my 'Social Realism' 14–15; Robert Regout 'Erasmus en de theorie van den rechtvaardigen oorlog' 167, 169; José A. Fernandez 'Erasmus on the Just War' 222–6; Rudolf Padberg 'Erasmus contra Augustinum: Das Problem des bellum justum in der erasmischen Friedensethik,' in *Coll Eras: Liège* 285–91. See Erasmus in reply to the Sorbonne and Alberto Pio LB 9:841A, 1192F-1193B, and his annotations on Luke 3:17 (John the Baptist and the soldiers) and 22:36 (selling cloaks to buy swords), in Reeve 171–2, 212.

30 A.G. Weiler 'The Turkish Argument and Christian Piety in Desiderius Erasmus' *Consultatio de Bello Turcis Inferendo* (1530),' in *Erasmus of Rot-*

terdam 30–9, and 'La Consultatio de bello Turcis inferendo: une oeuvre de
piété politique,' in Actes du Colloque International 99–108; ASD V-3 3–
82. Cf J.-C. Margolin 'Erasme et la guerre contre les Turcs,' in Erasme:
le prix des mots et de l'homme ch 11. Michael J. Heath sees providence as
a key idea of the Consultatio: Turkish success indicated God's displea-
sure with Christendom ('Erasmus and the Infidel,' in ERSY 16[1996]
19–33, esp 29–33).

31 Constantinescu Bagdat La 'Querela Pacis' 16, 133
32 Ferdinand Geldner Die Staatsauffassung und Fürstenlehre des Erasmus
    von Rotterdam 8, 31, 142–5
33 Tracy Politics 11–17, 20, 49–52, 56–9
34 Pierre Mesnard L'essor de la philosophie politique au XVIe siècle 86, 89.
    Maritain's book derived from lectures given at Santander in 1934 and
    first published in Spanish; for his ideal of 'integral humanism,' see
    Eng tr True Humanism xvi, 65, 70, 81.
35 Mesnard L'essor 87–8. On Imbart de la Tour, Man On His Own 233–5
36 Mesnard L'essor 130
37 Ibid 105–18
38 Jacques Madaule, quoted Margolin 'Hommage à Pierre Mesnard,
    philosophe et humaniste (1900–69)' BHR 31 (1969): 645–9, at 649
39 Eberhard von Koerber Die Staatstheorie des Erasmus von Rotterdam 5
40 Ibid 21–5, 30–1n
41 Ibid 26–8, 30–1, 70
42 Otto von Gierke Natural Law and the Theory of Society 1500 to 1800,
    trans Ernest Barker, Translator's Introduction 1:lxii–lxxiv, lxxx–lxxxv;
    Community in Historical Perspective: A Translation of Selections from Das
    deutsche Genossenschaftsrecht (The German Law of Fellowship) trans
    Mary Fischer, ed Antony Black 109, 112
43 Koerber Die Staatstheorie 95–102
44 R.W. Scribner 'The Social Thought of Erasmus' 11
45 Ibid 4–10. Scribner refers to Mestwerdt, Schottenloher, and Hyma. On
    the first two, Man On His Own 341–7, on Hyma, ch 1 above.
46 Scribner 'Social Thought' 14; E. Durkheim The Rules of Sociological
    Method 7
47 Scribner 'Social Thought' 16, 24–5
48 Marjorie O'Rourke Boyle 'Erasmus' Prescription for Henry VIII:
    Logotherapy' 163–6; Erasmus to Henry VIII 23 August 1523 Ep 1381
    Allen 5:316 lines 128–9, 141, CWE 10:65 lines 135–6, 148–9
49 Richard F. Hardin 'The Literary Conventions of Erasmus' Education of
    a Christian Prince: Advice and Aphorism' 155–8, 162
50 Geldner Die Staatsauffassung 83, 85, 88, 92, 135, 148–9, 162
51 Geldner Die Staatsauffassung 163; Mesnard L'essor 137–8
52 Guido Kisch Erasmus und die Jurisprudenz seiner Zeit 60, 62–4, 67, 118,
    121–3 (Wernle, Troeltsch, Köhler, Renaudet), 130 (Geldner); on
    Wernle and Troeltsch and Renaudet, Man On His Own 290–2, 311–14;

on Köhler, above ch 1; *Summum ius, summa iniuria, Adagia* I.x.25 CWE 32:244–5
53 My 'Social Realism' 15
54 Rudolf Liechtenhan 'Die politische Hoffnung des Erasmus und ihr Zusammenbruch,' in *Gedenkschrift* 144, 150–1, 160; Johan Huizinga 'Ce qu'Erasme ne comprenait pas,' in *Verzamelde Werken* 6 250 (first published in *Grotius: Annuaire international pour 1936*)
55 Fritz Caspari 'Erasmus on the Social Functions of Christian Humanism' 79–80, 82–3, 88–91, 97, 102
56 Reprinted in Hexter *The Vision of Politics on the Eve of the Reformation: More, Machiavelli, and Seyssel* 72
57 Ibid 82–4, 89–91, 102–4
58 See note 49 above.
59 Skinner *Foundations* 1:256–9
60 J.C. Davis 'Utopianism,' in *Cambridge History of Political Thought 1450–1700* 330–1, 334–5; George M. Logan *The Meaning of More's 'Utopia'* 60, 218, 243–4, 249. Cf Dominic Baker-Smith *More's 'Utopia'* 241–3.
61 ASD IV-1 121–2, 190–2, CWE 27:260–2. On background to the tax revision of 1514, see Tracy *Holland under Habsburg Rule, 1506–66: The Formation of a Body Politic* 26–8; on the *accijns*, Tracy *A Financial Revolution in the Habsburg Netherlands: 'Renten' and 'Renteniers' in the County of Holland, 1515–1565* 56–7n.
62 Margherita Isnardi-Parente 'Erasme, la République de Platon et la communauté des biens,' in *Erasmus of Rotterdam* 40–5; John C. Olin 'Erasmus' *Adagia* and More's *Utopia'*
63 Herding, ASD IV-1 211–13
64 Liechtenhan 'Die politische Hoffnung' 145; Bradshaw 'Transalpine Humanism' 121, 127; Renaudet 'Erasme économiste,' in *Mélanges Abel Lefranc* 130–41, and *Humanisme et Renaissance* 194–200; Renaudet *Etudes érasmiennes* 76, 114–15; Margolin 'Erasme et le problème social,' in *Erasme, le prix des mots et de l'homme* 90–5, 103–8. Erasmus on work and wealth, 'Convivium religiosum' and 'Exequiae seraphicae' ('The Seraphic Funeral'), in Thompson *Colloquies* 73, 513.
65 Elisabeth Schneider *Das Bild der Frau im Werk des Erasmus von Rotterdam* 50–64, 72
66 Erika Rummel *Erasmus on Women* Introduction 3–5, 9–10; Elizabeth McCutcheon 'Erasmus' Representation of Women and Their Discourses,' in ERSY 12 (1992): 64–86, at 65, 69; Anne M. O'Donnell 'Contemporary Women in the Letters of Erasmus,' in ibid 9 (1989) 34–72, at 67, 69–72; J.K. Sowards 'Erasmus and the Education of Women'
67 Albert Salomon 'Democracy and Religion in the Work of Erasmus' 227–31, 234–7, 240–2, 247; Günther Rudolph 'Das sozialökonomische Denken des Erasmus von Rotterdam' 1076, 1079–80, 1083, 1087–92
68 Caspari 'Social Functions' 105

CHAPTER THREE

1 Cf Lucien Febvre 'L'Erasme de Marcel Bataillon,' in *Au coeur religieux du XVIe siècle* 97. For Renaudet's own reflections on the meaning of 'Préréforme,' see his 'Paris from 1494 to 1517 – Church and University; Religious Reforms; Culture and the Humanists' Critiques,' in Werner L. Gundersheimer (ed) *French Humanism 1470–1560* 65–6.

2 Marcel Bataillon *Erasme et l'Espagne* 1:2, 11

3 Bataillon 'Préface' 1950 *Erasme et l'Espagne* 2:8; ibid 1:2, 186, 189, 199; 'A propos de l'influence d'Erasme' ibid 3:305; Lucien Febvre 'Une question mal posée: Les origines de la réforme française et le problème des causes de la réforme,' in *Au coeur* 3–70

4 Bataillon *Erasme et l'Espagne* 1:40–5, 47–8, 51–3, 73–5, 98–102, 190–6

5 Ibid 78–80, 123, 143, 151

6 Ibid vi–vii, 83, 162, 166–7, 205–6, 226

7 Ibid ch 5 (Valladolid), 304–39 (translations), 341–2 (comparison with France), 345 (reformed monks), 414 (imperial reform), 466 (retreat of Erasmians), 513–14 (persecution)

8 Ibid 614, 629, 2:339

9 Ibid 1:847–8

10 Alvaro Huerga 'Erasmismo y Alumbradismo,' in Manuel Revuelta Sañudo and Ciriaco Morón Arroyo (eds) *El Erasmismo en España* 340. Cf the remark of Ottavio di Camillo in 1988 that the 1952 article of Eugenio Asensio discussed below had been the only attempt at serious revision and was without successors, so that 'today "Erasmismo" in Spain is often confused with humanism and other Renaissance trends' ('Humanism in Spain,' in Albert Rabil Jr [ed] *Renaissance Humanism: Foundations, Forms, and Legacy* 2 106n).

11 Devoto 'Note préliminaire sur cette deuxième édition française' in Bataillon *Erasme et l'Espagne* 1:ix–xii

12 Bataillon *Erasme et l'Espagne* 2:9. Cf Rudolph Schevill's review of 1939, 'Erasmus and Spain.'

13 Eugenio Asensio 'El erasmismo y las corrientes espirituales afines (Conversos, franciscanos, italianizantes)' 44–5, 54, 62, 64. Cf Bataillon *Erasme et l'Espagne* 2:10. Huerga attributes Bataillon's overvaluing of Erasmus as a theologian of the mystical body to his not being a professional theologian ('Erasmismo y Alumbradismo' 346).

14 Asensio 'El erasmismo' 70, 72–3, 86, 97. Cf Margolin *Erasme, précepteur* 155.

15 Bataillon, *Erasme et l'Espagne* 2:7, 17–18. Cf Joseph Pérez '"El erasmismo y las corrientes espirituales afines,"' in Sañudo and Arroyo (eds) *El Erasmismo en España* 324. Pérez' essay revisits the themes of Asensio's 1952 article, especially by questioning the assumption of Bataillon's generation that the sixteenth century was the start of modernity.

16 Bataillon 'L'Espagne religieuse dans son histoire. Lettre ouverte à Américo Castro,' in *Erasme et l'Espagne* 3:12–13, 15. See Castro *The Spaniards: An Introduction to Their History* 332 'the Erasmian movement and the so-called Spanish pre-Reformation were based more on peculiar Spanish conditions than on apparently similar circumstances elsewhere in Europe.'

17 Bataillon 'L'Espagne religieuse' 17–18; 'Préface' *Erasme et l'Espagne* 2:8; Raymond Marcus 'Marcel Bataillon 1895–1977' 597; Huerga 'Erasmismo y Alumbradismo' 343. Cf Raymond Aron: 'L'historien tient à la fois du spectateur et de l'acteur, il cherche dans le passé et lui-même et l'autre que lui' (*Introduction à la philosophie de l'histoire* 60).

18 Devoto 'Note préliminaire' in Bataillon *Erasme et l'Espagne* 1:xiv; Marcus 'Marcel Bataillon' 598; Bataillon 'Préface' *Erasme et l'Espagne* 2:9

19 Bataillon's review of Nieto, ibid 2:506–7

20 José C. Nieto *Juan de Valdés and the Origins of the Spanish and Italian Reformations* 29–31, 34–7, 94, 119n, 136–7, and 'Luther's Ghost and Erasmus' Masks in Spain' 41–9. John E. Longhurst's *Erasmus and the Spanish Inquisition: The Case of Juan de Valdés* of 1950, which used the Inquisition records, had found in Valdés no contradiction with essential Catholic doctrine, but had recognized also a substantial debt to Erasmus and resemblances to illuminism (79–80).

21 Nieto *Juan de Valdés* 97n, 110–11, 135–6

22 Carlos Gilly 'Juan de Valdés: Übersetzer und Bearbeiter von Luthers Schriften in seinem *Diálogo de Doctrina*' 265–73, 278, 281–2, 286–7, 297, 300–1. On predecessors for Gilly's argument, ibid 297 n121. Cf Alastair Hamilton *Heresy and Mysticism in Spain: The 'Alumbrados'* 40–2, 80.

23 Ottavio di Camillo 'Interpretations of the Renaissance in Spanish Historical Thought: The Last Thirty Years' 382, with reference to the writings of José Luis Abellán in particular.

24 Lu Ann Homza 'Erasmus as Hero, or Heretic? Spanish Humanism and the Valladolid Assembly of 1527' 78–82, 115

25 Bataillon review of Nieto, in *Erasme et l'Espagne* 2:509, 512

26 Mann *Erasme et les débuts de la Réforme française* xix

27 Ibid 1, 3, 11–12, 14, 19, 31–9, 41

28 Ibid 47, 70, 73, 81, 88, 90. On Margaret, *Contemporaries* 2:386–8.

29 Mann *Erasme* 103, 112, 150, 167–9

30 Ibid xvii, 20

31 J.-C. Margolin 'Erasme et la France,' in *Erasmus und Europa* 58–9. The distinction is reduced by those, like A.H.T. Levi, who emphasize Erasmus' receptiveness to Neoplatonism. See A.H.T. Levi (ed) *Humanism in France at the End of the Middle Ages and in the Early Renaissance* 231–2.

32 Margolin 'Erasme et la France' 55, 69–73

33 G. Ritter *Erasmus und der deutsche Humanistenkreis am Oberrhein: Eine Gedenkrede* 11–16, 22, 27, 32, 38n
34 James D. Tracy 'Erasmus Becomes a German' 285–8; Peter G. Bietenholz 'Erasmus and the German Public, 1518–1520: The Question of the Authorized and Unauthorized Circulation of His Correspondence' esp 69; Lewis Spitz *The Religious Renaissance of the German Humanists* 5–7
35 B. Moeller 'The German Humanists and the Beginnings of the Reformation' 20, 32–3; Spitz *Religious Renaissance* 206, 212, 234–5
36 Heinz Holeczek *Erasmus Deutsch* 1:63
37 Ibid 12–13; R.W. Scribner *For the Sake of Simple Folk: Popular Propaganda for the German Reformation* 104–6
38 Holeczek *Erasmus Deutsch* 1:23
39 Ibid 16–18, 28–9, 36, 76, 91, 106, 114, 126–7
40 Eugène Honée 'Erasmus und die Religionsverhandlungen der deutschen Reichstage (1524–1530),' in M.E.H.N. Mout, H. Smolinsky, and J. Trapman (eds) *Erasmianism: Idea and Reality* 65–75; Heribert Smolinsky 'Erasmianismus in der Politik? Das Beispiel der vereinigten Herzogtümer Jülich-Kleve-Berg,' in ibid 77–89, esp 78–9, 82–4, 87–8; Barbara Henze 'Erasmianisch: Die "Methode," Konflikte zu lösen? Das Wirken Witzels und Cassanders,' in ibid 155–68, esp 158, 164, 168
41 D. Nauta 'De Reformatie in Nederland in de Historiografie' 69–71; James D. Tracy *Erasmus of the Low Countries* 13–14; Alastair Duke *Reformation and Revolt in the Low Countries* 5–8, 14, 47, 55–7; Johannes Trapman 'Le rôle des "sacramentaires" des origines de la Réforme jusqu'en 1530 aux Pays-Bas' 23, and ' "Erasmianism" in the Early Reformation in the Netherlands,' in Mout, Smolinsky, and Trapman (eds) *Erasmianism* 169–76; G.J. Hoenderdaal 'Erasmus en de nederlandse Reformatie' 132–4; for early twentieth-century Dutch historians, *Man On His Own* 306–9
42 Mestwerdt, *Man On His Own* 341–7; Hyma, ch 1 above; Post *The Modern Devotion: Confrontation with Reformation and Humanism* 7, 469, 549, 553–4, 562, 574, 579, 658–60. See also Reinhold Mokrosch 'Devotio Moderna und nordeuropäischer Humanismus' TRE 8:609–12.
43 Léon-E. Halkin 'Erasme et les Pays-Bas,' in *Erasmus und Europa* 36. Cf Halkin *Erasmus: A Critical Biography* 3–4.
44 A.G. Weiler 'Recent Historiography on the Modern Devotion: Some Debated Questions' 175
45 Alois Gerlo 'Erasme, homo batavus,' in *Commém Nat* 73, 80
46 J.J. Poelhecke 'The Nameless Homeland of Erasmus'; Ari Wesseling 'Are the Dutch Uncivilized? Erasmus on the Batavians and His National Identity,' in ERSY 13 (1993): 68–102, and 'Or Else I Become a Gaul: A Note on Erasmus and the German Reformation,' in ibid 15 (1995): 96–8; István Bejczy 'Erasmus Becomes a Netherlander'
47 See ch 5 below

48 I use the German edition, *Erasmus als Ketzer: Reformation und Inquisition im Italien des 16. Jahrhunderts* (Leiden 1993).

49 Seidel Menchi 'La fortuna di Erasmo in Italia: Confronto metodologico con la ricerca di Marcel Bataillon,' in *El Erasmismo en España* 23–4, 29–32, 35–9

50 Paul Oskar Kristeller 'Erasmus from an Italian Perspective,' on Erasmus' affinity with the Italian humanists and the evidences of Florentine Neoplatonist influence upon him; Raymond Marcel 'Les dettes d'Erasme envers l'Italie,' in *Actes* 159–73, who says: 'à mon avis toutes ses oeuvres, sans exception, ne sont que la suite logique des différentes initiatives des humanistes italiens,' perhaps a little tongue-in-cheek, for he immediately indicates how Erasmus gave 'another dimension' to those earlier initiatives (171–2. Cf review by A. Godin BHR 33 [1971]: 745–8); Léon-E. Halkin, 'Erasme en Italie,' in *Coll Tur* 1:37–53, harvesting economically what the sources recount of Erasmus' Italian journey; Eugenio Garin 'Erasmo e l'Umanesimo italiano,' identifying for study the relation between Leon Battista Alberti and Erasmus, especially over Lucian, refining the issues in Erasmus' relation to Pico and to Valla and emphasizing both Erasmus' debt to and distance from his Italian predecessors.

51 Renaudet *Erasme et l'Italie* x–xi

52 Ibid 205, 217–37. On Corsi, *Contemporaries* 1:344.

53 Renaudet *Erasme et l'Italie* x, 32, 96, 114, 246. On Colet, John B. Gleason *John Colet* 58–9, 62–4, 194–5; on Erasmus' dependence on and independence from Ficino, see Maria Cytowska 'Erasme de Rotterdam et Marcile Ficin son Maître.' In her Preface to the second edition of Renaudet's book, Seidel Menchi presents it as a challenge to Bataillon's shift of interest towards Spain, a recentring of humanist history and the Erasmus story on Italy and a restatement of the classic myth of the Renaissance as 'une apologie de la nature humaine' (*Erasme et l'Italie*, 2nd edn, ix–xvi, esp x, xv).

54 Paul and Marcella Grendler 'The Survival of Erasmus in Italy' 9–10; Myron P. Gilmore 'Italian Reactions to Erasmian Humanism,' in Heiko A. Oberman and Thomas A. Brady, Jr (eds) *Itinerarium Italicum: The Profile of the Italian Renaissance in the Mirror of Its European Transformations* 103–7. As a further antidote to any romanticizing of Erasmus' relation with Italy, see now István Beczy's 'Erasmus versus Italy,' which describes it as tense from the beginning.

55 Delio Cantimori 'Erasmo e la vita morale e religiosa italiana nel secolo XVI,' in *Gedenkschrift* 98–112, and *Umanesimo e religione nel Rinascimento* 40–59, at 40–3, 50, 57–8; Seidel Menchi 'La fortuna di Erasmo in Italia' 21–2. Cantimori's 'Note su Erasmo e l'Italia' (reprinted in *Umanesimo e religione* as 'Erasmo e l'Italia') emphasizes his alienation from the Italian humanists.

56 Seidel Menchi *Erasmus als Ketzer* 1–3, 132–5. Seidel Menchi refers to

the late Robert Scribner's pioneer work on the *Flugschriften*. Cf R.W. Scribner *For the Sake of Simple Folk: Popular Propaganda for the German Reformation*.

57 Seidel Menchi *Erasmus als Ketzer* 276–7; 'La fortuna' 38

58 Seidel Menchi *Erasmus als Ketzer* 3–5, 7. Since 1970 there has been a considerable extension in the availability of the Inquisition records.

59 See, eg, Scribner 'Is There a Social History of the Reformation?'

60 Seidel Menchi *Erasmus als Ketzer* 5–6, 8–9. Seidel Menchi refers also to the 'Erasmian school at Liège.'

61 Ibid 9–11, 142. Cf Silvana Seidel Menchi 'Erasme et son lecteur,' in *Coll Eras: Liège* 31–45, esp 36–41, for readers' radicalizing, but not necessarily their distorting, of Erasmus.

62 Seidel Menchi *Erasmus als Ketzer* 32, 38–41, 50–3, 60. That Erasmus was similarly received by humble radicals elsewhere is demonstrated in the bibliographically rich essay by Marc Lienhard 'Die Radikalen des 16. Jahrhunderts und Erasmus,' in Mout, Smolinsky, and Trapman (eds) *Erasmianism* 91–104, esp 97.

63 Seidel Menchi *Erasmus als Ketzer* 80–1, 85–6, 93, 97–103

64 Ibid., ch 4, esp 113–21, 124. Seidel Menchi notes that a theologically aware study of Erasmus' idea of evangelical freedom is required (ibid 126).

65 Ibid., ch 6, esp 169, 172, 176, 186, 188

66 Ibid., ch 8, esp 241–4, 247, 251, 254–5, 259

67 Ibid 139–42, 215, 219–20, 223–4, 233 (as against Margolin ASD V:1 367), 406–10, 417–21, 424

68 Ibid 281–7, 352, 362–4, 404–5, 427, 432, 447–9. I find Margolin's review ('Un Erasme revisité par une historienne italienne,' 1997) of Seidel Menchi's book (in its largely unchanged French translation, 1996) too polemical. He rightly questions her excessive criticism, even denunciation, of previous Erasmus scholarship and poses the issue of distinguishing between how Erasmus has been read in different historical circumstances and how we should read him in himself. He recognizes the interest of her methodology but gives it too little space in his twelve-page critique (but cf *Erasme, précepteur de l'Europe* ch 8).

69 *Times Literary Supplement* no. 1797 (11 July 1936)

70 D. Knowles *The Religious Orders in England* 3; A.G. Dickens *The English Reformation* (1964) 66–7. H.C. Porter's *Reformation and Reaction in Tudor Cambridge* (1958) sees his biblical work as preparatory.

71 McConica *English Humanists and Reformation Politics* ch 1

72 Ibid 16, 22–3, 32–3

73 Ibid 35, 42, 51, 57–8, 60, 68, 71–2

74 Ibid ch 4, esp 88–9

75 Ibid 106, 118, 120, 124, 144–5. The suggestion that the translation was by William Tyndale is discussed by David Daniell *William Tyndale: A Biography* 70–4.

76 McConica *English Humanists* 147–8, 151–2, 199, 215, 227, 240–8

77 Fox 'Facts and Fallacies: Interpreting English Humanism,' in Alistair Fox and John Guy *Reassessing the Henrician Age: Humanism, Politics and Reform 1500–1550* 11, 32, 48. The condemned contemporaries include Quentin Skinner.

78 Ibid 36, 51; Richard M. Douglas 'Talent and Vocation in Humanist and Protestant Thought,' in Theodore K. Rabb and Jerrold E. Seigel (eds) *Action and Conviction in Early Modern Europe: Essays in Memory of E.H. Harbison* 261–98. J.T. Rhodes ('Erasmus and English Readers of the 1530s') sees translations of Erasmus' works as supporting, but in an ancillary way, the Reformers' appeal to the laity in the 1530s.

79 On the *Epystle* and its translator Richard Taverner, McConica *English Humanists* 117–18

80 Maria Dowling *Humanism in the Age of Henry VIII* 37 and ch 2 *passim*; Craig W. D'Alton 'The Trojan War of 1518: Melodrama, Politics, and the Rise of Humanism.' For further discussion, see ch 6 below.

81 Christopher Haigh *The English Reformation Revised* Introduction and ch 1; McConica *English Humanists* 43, 281. This discussion attempts no more than to indicate the difficulties the revisionist historiography makes for an attempt to apply the Febvre/Bataillon model to the English case. For an exceedingly sober estimate, from the revisionist side, of Erasmus' significance, J.J. Scarisbrick *The Reformation and the English People* 46–7. For rebuttals of revisionism, A.G. Dickens 'The Early Expansion of Protestantism in England,' Daniell *William Tyndale* 94–100, 398–9. McConica's 1997 essay 'The English Reception of Erasmus,' in Mout, Smolinsky, and Trapman (eds) *Erasmianism* 37–46, demonstrates how 'Erasmian' ideas were in accord with early sixteenth-century intellectual and spiritual developments in the universities and at the English court, while holding to his position that they were largely to define the content of the religious settlement of Henry VIII's last years.

82 Maria Cytowska 'Erasme en Pologne avant l'époque du Concile de Trente' 11. What follows can be no more than a sketch. English readers now have James Tracy's 'Erasmus' Polish Readers,' in *Erasmus of the Low Countries* 191–203.

83 Cytowska 'Erasme en Pologne' 11–12; Jacqueline Glomski 'Erasmus and Cracow (1510–1530),' in ERSY 17 (1997): 1–18, at 6–8, 16–18

84 Cf Tracy *Erasmus of the Low Countries* 192–6; Cytowska 'Erasme en Pologne' 15–16; George H. Williams 'Erasmianism in Poland: An Account of a Major, Though Ever Diminishing, Current in Sixteenth-Century Polish Humanism and Religion, 1518–1605' 5–7, 10

85 Claude Backvis 'La fortune d'Erasme en Pologne,' in *Coll Eras: Mons* 176, 184

86 Cytowska 'Erasme en Pologne' 14; Backvis 'La fortune d'Erasme' 186, 189; Margolin *Erasme, précepteur de l'Europe* 205–8; Andrzej

Kempfi 'Erasme et la vie intellectuelle en Warmie au temps de Nicolas Copernic,' in *Coll Tur* 1:397–406

87 Tracy *Erasmus of the Low Countries* 200–2; *Contemporaries* 2:206–7 (Hosius), 297–301 (Laski); Williams 'Erasmianism' 15, 28–32 (Laski); Backvis 'La fortune d'Erasme' 190–5

88 Imre Trencsényi-Waldapfel 'L'humanisme belge et l'humanisme hongrois liés par l'esprit d'Erasme,' in *Commém Nat* 209–24; Tibor Kardos 'L'esprit d'Erasme en Hongrie,' in *Coll Tur* 1:187–214; Constantin Crisan 'Erasme en Roumanie: Approximations diachroniques et synchroniques,' in ibid 175–85

89 Backvis 'La fortune d'Erasme' 173, 196–8. Cf Margolin: 'on ne prête qu'aux riches' (*Erasme, précepteur* 216)

CHAPTER FOUR

1 C. Reedijk 'Erasmus in 1970' 455. Cf *Neuf années* no. 1376.

2 *Neuf années* no. 1095; Reedijk 'Erasmus in 1970' 456

3 Hayden White 'The Burden of History' (1966), in *Tropics of Discourse: Essays in Cultural Criticism* 50; Gilbert Allardyce 'The Rise and Fall of the Western Civilization Course'; William Bouwsma *A Usable Past: Essays in European Cultural History* 7

4 P.-H. Simon 'Allocution,' in *Coll Tur* 1:16

5 Reedijk 'Erasmus in 1970' 455; *Neuf années* nos 711, 748, 1017, 1222, 1514, 1551, 1566, 1568, 1575, 1619; N. van der Blom (ed) *Grepen uit de geschiedenis van het Erasmiaans Gymnasium 1328–1978* 199–201

6 *Neuf années* nos 333, 750, 1006, 1084, 1291, 1323–4, 1554, 1562, 1567, 1580, 1601, 1941

7 Margolin *Erasme et la musique* and 'Erasme et la musique,' in *Recherches érasmiennes* 85–97; Clement A. Miller 'Erasmus on Music'; R.B. Lenaerts 'Erasmus en de muziek,' summarized *Neuf années* no. 1260

8 André Chastel in *Le Monde*, summarized *Neuf années* no. 1091

9 Reedijk 'Erasmus in 1970' 460; *Neuf années* no. 1557

10 Reedijk 'Erasmus in 1970' 453, 461–2; ASD I-1 'General Introduction'; *Neuf années* no. 590; James K. McConica 'Erasmus in Amsterdam and Toronto,' in Erika Rummel (ed) *Editing Texts from the Age of Erasmus* 96–9; McConica and R.M. Schoeffel 'The Collected Works of Erasmus' 317

11 McConica 'Erasmus in Amsterdam and Toronto' 90–6

12 Max Drechsel 'Avant-Propos,' in *Coll Eras: Mons* vii–iii; Aloïs Gerlo 'Allocution d'acceuil – Begroeting,' in *Commém Nat* 1–2; M.M. Phillips 'The Erasmus Quincentenary: Europe,' *Erasmus in English* 1 (1970) n.p.; J.-C. Margolin 'Le douzième Stage international d'Etudes humanistes (Tours, 3–25 juillet 1969),' in *Coll Tur* 1:11

13 R.R. Post 'Quelques précisions sur l'année de la naissance d'Erasme (1469) et sur son éducation,' esp 489n (cf ASD I-1 xvn, xx); E.-W. Kohls

Notes to pages 83–7 249

'Das Geburtsjahr des Erasmus'; Post 'Nochmals Erasmus' Geburtsjahr'; Kohls 'Noch einmal das Geburtsjahr des Erasmus: Antwort an
R.R. Post'; A.C.F. Koch *The Year of Erasmus' Birth and Other Contributions to the Chronology of His Life*; Harry Vredeveld 'The Ages of Erasmus and the Year of His Birth,' esp 766–70. The argument from
Erasmus' 'plain statements' about his age rests in part on reading
expressions like 'accedere ad annum ... um' in a cardinal ('going on this
or that age'), not an ordinal ('approaching one's nth year'), sense (769).
14 J.-P. Massaut 'Les études érasmiennes à Liège' *Revue Universitaire de
Liège* 42–3 (1970–1): 51–4, summarized *Neuf années* no. 1820; F. Schalk
'Erasmus und die *Res publica literaria*,' in *Actes* 14–28; Allen 4:iii (cf
my 'Anguish of an Erasmian: P.S. Allen and the Great War'); Halkin
'Signification du Congrès érasmien,' in *Actes* 197; Bataillon 'Actualité
d'Erasme,' in *Coll Tur* 2:878–82, 884–6, and 'La situation présente du
message érasmien,' in *Coll Eras: Mons* 7–10. On Vatican 2, cf Reedijk
'Erasmus in 1970' 451–2, 466.
15 Margaret Mann Phillips *Erasmus and the Northern Renaissance* xxiv–
xxv, 22–3, 40, 43–4, 49
16 M.A. Screech 'Margaret Mann Phillips,' in ERSY 8 (1988): 1–4, at 3;
K.A. Meissinger *Erasmus von Rotterdam* 6, 411
17 Ibid 11, 13, 15, 22, 97–100. On the inaccessibility of Colet to European
scholars, including Meissinger, and their unawareness of Seebohm's
book, so influential in English-speaking countries, see Gleason *John
Colet* 13. Cf, against the trend, Raymond Marcel 'Les "Découvertes"
d'Erasme en Angleterre' and, of course, Renaudet, who, like Meissinger, saw his English associates as Erasmus' route to Italy (*Erasme et
l'Italie* 27–31).
18 Meissinger *Erasmus von Rotterdam* 17, 352, 356. Cf H.A. Oberman *The
Harvest of Medieval Theology: Gabriel Biel and Late Medieval Nominalism*;
William Courtenay 'Nominalism and Late Medieval Religion,' in
Charles Trinkaus with Heiko A. Oberman (eds) *The Pursuit of Holiness
in Late Medieval and Renaissance Religion* 26–59
19 Meissinger *Erasmus von Rotterdam* 37–9
20 Roland H. Bainton *Erasmus of Christendom* 8; *Pilgrim Parson: The Life of
James Herbert Bainton (1867–1942)* 101–7, 111–14, 127; Steven H. Simpler *Roland H. Bainton: An Examination of His Reformation Historiography* 4–10
21 Bainton *Erasmus of Christendom* 57, 87
22 Ibid 24, 55–6, 76, 80–3, 86
23 C. Béné, J. Hadot, in *Coll Eras: Mons* 65–6; Germain Marc'hadour
'Erasme et John Colet,' in *Coll Tur* 2:761–9
24 Denys Gorce 'La patristique dans la réforme d'Erasme,' in *Festgabe
Joseph Lortz* 1:233–76, esp 255–74. See ch 5 below for the work of John
Olin and others.
25 *Coll Eras: Mons* 32, 66–7. The Mons publication is unique among the

quincentenary publications in reporting the debates following the presentation of papers.

26 Charles Béné 'Saint Augustin dans la controverse sur les trois langues à Louvain en 1518 et 1519,' in ibid 20–32; *Erasme et Saint Augustin ou influence de Saint Augustin sur l'humanisme d'Erasme* 86–90, 100–3, 110–11, 139, 141, 143–4, 150, 181, 185, 220, 393, 419

27 Béné *Erasme et Saint Augustin* 91, 166, 231–2, 246, 342; Margolin, in *Actes* 107.

28 Ep 1211 Allen 4:507–14, CWE 8:225–32; Olin *Christian Humanism* 157–66; Meissinger *Erasmus von Rotterdam* 71–2, 98; Bainton *Erasmus of Christendon* 84–5

29 Godin 'De Vitrier à Origène: recherches sur la patristique érasmienne' *Coll Eras: Mons* 47–57, esp 52, 55–7; 'Jean Vitrier et la "Cénacle" de Saint-Omer' *Coll Tur* 2:781–805, esp 786, 804 n47 (Godin uses the expression 'mysterious alchemy' of Vitrier's sources; it seems equally applicable to Erasmus; see also Godin *Spiritualité franciscain en Flandre au XVIe siècle: L'Homéliaire de Jean Vitrier* 19); 'Erasme et la modèle origénien de la prédication' *Coll Tur* 2:807–20, esp 807–8, 811, 816–18; John B. Payne 'Toward the Hermeneutic of Erasmus,' in *Scrinium* 2:13–49 at 49

30 Godin *Erasme lecteur d'Origène* 2–3, 38, 63–4, 75, 110–11,160n, 164, 177, 180, 242–4, 302, 345–6, 355, 369, 396–7, 433

31 E.-W. Kohls 'La position théologique d'Erasme et la tradition dans le "De libero arbitrio,"' in *Coll Eras: Mons* 69–88, esp 71–2, 76–7, 79, 82, 86–7; J.-P. Massaut 'Erasme et Saint Thomas,' in *Coll Tur* 2:581–611, esp 582–3, 588, 590, 598, 603–5

32 Kohls *Die Theologie des Erasmus* 1:16, 24, 27–8, 30–1, 45, 55, 58, 67, 77, 84, 98, 115–16, 136, 163

33 Ibid 1:59, 150–1, 193, 196; 2:36, 45, 53, 63, 75

34 Payne *Erasmus: His Theology of the Sacraments* 10, 13, 19–23, 98, 238–9, 264, 266, 337

35 Ibid 36–9, 78–84, 220, 249; Kohls *Die Theologie* 2:94

36 Payne *Erasmus* 262. Cf ibid 88, 95.

37 See, eg, Mark U. Edwards Jr *Luther's Last Battles: Politics and Polemics 1531–46.*

38 Richard Newald *Erasmus Roterodamus* 299–301, 313, 323, 343

39 K.H. Oelrich *Der späte Erasmus und die Reformation* 3–4

40 Emile V. Telle 'Dolet et Erasme' *Coll Tur* 1:407–39, esp 424 (cf Telle [ed] *L'Erasmianus sive Ciceronianus d'Etienne Dolet (1535)*, in whose 'Avant-propos' [12–13] Telle emphasizes the *ad hominem* character of Erasmus' performance in his *Ciceronianus* and Dolet's rebuttal); J.V. Pollet 'Origine et structure du "De sarcienda ecclesiae concordia" (1533) d'Erasme,' in *Scrinium* 2:183–95

41 M.P. Gilmore 'Les limites de la tolérance dans l'oeuvre polémique d'Erasme,' in *Coll Tur* 2:713–36, esp 714–15, 717, 731–2

42 C. Reedijk 'Erasmus' Final Modesty,' in *Actes* 174–92, esp 176–8, 183, 186–7, 189, 191

43 Reedijk 'Das Lebenende des Erasmus'

44 In Margolin's catalogue for 1969, twenty-one pieces. See esp nos 1052, 1056, 1061–2.

45 Peter Bietenholz 'Erasmus und der Basler Buchhandel in Frankreich' *Scrinium* 1:293–323 (in French, *Coll Tur* 1:55–78). Cf his *Basle and France in the Sixteenth Century.*

46 M.A. Nauwelaerts 'Erasme à Louvain: Ephémérides d'un séjour de 1517 à 1521,' in *Scrinium* 1:3–24; Franz Bierlaire 'Le *Libellus Colloquiorum* de mars 1522 et Nicolas Baechem, dit *Egmondanus*,' in ibid 55–81 (cf *Contemporaries* 1:81–3 ['Nicolaas Baechem of Egmond']); R. Crahay 'Les censeurs louvanistes d'Erasme,' in ibid 1:221–49, esp 230–1, 235, 245, 248–9. For an analysis in detail of the treatment of Erasmus in the *Index expurgatorius* of 1571, and in particular of his New Testament edition, see G. van Calster 'La censure louvaniste du Nouveau Testament et la rédaction de l'index érasmien expurgatoire de 1571,' in ibid 2:379–436.

47 Roland Crahay and Marie-Thérèse Isaac 'Livres d'Erasme dans les bibliothèques anciennes du Hainaut,' in *Coll Eras: Mons* 203–44, esp 228–31; Ph. Lefèvre 'La lecture des oeuvres d'Erasme au sein du bas clergé durant la première moitié du XVIe siècle,' in *Scrinium* 1:83–91; G. Degroote 'Erasmofilie te Antwerpen in de eerste helft van de zestiende eeuw,' in *Commém Nat* 31–50 (French summary 50–1); M.A. Nauwelaerts 'Erasme et Gand,' in ibid 152–77. M. Sabbe had written of Erasmus' Antwerp friends in 1936 (see ch 1 above).

48 On Strasbourg, Erasmus to Jakob Wimpfeling 21 September 1514 Ep 305 Allen 2:19 lines 92–4, CWE 3:26 lines 99–101; Otto Herding 'Erasme et Wimpfeling,' in *Erasme, l'Alsace et son temps* 111–15; Jean Lebeau 'Erasme, Sebastian Franck et la tolérance,' in ibid 117–38; 'hungry tricksters,' ibid 134, Erasmus to Martin Bucer 2 March 1532 Ep 2615 Allen 9:454 line 364. On Erasmus and Franck, see further *Phoenix of His Age* 99–101.

49 Bernd Moeller *Reichstadt und Reformation* esp 48–9. Moeller's views on Erasmus were influenced by Maurer's *Das Verhältnis des Staates zur Kirche* (see ch 2 above).

50 Marie-Madeleine de la Garanderie 'Les relations d'Erasme avec Paris, au temps de son séjour aux Pays-Bas méridionaux (1516–1521),' in *Scrinium* 1:29–53, esp 43, 52. In her study of Budé and French humanism, Marie-Madeleine de la Garanderie summarizes the difference between Erasmus and Budé thus: they played the same experiences (the problematical relation between Christianity and humanism) on different registers, 'Erasmus more polemically, Budé with an unsurpassable inner intensity' (*Christianisme et lettres profanes: Essai sur l'humanisme français (1515–1535) et sur la pensée de Guillaume Budé* 383).

51 Marcel Bataillon 'Vers une définition de l'érasmisme,' in *Coll Tur* 1:21–34, esp 24–6, 29; 'Un problème d'influence d'Erasme en Espagne: L'*Eloge de la Folie*,' in *Actes* 136–47. A later version of this paper, in the 1991 edition of *Erasme et l'Espagne*: 'Erasmisme de *Lazarillo de Tormes* et de *Don Quichotte* en tant que créations littéraires (Un problème d'influence, etc.)' records later work confirming the influence (3:419–65, at 455).

52 Craig R. Thompson 'Erasmus and Tudor England,' in *Actes* 29–68 (Jewel at 60)

53 J.-C. Margolin 'L'inspiration érasmienne de Jacob Cats,' in *Commém Nat* 113–51, esp 114–17, 123, 128, 137, 140–1, 148, 150–1 (cf Margolin 'Erasme et la psychologie des peuples,' a survey of Erasmus' judgments and observations on the various peoples, which demonstrates the difficulty of interpreting his views and, perhaps, the inherent difficulty of 'ethnopsychology'); Irving L. Zupnick 'The Influence of Erasmus' *Enchiridion* on Bruegel's *Seven Virtues*,' in ibid 225–35; Gilbert Degroote 'Erasmiaanse echo's in de Gouden Eeuw in Nederland,' in *Scrinium* 1:391–421, esp 392, 402–9

54 M.A. Screech 'Folie érasmienne et folie rabelaisienne,' in *Coll Tur* 1:441–52, 'Comment Rabelais a exploité les travaux d'Erasme: quelques détails,' in ibid 453–61, esp 454; Margaret Mann Phillips 'Erasme et Montaigne,' in ibid 479–90 (cf Hugo Friedrich *Montaigne* 319–24).

55 Notably in the essay by Claude Backvis (see above, ch 3). There were numerous other pieces, many very short, on the theme 'Erasmus and Eastern Europe' in the quincentenary years. See *Neuf années* nos 642, 743–4, 746, 809, 889, 896, 899, 902, 992, 1026, 1147, 1185, 1226 (a Marxist assessment of the Tours meeting), 1252, 1451, 1487–91, 1721, 1921. Istvan (Stefan) Vida of Budapest, who wrote a number of these pieces on Erasmus and Eastern Europe, argues as well that Erasmus' religion was congenial to the Catholicism emerging from Vatican 2 (nos 742, 897–8, 1485, 1492, 1912–13).

56 Pierre Mesnard 'Le caractère d'Erasme,' in *Coll Eras: Mons* 327–32 (on Mesnard's death, *Coll Tur* 1:10–11); S. Dresden 'Présence d'Erasme,' in *Actes* 1–13, esp 2–3, 8, 10 (on Dresden further, see below).

57 Jean Hoyoux 'Les voyages d'Erasme et de Jérôme Aléandre: un chapitre de vie quotidienne,' in *Coll Eras: Mons* 315–25; Franz Bierlaire 'La *familia* d'Erasme,' in ibid 301–13, *La familia d'Erasme: Contribution à l'histoire d'humanisme*

58 Georges Chantraine 'Erasme théologien'

59 Jozef Coppens 'Où en est le portrait d'Erasme théologien?' in *Scrinium* 2:569–93, esp 582–4, 587–90, 593 (cf *Neuf années* no. 1102).

60 Robert Stupperich 'Die theologische Neuorientierung des Erasmus in der *Ratio seu Methodus* 1516–18,' in *Actes* 148–58; E.-W. Kohls 'Erasmus und die werdende evangelische Bewegung des 16. Jahrhunderts,' in *Scrinium* 1:203–19, esp 206–7, 212, 215 (cf 'Erasme et la

Réforme,' in *Coll Tur* 2:837–47); G.W. Locher 'Zwingli und Erasmus,' in *Scrinium* 2:325–50

61 Léon-E. Halkin 'La thème du pèlerinage dans les *Colloques* d'Erasme,' in *Actes* 88–98, esp 97–8, 'Erasme pèlerin,' in *Scrinium* 2:239–52, esp 251; 'enfant terrible,' *Neuf années* no. 1186, summarizing Halkin's article in the *Revue générale belge* (June 1969) 'Erasme, enfant terrible de l'Eglise romaine' (Halkin's monograph of the quincentenary years, *Erasme et l'humanisme chrétien*, recalls the diptych image: Erasmus was 'profondément pieux at farouchement anticlérical,' but not in contradiction with himself, as if half a Voltaire and half a Fénelon; he condemned the abuse and not the institution [6, 105, 122]); J.-P. Massaut 'Erasme, la Sorbonne at la nature de l'Eglise,' in *Coll Eras: Mons* 89–118, esp 92, 99, 105–6, 112–13. At Mons also, Marcelle Derwa, together with the doyenne of Erasmus studies at Liège, Marie Delcourt, presented 'Trois aspects humanistes de l'épicurisme chrétien,' on the epicureanism of Valla, More, and Erasmus: Erasmus' last colloquy *Epicureus* offered, in the manner of the Beatitudes, the paradox of the good life, the life of practical piety, as the highest pleasure (*Coll Eras: Mons* 119–33). Cf R. Bultot 'Erasme, Epicure et le "Contemptu Mundi,"' which finds in both the latter work and the *Epicureus* an essentially traditional understanding of the Christian, including the monastic, life, an understanding which, from the time of the Fathers, had appropriated the words of Epicurus about the true pleasures of life (*Scrinium* 2:205–38).

62 C.J. de Vogel 'Erasmus and His Attitude towards Church Dogma,' in *Scrinium* 2:101–32, esp 103–4, 106, 109, 114; C. Augustijn 'The Ecclesiology of Erasmus,' in ibid 135–55, esp 135, 139–41, 144, 154–5; 'I shall therefore tolerate,' *Hyperaspistes diatribae adversus Servum arbitrium Martini Lutheri*, in LB 10:1258A

63 J.K. McConica 'Erasmus and the Grammar of Consent,' in *Scrinium* 2:77–99, esp 79–81, 89–90, 95–6; 'consensus of whole Christian people,' Ep 1893 to Willibald Pirckheimer 19 October 1527, in Allen 7:216 lines 59–60, 'Summa nostrae religionis,' Ep 1334 to Jean de Carondelet 5 January 1523, in ibid 5:177 line 217, CWE 9:252 line 232

64 Otto Schottenloher 'Lex naturae und Lex Christi bei Erasmus,' in *Scrinium* 2:253–99, esp 254, 263–4, 270–1, 276, 280, 288–9 (against Geldner). Cf R. Padberg 'Pax Erasmiana: Das politische Engagement und die "politische Theologie" des Erasmus von Rotterdam,' in ibid 301–12, at 309 (correcting Koerber on Erasmus and natural law).

65 See ch 2 above.

66 S. Dresden 'Erasme, Rabelais et la "festivitas" humaniste,' in *Coll Tur* 1:463–78, esp 466–9, 472–3, 'Erasme et la notion de *Humanitas*,' in *Scrinium* 2:527–45, esp 536–7, 540, 544–5. Poetry was for Erasmus, says D.F.S. Thomson, 'on the whole a department of rhetoric' ('Erasmus as a Poet in the Context of Northern Humanism,' in *Commém Nat*

187–210, at 197). In his other paper at Tours ('Sagesse et folie d'après Erasme'), Dresden emphasizes the essentially Christian character of the Erasmian wisdom (*Coll Tur* 1:285–99).

67 Margaret Mann Phillips 'Erasmus and the Art of Writing,' in *Scrinium* 1:335–50, esp 349–50; J.-C. Margolin 'Erasme et la Verbe: De la rhétorique à l'herméneutique,' in *Erasme, l'Alsace, et son temps* 87–110, esp 89, 91, 94n, 99, 101–2, 'Erasme et la Vérité,' in *Coll Eras: Mons* 135–70, reprinted in *Recherches érasmiennes* 45–69
68 *Man On His Own* 134; Gérard Defaux 'Jean-Claude Margolin,' in ERSY 10 (1990): 1–8, esp 4
69 J.-C. Margolin 'L'idée de nature dans la pensée d'Erasme,' in *Recherches érasmiennes* 9–44; Michel Foucault *The Order of Things: An Archaeology of the Human Sciences* ch 2
70 Cf *Man On His Own* 373–5

CHAPTER FIVE

1 J.-B. Pineau *Erasme: Sa pensée religieuse* 27, 35, 40, 70, 131, 183, 268
2 Pineau *Erasme* 251, 253, 271; Godet DTC 5:1 col 396 (cf *Man On His Own* 227–8)
3 J. de Jong 'Het goddienstig standpunt van Erasmus' esp 318–19, 326–8, 336–8; P. Polman 'Erasmus en de theologie' esp 273, 279–80, 292; N. Greitemann 'Erasmus als exegeet' esp 365–6. On de Jong, *New Cath Enc* 7: 1098; on Wernle and Troeltsch, *Man On His Own*, 289–96.
4 R. Pfeiffer 'Die Einheit im geistigen Werk des Erasmus' esp 474, 477–8, 480–2
5 Pfeiffer *Humanitas Erasmiana* esp 8–9, 23–4; 'Die Einheit' 483; 'Erasmus und die Einheit der klassischen und der christlichen Renaissance' esp 184
6 Emile V. Telle *Erasme de Rotterdam et le septième sacrement: Etude d'évangélisme matrimonial au XVIe siècle et contribution à la biographie intellectuelle d'Erasme* 8
7 Joseph Lortz *The Reformation in Germany* 1:216–18, 435; Karl Meissinger *Erasmus von Rotterdam* 351
8 Lortz *Reformation in Germany* 135–44, 'Erasmus-kirchengeschichtlich' 273–4, 293, 301; Telle *Erasme de Rotterdam et le septième sacrement* 68, 99–102, 128, 142
9 Lortz 'Erasmus-kirchengeschichtlich' 275, 277–9; *Reformation* 145–6, 150
10 Lortz *Reformation* 147–8, 153; 'Erasmus-kirchengeschichtlich' 273, 293, 301, 310. Hubert Jedin has essentially shared Lortz's judgments and, if more mildly, given them further currency (*A History of the Council of Trent* 1: 156–61).
11 Telle *Erasme de Rotterdam et le septième sacrement* 5–6, 25, 64, 116, 125, 130, 136, 140, 143, 145

12 Ibid 180–1, 189, 209, 212, 228, 249, 263, 266, 291–2, 295, 308, 340, 345, 414
13 Ibid 347
14 Eugene Rice 'Erasmus and the Religious Tradition,' and *The Renaissance Idea of Wisdom* esp 28–30, 124, 159–63. Within the German literature, Karl Schlechta's elegant essay of 1948, *Erasmus von Rotterdam*, reaches the same conclusion as Rice (esp 20–3, 82–6).
15 Hans Baron 'Secularization of Wisdom and Political Humanism in the Renaissance'; R.W. Scribner 'The Power of Wisdom: The Social Thought of Erasmus 1489–1518' 343–6
16 Louis Bouyer *Autour d'Erasme: Etudes sur le christianisme des humanistes catholiques* 38, 123, 126–7, 129, 133–4, 144, 155
17 Alfons Auer *Die vollkommene Frömmigkeit des Christen* 24, 71, 103–8, 110, 117–19, 165
18 Ibid 12, 53–4, 58
19 Jacques Etienne *Spiritualisme érasmien et théologiens louvanistes: Un changement de problématique au début du XVIe siècle* esp 14–17, 28, 33, 36, 59–62
20 Auer *Die vollkommene Frömmigkeit* 63–4, 67–9, 80–1, 83, 89, 91, 96, 99, 102, 181
21 Ibid 119, 151, 155–6, 189–93, 202, 205
22 Kohls *Die Theologie* 2:94, 122 (cf 1:161–3). While Auer makes central to the *Enchiridion* the fifth rule of the Christian life (canon 5): moving from visible things to the invisible, Kohls privileges the fourth (canon 4), with its Christocentrism.
23 Margolin 'Interpretation d'un passage de l'*Enchiridion Militis Christiani, Canon Quintus,*' in *Actes* 99–115, at 112
24 Auer *Die vollkommene Frömmigkeit* 197–8; 'unicus scopus' Holborn 63, CWE 66:61
25 Wilhelm Shenk 'The Erasmian Idea' 263. Wallace Ferguson, in an article of 1954, 'Renaissance Tendencies in the Religious Thought of Erasmus,' finds laicization the key element in Renaissance religion, and of this Erasmus' religious thought was a reflection.
26 Jean Boisset *Erasme et Luther: Libre ou serf arbitre?* 6, 15, 34, 58–61, 80–2, 86, 126, 130, 142; on Blondel, John Macquarrie, in *Encyclopedia of Philosophy* 1:323–4
27 *Ratio verae theologiae*, in Holborn 180, lines 20–4
28 Harry J. McSorley *Luther: Right or Wrong? An Ecumenical-Theological Study of Luther's Major Work 'The Bondage of the Will'* 18, 279–89 (Erasmus); 21, 310–35, 353–5 (Luther); ix, 366 (ecumenical study and dialogue)
29 Ernst-Wilhelm Kohls *Luther oder Erasmus: Luthers Theologie in der Auseinandersetzung mit Erasmus* 1:xii–xiv, 2, 6, 11–12. In referring to the present 'Umbruchszeit,' is Kohls thinking of the student rebellions around 1970?

30 Ibid 3, 23–4, 39, 41, 54. There is a parallel in an important essay by the Lutheran historian Bernhard Lohse. Erasmus turned his back on philosophical treatments of the free-will issue, whether classical (as in Valla) or scholastic (as in John Fisher). He wished to build his case on the biblical evidence alone. This was the biblicism of the *Devotio moderna*, the noblest flowering of medieval piety, not the Bible as understood by the Reformers. Luther and Erasmus had different concerns, one with certainty of faith, the other with pastoral care (Lohse 'Marginalien zum Streit zwischen Erasmus und Luther' esp 13, 15, 20).

31 Kohls *Luther oder Erasmus* 1:xiii, xv, 48, 57, 162–3

32 *Quinze années* 602–3

33 Kohls *Luther oder Erasmus* 1:2. See Kohls' annexure 'Einen Autor besser verstehen, als er sich selbst verstanden hat,' a defence of the Rankean and empirical approach against the strongly interpretative tradition from Kant to Dilthey and Troeltsch (ibid 213–29).

34 Georges Chantraine *Erasme et Luther, libre et serf arbitre* v, xxxix, xliv

35 Ibid xlvi, 49, 84, 101, 128; Renaudet *Erasme et l'Italie* 160

36 Chantraine *Erasme et Luther* 268, 273, 276, 278–9, 283, 295–6

37 Ibid 314, 328–9, 445, 447, 449, 454–5; on Congar, 449n

38 John O'Malley 'Erasmus and Luther, Continuity and Discontinuity as Key to Their Conflict' 48–50, 54, 57–60, 65

39 B.A. Gerrish '*De Libero Arbitrio* (1524): Erasmus on Piety, Theology, and the Lutheran Dogma,' in Richard L. DeMolen (ed) *Essays on the Works of Erasmus* 187–209, esp 194, 196, 198, 202

40 Marjorie O'Rourke Boyle *Rhetoric and Reform: Erasmus' Civil Dispute with Luther* 5–6, 14–15, 33; further on More 173, n40

41 Ibid 23–4, 48–51, 53. Cf Boyle 'Stoic Luther: Paradoxical Sin and Necessity.' See the review by James Michael Weiss in SCJ 16 (1985): 571–2.

42 Boyle *Rhetoric and Reform* 41, 58–9, 70, 107, 112–16

43 Karl Heinz Oelrich *Der späte Erasmus und die Reformation* 10, 35, 51, 118 (empirical observer); 14, 37 (Erasmus *Städter*); 17, 53–67, 98, 103, 112 (observation of events and their consequences); 62–7 (causes of catastrophe)

44 Ibid 11, 134–59

45 C. Augustijn *Erasmus en de Reformatie: Een onderzoek naar de houding die Erasmus ten opzichte van de Reformatie heeft aangenomen* 11, 14–17. On Lindeboom and Huizinga, see *Man On His Own* 307–9, 368–72.

46 Augustijn *Erasmus en de Reformatie* 28, 42, 46, 63, 88

47 Ibid 66–7; Heinz Holeczek 'Die Haltung des Erasmus zu Luther nach dem Scheitern seiner Vermittlungspolitik 1520/1' esp 107–11; Erasmus to Justus Jonas 10 May 1521 Ep 1202 Allen 4:486–93, CWE 8: 201–11

48 Augustijn *Erasmus en de Reformatie* 100, 102, 115, 143–5, 159. Cf Boyle 'Erasmus and the "Modern" Question: Was He Semi-Pelagian?'

49 Augustijn *Erasmus en de Reformatie* 174–5, 180, 184–5. Augustijn refers to the famous Erlangen dissertation of G. Krodel 'Die Abendmahlslehre des Erasmus von Rotterdam und seine Stellung am Anfang des Abendsmahlsstreites der Reformatoren,' which I have not seen.

50 Augustijn *Erasmus en de Reformatie* 226, 231–2, 281–2, 301

51 Cornelis Augustijn *Erasmus: His Life, Works and Influence* chs 10–12, esp 132–3, 138–9, 150–2, 158

52 See ch 3 above.

53 Eg, James D. Tracy *Erasmus of the Low Countries*, discussed in ch 7 below.

54 Austin Flannery (gen ed) *Vatican Council II: The Conciliar and Post Conciliar Documents* 363 (biblical references omitted)

55 Coppens *Scrinium* 2:589–90, esp 590n

56 Karl Schätti *Erasmus von Rotterdam und die Römische Kurie* 16–17, 61–2, 75, 77, 85–6, 136–7

57 Georg Gebhart *Die Stellung des Erasmus von Rotterdam zur Römische Kirche* 26, 332–9

58 Ibid 31, 66, 106–7. One reference is to Erasmus' exposition of Psalm 1: 'Happy the man, therefore, who has always taken his stand on Christ, always clung to the evidence of Holy Writ, always accepted the decrees of the church, and never "walked in the council of the impious"' (CWE 63:17).

59 Gebhart *Die Stellung* 159, 163

60 Ibid 218–19. Gebhart follows Hans Baron 'Erasmus-Probleme im Spiegel des Colloquium "Inquisitio de Fide."' Cf George Hunston Williams 'Erasmus and the Reformers on Non-Christian Religions and *Salus extra Ecclesiam*,' in Theodore K. Rabb and Jerrold E. Seigel (eds) *Action and Conviction in Early Modern Europe: Essays in Memory of E.H. Harbison* 324–37, which links Erasmus' views on this subject to his 'doctrinal simplification of Christianity.'

61 Gebhart *Die Stellung* 231, 269–70, 274, 287. Cf H.J. McSorley's 'Erasmus and the Primacy of the Roman Pontiff: Between Conciliarism and Papalism,' which sets out 'to demonstrate that Erasmus was clearly influenced by both conciliarism and papalism but was an uncritical follower of neither' (38n).

62 I follow a comment of the late Robert Scribner's. I have not seen Willi Hentze *Kirche und kirchliche Einheit bei Desiderius Erasmus von Rotterdam* (Paderborn 1974), which presents itself as a 'theologiegeschichtliche bzw. ekklesiologiegeschichtlich systematische Arbeit' and also concludes that Erasmus held 'eine gut katholische Einstellung' (ARG *Literaturbericht* 4 [1975]: 60–1).

63 Otto Schottenloher 'Erasmus und die *Respublica Christiana*' 296–301. Cf my 'The Three Circles of Erasmus of Rotterdam.'

64 Schottenloher 'Erasmus und die *Respublica Christiana*' 302–8, 319–21. *Paraclesis* Holborn 145 lines 6–7, Olin *Christian Humanism* 104. Mc-

Conica, too, returned to his quincentenary theme by demonstrating how, in the *Julius Exclusus*, Erasmus took a view of the church quite different from late-medieval ones, whether papalist or conciliarist, a view McConica describes as humanist and evangelical ('Erasmus and the "Julius": A Humanist Reflects on the Church,' in Charles Trinkaus with Heiko A. Oberman [eds] *The Pursuit of Holiness in Late Medieval and Renaissance Religion* 444–67). It is not possible in this study to enter into the subject of the *Julius Exclusus*. McConica reviews the literature up to the time of his essay in an appendix (ibid 467–71). In his *Erasmus* of 1991 he suggests the essential radicalism of the three-circles image (61–2).

65 Manfred Hoffmann 'Erasmus on Church and Ministry,' in ERSY 6 (1986): 1–30; Hilmar M. Pabel 'The Peaceful People of Christ: The Irenic Ecclesiology of Erasmus of Rotterdam,' in Pabel (ed) *Erasmus' Vision of the Church* 57–93

66 Germain Marc'hadour 'Erasmus as Priest: Holy Orders in His Vision and Practice,' in Pabel (ed) *Erasmus' Vision* 115–49, esp 129, 140, 146

67 Hoffmann 'Erasmus on Church and Ministry' 2–3

68 Margolin says of Screech that 'le fougueux et enthousiaste savant brittanique' loves to cross swords with his Erasmian colleagues (*Quinze années* 610).

69 Kohls *Theologie* 1:16

70 Manfred Hoffmann *Erkenntnis und Verwirklichung der wahren Theologie nach Erasmus von Rotterdam* 28–36

71 Georges Chantraine *'Mystère et 'Philosophie du Christ' selon Erasme* 14, 206–7, 224; Marjorie O'Rourke Boyle *Erasmus on Language and Method in Theology* 108

72 Chantraine *'Mystère'* 282, 298, 307–8; Boyle 74–81, 91, 93

73 Chantraine *'Mystère'* 6. On mystery, 'one of the most important keywords of Christianity and its theology,' see Karl Rahner in *Encyclopedia of Theology: The Concise Sacramentum Mundi* 1000–4.

74 Chantraine *'Mystère'* 158, 179; Boyle *Erasmus on Language* xiii, 9, 30, 36–7, 40–1, 52–3, 199 n132

75 Chantraine *'Mystère'* 259n; Boyle *Erasmus on Language* 244n

76 Hoffmann *Erkenntnis* 8, 48–9, 58–9, 64–5

77 Ibid 38n, 50, 57, 61–4, 79, 87–8, 99, 168

78 Ibid 40, 65–8; Boyle *Erasmus on Language* 84–5, 92, 98–108

79 Chantraine *'Mystère'* 86, 139, 141–2, 145–6, 184–5, 235, 378–9

80 Godin *Erasme lecteur d'Origène* 508–9, 524

81 Chantraine 'L'Apologia ad Latomum. Deux conceptions de théologie,' in *Scrinium* 2:51–75; Godin *Erasme lecteur d'Origène* 169, 207, 238–9. Godin shows more sympathy for Boyle's work, while asking how *logos* can be central when the word appears so rarely in Erasmus' writing (ibid 502n).

82 Cf the remark of Henri de Lubac, Chantraine's mentor: Erasmus did

not reject the old teaching on the four senses of scripture, rather he attempted to snatch it from death (*Exégèse médiévale. Les quatre sens de L'Ecriture* IV.2 436). Margolin suggests some parallels between Erasmus' position in these early sixteenth-century controversies and the 'modernism' of Alfred Loisy in the early twentieth century (*Erasme, précepteur* 366).

83 Godin *Erasme lecteur d'Origène* 169, 197–201, 209. Jacques Lacan asks how Erasmus could occupy a revolutionary place in history and answers that 'the slightest alteration in the relation between man and the signifier, in this case in the procedures of exegesis, changes the whole course of history by modifying the moorings that anchor his being' (*Ecrits: A Selection* [trans Alan Sheridan] 174. Reference owed to Nicholas Mansfield).

84 Godin *Erasme lecteur d'Origène* 3, 48–9, 54n, 69

85 M.A. Screech *Ecstasy and the Praise of Folly* 11, 202–10

86 Ibid xix, 3–4, 62. On the 1514 edition, cf Clarence H. Miller 'Introduction' ASD IV-3 29–31.

87 Cf A.H.T. Levi 'Introduction' *Praise of Folly* 15–16

88 For a compendium to the late 1960s, Kathleen Williams (ed) *Twentieth Century Interpretations of 'The Praise of Folly': A Collection of Critical Essays*.

89 Geraldine Thompson *Under Pretext of Praise: Satiric Mode in Erasmus' Fiction* 53, 55, 72, 84; A.E. Douglas 'Erasmus as Satirist,' in T.A. Dorey (ed) *Erasmus* 31–54, whose opinion of the *Folly* is not high.

90 Walter Kaiser *Praisers of Folly: Erasmus, Rabelais, Shakespeare* 37, 51–2

91 Ibid 46–50; Hoyt Hopewell Hudson 'Analysis' *Praise of Folly* 129–42. For further bibliography, see Miller ASD IV-3 18nn.

92 Clarence H. Miller 'Some Medieval Elements and Structural Unity in Erasmus' *Praise of Folly*'

93 W.A. Rebhorn 'The Metamorphoses of Moria: Structure and Meaning in *The Praise of Folly*' argues for its intentional unity, as does Richard Sylvester, who finds 'a kind of Hegelian pattern' in the work's three stages ('The Problem of Unity in the *Praise of Folly*' 138). Cf Zoja Pavlovskis *The Praise of Folly: Structure and Irony* (1983).

94 Miller ASD IV-3 20 and note

95 Screech *Ecstasy* 13, 20–6, 37, 55–6, 64, 75–7, 89 (on Ficino), 114, 116

96 Ibid 46, 50, 57–8, 68, 92, 128, 141, 194–202

97 Ibid 239

98 Ibid 69, 71

99 'Gaudium et spes,' in Flannery (ed) *Vatican Council II Documents* 932

100 CWE 49:18–19, LB 7:161A

101 John C. Olin *Six Essays on Erasmus* 67

102 Denys Gorce 'La patristique dans la réforme d'Erasme,' in *Festgabe Joseph Lortz* 1:233–76 at 233–8, 254

103 Ibid 242, 250: Pierre Imbart de la Tour *Les Origines de la Réforme* 3 (cf *Man On His Own* 233–5).

104 Eg, Olin 'Erasmus and Saint Jerome: The Close Bond and Its Significance,' in ERSY 7 (1987): 33–53, at 44, 50

105 de Lubac *Exégèse médiévale* IV.2 429–31, 442, 463–5

106 Olin 'Erasmus and St. Ignatius Loyola,' in *Six Essays* 75–92, at 81–2. See the literature there referred to (esp at 86–8), which cannot be reviewed here. Bataillon *Erasme et l'Espagne* 1:631. Cf 'D'Erasme à la Compagnie de Jésus,' in ibid 3:279–304, which demonstrates the Jesuit indifference, or resistance, to many elements in the monastic tradition, to which Erasmus also was cool.

107 Olin *Erasmus, Utopia, and the Jesuits: Essays on the Outreach of Humanism* xiii–xiv, 96, and 'Erasmus and St. Ignatius' 81

108 de Lubac *Exégèse* IV.2 459

109 Anthony Grafton and Lisa Jardine *From Humanism to the Humanities: Education and Liberal Arts in Fifteenth- and Sixteenth-Century Europe* 144

110 Henk Jan de Jonge '*Novum Testamentum a nobis versum*: The Essence of Erasmus' Edition of the New Testament' 395, 401, 403, 405–6, 412

111 Andrew J. Brown 'The Date of Erasmus' Latin Translation of the New Testament' 351–2, 360, 364, 368, 371–2. Correspondence: Erasmus to Reuchlin August 1514 Ep 300 Allen 2:4–5 lines 31–3; Erasmus to Wimpfeling 21 September 1514 Ep 305 ibid 23 lines 222–4 (respectively, CWE 3:7 lines 33–5, 32 lines 228–9). A later intervention by de Jonge demonstrates at least a start by 1512. He relies on Erasmus' use of the words *castigare* and *castigatio* in correspondence from 1512 (eg, in his letter to Pieter Gillis of autumn 1512: 'Absolvam castigationem Novi Testamenti' [Ep 264 Allen 1:517 lines 13–14, CWE 2:234 line 16]) ('Wann ist Erasmus' Übersetzung des Neuen Testaments entstanden,' in *Erasmus of Rotterdam* 151–7).

112 Erika Rummel *Erasmus' 'Annotations' on the New Testament: From Philologist to Theologian* 24–5

113 Catherine A.L. Jarrott 'Erasmus's Annotations and Colet's Commentaries on Paul: A Comparison of Some Theological Themes,' in DeMolen (ed) *Essays* 125

114 Jarrott 'Erasmus' Biblical Humanism' 151

115 Research has been promoted by the publication in facsimile of the final Latin text with all earlier variants: Reeve; Reeve and Screech.

116 John B. Payne 'Erasmus and Lefèvre d'Etaples as Interpreters of Paul' 62–4; Jerry H. Bentley 'Erasmus' *Annotationes in Novum Testamentum* and the Textual Criticism of the Gospels' 38–41, 44–6, and *Humanists and Holy Writ: New Testament Scholarship in the Renaissance* 184–90; Rummel *Erasmus' 'Annotations'* 62

117 Albert Rabil Jr *Erasmus and the New Testament: The Mind of a Christian Humanist* 100–3; Bentley 'Erasmus' *Annotationes*' 42–4, and *Humanists* 187–8; Payne 'Erasmus and Lefèvre d'Etaples' 65

118 Payne 'Erasmus: Interpreter of Romans' 17–25. Cf 'Toward the Hermeneutics of Erasmus,' in *Scrinium* 2:13–49, and Bentley *Humanists* 189–91. Writing from a Reformed standpoint, T.F. Torrance, well grounded in Erasmus but without reference to scholarship since 1955, writes about Erasmus' hermeneutic with understanding (eg, of his exalted view of the proclaimed Word), but makes an inappropriate distinction between the 'ethical and social' and the 'evangelical and theological,' associating Erasmus essentially with the former ('The Hermeneutics of Erasmus,' in Elsie Anne McKee and Brian G. Armstrong (eds) *Probing the Reformed Tradition: Historical Studies in Honor of Edward A. Dowey, Jr.* 48–76, esp 49, 65).

119 Payne 'The Significance of Lutheranizing Changes in Erasmus' Interpretation of Paul's Letters to the Romans and Galatians in his *Annotationes* (1527) and *Paraphrases* (1532),' in Olivier Fatio and Pierre Fraenkel (eds) *Histoire de l'exégèse au XVIe siècle* 312–30, at 330; Rabil *Erasmus and the New Testament* 137–9; Bentley *Humanists* 191

120 See Friedhelm Krüger *Humanistische Evangelienauslegung* 239–46 (Conclusion).

121 Rummel *Erasmus' 'Annotations'* 52–74

122 Bentley 'Biblical Philology and Christian Humanism: Lorenzo Valla and Erasmus as Scholars of the Gospels' 19, 26–7, and *Humanists* 140–2 (cf Godin *Erasme lecteur* 144); Jacques Chomarat 'Les *Annotations* de Valla, celles d'Erasme et la grammaire,' in Fatio and Fraenkel *Histoire de l'exégèse* 208, 215–17, 223, 226. Rummel, following Erasmus himself, diminishes his debt to Valla (*Erasmus' 'Annotations'* 12–15, 49–50, 85–8).

123 Heinz Holeczek *Humanistische Bibelphilologie als Reformproblem bei Erasmus von Rotterdam, Thomas More und William Tyndale* 83, 88–9 (Valla), 92, 98 (discussion of Erasmus based on his dedication to Christopher Fisher of his edition of Valla's annotations: Ep 182 Allen 1:406–12 CWE 2:89–97); Werner Schwarz *Principles and Problems of Biblical Translation: Some Reformation Controversies and Their Background* 146

124 Chomarat 'Les *Annotations'* 209–10

125 Holeczek *Humanistische Bibelphilologie* 92, 98, 130, 133, 135–7

126 Bo Reicke 'Erasmus und die neutestamentliche Textgeschichte'; Holeczek *Humanistische Bibelphilologie* 115; Bentley *Humanists* 137–9, 193; Rummel *Erasmus' 'Annotations'* 41–2

127 Bentley *Humanists* 144–5, 153–5, and 'Erasmus, Jean Le Clerc, and the Principle of the Harder Reading'

128 Review of *Scrinium* in *Revue d'histoire et de philosophie religieuses* 51 (1971): 106

129 J.W. O'Malley 'Introduction' CWE 66:xi–xii, xvii, xix, xxiii

130 Ibid xxix

131 See note 109 above.

132 On Dilthey, Troeltsch, and Wernle, *Man On His Own* 285–92. See also Johannes von Walter 'Das Ende der Erasmusrenaissance,' in *Christentum und Frömmigkeit: Gesämmelte Verträge und Aufsätze* 153–62.
133 Renaudet *Erasme et l'Italie* xi, 200–1
134 J.V.M. Pollet 'Easmiana: Quelques aspects du problème érasmien d'après les publications récentes' 387
135 Trevor-Roper 'Desiderius Erasmus' 64–6. On Gibbon, *Man On His Own* 34–5
136 H.A. Enno van Gelder *The Two Reformations in the 16th Century: A Study of the Religious Aspects and Consequences of Renaissance and Humanism*. On Erasmus, ch 4. For a contemporary reiteration of the case, Siegfried Wollgast 'Erasmianer und die Geschichte des Nonkonformismus. Aspekte,' in Mout, Smolinsky and Trapman (eds) *Erasmianism* 105–26. It finishes: 'Erasmus supplied ammunition for emancipation struggles which went far beyond the Reformation of Luther, Zwingli and Calvin' (126).
137 Padberg *Erasmus als Katechet. Der literarische Beitrag des Erasmus von Rotterdam zur katholischen Katechese des 16. Jahrhunderts. Eine Untersuchung zum Geschichte der Katechese*, esp 46–7, 50, 52, 64, 76, 79, 82, 101. Padberg himself notices the literary contrast (ibid 73n). The two catechetical works are *Christiani hominis institutum* (1513–14) (CWE 85:92–107), and *Explanatio symboli apostolorum sive catechismus* (1533) (CWE 70:231–387).
138 Donald Nugent 'The Erasmus Renaissance' 37
139 O'Malley 'Introduction' CWE 66:xv

CHAPTER SIX

1 James J. Murphy (ed) *Renaissance Eloquence: Studies in the Theory and Practice of Renaissance Rhetoric* 29. Cf Don Paul Abbott 'The Renaissance,' in Winifred Bryan Horner (ed) *The Present State of Scholarship in Historical and Contemporary Rhetoric* 75–100.
2 John O. Ward 'Renaissance Commentators on Ciceronian Rhetoric,' in Murphy *Renaissance Eloquence* 126–7, 168; W. Keith Percival 'Grammar and Rhetoric in the Renaissance,' in ibid 307, 329; Hanna H. Gray 'Renaissance Humanism: The Pursuit of Eloquence'; Paul Oskar Kristeller 'Rhetoric in Medieval and Renaissance Culture,' in Murphy 1–19 (cf 'Humanism and Scholasticism in the Italian Renaissance,' based on a lecture given at Brown University in December 1944, in *Renaissance Thought: The Classic, Scholastic, and Humanist Strains* 98–9, 150).
3 Roland Barthes (1977), quoted in Patrick Fuery and Nick Mansfield *Cultural Studies and the New Humanities: Concepts and Controversies* 66
4 Bouwsma 'The Renaissance and the Drama of Western History,' in *A Usable Past: Essays in European Cultural History* 348–65, esp 357–60.

Cf 'From History of Ideas to History of Meaning,' in ibid 336–47, first published in *Journal of Interdisciplinary History* 12 (1981): 279–91.

5 John E. Toews 'Intellectual History after the Linguistic Turn' esp 898–9. See also Dominick LaCapra *Rethinking Intellectual History: Texts, Contexts, Language* and *History and Criticism*.

6 Among recent studies, see, eg, John Monfasani 'Humanism and Rhetoric,' in Albert Rabil Jr (ed) *Renaissance Humanism: Foundations, Forms, and Legacy* 3 *Humanism and the Disciplines* 171–235; Peter Mack 'Humanist Rhetoric and Dialectic,' in Jill Kraye (ed) *The Cambridge Companion to Renaissance Humanism* 82–99; Kathy Eden *Hermeneutics and the Rhetorical Tradition: Chapters in the Ancient Legacy and Its Humanist Reception*.

7 Toews 'Intellectual History' 906

8 Kenneth Gouwens 'Perceiving the Past: Renaissance Humanism after the "Cognitive Turn,"' drawing on the cognitive psychology of Jerome Bruner, esp his *Culture of Education* (1996). Both Gouwens and Bruner accept the idea of 'dialogue' with the past.

9 Chomarat does not make extensive reference to predecessors.

10 Margaret Mann Phillips 'Erasmus and the Classics,' in T.A. Dorey (ed) *Erasmus* 1–30; Rudolf Pfeiffer *History of Classical Scholarship from 1300 to 1850* 71–81, esp 74

11 Walter Rüegg *Cicero und der Humanismus* vii–xiii, xxii–xxiii, xxviii–xxx

12 Ibid 67–70

13 Ibid 76; Ep 152, to James Voecht (Jakob Voogd) 28/4/[1501] Allen 1:355–7, CWE 2:29–32

14 Rüegg *Cicero und der Humanismus* 82, 85–7, 90, 107, 117–18

15 Ibid 111

16 J.K. Sowards 'Erasmus and the Apologetic Textbook: A Study of the *De duplici Copia verborum ac rerum*' 126–8, 134

17 Guilio Vallese 'Erasme et le *De duplici Copia verborum ac rerum*,' in *Coll Tur* 1:233–9, at 239. For a review of twentieth-century references to *De Copia*, see Virginia W. Callahan 'The *De Copia*: The Bounteous Horn,' in Richard L. DeMolen (ed) *Essays on the Works of Erasmus* 99–109

18 Terence Cave speaks of the 'duplicity' of *copia*, for the versatility of language obscures the wavering in the meaning of *res* between 'object-thing' and 'word-thing' (*The Cornucopian Text: Problems of Writing in the French Renaissance* 22, 34).

19 Chomarat *Grammaire et rhétorique chez Erasme* 2:719, 731, 733, 758

20 Ibid 767. Admittedly, the treatment of the *Adagia* is limited to his theme at that point in his book: 'Style and art of writing.'

21 Margaret Mann Phillips *The 'Adages' of Erasmus* 5–8

22 Ibid 102, 104, 107, 112

23 Chomarat *Grammaire et rhétorique* 1:156, 159, 161; 2:962–70. Reference on these themes is also to *De recta latini graecique sermonis pronuntiatione dialogus*.

24 Jean-Claude Margolin *Erasme: Declamatio de pueris statim ac liberaliter instituendis: Etude critique, traduction et commentaire* 20, 22, 41, 45, 49–50, 56
25 Ibid 65, 72, 76–82, 94–5
26 Anthony Grafton and Lisa Jardine *From Humanism to the Humanities: Education and the Liberal Arts in Fifteenth- and Sixteenth-Century Europe* xvi, 23–4, 134, 136, 138–9, 141, 144–5, 148
27 Margolin *Erasme: De pueris* 45, 85
28 Peter Bietenholz *History and Biography in the Work of Erasmus of Rotterdam* 12–17, 19, 25, 28–9, 35, 38, 40 (*kairoi*), 45
29 Ibid 37, 39, 41, 43–4
30 Ibid 12, 61–2, 69, 73–4, 79, 85–7
31 Ibid 91–4, 98; 'Life of Jerome' CWE 61:19–62. Cf John B. Maguire 'Erasmus' Biographical Masterpiece: *Hieronymi Stridonensis Vita.*'
32 M.P. Gilmore '*Fides et Eruditio*: Erasmus and the Study of History,' in *Humanists and Jurists: Six Studies in the Renaissance* 87–114, esp 108. Bietenholz is aware of his difference from Gilmore over Erasmus' sense of historical development (*History and Biography* 29n).
33 J. IJsewijn and C. Matheeussen 'Erasme et l'historiographie,' in G. Verbeke and J. IJsewijn (eds) *The Late Middle Ages and the Dawn of Humanism outside Italy* 31–43. Cf *Enarratio Psalmi XXXIII* LB 5:371DE, 373DE, 378AB
34 G.W. Pigman III 'Imitation and the Renaissance Sense of the Past: The Reception of Erasmus' *Ciceronianus*' 158–9, 161, 171, 175
35 Chomarat 2:828, 832–3, 841–3
36 Z.S. Schiffman 'Renaissance Historicism Reconsidered'
37 Chomarat *Grammaire et rhétorique* 2:848. On the three functions, Quintilian *Institutio oratoria* III.v.2.
38 His documentation is to the Amsterdam edition (ASD I–3, 1972), edited by Bierlaire, L.-E. Halkin, and R. Hoven, which gives the text of the first edition of each colloquy (Bierlaire *Erasme et ses Colloques* 9–10).
39 Ibid 10, 14–19, 24–5, 42, 51
40 Ibid 45. Cf *Les Colloques d'Erasme* 75.
41 *Les Colloques* 75–80, 101, 131–2, 140
42 Ibid 224–6, 262, 290. Cf 241 (on sacraments), 254 (on monasticism), 264 (on ceremonies).
43 Ibid 262
44 Ibid 189, 199. I take the English titles from C.R. Thompson's translation.
45 An even more unitary view than Bierlaire's has been put (Geraldine Thompson 'As Bones to the Body: The Scope of *Inventio* in the *Colloquies* of Erasmus,' in De Molen (ed) *Essays* 163–78, esp 170.
46 Terence Cave *The Cornucopian Text: Problems of Writing in the French Renaissance* 107

47 Bierlaire *Les Colloques* 165–6, 168–70, 307
48 Chomarat *Grammaire et rhétorique* 2:871, 887, 891–2, 896, 916, 926, 929.
   Erasmus uses the image of the cuttlefish in the colloquy 'The Lover of
   Glory' (*Philodoxus*) (Thompson *Colloquies* 484). Cf, for other uses,
   Chomarat *Grammaire et rhétorique* 2:929n368.
49 J.W. Binns 'The Letters of Erasmus,' in T.A. Dorey (ed) *Erasmus* 55–79,
   at 60
50 Judith Rice Henderson 'Erasmus on the Art of Letter-Writing,' in
   Murphy (ed) *Renaissance Eloquence* 331–55, at 331–2
51 Binns 'Letters,' esp 71–2; Henderson 'Erasmus on the Art of Letter-
   Writing,' esp 350–3; Aloïs Gerlo 'The *Opus de conscribendis epistolis* of
   Erasmus and the Tradition of the *Ars epistolica*,' in R.R. Bolgar (ed)
   Classical Influences on European Culture AD 500–1500 esp 107–8; Léon-
   E. Halkin 'Erasme éditeur de sa correspondance: le cas de l'*Auctarium*' 240; above all, M. Fumaroli 'Genèse de l'epistolographie classique: rhétorique humaniste de la lettre, de Pétrarque à Juste Lipse.'
   Cf Chomarat *Grammaire et rhétorique* 2:1010, 1014, 1016, 1020, 1026,
   1032, 1051. On Erasmus' own published collections, see Halkin *Erasmus ex Erasmo: Erasme éditeur de sa correspondance*.
52 Chomarat *Grammaire et rhétorique* 2:1059. Charles Béné's explanation
   is that preaching was too new a subject for Erasmus, and one on
   which he could not turn to Augustine's *De doctrina christiana* (*Erasme
   et Saint Augustin* 375). Chomarat was finally to prepare the *Ecclesiastes*
   for the Amsterdam edition: ASD V-4/5.
53 Robert G. Kleinhans '*Ecclesiastes sive de Ratione Concionandi*,' in De
   Molen (ed) *Essays* 253–66; James M. Weiss '*Ecclesiastes* and Erasmus:
   The Mirror and the Image'
54 Kleinhans '*Ecclesiastes*' 255, 261–3
55 Weiss '*Ecclesiastes* and Erasmus' 90–3, 97, 99n, 102. Cf Jacques Etienne
   Spiritualisme érasmien et théologiens louvanistes 59–60.
56 Weiss '*Ecclesiastes* and Erasmus' 90, 96. Weiss thinks especially of
   rhetoric's relation to grammar and dialectic. Cf J.W. O'Malley's contention that Erasmus subordinated rhetoric to grammar, part of a
   larger argument about his preference for the contemplative over the
   public and active life, which seems to underestimate his role as a
   public intellectual ('Grammar and Rhetoric in the *pietas* of Erasmus').
   O'Malley's own article on the *Ecclesiastes* emphasizes its originality,
   its break from the scholastic, thematic sermon towards something
   more didactic and homiletic and, therefore, pastoral. Erasmus' ideal
   of preaching anticipated that of later, even the Counter-Reformation,
   preachers ('Erasmus and the History of Sacred Rhetoric: The *Ecclesiastes* of 1535,' in ERSY 5 [1985]: 1–29, at 13–15, 24–5, 28–9).
57 Kleinhans '*Ecclesiastes*' 254, 265n
58 Chomarat *Grammaire et rhétorique* 2:1063; Erasmus at ASD V-4 248–51,
   esp lines 30–40

59 Chomarat *Grammaire et rhétorique* 2:1071–85
60 Ibid 1101–2, 1109–10, 1142–3; Quintilian *Institutio* VI.v.11, XI.i.42–7
61 See above ch 5.
62 Marjorie O'Rourke Boyle *Christening Pagan Mysteries* 7–11, 15, 17
63 Ibid 28, 30–2, 34, 38, 41, 47, 58
64 Ibid 68, 85, 87
65 Cf Chomarat *Grammaire et rhétorique* 1:586
66 J.-C. Margolin, in BHR 60 (1998): 815–16, ERSY 19 (1999): 111–13
67 Chomarat *Grammaire et rhétorique* 1:16–20, 165–6, 403; on Béné, 167–79; on Horace, Eckhart Shäfer 'Erasmus und Horaz'
68 Chomarat *Grammaire et rhétorique* 1:25, 29, 36, 39, 66, 73–4, 435; 2:905, 1161
69 Ibid 1:61, 71, 73, 692, 695 (on the Psalms commentaries); 2:914, 988–9
70 Ibid 2:1150, where Chomarat puts the matter in tabular form.
71 Ibid 1:698, 700
72 Ibid 1:71, 91, 93, 99–101, 103, 149–50; 2:1164
73 Ibid 1:148, 550
74 Ibid 2:815, 820–1
75 Ibid 1:378
76 Ibid 1:553, 2:841–3
77 Ibid 1:525–6; 2:1159
78 Ibid 1:224, 259–61, 263, 276
79 Ibid 1:387–8, 392
80 Ibid 1:38n, 177, 263, 338, 341–2, 430–1, 433
81 Ibid 1:499, 501–2, 562, 564, 570, 576, 584–5
82 Ibid 2:1160
83 Ibid 1:651–4; 2:1162–3, 1168
84 Ibid 2:1165. That Chomarat makes a cross-reference to Erik Erikson's work on the young Luther is not altogether reassuring about this line of argument.
85 Ibid 2:1161
86 Ibid 2:1162
87 See ch 3 above.
88 Eg, Manfred Hoffmann in ERSY 5 (1985): 65–83, at 82: Erasmus' 'tendency toward refinement, toward intellectualizing, moralizing, and spiritualizing is grossly blown out of proportion.'
89 Walter M. Gordon *Humanist Play and Belief: The Seriocomic Art of Desiderius Erasmus* 11, 259–60
90 Quoted Marie-Dominique Chenu *Nature, Man, and Society in the Twelfth Century: Essays on New Theological Perspectives in the Latin West* 117
91 Ibid 118
92 Hans Urs von Balthasar *The Glory of the Lord: A Theological Aesthetics* 1 *Seeing the Form* 77
93 Huizinga *Homo Ludens: A Study of the Play-Element in Culture* 14–19

94 Gordon *Humanist Play* 164–9
95 Ibid 92–3, 120
96 Ibid 100, 111, 115, 117–18, 130–8
97 Ibid 161. Cf Chantraine *Mystère* 275, 282, 295 (see also ch 5 above).
98 Gordon *Humanist Play* 181–2
99 Ibid 189; ASD IV-3 104–6, CWE 27:103–4
100 Gordon *Humanist Play* 201, 205, 210–11
101 Mikhail Bakhtin *Rabelais and His World* 11, 14; Donald Gwynn Watson 'Erasmus' *Praise of Folly* and the Spirit of Carnival'
102 Gordon *Humanist Play* 215–17. Cf Screech *Ecstasy* 24–5, 37–8.
103 Gordon *Humanist Play* 223–6, 229, 231, 242–5, 252–3
104 Note the difference between Gordon's and Chomarat's comments on Erasmus' attitude to the resurrection of the body: Gordon *Humanist Play* 245–6; Chomarat *Grammaire et rhétorique* 2:912, 914, 961. Gordon follows the *Paraphrase* of 1 Corinthians 15 (LB 7:909 D–F). Cf David Marsh 'Erasmus on the Antithesis of Body and Soul.'
105 Manfred Hoffmann *Rhetoric and Theology: The Hermeneutic of Erasmus* 17–18
106 Hoffmann ERSY 5 (1985): 71
107 Hoffmann *Rhetoric and Theology* 3–4, 8–9
108 Ibid 62–3
109 Ibid 9, 11. For a summary of Erasmus' approach to the fourfold sense of scripture, 104.
110 Ibid 126
111 Ibid 82, 97
112 Ibid 23–7, 73, 88–9
113 Erasmus to Johann von Botzheim 30 January 1523 Ep 1341A CWE 9:340
114 Hoffmann *Rhetoric and Theology* 6, 152
115 Cf ibid 272 n86, which refers to the two circles or spheres, the heavenly and the earthly, that Erasmus mentions in the letter to the reader concluding his *Paraphrase on John*. He says there: 'Neither of these can be pointed to with a finger, but each resides in our deepest feelings, though sometimes showing itself in our very actions, except in so far as actions are also pretended' (CWE 46:226). The better-known image of the three circles deals with the dilemma of love and justice (see my 'The Three Circles of Erasmus of Rotterdam').
116 Lisa Jardine *Erasmus, Man of Letters: The Construction of Charisma in Print* 13, 23, 29–30, 47–8
117 Ibid 74, 145
118 Ibid 13, 147
119 Ibid 23, 43, 93, 95, 110–11. In a study of Dürer's famous engraving of Erasmus, Andrée Hayum finds a bond between them in their common devotion to the printing medium and the power of the 'exactly

repeatable image' ('Dürer's Portrait of Erasmus and the Ars Typographorum').

120 Jardine *Erasmus, Man of Letters* 59, 62–3
121 Léon-E. Halkin *Erasmus ex Erasmo: Erasme éditeur de sa correspondance* 32, 36, 39, 61, 64, 205–10
122 Jardine *Erasmus, Man of Letters* 153, 227n25
123 Ibid 118, 122, 129
124 Ibid 187. As a further example, see Jardine 'Penfriends and Patria: Erasmian Pedagogy and the Republic of Letters,' in ERSY 16 (1996): 1–18, which, in particular, deconstructs the publications, especially *De Copia*, surrounding Erasmus' renowned visit to Strasbourg in 1514.
125 Jardine *Erasmus, Man of Letters* 149
126 Ibid 153, 162
127 Tracy 'Erasmus among the Postmodernists,' in Hilmar M. Pabel (ed) *Erasmus' Vision of the Church* 1–40
128 Ibid 11. Tracy follows Chomarat, who speaks of the 'pious lie' *Grammaire et rhétorique* (2:929).
129 Tracy 'Erasmus among the Postmodernists' 8; Hans-Georg Gadamer *Truth and Method* 236, 238, 245, 261, 269–73
130 Halkin *Erasmus ex Erasmo* 209
131 Tracy 'Erasmus among the Postmodernists' 18
132 Ibid 26. Cf Tracy 'From Humanism to the Humanities: A Critique of Grafton and Jardine.' Marie-Madeleine de la Garanderie poses more starkly than Grafton and Jardine the problematic of the Christian and the classical in humanism, at best 'an unstable equilibrium' (*Christianisme et lettres profanes* 10).
133 Tracy 'Erasmus among the Postmodernists' 27
134 Ibid 29; Norbert Elias *The Civilizing Process: The History of Manners* ch 2
135 Tracy 'Erasmus among the Postmodernists' 38
136 For an attempt along this line in relation to the spiritualizing and realistic elements in his social thought, see my 'The Social Thought of Erasmus.'
137 But notice Jean-Claude Margolin's 'Tribut d'un antihumaniste aux études d'humanisme et Renaissance: Note sur l'oeuvre de Michel Foucault' of 1967, another arrow in Margolin's quiver from the time of the quincentenary. He notes the attraction Foucault feels for Erasmus' Folly, with her two-faced judgments on human weaknesses and illusions, even if, for Foucault, the humanist understanding of folly was a thinning out and weakening of the late-medieval understanding, which was tragic, cosmic, and eschatological (702–5; Michel Foucault *Histoire de la Folie à l'âge classique* 33–7, 48, 50); in face of Foucault's depiction (in his 'The Prose of the World,' chapter 2 of *The Order of Things: An Archaeology of the Human Sciences*) of the

sixteenth century as a world of signs and resemblances, impersonal and beyond man, Margolin defends the Renaissance idea of the primacy, the indispensability, of human language (705–6); indeed, he sees the possibility of a coalescence, on the language problem, between Foucault and the Erasmus of the *Lingua* of 1525 (710).

138 But see Charles Witke 'Erasmus Autor et Actor,' in ERSY 15 (1995): 26–52, which builds on Jardine's insight that 'nothing Erasmus does seems gratuitous or unpurposeful in regard to a larger strategy' and demonstrates the encompassing presence of his persona in two of his smaller commentaries; Erasmus thus broke with the traditional understanding of commentary as facilitator to a canonical text and made his commentary an independent text of status; that was part of a strategy of self-construction in and through print (26–9).

CHAPTER SEVEN

1 *Praemium Erasmianum MCMLXXXVI* 9, 13
2 Ibid 34–5, 44–5
3 Václav Havel *Disturbing the Peace: A Conversation with Karel Hvízdala* 62–6. Cf John Keane *Václav Havel: A Political Tragedy in Six Acts* 315–16.
4 *Praemium Erasmianum* 29, 45. Jan Patocka was a distinguished philosopher who 'died after a police interrogation about his work as Charter 77 spokesperson' in 1977 (Havel *Disturbing the Peace* 214).
5 *Erasmus Universiteit Rotterdam: In Vogelvlucht* [1986]
6 *Gymnasium Erasmianum Rotterdam: Voorlichtingsboekje* [1986] 2–3
7 J. Nuchelmans *Erasmus en de muziek* (reprinted in J. Sperna Weiland et al *Erasmus: De actualiteit van zijn denken* 113–36)
8 Programs in Nuchelmans *Erasmus en de muziek* np. Performers included Ton Koopman and the Royal Consort, Eveline Juten (lute), and singers from the Festival of Old Music Utrecht.
9 A.M. Koldeweij *Erasmus: zicht op een geleerde in zijn tijd* np (reprinted in Sperna Weiland *Erasmus: De actualiteit van zijn denken* 137–80, at 138); Erwin Panofsky 'Erasmus and the Visual Arts' 204
10 *Erasmus: zicht op een geleerde* 'Catalogus' np; Jardine 47–8
11 Jardine *Erasmus, Man of Letters* 41–5
12 Blockmans, in Sperna Weiland *Erasmus: De actualiteit van zijn denken* 63–4, 67, 70, 72n46
13 Sperna Weiland, in ibid 79, 89
14 For appreciations of Halkin (1906–98), see René Hoven in ERSY 19 (1999): 111, and James McConica, in Erika Rummel (ed) *Editing Texts from the Age of Erasmus* 95.
15 Jean-Pierre Massaut *Coll Eras: Liège* Preface vii–viii
16 J.-C. Margolin to author February 1986; *Actes du Colloque International* 'Avant-propos' (Margolin)

17 Massaut (ed) *Coll Eras: Liège* 251–77
18 See Cornelis Reedijk 'The Leiden Edition of Erasmus' *Opera omnia* in a European Context,' in *Erasmus und Europa* 163–82, esp 180. Cf *Phoenix of His Age* 251–8.
19 Jean-Claude Margolin 'Avant-propos,' in *Actes du Colloque International* vii; Jean-Pierre Massaut 'Preface,' in *Coll Eras: Liège* viii–ix
20 Aloïs Gerlo 'Marie Delcourt, traductrice d'Erasme,' in *Actes du Colloque International* 387–92
21 Godin 'Une biographie en quête d'auteur: le *Compendium vitae Erasmi*,' in *Coll Eras: Liège* 203, 210–12; Roland Crahay 'Recherches sur le "Compendium vitae" attribué à Erasme.' As it happens, Crahay also contributed an essay to the Liège volume.
22 Margaret Mann Phillips 'Visages d'Erasme,' in *Coll Eras: Liège* 22–4. Cf Phillips 'P.S. Allen: A Lifetime of Letters,' in ERSY 9 (1989): 91–105.
23 Phillips 'Visages' 29
24 Needless to say, the above paragraphs are not a systematic study of generational change in Erasmus scholarship. They simply use the Erasmus commemorations as markers and should be read against the study of individual writers elsewhere in the volume.
25 Craig R. Thompson 'Three American Erasmians,' in ERSY 4 (1984), esp 4, 6, 15, 28
26 See *Quatorze années* nos 907–8, 972–3.
27 Nelson H. Minnich and W.W. Meissner 'The Character of Erasmus' 599–602, 604–5, 611–12, 618–20
28 John C. Olin *Six Essays on Erasmus* 68–72. This controversy is reminiscent of that over Erik Erikson's *Young Man Luther*. See Roger A. Johnson (ed) *Psychohistory and Religion: The Case of Young Man Luther*, in which collection Roland Bainton (19–56) and Lewis Spitz (57–87) play a critical role like Olin's, though with less anger. Meissner, psychiatrist and Jesuit, is also a contributor ('Faith and Identity' 97–126). I have taken Olin as representative of the critical view. Halkin's essay 'La psychohistoire et le caractère d'Erasme' is more substantial and more accommodating, but generally shares Olin's positions.
29 Yvonne Charlier *Erasme et l'amitié d'après sa correspondance* 184
30 Ibid 83, 107, 139
31 Ibid 125, 300, 306, 330–2
32 Ibid 107–11 (Batt), 206–7, 217 (Budé), 224–7 (Vives)
33 D.F.S. Thomson 'Erasmus as a Poet in the Context of Northern Humanism,' in *Commém Nat* 195–6. Cf C. Reedijk (ed) *The Poems of Desiderius Erasmus* 57, 143; CWE 86:625–6. For an overstatement of the view that Erasmus' writings of the monastic years, except for the *Antibarbari*, were literary exercises, see J.K. Sowards 'The Youth of Erasmus: Some Reconsiderations,' in ERSY 9 (1989): 18–20.
34 Charlier *Erasme et l'amitié* 72–81
35 Ibid 158–62, 328

36 André Godin 'Erasme, Aléandre: une étrange familiarité,' in *Actes du Colloque International* 249–74, at 252, 254–5, 257, 268
37 Charlier *Erasme et l'amitié* 303–4
38 Godin 'Erasme, Aléandre' 265–9, dealing with the MS 'Racha,' probably by Aleander
39 Ibid 271. See Michel Magnien 'Introduction à l'*Oratio prima,'* in Jules-César Scaliger *Orationes duae contra Erasmum* 56.
40 Godin 'Erasme, Aléandre' 273. See 2 Samuel 16:11–12; to Melanchthon, 6 June 1536, Allen Ep 3127, 11:334.
41 Godin 'Une biographie en quête d'auteur' 220. In another connection, a critique of passages in Godin's *Erasme lecteur d'Origène* concerning translations of Origen, Jacques Chomarat criticizes him for treating intellectual errors as symptoms, a procedure, he says, seductive but perilous ('Sur Erasme et Origène: Plaidoyer,' in *Coll Eras: Liège* 92).
42 Godin 'Une biographie' 197–8, 212–16, 218; G. Avarucci 'Due codici scritti da "Gerardus Helye" padre di Erasmo.' That the *Compendium vitae* offers a romanticized version is confirmed by the absence from it of Erasmus' older brother Pieter. Whether his father was a priest at the time of his conception and birth is a separate question. James McConica has argued that the phrase in the papal dispensation of 1517 taken to demonstrate that he was a priest referred, if its canonical background were correctly understood, not to clerical status, but to 'some relationship of consanguinity or affinity' (CWE 4:189–90). This argument has received some, but not universal, support. Cf Chomarat in *Actes du Colloque International* 248; Chomarat has not fully taken McConica's point.
43 McConica contested this interpretation of canon law when it was first enunciated by Robert Stupperich in 1974 ('Zur Biographie des Erasmus von Rotterdam: Zwei Untersuchungen' 22): a bishop could give the necessary dispensations for ordination to the priesthood (CWE 4:401).
44 Chomarat 'Pourquoi Erasme s'est-il fait moine?,' in *Actes du Colloque International* 234–5, 238–9, 241–7
45 Ibid 239
46 J.K. Sowards 'The Youth of Erasmus: Some Reconsiderations' 17n
47 Chomarat 'Sur Erasme et Origène' 99
48 Sowards 'The Youth of Erasmus' 9
49 Richard L. DeMolen 'Erasmus as Adolescent: "Shipwrecked am I, and lost, Mid waters chill"' 14. For DeMolen's own speculation that Erasmus agonized over the eternal fate of his parents, there is, as Sowards says, no evidence (as with so much else) (DeMolen 'Erasmus as Adolescent' 13, Sowards 'The Youth of Erasmus' 17n).
50 Sowards 'The Youth of Erasmus' 33; Chomarat 'Pourquoi Erasme s'est-il fait moine?' 237
51 Jean-Pierre Vanden Branden 'Le "Corpusculum" d'Erasme,' in *Actes*

du Colloque International 215–31. Cf Maria Cytowska 'Erasme et son petit corps,' which studies Erasmus' use of 'corpusculum' in the context of his use of Latin diminutives generally. In this case, the use is mostly pejorative, so that the meaning is not (affectionately) 'little body,' but (dismissively) 'poor body' (cf Huizinga *Erasmus of Rotterdam* 118: 'He always speaks in a coddling tone about his little body').

52 J. den Boeft '"Illic aureum quoddam ire flumen": Erasmus' enthusiasm for the patres,' in *Erasmus of Rotterdam* 172–81; John C. Olin 'Erasmus and Saint Jerome: An Appraisal of the Bond,' in ibid 182–6

53 M.A. Screech *Ecstasy and the Praise of Folly* 248–9

54 Rodemaker 'Erasmus and the Psalms: His Commentary on Psalm 86 (85),' in *Erasmus of Rotterdam* 187–94, esp 193

55 C. Béné 'Le *De puritate Tabernaculi*: testament spirituel d'Erasme?,' in *Actes du Colloque International* 199–212. See Béné, further, 'Introduction générale' ASD V-2, and now also Dominic Baker-Smith 'Introduction' CWE 63 *Expositions of the Psalms*.

56 Richard L. DeMolen 'First Fruits: The Place of *Antibarborum Liber* and *De Contemptu Mundi* in the Formulation of Erasmus' *Philosophia Christi*,' in *Coll Eras: Liège* 178; Ernst-Wilhelm Kohls 'Die Neuentdeckung der Theologie des Erasmus,' in ibid 241, 243, 249

57 Kohls 'Die Neuentdeckung' 243

58 DeMolen 'Erasmus as Adolescent' 24–5. The evidence DeMolen adduces does not always confirm his positions. Thus the letter to Hector Boece 8 November [1495] (Ep 47 Allen 1:154–8; CWE 1:94–7) does not confirm that Erasmus was by then exclusively committed to holiness ('First Fruits' 178).

59 C. Augustijn 'Erasmus und seine Theologie. Hatte Luther Recht?,' in *Coll Eras: Liège* 62–8

60 Ibid 64; Marie-Madeleine de La Garanderie 'Erasme et Luther commentateurs de la première épître de Saint-Jean (I, 1–7): "Dieu est lumière,"' in *Coll Eras: Liège* 161–75, and 'Erasme à l'épreuve des textes de saint Jean,' in *Actes du Colloque International* 127–40, esp 134

61 James D. Tracy *Erasmus: The Growth of a Mind* 10, 18–19

62 Ibid 10. Perhaps there are traces of his original, more abstract project (for this Princeton dissertation), an inquiry into 'differences in intellectual outlook between humanists who became Protestant and those who remained Catholic' (10n).

63 Ibid 10–14, 158

64 Ibid 97, 146

65 Ibid 133n, 151. On Treinen, see ch 2 above.

66 Ibid 93 and 93n, referring to Rudolf Padberg *Personaler Humanismus: das Bildungsverständnis des Erasmus* (1964)

67 Tracy *Erasmus: Growth of a Mind* 52, 62, 160, 235. On Lindeboom, *Man On His Own* 307–9.

68 Tracy *Erasmus: The Growth of a Mind* 182. See ch 6 above and also

Robert G. Kleinhans 'Luther and Erasmus: Another Perspective,' which dates the changes to 1522–3, and CWE 42:xxxv (John B. Payne, Albert Rabil Jr, and Warren S. Smith Jr).

69 Tracy *Erasmus: The Growth of a Mind* 236
70 Manfred Hoffmann 'Erasmus and Religious Toleration,' in ERSY 2 (1982): 80–106, at 83, 105–6
71 John W. O'Malley 'Erasmus and the History of Sacred Rhetoric: The *Ecclesiastes* of 1535,' in ERSY 5 (1985): 1–29, esp 18–25, 29. This was the inaugural Bainton Presidential Lecture of the Erasmus of Rotterdam Society.
72 See ch 2 above.
73 Rudolf Padberg 'Erasmus contra Augustinum: Das Problem des bellum justum in der erasmischen Friedensethik,' in *Coll Eras: Liège* 279–96, esp 286–8, 290, 292–4
74 For example, his annotation on Jesus' admonition to his disciples at Luke 22:36: 'he that hath no sword, let him sell his garment, and buy one.' Erasmus, as Padberg notes, rejected any suggestion of armed defence of the gospel and read the text symbolically as Jesus' psychological preparation of the disciples for coming persecution. But, in later additions to the original annotation, he accepted Ambrose's praise of those who fought to preserve the Christian peace (Reeve 209–13).
75 On the Roman empire and attempts to revive universal empire, see James S. Hirstein 'Erasme, l'*Histoire Auguste* et l'Histoire,' in *Actes du Colloque International* 71–95, esp 90–5, referring above all to Erasmus' preface to Froben's edition (1518) of Suetonius and the so-called and controverted *Historia Augusta* on the Roman emperors from Hadrian on (Ep 586 Allen 2:578–86, CWE 4:373–83). This paper also presents Erasmus as 'a very exacting reader of history' (72).
76 A.G. Weiler 'The Turkish Argument and Christian Piety in Desiderius Erasmus' *Consultatio de Bello Turcis Inferendo* (1530),' in *Erasmus of Rotterdam* 30–9, and 'La *Consultatio de Bello Turcis inferendo*: une oeuvre de piété politique,' in *Actes du Colloque International* 99–108. Cf also ch 2 above.
77 Margherita Isnardi-Parente 'Erasme, la République de Platon et la communauté des biens,' in *Erasmus of Rotterdam* 40–5
78 Willem Frijhoff 'Erasme, l'éducation et le monde scientifique de son temps – rapport introductif,' in ibid 101–8, and G. Chantraine 'Quelle intelligence de son temps Erasme nous donne-t-il?,' in ibid 109–16, esp 111–14
79 J.K. Sowards 'Erasmus as a Practical Educational Reformer,' in ibid 123–31. According to a paper by Jacques Chomarat, 'La philosophie de l'histoire d'Erasme d'après ses réflexions sur l'histoire romaine,' Erasmus placed history at the apex of (in modern terminology) 'les sciences socio-culturelles'; in that respect, he was an innovator.

Unfortunately, Chomarat's paper was included in neither the published nor the preliminary photocopied collections of the Rotterdam symposium (summary by Frijhoff at ibid 107). Despite the generally accepted and justified view that Erasmus had little interest in scientific inquiry, evidence was adduced at Rotterdam that he thought more highly of Galen's medical-scientific writings than of his philosophical ones (B. Ebels-Hoving and E.J. Ebels 'Erasmus and Galen,' in ibid 132–42).

80 Cornelis Augustijn *Erasmus, His Life, Works, and Influence* 26
81 Ibid 39, 104, 109, 190–1, 193
82 Ibid 192. The distinction was used in other connections in Marxist historiography (see G. Zschäbitz *Martin Luther: Grösse und Grenze* 6).
83 Augustijn *Erasmus, His Life* 41, 46–50, 68, 102–3 (on scholasticism, against Christian Dolfen)
84 Ibid 53–4, 88. Renaudet *Préréforme et humanisme à Paris pendant les premières guerres d'Italie (1494–1517)* 435
85 Augustijn *Erasmus, His Life* 48, 55, 182
86 Ibid 40. On Huizinga, 3–4.
87 A theme not captured by the title of the English translation by John Tonkin: *Erasmus: A Critical Biography.*
88 On Erasmus' Christocentrism, see Halkin *Erasmus: A Critical Biography* 119, 230, 285. The sincerity of Erasmus' pious expressions is accepted at all times, even those from his early days, when other explanations offer themselves (see 20, 26).
89 Ibid 12, 87, 280
90 Ibid 13, 275–6.
91 Ibid 107, 292. Concerning popular devotions, see, on pilgrimages 39, on Mariology 223–30.
92 Ibid 181, 283–5. On Trent 287 (there were issues on which the Council followed Erasmus 191, 259).
93 Reflections based on ch 24, 'Erasmus's Personality'
94 Augustijn *Erasmus, His Life* 15; Halkin *Erasmus: A Critical Biography* 4, 268. De Molen makes the same points as Halkin, if even more categorically (*The Spirituality of Erasmus of Rotterdam* 35–6).
95 Alain Michel 'La parole et la beauté chez Erasme,' in *Actes du Colloque International* 3–17, esp 6–11, 15
96 Jorge Alves Osorio 'Enoncé et dialogue dans les *Colloques* d'Erasme,' in ibid 19–34, esp 22, 25–7, 29
97 Daniel Kinney 'Erasmus and the Latin Comedians,' in ibid 57–69, esp 66–9. Erasmus' contention that the *Folly* and the *Enchiridion* treat the same subject is in his letter to Maarten van Dorp (1515) Ep 337 Allen 2:93, CWE 3:115.
98 Sem Dresden 'Erasme et les belles-lettres,' in *Coll Eras: Liège* 3–16, esp 5–7, 9–11. In his introduction to the ASD edition of *De contemptu mundi*, Dresden says that detachment from the world is a consistent

idea of Erasmus' through his life, achievable both in the monastery and elsewhere (ASD V-1 23, 25, 28–9, 32–4).

99 Betty I. Knott 'Erasmus' Working Methods in "De Copia,"' in *Erasmus of Rotterdam* 143–50, esp 146

100 As in Method 10 of Part II (see CWE 24:595–7).

101 T.O. Sloane 'Schoolbooks and Rhetoric: Erasmus's *Copia*' 114, 118, 120, 129. Gérard Defaux draws the same conclusion about *copia* ('True *copia*, genuine abundance, is not copia [sic] of words but of things. ... *Elocutio* is the daughter of *inventio*') in arguing against Jacques Derrida's view that writing is downgraded in the Western tradition, seen as mere 'dead letter' over against spirit, expressed essentially in speech. On the contrary, for humanists like Erasmus the person was as fully present in writing, in texts, as in speech ('Against Derrida's "Dead Letter": Christian Humanism and the Valorization of Writing,' esp 174, 179, 181).

102 Silvana Seidel Menchi 'Erasme et son lecteur: à propos du rapport auteur-public au XVIe siècle,' in *Coll Eras: Liège* 31–45, esp 34, 36–7, 39–41

103 Cf ch 3 above.

104 L. Voet 'Erasmus and His Correspondents,' in *Erasmus of Rotterdam* 195–202

105 We remain, as one writer puts it, 'on thin ice' (Hubertus Schulte Herbrüggen 'Erasmus und England: Erasmus und Morus,' in *Erasmus und Europa* 109).

106 R.J. Schoeck 'Erasmus as Latin Secretary to the Bishop of Cambrai: Erasmus' Introduction to the Burgundian Court,' in *Erasmus of Rotterdam* 7–14 (another version of this text in Schoeck *Erasmus Grandescens: The Growth of a Humanist's Mind and Spirituality* 90–101)

107 Germain Marc'hadour 'Thomas More in Emulation and Defense of Erasmus,' in *Erasmus of Rotterdam* 203–14 (an essay primarily about the continuing 'fellow-work' of More and Erasmus, to use Frederic Seebohm's famous expression), at 207; Herbrüggen 'Erasmus und England,' in *Erasmus und Europa* 103. Marc'hadour refers to passages in Epp 999 and 1233, respectively to Ulrich von Hutten, 23 July 1519, CWE 7:24, and Guillaume Budé, [c September] 1521, CWE 8:295–7.

108 I must emphasize that it is impossible to encompass here the literature on these and other personal relationships of Erasmus. Naturally, studies of the partner in the relationship deal with Erasmus and his influence. On Tyndale, there is, most recently, David Daniell *William Tyndale: A Biography.*

109 G. Marc'hadour 'William Tyndale entre Erasme et Luther,' in *Actes du Colloque International* 185–98 at 193. Marc'hadour accepts Rainer Pineas' demonstration of Tyndale's avowed debt to Erasmus in 'William Tyndale and More's 1529 *Dialogue*,' *Moreana* 75–6 (1982): 57–8

(quoted ibid 192). For the *Paraclesis*, ibid 186, and More's 'Trojan horse,' 187.

110 J.M. Weiss 'Melanchthon and the Heritage of Erasmus: *Oratio de Puritate Doctrinae* (1536) and *Oratio de Erasmo Roterodamo* (1557),' in ibid 293–306, at 300.

111 Ibid 295–7, 301–2, 304. Weiss advances beyond previous commentators on the 1557 oration, including this author's (*Phoenix of His Age* 89–93), by drawing out its rhetorical character and relating it to a precise academic context ('Melanchthon and the Heritage of Erasmus' 300).

112 Epp 2296 (28 March 1530) and 2442 (6 March 1531) Allen 8:397–8, 9:156–7

113 He warned against writing anything that would appear damaging in other hands (Ep 2442 Allen 9:157 lines 23–5). The bishop of Arles was said to have ordered the seizure of all Erasmus' books in his diocese (Jan N. Pendergrass 'Cassander de Colmars, un correspondant d'Erasme,' in *Actes du Colloque International* 277–91, at 279).

114 Pendergrass 'Cassander' 278, 281–4

115 Jean-Claude Margolin 'Erasme et Ferdinand de Habsbourg d'après deux lettres inédites de l'Empereur à l'humaniste,' in *Erasmus of Rotterdam* 15–29. On Ferdinand and Erasmus, see further Paula Sutter Fichtner *Ferdinand I of Austria: The Politics of Dynasticism in the Age of the Reformation* 6.

116 Nelson H. Minnich 'Erasmus and the Fifth Lateran Council (1512–17),' in *Erasmus of Rotterdam* 46–60. Cf ch 5 above.

117 Minnich 'Erasmus and the Fifth Lateran Council' 52–3

118 Ibid 46–7, 49, 54–5

119 Chris L. Heesakkers 'Argumentatio a persona in Erasmus' Second Apology against Alberto Pio,' in ibid 79–87

120 M. Gielis 'Erasme, Latomus et le martyre de deux augustins luthériens à Bruxelles en 1523,' in ibid 61–8, esp 66

121 Erika Rummel *Erasmus and His Catholic Critics* 1 *1515–1522* ch 4; Masson saw the former as 'dangerous material, to be handled only by experienced theologians' (ibid 83).

122 Rummel 'Erasmus and the Valladolid Articles: Intrigue, Innuendo, and Strategic Defense,' in *Erasmus of Rotterdam* 69; on general application, my MS notes of Rotterdam conference

123 Ibid. On Lee, see also Rummel *Erasmus and His Catholic Critics* 1 ch 5; R. Coogan 'The Pharisee against the Hellenist: Edward Lee versus Erasmus.'

124 Rummel 'Erasmus and the Valladolid Articles' 70–1, 74–6

125 Heesakkers 'Argumentatio' 85. The Liège volume carries evidence of the character of these controversies in H.J. de Jonge's 'Four Unpublished Letters on Erasmus from J.L. Stunica to Pope Leo X,' in *Coll Eras: Liège* 147–60.

126 On the Lutheranism charge, see Rummel *Erasmus and His Catholic Critics* 2:34–5, 54. I realize that this broad-brush judgment does not do justice to scholasticism and its sixteenth-century heirs. For balance, see Rummel's judicious conclusion to volume 1 185–90 and James K. Farge 'Erasmus, the University of Paris, and the Profession of Theology,' in ERSY 19 (1999): 18–46. See also Erika Rummel *The Humanist-Scholastic Debate in the Renaissance and Reformation.*

127 Roland Crahay 'Le procès d'Erasme à la fin du XVIe siècle: position de quelques jésuites,' in *Coll Eras: Liège* 115–33. Cf *Phoenix of His Age* 48–53.

128 M.A. Screech 'Erasmus and the *Concordia* of Cornelius Jansenius, Bishop of Ghent: Christian Folly and Catholic Orthodoxy,' in *Coll Eras: Liège* 297–307. On the suppression of his name and personality, see Jean Céard's essay in the Tours volume on the expurgated edition of the *Adages* (Florence 1575): every personal reference was effaced, all material critical of secular and ecclesiastical authority, also, and anything suggesting rapprochement between classical wisdom and Christian belief ('La censure tridentine et l'édition florentine des *Adages* d'Erasme,' in *Actes du Colloque International* 337–50). Another contribution at Tours shows how, even in the unpromising atmosphere of Italy in the 1540s, his ideas could, suitably camouflaged, find an outlet: Lucia Gualdo Rosa 'L'Institutio "del prencipe christiano" de Mambrino Roseo de Fabriano entre Antonio de Guevara et Erasme,' in ibid 307–24.

129 Charles Béné 'Saint François de Sales et Erasme,' in ibid 69–85

130 See my 'Erasmus and Frederic Seebohm: "The Oxford Reformers," Down but Not Out?' 25–6.

131 August Buck (ed) *Erasmus und Europa* 7–12

132 Halkin 'Erasme et les Pays-Bas,' in ibid 36, 39–40. Cf ch 3 above.

133 Margolin, in ibid 55, 58–61, 72–3

134 The essay by H. Schulte Herbrüggen, in ibid 91–110 (see above).

135 Bengt Hägglund 'Erasmus und die Reformation,' in ibid 139–47, at 140, 142–3. See *Paraphrase on John* CWE 46:15, 22–3. On justification, the lines Hägglund quotes (ibid 147–8) from a letter of 1527 to Thomas More, favouring the Scotist emphasis on human powers, are followed immediately by a warning 'that we do not arrogate to our strength what we owe wholly to divine liberality' (30 March 1527 Allen Ep 1804, 7:8 lines 91–9).

136 Dietrich Briesemeister 'Erasmus und Spanien,' in *Erasmus und Europa* 75–90, at 75, 78–80, 82, 84, 88

137 Agnes Ritoók-Szalay 'Erasmus und die ungarischen Intellektuellen des 16. Jahrhunderts,' in ibid 111–28, at 116–19

138 Ibid 122–4, 126–8. For the quincentenary essays, see ch 3 above.

139 Briesemeister 'Erasmus und Spanien' 90

140 P.P.J.L. van Peteghem's Rotterdam paper 'Erasmus' Last Will, the

Holy Roman Empire and the Low Countries' uses the history of his testamentary dispositions to demonstrate the complexity, 'the labyrinthine state,' of law and the administration of justice in Easmus' time, as between Roman, customary and canon law; there were also political implications (*Erasmus of Rotterdam* 88–97).

141 Notable in 1969 was Craig Thompson's treatment of Anglican and Jesuit images in the Elizabethan age ('Erasmus and Tudor England,' in *Actes* 57–64).

142 See section V above.

143 Phillips 'Visages d'Erasme,' in *Coll Eras: Liège* 17–29 (on Amiel, *Man On His Own* 148–50).

144 Augustijn 'Vir duplex: German Interpretations of Erasmus,' in *Erasmus of Rotterdam* 219–27

145 Van der Blom 'Rotterdam and Erasmus: Some Remarks,' in ibid 240–52

146 On the latter, see my 'Erasmus in the Age of Revolutions,' in ibid 228–39.

147 Werner Kaegi 'Erasmus im achtzehnten Jahrhundert,' in *Gedenkschrift* 205–27

148 J.-C. Margolin 'Guy Patin, lecteur d'Erasme,' in *Coll Tur* 1:323–58; André Stegmann 'La réhabilitation de l'orthodoxie chez Erasme par Jean Richard (1688),' in ibid 2:867–76 (Stegmann underestimates Richard's Jansenist connections). Cf *Phoenix of His Age* 155–6, 163–9.

149 P. Mesnard 'La dernière traduction française de l'Enchiridion,' in *Scrinium* 1:325–32

150 Quoted ibid 328

151 Margolin 'La religion d'Erasme et l'Allemagne des Lumières,' on the theses pronounced at Hamburg in 1717 by Johann Klefeker

152 Margolin 'Erasme à l'époque des "Lumières": Une traduction française inédite du *De contemptu mundi*,' in *Actes du Colloque International* 351–86. Margolin demonstrates that Mesnard (along with, I must add, the present author) was mistaken to identify the translator as Du Bosc de Montrandré (d 1690). He was the *parlementaire* Claude Bosc (d 1715) (ibid 357); cf *Phoenix of His Age* 189).

153 It was not published but is in MS, in another hand than Devoyo's (dated 1821), in the Municipal Library of Dijon (Margolin 'Erasme à l'époque des "Lumières"' ibid 366–7).

154 Ibid 368–9, 375, 382–4

155 In a correction of Kaegi's remark that the seventeenth century knew Erasmus as but a master of Latinity, Reedijk draws attention to the numerous editions of his religio-ethical works in the seventeenth-century Netherlands (see Reedijk *Tandem bona causa triumphat: Zur Geschichte des Gesamtwerkes des Erasmus von Rotterdam* 36).

156 Cornelis Reedijk 'The Leiden Edition of Erasmus' *Opera Omnia* in a European Context,' in *Erasmus und Europa* 163–82, esp 178–81

157 Cf Reedijk *Tandem bona causa* 44: if the Basel edition of the *Opera*

omnia (1540) appeared when the tide of toleration was ebbing, Le Clerc's caught it at the turn: the Leiden edition led in a new age. In the final essay of the Tours volume, Klaus Garber follows the idea of peace in humanism through to the Enlightenment ('humanisme tardif'), Erasmus occupying a central position in the story with his looking back to the apostolic witness to peace and forward to the political programs of Leibniz and Kant ('L'humanisme européen et l'utopie pacifiste: essai de reconstitution historique,' in *Actes du Colloque International* 393–425, esp 408–13, 424).

158 See especially Schoeck 'Humanism in Renaissance England,' in Albert Rabil, Jr (ed) *Renaissance Humanism: Foundations, Forms, and Legacy* 2:5–38, and 'Humanism and Jurisprudence' in ibid 3:310–26

159 Schoeck *Erasmus of Europe* 2:293, quoting W.S. Heckscher 'Reflections on Seeing Holbein's Portrait of Erasmus at Longford Castle,' in *Essays in the History of Art Presented to Rudolf Wittkower*, 132, 144–5

160 Schoeck *Erasmus of Europe* 1:xiii, 26–7, 30–1, 53 (childhood); *Erasmus Grandescens* 7–9, 89–90 (growth and liminality); *Erasmus of Europe* 2:74–5 (*Adagia*); ibid 1:239, 250, 256 (the year 1500), 224–6, 230–1, 2:x, 8 (Colet and Vitrier; cf John B. Gleason *John Colet* and André Godin, in *Contemporaries* 3 408–9). On liminality, it is interesting that Schoeck appends to his book of poems *The Eye of a Traveller: Landscapes and Seascapes* (1992) an essay on 'Crossing Borders,' with a motto from A.S. Byatt's *Possession*: 'I write about liminality. Thresholds. Bastions. Fortresses.'

161 Schoeck *Erasmus of Europe* 1:112 (independence), 129, 156, 268 (monasticism and canons regular), 2 ch 29 ('Vocation and Lifestyle'), esp 147 ('independent cleric'; cf Halkin's expression: after leaving the monastery, Erasmus became 'le prêtre libre qu'il voulait être' ['La piété d'Erasme' 674]), 37, 200 (laity); Richard L. DeMolen 'Erasmus' Commitment to the Canons Regular of St. Augustine'

162 Schoeck *Erasmus of Europe* 1:15, 24, 43, 48, 123–4; 2:218, 297 (*Devotio moderna*); *Erasmus Grandescens* 37 (*Devotio moderna*); ibid 19, 21–2, 24, 27 (tradition, More); ibid 112 ('received medievalism'); *Erasmus of Europe* 1:63; 2:80, 310 (classical tradition); ibid 1:xii, 51, 187 (*philosophia Christi*); *Erasmus Grandescens* 44, 114, 123n (exuberance in living, etc.)

163 Schoeck *Erasmus of Europe* 1:67, 242; 2:234, 291; *Erasmus Grandescens* 12, 132. See also Schoeck '*In loco intertexantur*: Erasmus as Master of Intertextuality,' in Heinrich F. Plett (ed) *Intertextuality* 181–91. Schoeck compares intertextuality with 'a galaxy of mobiles' (189).

164 Schoeck *Erasmus of Europe* 2:310, 353

165 McConica *Erasmus* 15 (cf *Antibarbari* CWE 23:105), 17, 23

166 McConica *Erasmus* 46–7, 50–1, 55–6, 60–2, 76–8, 84–5. There is here recall of McConica's great essay 'Erasmus and the Grammar of Consent.'

167 Schoeck *Erasmus of Europe* 1:3–4, 6
168 James D. Tracy *Erasmus of the Low Countries* 38, 80–1, 90, 93–4, 106, 108, 111, 113, ch 11 ('A Reformation Gone Wrong'), 163, 171, 173–4. On Erasmus' tendency to view all acts of the powerful with suspicion, see Tracy *Holland under Habsburg Rule, 1506–1566: The Formation of a Body Politic* 65–70. Turchetti's article carries conviction over all, but he himself quotes a text which seems to take Erasmus beyond the 'condescension' (or 'bearing with') his argument alone allows and towards a policy of reciprocal concession (389, from *De amabili ecclesiae concordia* LB 5:500).
169 Tracy *Erasmus of the Low Countries* 147
170 Schoeck *Erasmus Grandescens* 123n, Tracy *Erasmus of the Low Countries* 34, McConica *Erasmus* 89
171 Schoeck *Erasmus of Europe* 2:135, 138–9; Tracy *Erasmus of the Low Countries* 100–2. For a recent review of the literature on Erasmus' anti-Semitism, see Hilmar M. Pabel 'Erasmus of Rotterdam and Judaism: A Reexamination in the Light of New Evidence.' Pabel assembles and presses hard on the evidence from the *Paraphrases* to support a negative judgment of Erasmus on this matter. He agrees with the unfavourable judgments of Guido Kisch (*Erasmus' Stellung zu Juden und Judentum* 1969) and Heiko A. Oberman (*The Roots of Anti-Semitism in the Age of Renaissance and Reformation* 1984 38–40), against the favourable (or at least neutral) ones of Shimon Markish (*Erasmus and the Jews* 1986) and Augustijn, as in *Erasmus, His Life, Works, and Influence* 48–9, 80–1. Schoeck's view that 'Judaism' was a metaphor for ceremonial Christianity was apparently first put by Gerhard Winkler in 1970, in an article 'Erasmus und die Juden' (reference Pabel 'Erasmus of Rotterdam' 13), which I have not seen. For Erasmus on Pfefferkorn, see Ep 694 to Willibald Pirckheimer 2 November 1517 Allen 3:116–19, CWE 5:164–71. To be added now: the comprehensive and finely balanced judgments of Dominic Baker-Smith in his Introduction to the *Expositions of the Psalms* (CWE 63:xlix–lvi).
172 Tracy *Erasmus of the Low Countries* 173
173 Quoted *Phoenix of His Age* 282. In general, on Jortin, ibid 275–85, Burigny 285–95.
174 Jozef IJsewijn 'Humanism in the Low Countries,' in Rabil (ed) *Renaissance Humanism* 2:167
175 See now Hilmar M. Pabel *Conversing with God: Prayer in Erasmus' Pastoral Writings*

CONCLUSION

1 See Alan W. Reese 'Learning Virginity: Erasmus' Ideal of Christian Marriage,' which weights the balance towards the 'more serious' works rather than the more exuberant ones.

2 Pabel *Conversing with God* 8, 14, 25, 191–2, 196, 202
3 See my 'A Not Exclusive Truth: An Early Nineteenth-Century Pastoral Theology and Erasmus,' in Nigel Aston (ed) *Religious Change in Europe 1650–1914: Essays for John McManners* 275–97
4 Notice the expressions used by M.E.H.N. Mout in her essay 'Erasmianism in Modern Dutch Historiography': 'Erasmianism has been ghosting around Dutch modern historiography for quite a while, but it has never been properly studied or even defined in relation to its different uses' (Mout, Smolinsky, and Trapman [eds] *Erasmianism* 189–98, at 197).
5 Ibid 198; Silvana Seidel Menchi 'Do We Need the 'ism'? Some Mediterranean Perspectives,' in ibid 47–64. Cf Cornelis Augustijn 'Verba valent usu: was ist Erasmianismus?,' in ibid 5–14, at 11–13.
6 Jan van Dorsten '"The Famous Clerk Erasmus"'; R.J. Schoeck *Erasmus Grandescens* 137–43. On van Dorsten, see Mout *Erasmianism* 189–90.
7 Godin 'Jean Vitrier,' in *Coll Tur* 2:804 n47
8 Kathy Eden '"Between Friends All Is Common": The Erasmian Adage and Tradition'; Eva Kushner 'Erasmus and the Paradox of Subjectivity,' in ERSY 18 (1998): 1–20; Laurel Carrington 'The Boundaries between Text and Reader: Erasmus's Approach to Reading Scripture'; Charles Witke 'Erasmus Auctor et Actor,' in ERSY 15 (1995): 26–52
9 *Phoenix of His Age* 300
10 Locher 'Zwingli und Erasmus,' in *Scrinium* 2:349
11 Bataillon 'Actualité d'Erasme,' in *Coll Tur* 2:884

Bibliography

WORKS ON ERASMUS

Adams, Robert P. *The Better Part of Valor: More, Erasmus, Colet, and Vives on Humanism, War, and Peace, 1496–1535* Seattle 1962

Anon 'Erasmus in Praise of England: The Journalism of Scholarship' *Times Literary Supplement* No. 1797 (11 July 1936): 569–70

Asensio, Eugenio 'El erasmismo y las corrientes espirituales afines (Conversos, franciscanos, italianizantes)' *Revista de filología española* 36 (1952): 31–99

Auer, Alfons *Die vollkommene Frömmigkeit des Christen: Nach dem Enchiridion militis christiani des Erasmus von Rotterdam* Düsseldorf 1954

Augustijn, Cornelis 'The Ecclesiology of Erasmus' in *Scrinium* 2:135–55

– *Erasmus en de Reformatie: Een onderzoek naar de houding die Erasmus ten opzichte van de Reformatie heeft aangenomen* Amsterdam 1962

– *Erasmus, His Life, Works, and Influence* Toronto 1991

– 'Erasmus und seine Theologie. Hatte Luther Recht?' in *Coll Eras: Liège* 49–68

– 'Verba valent usu: was ist Erasmianismus?' in Mout, Smolinsky, and Trapman (eds) *Erasmianism* 5–14

– 'Vir duplex: German Interpretations of Erasmus,' in *Erasmus of Rotterdam* 219–27

Avarucci, G. 'Due codici scritti da "Gerardus Helye" padre di Erasmo' *Italia medioevale e humanistica* 26 (1983): 215–55

Backvis, Claude 'La fortune d'Erasme en Pologne,' in *Coll Eras: Mons* 173–202

Bainton, Roland H. 'The *Complaint of Peace* of Erasmus, Classical and Christian Sources' in *Collected Papers in Church History* 1, London 1965, 217–35

– *Erasmus of Christendom* London 1970

Bakel, H.A. van 'Erasmus en Luther' *Nieuw Theologisch Tijdschrift* 25 (1936): 211–46

Baker-Smith, Dominic *More's 'Utopia'* London 1991 (paperback Toronto 2000)
- 'Introduction' CWE 63:xiii–lxxii
Baron, Hans 'Erasmus-Probleme im Spiegel des Colloquium "Inquisitio de Fide"' ARG 43 (1952): 254–63
- 'Secularization of Wisdom and Political Humanism in the Renaissance' *Journal of the History of Ideas* 21 (1960): 131–50
Bataillon, Marcel 'Actualité d'Erasme' in *Coll Tur* 2:877–89
- 'A propos de l'influence d'Erasme' in *Erasme et l'Espagne* 3:305–12
- 'D'Erasme à la Compagnie de Jésus' in *Erasme et l'Espagne* 3:279–304
- *Erasme et l'Espagne,* 2nd French edn, ed Daniel Devoto 3 vols, Geneva 1991
- 'Un problème d'influence d'Erasme en Espagne: L'*Eloge de la Folie*' in *Actes* 136–47 (later version: 'Erasmisme de *Lazarillo de Tormes* et de *Don Quichotte* en tant que créations littéraires [Un problème d'influence, etc.],' in *Erasme et l'Espagne* 3:419–65)
- 'La situation présente du message érasmien,' in *Coll Eras: Mons* 3–16
- 'Vers une définition de l'érasmisme,' in *Coll Tur* 1:21–34
Bejczy, István 'Erasmus Becomes a Netherlander' SCJ 28 (1997): 387–99
- 'Erasmus versus Italy' *Medievalia et Humanistica: Studies in Medieval and Renaissance Culture* ns 24 (1997): 123–45
Béné, Charles *Erasme et Saint Augustin ou influence de Saint Augustin sur l'humanisme d'Erasme* Geneva 1969
- 'Le *De puritate Tabernaculi*: testament spirituel d'Erasme?' in *Actes du Colloque International* 199–212
- 'Saint Augustin dans la controverse sur les trois langues à Louvain en 1518 et 1519,' in *Coll Eras: Mons* 20–32
- 'Saint François de Sales et Erasme,' in *Coll Eras: Liège* 69–85
Bentley, Jerry H. 'Biblical Philology and Christian Humanism: Lorenzo Valla and Erasmus as Scholars of the Gospels' SCJ 8 (1977): 9–28
- 'Erasmus' *Annotationes in Novum Testamentum* and the Textual Criticism of the Gospels' ARG 67 (1976): 33–53
- 'Erasmus, Jean Le Clerc, and the Principle of the Harder Reading' RQ 31 (1978): 309–21
- *Humanists and Holy Writ: New Testament Scholarship in the Renaissance* Princeton 1983
Bierlaire, Franz *Erasme et ses Colloques: le livre d'une vie* Geneva 1977
- 'La *familia* d'Erasme,' in *Coll Eras: Mons* 301–13
- *La familia d'Erasme: Contribution à l'histoire d'humanisme* Paris 1968
- 'Le *Libellus Colloquiorum* de mars 1522 et Nicolas Baechem, dit *Egmondanus*,' in *Scrinium* 1:55–81
- *Les Colloques d'Erasme: réforme des études, réforme des moeurs et réforme de l'Eglise au XVIe siècle* Paris 1978
Bietenholz, Peter G. 'Erasmus and the German Public, 1518–1520: The Question of the Authorized and Unauthorized Circulation of His Correspondence' SCJ 8 (1977): 61–78

– 'Erasmus und der Basler Buchhandel in Frankreich,' in *Scrinium* 1:293–
  323 (in French, *Coll Tur* 1:55–78)
– *History and Biography in the Work of Erasmus of Rotterdam* Geneva 1966
Binns, J.W. 'The Letters of Erasmus,' in T.A. Dorey (ed) *Erasmus* 55–79
Blom, Nicolaas van der 'The Erasmus Statues in Rotterdam' *Erasmus in
  English* 6 (1973): 5–9
– 'Rotterdam and Erasmus: Some Remarks,' in *Erasmus of Rotterdam*
  240–52
Boeft, J. den '"Illic aureum quoddam ire flumen": Erasmus' enthusiasm
  for the patres,' in *Erasmus of Rotterdam* 172–81
Boisset, Jean *Erasme et Luther: Libre ou serf arbitre?* Paris 1962
Born, Lester K. 'Erasmus on Political Ethics: The *Institutio Principis Chris-
  tiani' Political Science Quarterly* 43 (1928): 520–43
– 'Some Notes on the Political Theories of Erasmus' *Journal of Modern
  History* 2 (1930): 226–36
Born, Lester K. (ed) *The Education of a Christian Prince by Desiderius Eras-
  mus* New York 1936 (reprint 1965)
Bouyer, Louis *Autour d'Erasme: Etudes sur le christianisme des humanistes
  catholiques* Paris 1955
Boyle, Marjorie O'Rourke *Christening Pagan Mysteries: Erasmus in Pursuit
  of Wisdom* Toronto 1981
– 'Erasmus and the "Modern" Question: Was He Semi-Pelagian?' ARG
  75 (1984): 59–77
– *Erasmus on Language and Method in Theology* Toronto 1977
– 'Erasmus' Prescription for Henry VIII: Logotherapy' RQ 31 (1978):
  161–72
– *Rhetoric and Reform: Erasmus' Civil Dispute with Luther* Cambridge,
  Mass/London 1983
Brachin, Pierre 'Vox clamantis in deserto: Réflexions sur le pacifisme
  d'Erasme,' in *Coll Tur* 1:247–75
Bradshaw, Brendan 'Transalpine Humanism,' in J.H. Burns (ed), *The
  Cambridge History of Political Thought 1450–1700* 95–131
Briesemeister, Dietrich 'Erasmus und Spanien,' in *Erasmus und Europa*
  75–90
Brown, Andrew J. 'The Date of Erasmus' Latin Translation of the New
  Testament' *Transactions of the Cambridge Bibliographical Society* 8 (1984):
  351–80
Bultot, R. 'Erasme, Epicure et le "Contemptu Mundi,"' in *Scrinium* 2:205–
  38
Burns J.H. (ed), with Mark Goldie, *The Cambridge History of Political
  Thought 1450–1700* Cambridge 1991
Callahan, Virginia W. 'The *De Copia*: The Bounteous Horn,' in DeMolen
  (ed) *Essays on the Works of Erasmus* 99–109
Calster, G. van 'La censure louvaniste du Nouveau Testament et la rédac-
  tion de l'index érasmien expurgatoire de 1571,' in *Scrinium* 2:379–436

Cantimori, Delio 'Erasmo e l'Italia' in *Umanesimo e religione nel Rinascimento* Turin 1975, 60–87
- 'Erasmo e la vita morale e religiosa italiana nel secolo XVI,' in *Gedenkschrift* 98–112, and *Umanesimo e religione nel Rinascimento* Turin 1975, 40–59
Carrington, Laurel 'The Boundaries between Text and Reader: Erasmus' Approach to Reading Scripture' ARG 88 (1997): 5–22
Caspari, Fritz 'Erasmus on the Social Functions of Christian Humanism' *Journal of the History of Ideas* 8 (1947): 78–106
Céard, Jean 'La censure tridentine et l'édition florentine des *Adages* d'Erasme,' in *Actes du Colloque International* 337–50
Chantraine, Georges *Erasme et Luther, libre et serf arbitre* Paris/Namur 1981
- 'Erasme théologien' *Revue d'histoire ecclésiastique* 64 (1969): 811–20
- 'L'Apologia ad Latomum. Deux conceptions de théologie,' in *Scrinium* 2:51–75
- *'Mystère' et 'Philosophie du Christ' selon Erasme* Namur/Gembloux 1971
- 'Mysterium et sacramentum dans le "Dulce bellum inexpertis,"' in *Coll Eras: Mons* 33–45
- 'Quelle intelligence de son temps Erasme nous donne-t-il?' in *Erasmus of Rotterdam* 109–16
Charlier, Yvonne *Erasme et l'amitié d'après sa correspondance* Paris 1977
Chomarat, Jacques *Grammaire et rhétorique chez Erasme* 2 vols, Paris 1981
- 'Les *Annotations* de Valla, celles d'Erasme et la grammaire,' in Olivier Fatio and Pierre Fraenkel (eds) *Histoire de l'exégèse au XVIe siècle* Geneva 1978, 202–28
- 'Pourquoi Erasme s'est-il fait moine?' in *Actes du Colloque International* 233–48
- 'Sur Erasme et Origène: Plaidoyer,' in *Coll Eras: Liège* 87–113
Constantinescu Bagdat, Elise *La 'Querela Pacis' d'Erasme (1517)* Paris 1924
Coogan, R. 'The Pharisee against the Hellenist: Edward Lee versus Erasmus' RQ 39 (1986): 476–506
Coppens, Jozef 'Où en est le portrait d'Erasme théologien?' in *Scrinium* 2:569–93
Cowell, Henry J. 'Erasmus' Personal and Literary Associations with England' *Proceedings of the Huguenot Society of London* 15 (1936): 428–55
Crahay, Roland 'Le procès d'Erasme à la fin du XVIe siècle: position de quelques jésuites,' in *Coll Eras: Liège* 115–33
- 'Les censeurs louvanistes d'Erasme,' in *Scrinium* 1:221–49
- 'Recherches sur le "Compendium vitae" attribué à Erasme' *Humanisme et Renaissance* 6 (1939): 7–19, 135–53
Crahay, Roland, and Marie-Thérèse Isaac 'Livres d'Erasme dans les bibliothèques anciennes du Hainaut,' in *Coll Eras: Mons* 203–44
Crisan, Constantin 'Erasme en Roumanie: Approximations diachroniques et synchroniques,' in *Coll Tur* 1:175–85

Cytowska, Maria 'Erasme de Rotterdam et Marcile Ficin son Maître' *Eos* 63 (1975): 165–79
– 'Erasme en Pologne avant l'époque du Concile de Trente' *Erasmus in English* 5 (1972): 10–16
– 'Erasme et son petit corps' *Eos* 62 (1974): 129–38
Damme, Daniel van *Une heure à la maison d'Erasme et au vieux béguinage d'Anderlecht* Anderlecht 1964
Davis, J.C. 'Utopianism,' in J.H. Burns (ed) *Cambridge History of Political Thought 1450–1700* 329–44
Degroote, Gilbert 'Erasmofilie te Antwerpen in de eerste helft van de zestiende eeuw,' in *Commém Nat* 31–50 (French summary 50–1)
– 'Erasmiaanse echo's in de Gouden Eeuw in Nederland,' in *Scrinium* 1:391–421
DeMolen, Richard L. 'Erasmus as Adolescent: "Shipwrecked am I, and lost, Mid waters chill"' BHR 38 (1976): 7–25, and in *The Spirituality of Erasmus of Rotterdam* 15–34
– 'Erasmus' Commitment to the Canons Regular of St. Augustine' RQ 26 (1973): 437–43, and *Spirituality of Erasmus of Rotterdam* 191–7
– *Essays on the Works of Erasmus* New Haven/London 1978
– 'First Fruits: The Place of *Antibarborum Liber* and *De Contemptu Mundi* in the Formulation of Erasmus' *Philosophia Christi*,' in *Coll Eras: Liège* 177–96
– *The Spirituality of Erasmus of Rotterdam* Nieuwkoop 1987
Derwa, Marcelle, and Marie Delcourt 'Trois aspects humanistes de l'épicurisme chrétien,' in *Coll Eras: Mons* 119–33
Dickens, A.G. *The English Reformation* London 1964
Dolfen, Christian *Die Stellung des Erasmus von Rotterdam zur scholastischen Methode* Osnabrück 1936
Dorsten, J. van '"The Famous Clerk Erasmus"' *Dutch Quarterly Review of Anglo-American Letters* 10 (1980): 296–305
Douglas, A.E. 'Erasmus as Satirist,' in T.A. Dorey (ed) *Erasmus* London 1970, 31–54
Douglas, Richard M. 'Talent and Vocation in Humanist and Protestant Thought,' in Theodore K. Rabb and Jerrold E. Seigel (eds) *Action and Conviction in Early Modern Europe: Essays in Memory of E.H. Harbison* Princeton 1969, 261–98
Dresden, S. 'Erasme et la notion de *Humanitas*,' in *Scrinium* 2:527–45
– 'Erasme et les belles-lettres,' in *Coll Eras: Liège* 3–16
– 'Erasme, Rabelais et la "festivitas" humaniste,' in *Coll Tur* 1:463–78
– 'Présence d'Erasme,' in *Actes* 1–13
– 'Sagesse et folie d'après Erasme,' in *Coll Tur* 1:285–99
Drummond, R.B. *Erasmus: His Life and Character As Shown in His Correspondence and Works* 2 vols, London 1873
Duinkerken, Anton van 'Nieuwe Erasmiana' *De Gids* 100 (1936): 225–39

Ebels-Hoving, B., and E.J. Ebels 'Erasmus and Galen,' in *Erasmus of Rotterdam* 132–42

Eden, Kathy '"Between Friends All Is Common": The Erasmian Adage and Tradition' *Journal of the History of Ideas* 59 (1998): 405–19

– *Hermeneutics and the Rhetorical Tradition: Chapters in the Ancient Legacy and Its Humanist Reception* New Haven/London 1997

Elias, Norbert *The Civilizing Process: The History of Manners* Oxford 1977

Enno van Gelder, H.A. *The Two Reformations in the 16th Century: A Study of the Religious Aspects and Consequences of Renaissance and Humanism* The Hague 1961

Estes, James M. *'Officium principis christiani*: Erasmus and the Origins of the Protestant State Church' ARG 83 (1992): 49–72

– 'Erasmus, Melanchthon and the Office of Christian Magistrate,' in ERSY 18 (1998): 24–39

Etienne, Jacques *Spiritualisme érasmien et théologiens louvanistes: Un changement de problématique au début du XVIe siècle* Louvain 1956

Farge, James K. 'Erasmus, the University of Paris, and the Profession of Theology,' in ERSY 19 (1999): 18–46

Febvre, Lucien 'L'Erasme de Marcel Bataillon,' in *Au coeur religieux du XVIe siècle* Paris 1957, 93–111

Ferguson, W.K. 'Renaissance Tendencies in the Religious Thought of Erasmus' *Journal of the History of Ideas* 15 (1954): 499–509

Ferguson, W.K. review of Adams *Better Part of Valor* AHR 68 (1963): 720–1

Fernandez, José A. 'Erasmus on the Just War' *Journal of the History of Ideas* 34 (1973): 209–26

Fox, Alistair 'Facts and Fallacies: Interpreting English Humanism,' in Alistair Fox and John Guy *Reassessing the Henrician Age: Humanism, Politics and Reform 1500–1550* Oxford 1986

Frijhoff, Willem 'Erasme, l'éducation et le monde scientifique de son temps – rapport introductif,' in *Erasmus of Rotterdam* 101–8

Fumaroli, M. 'Genèse de l'epistolographie classique: rhétorique humaniste de la lettre, de Pétrarque à Juste Lipse' *Revue d'histoire littéraire de la France* 78 (1978): 886–905

Garber, Klaus 'L'humanisme européen et l'utopie pacifiste: essai de reconstitution historique,' in *Actes du Colloque International* 393–425

Garin, Eugenio 'Erasmo e l'Umanesimo italiano' BHR 33 (1971): 7–17

Gebhart, Georg *Die Stellung des Erasmus von Rotterdam zur Römische Kirche* Marburg an der Lahn 1966

Geldner, Ferdinand *Die Staatsauffassung und Fürstenlehre des Erasmus von Rotterdam* Berlin 1930

Gerlo, Aloïs 'Erasme, homo batavus,' in *Commém Nat* 61–80

– 'Marie Delcourt, traductrice d'Erasme' in *Actes du Colloque International* 387–92

– 'The *Opus de conscribendis epistolis* of Erasmus and the Tradition of the

Ars epistolica,' in R.R. Bolgar (ed) *Classical Influences on European Culture AD 500–1500* Cambridge 1971, 103–14

Gerrish, B.A. *'De Libero Arbitrio* (1524): Erasmus on Piety, Theology, and the Lutheran Dogma,' in DeMolen (ed) *Essays on the Works of Erasmus* 187–209

Gielis, M. 'Erasme, Latomus et le martyre de deux augustins luthériens à Bruxelles en 1523,' in *Erasmus of Rotterdam* 61–8

Gilmore, Myron P. *'Fides et Eruditio*: Erasmus and the Study of History,' in Gilmore *Humanists and Jurists: Six Studies in the Renaissance* Cambridge, Mass 1963, 87–114

– 'Italian Reactions to Erasmian Humanism,' in Heiko A. Oberman and Thomas A. Brady, Jr (eds) *Itinerarium Italicum: The Profile of the Italian Renaissance in the Mirror of Its European Transformations* Leiden 1975, 61–115

– 'Les limites de la tolérance dans l'oeuvre polémique d'Erasme,' in *Coll Tur* 2:713–36

Gleason, John B. *John Colet* Berkeley 1989

Glomski, Jacqueline 'Erasmus and Cracow (1510–1530),' in ERSY 17 (1997): 1–18

Godin, André 'De Vitrier à Origène: recherches sur la patristique érasmienne,' in *Coll Eras: Mons* 47–57

– 'Erasme, Aléandre: une étrange familiarité,' in *Actes du Colloque International* 249–74

– 'Erasme et la modèle origénien de la prédication,' in *Coll Tur* 2:807–20

– *Erasme lecteur d'Origène* Geneva 1982

– 'Jean Vitrier et la "Cénacle" de Saint-Omer,' in *Coll Tur* 2:781–805

– 'Une biographie en quête d'auteur: le *Compendium vitae Erasmi,'* in *Coll Eras: Liège* 197–221

Gorce, Denys 'La patristique dans la réforme d'Erasme' in *Festgabe Joseph Lortz* 2 vols, Baden-Baden 1958, 1:233–76

Gordon, Walter M. *Humanist Play and Belief: The Seriocomic Art of Desiderius Erasmus* Toronto 1990

Grafton, Anthony, and Lisa Jardine *From Humanism to the Humanities: Education and Liberal Arts in Fifteenth-and Sixteenth-Century Europe* London 1986

Greitemann, N. 'Erasmus als exegeet' *Studia Catholica* 12 (1936): 294–305

Grendler, Paul and Marcella 'The Survival of Erasmus in Italy' *Erasmus in English* 8 (1976): 2–22

Gualdo Rosa, Lucia 'L'Institutio "del prencipe christiano" de Mambrino Roseo de Fabriano entre Antonio de Guevara et Erasme,' in *Actes du Colloque International* 307–24

Gunning, J.H. 'Desiderius Erasmus, 27 October 1466(?)–12 Juli 1536' *Paedagogische Studiën* 17 (1936): 129–41

Hägglund, Bengt 'Erasmus und die Reformation,' in *Erasmus und Europa* 139–47

Halkin, Léon-E. *Erasmus: A Critical Biography* Oxford 1993
- 'Erasme éditeur de sa correspondance: le cas de l'*Auctarium*' BHR 40 (1978): 239–47
- 'Erasme en Italie,' in *Coll Tur* 1:37–53
- 'Erasme et les Pays-Bas,' in *Erasmus und Europa* 33–46
- *Erasme et l'humanisme chrétien* Paris 1969
- *Erasmus ex Erasmo: Erasme éditeur de sa correspondance* Aubel 1983
- 'Erasme pèlerin,' in *Scrinium* 2:239–52
- 'La piété d'Erasme' *Revue d'histoire ecclésiastique* 79 (1984): 671–708
- 'La psychohistoire et le caractère d'Erasme' *Storia della Storiografia* 8 (1985): 73–90
- 'Signification du Congrès érasmien,' in *Actes* 193–8
- 'La thème du pèlerinage dans les *Colloques* d'Erasme,' in *Actes* 88–98
Hardin, Richard F. 'The Literary Conventions of Erasmus' *Education of a Christian Prince*: Advice and Aphorism' RQ 35 (1982):151–63
Hayum, Andrée 'Dürer's Portrait of Erasmus and the Ars Typographorum' RQ 38 (1985): 650–87
Headley, John M. 'Gattinara, Erasmus, and the Imperial Configurations of Humanism' ARG 71 (1980): 64–98
Heath, Michael J. 'Erasmus and the Infidel,' in ERSY 16(1996): 19–33
Heesakkers, Chris L. 'Argumentatio a persona in Erasmus' Second Apology against Alberto Pio,' in *Erasmus of Rotterdam* 79–87
Heijden, J.N. van der 'Erasmus als pacifist' *Kerk en Wereld* 28 (1936): 5–6
Henderson, Judith Rice 'Erasmus on the Art of Letter-Writing,' in Murphy (ed) *Renaissance Eloquence* 331–55
Henze, Barbara 'Erasmianisch: Die "Methode", Konflikte zu lösen? Das Wirken Witzels und Cassanders,' in Mout, Smolinsky, and Trapman (eds) *Erasmianism* 155–68
Herbrüggen, Hubertus Schulte 'Erasmus und England: Erasmus und Morus,' in *Erasmus und Europa* 91–110
Herding, Otto 'Erasme et Wimpfeling,' in *Erasme, l'Alsace et son temps* Strasbourg 1971, 111–15
- 'Isokrates, Erasmus und die Institutio principis christiani,' in Rudolf Vierhaus and Manfred Botzenhart (eds) *Dauer und Wandel der Geschichte: Aspekte europäischer Vergangenheit* Münster 1966, 101–43
Hermant, P. 'Le folklore dans les écrits d'Erasme' *Le Folklore Brabançon* 14 (1935): 5–69
Hexter, J.H. *The Vision of Politics on the Eve of the Reformation: More, Machiavelli, and Seyssel* London 1973
Hirstein, James S. 'Erasme, l'*Histoire Auguste* et l'histoire,' in *Actes du Colloque International* 71–95
Hoenderdaal, G.J. 'Erasmus en de nederlandse Reformatie' *Vox Theologica* 39 (1969): 126–44
Hoffmann, Manfred 'Erasmus and Religious Toleration,' in ERSY 2 (1982): 80–106

- 'Erasmus on Church and Ministry,' in ERSY 6 (1986): 1–30
- *Erkenntnis und Verwirklichung der wahren Theologie nach Erasmus von Rotterdam* Tübingen 1972
- *Rhetoric and Theology: The Hermeneutic of Erasmus* Toronto 1994
- review of Chomarat in ERSY 5 (1985): 65–83

Holeczek, Heinz *Erasmus Deutsch: Die volkssprachliche Rezeption des Erasmus von Rotterdam in der reformatorischen Öffentlichkeit* 1, Stuttgart-Bad Cannstatt 1983
- 'Die Haltung des Erasmus zu Luther nach dem Scheitern seiner Vermittlungspolitik 1520/1' ARG 64 (1973): 85–112
- *Humanistische Bibelphilologie als Reformproblem bei Erasmus von Rotterdam, Thomas More und William Tyndale* Leiden 1975

Homza, Lu Ann 'Erasmus as Hero, or Heretic? Spanish Humanism and the Valladolid Assembly of 1527' RQ 50 (1997): 78–118

Honée, Eugène 'Erasmus und die Religionsverhandlungen der deutschen Reichstage (1524–1530),' in Mout, Smolinsky, and Trapman (eds) 65–75

Hoyoux, Jean 'Les voyages d'Erasme et de Jérôme Aléandre: un chapitre de vie quotidienne,' in *Coll Eras: Mons* 315–25

Hudson, Hoyt Hopewell 'Analysis' *Praise of Folly*, Modern Library, New York nd, 129–42

Huerga, Alvaro 'Erasmismo y Alumbradismo,' in Revuelta Sañudo and Morón Arroyo (eds) *El Erasmismo en España* 339–55

Huizinga, Johan 'Ce qu'Erasme ne comprenait pas,' in *Verzamelde Werken* 6:247–51
- *Erasmus of Rotterdam* London 1952
- 'In Commemoration of Erasmus' in Huizinga *Men and Ideas: History, the Middle Ages, the Renaissance* New York 1959, 310–26

Hyma, Albert *The Christian Renaissance: A History of the 'Devotio Moderna'* 2nd edn, Hamden, Conn 1965
- 'Erasmus and the Oxford Reformers (1493–1503),' in Hyma *Renaissance to Reformation* Grand Rapids 1951, 209–49
- *The Youth of Erasmus* Ann Arbor 1930

IJsewijn, J. 'Humanism in the Low Countries,' in Rabil (ed) *Renaissance Humanism* 2:156–215

IJsewijn, J., and C. Matheeussen 'Erasme et l'historiographie,' in G. Verbeke and J. IJsewijn (eds) *The Late Middle Ages and the Dawn of Humanism outside Italy* The Hague 1972, 31–43

Imbart de la Tour, Pierre *Les Origines de la Réforme* 3 *L'Evangélisme (1521–38)* Paris 1914

Isnardi-Parente, Margherita 'Erasme, la République de Platon et la communauté des biens,' in *Erasmus of Rotterdam* 40–5

Jardine, Lisa *Erasmus, Man of Letters: The Construction of Charisma in Print* Princeton 1993
- 'Penfriends and Patria: Erasmian Pedagogy and the Republic of Letters,' in ERSY 16 (1996): 1–18

Jarrott, Catherine A.L. 'Erasmus's Annotations and Colet's Commentaries on Paul: A Comparison of Some Theological Themes,' in DeMolen (ed) *Essays on the Works of Erasmus*, 125–44

– 'Erasmus' Biblical Humanism' *Studies in the Renaissance* 17 (1970): 119–52

Jedin, Hubert *A History of the Council of Trent* 1, Edinburgh/London 1957

Jong, J. de 'Het goddienstig standpunt van Erasmus' *Historisch Tijdschrift* 11 (1932): 317–39

Jonge, Henk Jan de 'Four Unpublished Letters on Erasmus from J.L. Stunica to Pope Leo X,' in *Coll Eras: Liège* 147–60

– '*Novum Testamentum a nobis versum*: The Essence of Erasmus' Edition of the New Testament' *Journal of Theological Studies* ns 35 (1984): 394–413

– 'Wann ist Erasmus' Übersetzung des Neuen Testaments entstanden,' in *Erasmus of Rotterdam* 151–7

Jung, Gertrud 'Erasmus und Vives,' in *Gedenkschrift* 130–43

Kaegi, Werner 'Erasmus im achtzehnten Jahrhundert,' in *Gedenkschrift* 205–27

Kaiser, Walter *Praisers of Folly: Erasmus, Rabelais, Shakespeare* Cambridge, Mass 1964

Kardos, Tibor 'L'esprit d'Erasme en Hongrie,' in *Coll Tur* 1:187–214

Kempfi, Andrzej 'Erasme et la vie intellectuelle en Warmie au temps de Nicolas Copernic,' in *Coll Tur* 1:397–406

Kinney, Daniel 'Erasmus and the Latin Comedians,' in *Actes du Colloque International* 57–69

Kisch, Guido *Erasmus und die Jurisprudenz seiner Zeit: Studien zum humanistischen Rechtsdenken* Basel 1960

– *Erasmus' Stellung zu Juden und Judentum* Tübingen 1969

Kleinhans, Robert G. '*Ecclesiastes sive de Ratione Concionandi*,' in DeMolen (ed) *Essays on the Works of Erasmus* 253–66

– 'Luther and Erasmus: Another Perspective' *Church History* 39 (1970): 459–69

Kluge, Otto *Erasmus damals und heute* Leipzig [1936]

Knott, Betty I. 'Erasmus' Working Methods in "De Copia,"' in *Erasmus of Rotterdam* 143–50

Knowles, D. *The Religious Orders in England* 3, Cambridge 1957

Koch, A.C.F. *The Year of Erasmus' Birth and Other Contributions to the Chronology of His Life* Utrecht 1969

Koerber, Eberhard von *Die Staatstheorie des Erasmus von Rotterdam* Berlin 1967

Köhler, Walter 'Erasmus von Rotterdam als religiöse Persönlichkeit' *Bijdragen voor Vaderlandsche Geschiedenis en Oudheidkunde* 7th series 7 (1936): 213–25

Kohls, E.-W. 'Erasmus und die werdende evangelische Bewegung des

16. Jahrhunderts,' in *Scrinium* 1:203–19, and 'Erasme et la Réforme,' in *Coll Tur* 2:837–47

- 'Das Geburtsjahr des Erasmus' *Theologische Zeitschrift* 22 (1966): 95–121
- *Luther oder Erasmus: Luthers Theologie in der Auseinandersetzung mit Erasmus* 1, Basel 1972
- 'Die Neuentdeckung der Theologie des Erasmus,' in *Coll Eras: Liège* 234–50
- 'Noch einmal das Geburtsjahr des Erasmus: Antwort an R.R. Post' *Theologische Zeitschrift* 22 (1966): 347–59
- 'La position théologique d'Erasme et la tradition dans le "De libero arbitrio,"' in *Coll Eras: Mons* 69–88
- *Die Theologie des Erasmus* 2 vols, Basel 1966

Koldeweij, A.M. *Erasmus: zicht op een geleerde in zijn tijd* Amsterdam 1986, and in Sperna Weiland (ed) *Erasmus: De actualiteit van zijn denken* 137–80

Kristeller, Paul Oskar 'Erasmus from an Italian Perspective' *RQ* 23 (1970): 1–14

Krüger, Friedhelm *Humanistische Evangelienauslegung: Desiderius Erasmus von Rotterdam als Ausleger der Evangelien in seinen Paraphrasen* Tübingen 1986

Kushner, Eva 'Erasmus and the Paradox of Subjectivity,' in *ERSY* 18 (1998): 1–20

La Garanderie, Marie-Madeleine de *Christianisme et lettres profanes: Essai sur l'humanisme français (1515–1535) et sur la pensée de Guillaume Budé* Paris 1995

- 'Erasme à l'épreuve des textes de saint Jean,' in *Actes du Colloque International* 127–40
- 'Erasme et Luther commentateurs de la première épître de Saint-Jean (I, 1–7): "Dieu est lumière,"' in *Coll Eras: Liège* 161–75
- 'Les relations d'Erasme avec Paris, au temps de son séjour aux Pays-Bas méridionaux (1516–1521),' in *Scrinium* 1:29–53

Lebeau, Jean 'Erasme, Sebastian Franck et la tolérance,' in *Erasme, l'Alsace et son temps* Strasbourg 1971, 117–38

Lefèvre, Ph. 'La lecture des oeuvres d'Erasme au sein du bas clergé durant la première moitié du XVIe siècle,' in *Scrinium* 1:83–91

Levi, A.H.T. 'Introduction' *Praise of Folly*, Penguin Classics, Harmondsworth 1971

Liechtenhan, Rudolf 'Die politische Hoffnung des Erasmus und ihr Zusammenbruch,' in *Gedenkschrift* 144–65

Lienhard, Marc 'Die Radikalen des 16. Jahrhunderts und Erasmus,' in Mout, Smolinsky, and Trapman (eds) *Erasmianism* 91–104

Ligt, Bart de 'Erasmiana' *De Stem* 16 (1936): 649–72

Lindeboom, G.A. 'Erasmus in zorgen' *Hermeneus* 8 (1936): 167–72

Lindeboom, J. 'Erasmus in de Waardeering van het Nageslacht' *Bijdragen voor Vaderlandsche Geschiedenis en Oudheidkunde* 7th series 7 (1936): 117–31

Locher, G.W. 'Zwingli und Erasmus,' in *Scrinium* 2:325–50

Lohse, Bernhard 'Marginalien zum Streit zwischen Erasmus und Luther' *Luther: Zeitschrift der Luther Gesellschaft* 46 (1975): 5–24

Longhurst John E. *Erasmus and the Spanish Inquisition: The Case of Juan de Valdés* Albuquerque 1950

Lortz, Joseph 'Erasmus-kirchengeschichtlich,' in T. Steinbüchel and T. Müncker (eds) *Aus Theologie und Philosophie: Festschrift für Fritz Tillmann zu seinem 75. Geburtstag* Düsseldorf 1950, 271–326

– *The Reformation in Germany* 1, London/New York 1968

Lubac, Henri de *Exégèse médiévale. Les quatre sens de l'Ecriture* IV.2, Paris 1964

Magnien, Michel 'Introduction à l'*Oratio prima*,' in Jules-César Scaliger *Orationes duae contra Erasmum* Geneva 1999

Maguire, John B. 'Erasmus' Biographical Masterpiece: *Hieronymi Stridonensis Vita*' RQ 26 (1973): 265–73

Major, Emil 'Die Grabstätte des Erasmus,' in *Gedenkschrift* 299–315

Mangan, John Joseph *Life, Character and Influence of Desiderius Erasmus of Rotterdam* 2 vols, New York 1927

Mann, Margaret (Phillips) 'Autour du Paris d'Erasme,' in *Mélanges offerts à M. Abel Lefranc par ses élèves et ses amis* Paris 1936, 113–29

– *Erasme et les débuts de la Réforme française (1517–1536)* Paris 1934 (reprint Geneva 1978)

Mansfield, Bruce 'Erasmus in the Age of Revolutions,' in *Erasmus of Rotterdam* 228–39

– 'Erasmus and Frederic Seebohm: The "Oxford Reformers", Down but Not Out?' *Lucas: An Evangelical History Review* 17 (1994): 19–30

– 'A Not Exclusive Truth: An Early Ninetenth-Century Pastoral Theology and Erasmus,' in Nigel Aston (ed) *Religious Change in Europe 1650–1914: Essays for John McManners* Oxford 1997, 275–97

– 'The Social Realism of Erasmus: Some Puzzles and Reflections,' in ERSY 14 (1994): 1–23

– 'The Three Circles of Erasmus of Rotterdam' *Colloquium: The Australian and New Zealand Theological Review* 4 (1972): 4–11

Marc'hadour, Germain 'Erasmus as Priest: Holy Orders in His Vision and Practice,' in Pabel (ed) *Erasmus' Vision of the Church* 115–49

– 'Erasme et John Colet,' in *Coll Tur* 2:761–9

– 'Thomas More in Emulation and Defense of Erasmus,' in *Erasmus of Rotterdam* 203–14

– 'William Tyndale entre Erasme et Luther,' in *Actes du Colloque International* 185–98

Marcel, Raymond 'Les "Découvertes" d'Erasme en Angleterre' BHR 14 (1952): 117–23

– 'Les dettes d'Erasme envers l'Italie,' in *Actes* 159–73

Margolin, Jean-Claude *Erasme: Declamatio de pueris statim ac liberaliter instituendis: Etude critique, traduction et commentaire* Geneva 1966
- 'Le douzième Stage international d'Etudes humanistes (Tours, 3–25 juillet 1969),' in *Coll Tur* 1:9–12
- 'Erasme à l'époque des "Lumières": Une traduction française inédite du *De contemptu mundi*,' in *Actes du Colloque International* 351–86
- 'Erasme et Ferdinand de Habsbourg d'après deux lettres inédites de l'Empereur à l'humaniste,' in *Erasmus of Rotterdam* 15–29
- 'Erasme et la France,' in *Erasmus und Europa* 47–73
- 'Erasme et la guerre contre les Turcs,' in Margolin *Erasme: le prix des mots et de l'homme* ch 11
- *Erasme et la musique* Paris 1965, and 'Erasme et la musique,' in *Recherches érasmiennes* 85–97
- *Erasme, précepteur de l'Europe* Paris 1995
- *Erasme: le prix des mots et de l'homme* London 1986
- 'Erasme et le problème social,' in *Erasme: le prix des mots et de l'homme* ch 10
- 'Erasme et la psychologie des peuples' *Ethnopsychologie: revue de Psychologie des peuples* 25 (1970): 373–424
- 'Erasme et la Verbe: De la rhétorique à l'herméneutique,' in *Erasme, l'Alsace, et son temps* Strasbourg 1971, 87–110
- 'Erasme et la Vérité,' in *Coll Eras: Mons* 135–70, reprinted in *Recherches érasmiennes* 45–69
- *Guerre et paix dans la pensée d'Erasme* Paris 1973
- 'Guy Patin, lecteur d'Erasme,' in *Coll Tur* 1:323–58
- 'L'idée de nature dans la pensée d'Erasme,' in *Recherches érasmiennes* 9–44
- 'L'inspiration érasmienne de Jacob Cats,' in *Commém Nat* 113–51
- 'Interpretation d'un passage de l'*Enchiridion Militis Christiani, Canon Quintus*,' in *Actes* 99–115
- *Recherches érasmiennes* Geneva 1969
- 'La religion d'Erasme et l'Allemagne des Lumières' *ARG* 72 (1981): 197–231
- 'Un Erasme revisité par une historienne italienne' *BHR* 59 (1997): 687–98
Markish, Shimon *Erasmus and the Jews* Chicago 1986
Marsh, David 'Erasmus on the Antithesis of Body and Soul' *Journal of the History of Ideas* 37 (1976): 673–88
Massaut, J.-P. 'Erasme et Saint Thomas,' in *Coll Tur* 2:581–611
- 'Erasme, la Sorbonne et la nature de l'Eglise,' in *Coll Eras: Mons* 89–118
Maurer, Wilhelm *Das Verhältnis des Staates zur Kirche nach humanistischer Anschauung, vornehmlich bei Erasmus* Giessen 1930
McConica, James Kelsey *English Humanists and Reformation Politics under Henry VIII and Edward VI* Oxford 1965
- 'The English Reception of Erasmus,' in Mout, Smolinsky, and Trapman (eds) *Erasmianism* 37–46

- *Erasmus* Oxford 1991
- 'Erasmus and the Grammar of Consent,' in *Scrinium* 2:77–99
- 'Erasmus and the "Julius": A Humanist Reflects on the Church,' in Charles Trinkaus with Heiko A. Oberman (eds) *The Pursuit of Holiness in Late Medieval and Renaissance Religion* Leiden 1974, 444–71
- 'Erasmus in Amsterdam and Toronto,' in Erika Rummel (ed) *Editing Texts from the Age of Erasmus* Toronto 1996, 81–100
McConica, J.K., and R.M. Schoeffel 'The Collected Works of Erasmus' *Scholarly Publishing* July 1979: 313–24
McCutcheon, Elizabeth 'Erasmus' Representation of Women and Their Discourses,' in ERSY 12 (1992): 64–86
McSorley H.J. 'Erasmus and the Primacy of the Roman Pontiff: Between Conciliarism and Papalism' ARG 65 (1974): 37–54
- *Luther: Right or Wrong? An Ecumenical-Theological Study of Luther's Major Work The Bondage of the Will* New York/Minneapolis 1969
Meertens, P.J. 'Erasmus en Zeeland' *Provinciale Zeeuwsche en Middelburgsche Courant* 10, 11 July 1936
Meissinger, Karl A. *Erasmus von Rotterdam* Berlin 1948
Mesnard, Pierre 'Le caractère d'Erasme,' in *Coll Eras: Mons* 327–32
- 'La dernière traduction française de l'Enchiridion,' in *Scrinium* 1:325–32
- *L'essor de la philosophie politique au XVIe siècle* Paris 1951
- 'L'expérience politique de Charles-Quint et les enseignements d'Erasme,' in Jean Jacquot (ed) *Fêtes et cérémonies au temps de Charles-Quint* Paris 1960, 45–56
Michel, Alain 'La parole et la beauté chez Erasme,' in *Actes du Colloque International* 3–17
Miller, Clarence H. 'Some Medieval Elements and Structural Unity in Erasmus' *Praise of Folly*' RQ 27 (1974): 499–511
Miller, Clement A. 'Erasmus on Music' *Musical Quarterly* 52 (1966): 332–49
Minnich, Nelson H. 'Erasmus and the Fifth Lateran Council (1512–17),' in *Erasmus of Rotterdam* 46–60
Minnich, Nelson H., and W.W. Meissner 'The Character of Erasmus' AHR 83 (1978): 598–624
Moore, W.G. 'The Search for Erasmus' *Hibbert Journal* 34 (1936): 522–8
Mout, M.E.H.N. 'Erasmianism in Modern Dutch Historiography,' in Mout, Smolinsky, and Trapman (eds) *Erasmianism* 189–98
Mout, M.E.H.N., H. Smolinsky, and J. Trapman (eds) *Erasmianism: Idea and Reality* Amsterdam 1997
Nauwelaerts, M.A. 'Erasme à Louvain: Ephémérides d'un séjour de 1517 à 1521,' in *Scrinium* 1:3–24
- 'Erasme et Gand,' in *Commém Nat* 152–77
Newald, Richard *Erasmus Roterodamus* Freiburg-im-Breisgau 1947
Nieto, José C. 'Luther's Ghost and Erasmus' Masks in Spain' BHR 39 (1977): 33–49

Noordenbos, Oene 'Erasmus en de Nederlanden' *Bijdragen voor Vader-landsche Geschiedenis en Oudheidkunde* 7th series 7 (1936): 193–212

Nuchelmans, J. *Erasmus en de muziek* Amsterdam 1986, and in Sperna Weiland (ed) *Erasmus: De actualiteit van zijn denken* 113–36

Nugent, Donald 'The Erasmus Renaissance' *Month* 2229 (1970): 36–45

O'Donnell, Anne M. 'Contemporary Women in the Letters of Erasmus,' in ERSY 9 (1989): 34–72

Oberman, Heiko A. *The Roots of Anti-Semitism in the Age of Renaissance and Reformation* Philadelphia 1984

Oelrich, K.H. *Der späte Erasmus und die Reformation* Münster 1961

Olin, John C. 'Erasmus' *Adagia* and More's *Utopia' Moreana* 100 (vol. 26) *Mélanges Marc'hadour* (1989): 127–36

– 'Erasmus and Saint Jerome: An Appraisal of the Bond,' in *Erasmus of Rotterdam* 182–6

– 'Erasmus and Saint Jerome: The Close Bond and Its Significance,' in ERSY 7 (1987): 33–53

– *Erasmus, Utopia, and the Jesuits: Essays on the Outreach of Humanism* New York 1994

– *Six Essays on Erasmus* New York 1979

O'Malley, John W. 'Erasmus and the History of Sacred Rhetoric: The *Ecclesiastes* of 1535,' in ERSY 5 (1985): 1–29

– 'Erasmus and Luther, Continuity and Discontinuity as Key to Their Conflict' SCJ 5 (1974): 47–65

– 'Grammar and Rhetoric in the *pietas* of Erasmus' *Journal of Medieval and Renaissance Studies* 18 (1988): 81–98, and in *Religious Culture in the Six-teenth Century: Preaching, Rhetoric, Spirituality, and Reform* Aldershot 1993 ch 8

– 'Introduction' CWE 66:ix–li

Osorio, Jorge Alves 'Enoncé et dialogue dans les *Colloques* d'Erasme,' in *Actes du Colloque International* 19–34

Pabel, Hilmar M. *Conversing with God: Prayer in Erasmus' Pastoral Writ-ings* Toronto 1997

– 'Erasmus of Rotterdam and Judaism: A Reexamination in the Light of New Evidence' ARG 87 (1996): 9–37

– *Erasmus' Vision of the Church* Kirksville 1995

– 'The Peaceful People of Christ: The Irenic Ecclesiology of Erasmus of Rotterdam,' in Pabel (ed) *Erasmus' Vision of the Church* 57–93

Padberg, Rudolf *Erasmus als Katechet. Der literarische Beitrag des Erasmus von Rotterdam zur katholischen Katechese des 16. Jahrhunderts. Eine Unter-suchung zum Geschichte der Katechese* Freiburg-im-Breisgau 1956

– 'Erasmus contra Augustinum: Das Problem des bellum justum in der erasmischen Friedensethik,' in *Coll Eras: Liège* 279–96

– 'Pax Erasmiana: Das politische Engagement und die "politische Theol-ogie" des Erasmus von Rotterdam,' in *Scrinium* 2:301–12

Panofsky, Erwin 'Erasmus and the Visual Arts' *Journal of the Warburg and Courtauld Institutes* 32 (1969): 200–27

Pas, W.M. van de 'De onbekende Erasmus' *Het Katholieke Schoolblad* 3 (1936): 73–6

Pavlovskis, Zoja *The Praise of Folly: Structure and Irony* Leiden 1983

Payne, John B. 'Erasmus and Lefèvre d'Etaples as Interpreters of Paul' *ARG* 65 (1974): 54–83

- *Erasmus: His Theology of the Sacraments* 1970
- 'Erasmus: Interpreter of Romans' *Sixteenth Century Essays and Studies* 2 (1971): 1–35
- 'The Significance of Lutheranizing Changes in Erasmus' Interpretation of Paul's Letters to the Romans and Galatians in His *Annotations* (1527) and *Paraphrases* (1533),' in Olivier Fatio and Pierre Fraenkel (eds) *Histoire de l'exégèse au XVIe siècle* Geneva 1978, 312–30
- 'Toward the Hermeneutics of Erasmus,' in *Scrinium* 2:13–49

Pendergrass, Jan N. 'Cassander de Colmars, un correspondant d'Erasme,' in *Actes du Colloque International* 277–91

Pérez, Joseph '"El erasmismo y las corrientes espirituales afines,"' in Revuelta Sañudo and Morón Arroyo (eds) *El Erasmismo en España* 323–38

Peteghem, P.P.J.L. van 'Erasmus' Last Will, the Holy Roman Empire and the Low Countries,' in *Erasmus of Rotterdam* 88–97

Pfeiffer, Rudolf 'Die Einheit im geistigen Werk des Erasmus' *Deutsche Vierteljahrsschrift für Literaturwissenschaft und Geistesgeschichte* 15 (1937): 473–87

- 'Erasmus und die Einheit der klassischen und der christlichen Renaissance' *Historisches Jahrbuch* 74 (1955): 175–88
- *History of Classical Scholarship from 1300 to 1850* Oxford 1976
- *Humanitas Erasmiana* Leipzig/Berlin 1931
- 'Die Wandlung der "Antibarbari,"' in *Gedenkschrift* 50–67

Phillips, Margaret Mann *The 'Adages' of Erasmus* Cambridge 1964

- 'Erasmus and the Art of Writing,' in *Scrinium* 1:335–50
- 'Erasmus and the Classics,' in T.A. Dorey (ed) *Erasmus* 1–30
- 'Erasme et Montaigne,' in *Coll Tur* 1:479–90
- *Erasmus and the Northern Renaissance* London 1949
- 'The Erasmus Quincentenary: Europe' *Erasmus in English* 1 (1970) n.p.
- 'Visages d'Erasme,' in *Coll Eras: Liège* 17–29

Pigman, G.W., III 'Imitation and the Renaissance Sense of the Past: The Reception of Erasmus' *Ciceronianus' Journal of Medieval and Renaissance Studies* 9 (1979): 155–77

Pineau, J.-B. *Erasme: Sa pensée religieuse* Paris 1924

Poelhecke, J.J. 'The Nameless Homeland of Erasmus' *Acta Historiae Neerlandicae* 7 (1974): 54–87

Pollet, J.V.M. 'Erasmiana: Quelques aspects du problème érasmien d'après les publications récentes' *Revue des sciences religieuses* 26 (1952): 387–404

- 'Origine et structure du "De sarcienda ecclesiae concordia" (1533) d'Erasme,' in *Scrinium* 2:183–95
Polman, P. 'Erasmus en de theologie' *Studia Catholica* 12 (1931): 273–93
Porter, H.C. *Reformation and Reaction in Tudor Cambridge* Cambridge 1958
Post, R.R. *The Modern Devotion: Confrontation with Reformation and Humanism* Leiden 1968
- 'Nochmals Erasmus' Geburtsjahr' *Theologische Zeitschrift* 22 (1966): 319–33
- 'Quelques précisions sur l'année de la naissance d'Erasme (1469) et sur son éducation' BHR 26 (1964): 489–509
Praemium Erasmianum MCMLXXXVI Amsterdam 1986
Rabil, Albert, Jr *Erasmus and the New Testament: The Mind of a Christian Humanist* San Antonio 1972
Rabil, Albert, Jr (ed) *Renaissance Humanism: Foundations, Forms, and Legacy* 3 vols, Philadelphia 1988
Rademaker, C.S.M. 'Erasmus and the Psalms: His Commentary on Psalm 86 (85),' in *Erasmus of Rotterdam* 187–94
Rebhorn, W.A. 'The Metamorphoses of Moria: Structure and Meaning in *The Praise of Folly*' *Publications of the Modern Language Association* 89 (1974): 463–76
Reedijk, Cornelis 'Erasmus' Final Modesty,' in *Actes* 174–92
- 'Erasmus in 1970' BHR 32 (1970): 449–66
- 'Das Lebenende des Erasmus' *Basler Zeitschrift für Geschichte und Altertumskunde* 57 (1958): 23–66
- 'The Leiden Edition of Erasmus' *Opera omnia* in a European Context,' in *Erasmus und Europa* 163–82
- *The Poems of Desiderius Erasmus* Leiden 1956
- *Tandem bona causa triumphat: Zur Geschichte des Gesamtwerkes des Erasmus von Rotterdam* Basel 1980
Reese, Alan W. 'Learning Virginity: Erasmus' Ideal of Christian Marriage' BHR 57 (1995): 551–67
Regout, Robert 'Erasmus en de theorie van den rechtvaardigen oorlog' *Bijdragen voor Vaderlandsche Geschiedenis en Oudheidkunde* 7th series 7 (1936): 155–71
Reicke, Bo 'Erasmus und die neutestamentliche Textgeschichte' *Theologische Zeitschrift* 22 (1966): 254–65
Reijnen H. 'Erasmus en Luther' *Het Schild* 18 (1936): 7–17, 63–76, 158–77
- 'R.K. beoordeeling van Erasmus' *Het Schild* 17 (1936): 345–55
Renaudet, Augustin 'Erasme économiste,' in *Mélanges Abel Lefranc* Paris 1936, 130–41, and *Humanisme et Renaissance* Geneva 1958, 194–200
- *Erasme et l'Italie* Geneva 1954 (2nd edn, ed Silvana Seidel Menchi, Geneva 1998)
- *Etudes érasmiennes (1521–1529)* Paris 1939
Revuelta Sañudo, Manuel, and Ciriaco Morón Arroyo (eds) *El Erasmismo en España* Santander 1986

Rhodes, J.T. 'Erasmus and English Readers of the 1530s' *Durham University Journal* 71 (1979): 17–25

Rice, Eugene 'Erasmus and the Religious Tradition' *Journal of the History of Ideas* 11 (1950): 387–411

- *The Renaissance Idea of Wisdom* Cambridge, Mass 1958

Ritoók-Szalay, Agnes 'Erasmus und die ungarischen Intellektuellen des 16. Jahrhunderts,' in *Erasmus und Europa* 111–28

Ritter, G. *Erasmus und der deutsche Humanistenkreis am Oberrhein: Eine Gedenkrede* Freiburg im Breisgau 1937

Roth, Carl 'Das Legatum Erasmianum,' in *Gedenkschrift* 282–98

Roth, Paul 'Die Wohnstätten des Erasmus in Basel,' in *Gedenkschrift* 270–81

Rudolph, Günther 'Das sozialökonomische Denken des Erasmus von Rotterdam' *Deutsche Zeitschrift für Philosophie* 17 (1969): 1076–92

Rüegg, Walter *Cicero und der Humanismus: Formale Untersuchungen über Petrarca und Erasmus* Zürich 1946

Rummel, Erika *Erasmus' 'Annotations' on the New Testament: From Philologist to Theologian* Toronto 1986

- *Erasmus and His Catholic Critics* 2 vols, Nieuwkoop 1989

- 'Erasmus and the Valladolid Articles: Intrigue, Innuendo, and Strategic Defense,' in *Erasmus of Rotterdam* 69–78

Rummel, Erika (ed) *Editing Texts from the Age of Erasmus* Toronto 1996

- *Erasmus on Women* Toronto 1996

Sabbe, Maurits 'Erasmus en zijn Antwerpsche Vrienden' *De Gids* 100 (1936): 49–64

Salomon, Albert 'Democracy and Religion in the Work of Erasmus' *Review of Religion* 14 (1950): 227–49

Schalk, F. 'Erasmus und die *Res publica literaria*,' in *Actes* 14–28

Schätti, Karl *Erasmus von Rotterdam und die Römische Kurie* Basel 1954

Schevill, Rudolph 'Erasmus and Spain' *Hispanic Review* 7 (1939): 93–116

Schlechta, Karl *Erasmus von Rotterdam* Hamburg 1948

Schneider, Elisabeth *Das Bild der Frau im Werk des Erasmus von Rotterdam* Basel/Stuttgart 1955

Schoeck, R.J. 'Erasmus as Latin Secretary to the Bishop of Cambrai: Erasmus' Introduction to the Burgundian Court,' in *Erasmus of Rotterdam* 7–14

- *Erasmus Grandescens: The Growth of a Humanist's Mind and Spirituality* Nieuwkoop 1988

- *Erasmus of Europe* 1 *The Making of a Humanist 1467–1500* Edinburgh 1990, 2 *The Prince of Humanists 1501–1536* Edinburgh 1993

- '*In loco intertexantur*: Erasmus as Master of Intertextuality,' in Heinrich F. Plett (ed) *Intertextuality* Berlin 1991, 181–91

Schottenloher, Otto 'Erasmus und die *Respublica Christiana*' *Historische Zeitschrift* 210 (1970): 295–323

- 'Lex naturae und Lex Christi bei Erasmus,' in *Scrinium* 2:253–99

Schwarz, Werner *Principles and Problems of Biblical Translation: Some Reformation Controversies and Their Background* Cambridge 1955

Screech, M.A. *Ecstasy and the Praise of Folly* London 1980

– 'Erasmus and the *Concordia* of Cornelius Jansenius, Bishop of Ghent: Christian Folly and Catholic Orthodoxy,' in *Coll Eras: Liège* 297–307

– 'Folie érasmienne et folie rabelaisienne,' in *Coll Tur* 1:441–52, and 'Comment Rabelais a exploité les travaux d'Erasme: quelques détails,' in ibid 453–61

Scribner, R.W. 'The Power of Wisdom: The Social Thought of Erasmus 1489–1518' unpublished thesis, University of Sydney 1967

'The Social Thought of Erasmus' *Journal of Religious History* 6 (1970): 3–26

Seidel Menchi, Silvana 'Do We Need the "ism"? Some Mediterranean Perspectives,' in Mout, Smolinsky, and Trapman (eds) *Erasmianism* 47–64

– *Erasmus als Ketzer: Reformation und Inquisition im Italien des 16. Jahrhunderts* Leiden 1993

– 'Erasme et son lecteur: à propos du rapport auteur-public au XVIe siècle,' in *Coll Eras: Liège* 31–45

– 'La fortuna di Erasmo in Italia: Confronto metodologico con la ricerca di Marcel Bataillon,' in Revuelta Sañudo and Morón Arroyo (eds) *El Erasmismo en España* 21–39

Shäfer, Eckhart 'Erasmus und Horaz' *Antike und Abendland* 16 (1970): 54–67

Shenk, Wilhelm 'The Erasmian Idea' *Hibbert Journal* 48 (1950): 256–65

Skinner, Quentin *The Foundations of Modern Political Thought* 2 vols, Cambridge 1978

Sloane, T.O. 'Schoolbooks and Rhetoric: Erasmus's *Copia' Rhetorica* 9 (1991): 113–29

Smolinsky, Heribert 'Erasmianismus in der Politik? Das Beispiel der vereinigten Herzogtümer Jülich-Kleve- Berg,' in Mout, Smolinsky, and Trapman (eds) *Erasmianism* 77–89

Sowards, J.K. 'Erasmus and the Apologetic Textbook: A Study of the *De duplici Copia verborum ac rerum' Studies in Philology* 55 (1958): 122–35

– 'Erasmus and the Education of Women' SCJ 13 (1982): 77–89

– 'Erasmus as a Practical Educational Reformer,' in *Erasmus of Rotterdam* 123–31

– 'The Youth of Erasmus: Some Reconsiderations,' in ERSY 9 (1989): 1–33

Sperna Weiland, J. (ed) *Erasmus: De actualiteit van zijn denken* Amsterdam 1986

Spitz, Lewis W. *The Religious Renaissance of the German Humanists* Cambridge, Mass 1963

Staehelin, Ernst 'Erasmus und Ökolampad in ihrem Ringen um die Kirche Jesu Christi,' in *Gedenkschrift* 166–82

Stegmann, André 'La réhabilitation de l'orthodoxie chez Erasme par Jean Richard (1688),' in *Coll Tur* 2:867–76

Stupperich, Robert 'Die theologische Neuorientierung des Erasmus in der *Ratio seu Methodus* 1516–18,' in *Actes* 148–58

– 'Zur Biographie des Erasmus von Rotterdam: Zwei Untersuchungen'
  ARG 65 (1974): 18–36
Sylvester, Richard S. 'The Problem of Unity in the *Praise of Folly*' *English Literary Renaissance* 6 (1976): 125–39
Telle, Emile V. 'Dolet et Erasme,' in *Coll Tur* 1:407–39
– *Erasme de Rotterdam et le septième sacrament: Etude d'évangélisme matrimonial au XVIe siècle et contribution à la biographie intellectuelle d'Erasme* Geneva 1954
Telle, Emile V. (ed) *L'Erasmianus sive Ciceronianus d'Etienne Dolet (1535)* Geneva 1974
Thompson, Craig R. 'Erasmus and Tudor England,' in *Actes* 29–68
– 'Erasmus as Internationalist and Cosmopolitan' ARG 46 (1955): 167–95
Thompson, Geraldine 'As Bones to the Body: The Scope of *Inventio* in the *Colloquies* of Erasmus,' in DeMolen (ed) *Essays on the Works of Erasmus* 163–78
– *Under Pretext of Praise: Satiric Mode in Erasmus' Fiction* Toronto 1973
Thomson, D.F.S. 'Erasmus as a Poet in the Context of Northern Humanism,' in *Commém Nat* 187–210
Torrance T.F. 'The Hermeneutics of Erasmus,' in Elsie Anne McKee and Brian G. Armstrong *Probing the Reformed Tradition: Historical Studies in Honor of Edward A. Dowey, Jr* Louisville 1989, 48–76
Tracy, James D. 'Erasmus among the Postmodernists: *Dissimulatio, Bonae Literae,* and *Docta Pietas* Revisited,' in Pabel (ed) *Erasmus' Vision of the Church* 1–40
– 'Erasmus Becomes a German' RQ 21 (1968): 281–8
– *Erasmus: The Growth of a Mind* Geneva 1972
– *Erasmus of the Low Countries* Berkeley 1996
– 'From Humanism to the Humanities: A Critique of Grafton and Jardine' *Modern Language Quarterly* 51 (1990): 122–43
– *The Politics of Erasmus: A Pacifist Intellectual and His Political Milieu* Toronto 1978
Trapman, Johannes '"Erasmianism" in the Early Reformation in the Netherlands,' in Mout, Smolinsky, and Trapman (eds) *Erasmianism* 169–76
– 'Le rôle des "sacramentaires" des origines de la Réforme jusqu'en 1530 aux Pays-Bas' *Nederlands Archief voor Kerkgeschiedenis* 63 (1983): 1–24
Treinen, Hans *Studien zur Idee der Gemeinschaft bei Erasmus von Rotterdam and zu ihrer Stellung in der Entwicklung des humanistischen Universalismus* Saarlouis 1955
Trencsényi-Waldapfel, Imre 'L'humanisme belge et l'humanisme hongrois liés par l'esprit d'Erasme,' in *Commém Nat* 209–24
Trevor-Roper, H.R. 'Desiderius Erasmus' *Encounter* 20 (1955): 57–68
Turchetti, Mario 'Une question mal posée: Erasme et la tolérance. L'idée de *sygkatabasis*' BHR 53 (1991): 379–95
Vallese, Giulio 'Erasme et le *De duplici Copia verborum ac rerum*' in *Coll Tur* 1:233–9

Vanden Branden, Jean-Pierre 'Le "Corpusculum" d'Erasme' in *Actes du Colloque International* 215–31

Voet, L. 'Erasmus and His Correspondents,' in *Erasmus of Rotterdam* 195–202

Vogel, C.J. de 'Erasmus and His Attitude towards Church Dogma,' in *Scrinium* 2:101–32

Vredeveld, Harry 'The Ages of Erasmus and the Year of His Birth' RQ 46 (1993): 754–809

Walter, Johannes von 'Das Ende der Erasmusrenaissance,' in Walter *Christentum und Frömmigkeit: Gesämmelte Verträge und Aufsätze* Gutersloh 1941, 153–62

Watson, Donald Gwynn 'Erasmus' *Praise of Folly* and the Spirit of Carnival' RQ 32 (1979): 333–53

Weiler, A.G. 'The Turkish Argument and Christian Piety in Desiderius Erasmus' *Consultatio de Bello Turcis Inferendo* (1530),' in *Erasmus of Rotterdam* 30–9, and 'La *Consultatio de bello Turcis inferendo:* une oeuvre de piété politique,' in *Actes du Colloque International* 99–108

Weiss, James M. '*Ecclesiastes* and Erasmus: The Mirror and the Image' ARG 65 (1974): 83–108

– 'Melanchthon and the Heritage of Erasmus: *Oratio de Puritate Doctrinae* (1536) and *Oratio de Erasmo Roterodamo* (1557),' in *Actes du Colloque International* 293–306

Wendel, François, review of *Scrinium* in *Revue d'histoire et de philosophie religieuses* 51 (1971): 106–10

Wesseling, Ari 'Are the Dutch Uncivilized? Erasmus on the Batavians and His National Identity,' in ERSY 13 (1993): 68–102, and 'Or Else I Become a Gaul: A Note on Erasmus and the German Reformation,' in ibid 15 (1995): 96–8

Williams, George Hunston 'Erasmianism in Poland: An Account of a Major, though Ever Diminishing, Current in Sixteenth-Century Polish Humanism and Religion, 1518–1605' *Polish Review* 22 (1977): 3–50

– 'Erasmus and the Reformers on Non-Christian Religions and *Salus extra Ecclesiam*,' in Theodore K. Rabb and Jerrold E. Seigel (eds) *Action and Conviction in Early Modern Europe: Essays in Memory of E.H. Harbison* Princeton 1969, 319–70

Williams, Kathleen (ed) *Twentieth Century Interpretations of 'The Praise of Folly': A Collection of Critical Essays* Englewood Cliffs 1969

Witke, Charles 'Erasmus Autor et Actor,' in ERSY 15 (1995): 26–52

Wollgast, Siegfried 'Erasmianer und die Geschichte des Nonkonformismus. Aspekte,' in Mout, Smolinsky, and Trapman (eds) *Erasmianism* 105–26

Zupnick, Irving L. 'The Influence of Erasmus' *Enchiridion* on Bruegel's *Seven Virtues*,' in *Commém Nat* 225–35

Zweig, Stefan *Triumph und Tragik des Erasmus von Rotterdam* Vienna 1935 (Eng trans Eden and Cedar Paul *Erasmus* London 1951; both editions first published 1934)

OTHER WORKS CITED

Abbott, Don Paul 'The Renaissance,' in Winifred Bryan Horner (ed) *The Present State of Scholarship in Historical and Contemporary Rhetoric* Columbia/London 1983, 75–100

Allardyce, Gilbert 'The Rise and Fall of the Western Civilization Course' *AHR* 87 (1982): 695–725

Allen, J.W. *A History of Political Thought in the Sixteenth Century* London 1928

Aron, Raymond *Introduction à la philosophie de l'histoire: Essai sur les limites de l'objectivité historique* Paris 1948

Bainton, Roland H. *Pilgrim Parson: The Life of James Herbert Bainton (1867–1942)* New York 1958

Bakhtin, Mikhail *Rabelais and His World* Bloomington 1984

Balthasar, Hans Urs von *The Glory of the Lord: A Theological Aesthetics* 1 *Seeing the Form* Edinburgh 1982

Bataillon, Marcel 'L'Espagne religieuse dans son histoire. Lettre ouverte à Américo Castro' in *Erasme et l'Espagne* 3:9–30

– review of José C. Nieto *Juan de Valdés* in *Erasme et l'Espagne* 2:505–14

Bietenholz, P.G. *Basle and France in the Sixteenth Century* Geneva 1971

Blom, N. van der (ed) *Grepen uit de geschiedenis van het Erasmiaans Gymnasium 1328–1978* Rotterdam 1978

Bouwsma, William 'From History of Ideas to History of Meaning,' in *A Usable Past* 336–47

– 'The Renaissance and the Drama of Western History,' in *A Usable Past* 348–65

– *A Usable Past: Essays in European Cultural History* Berkeley 1990

Boyle, Marjorie O'Rourke 'Stoic Luther: Paradoxical Sin and Necessity' *ARG* 73 (1982): 69–93

Camillo, Ottavio di 'Humanism in Spain,' in Albert Rabil Jr (ed) *Renaissance Humanism: Foundations, Forms, and Legacy* 2:55–108

– 'Interpretations of the Renaissance in Spanish Historical Thought: The Last Thirty Years' *RQ* 49 (1996): 360–83

Castro, Américo *The Spaniards: An Introduction to Their History* Berkeley 1971

Cave, Terence *The Cornucopian Text: Problems of Writing in the French Renaissance* Oxford 1979

Chenu, Marie-Dominique *Nature, Man, and Society in the Twelfth Century: Essays on New Theological Perspectives in the Latin West* Chicago 1968

Courtenay, William 'Nominalism and Late Medieval Religion,' in Charles Trinkaus with Heiko A. Oberman (eds) *The Pursuit of Holiness in Late Medieval and Renaissance Religion* Leiden 1974, 26–59

D'Alton, Craig W. 'The Trojan War of 1518: Melodrama, Politics, and the Rise of Humanism' *SCJ* 28 (1997): 727–38

Daniell, David *William Tyndale: A Biography* New Haven/London 1994

Defaux, Gérard 'Against Derrida's "Dead Letter": Christian Humanism and the Valorization of Writing' *French Forum* 13 (1988): 167–85
– 'Jean-Claude Margolin,' in ERSY 10 (1990): 1–8
Dewald, Jonathan *The European Nobility 1400–1800* Cambridge 1996
Dickens, A.G. 'The Early Expansion of Protestantism in England' ARG 78 (1987): 187–223
Doran, Susan *England and Europe in the Sixteenth Century* London 1999
Dowling, Maria *Humanism in the Age of Henry VIII* London 1986
Duke, Alistair *Reformation and Revolt in the Low Countries* London 1990
Durkheim, E. *The Rules of Sociological Method* New York 1964
Edwards, Mark U., Jr *Luther's Last Battles: Politics and Polemics 1531–46* Leiden 1983
Febvre, Lucien 'Une question mal posée: Les origines de la réforme française et le problème des causes de la réforme', in *Au coeur religieux du XVIe siècle* Paris 1957, 3–70
Fichtner, Paula Sutter *Ferdinand I of Austria: The Politics of Dynasticism in the Age of the Reformation* New York 1982
Flannery, Austin (gen ed) *Vatican Council II: The Conciliar and Post Conciliar Documents* Dublin 1975
Foucault, Michel *Histoire de la Folie à l'âge classique* Paris 1972
– *The Order of Things: An Archaeology of the Human Sciences* London 1970
Friedrich, Hugo *Montaigne* Paris 1968
Fuery, Patrick, and Nick Mansfield *Cultural Studies and the New Humanities: Concepts and Controversies* Melbourne 1997
Gadamer, Hans-Georg *Truth and Method* London 1979
Gierke, Otto von *Community in Historical Perspective: A Translation of Selections from Das deutsche Genossenschaftsrecht (The German Law of Fellowship)*, trans Mary Fischer, ed Antony Black, Cambridge 1990
– *Natural Law and the Theory of Society 1500 to 1800*, trans Ernest Barker Cambridge 1934
Gilly, Carols 'Juan de Valdés: Übesetzer and Bearbeiter von Luthers Sohriften in seinem *Diálogo de Doctrina*' ARG 74 (1983): 257–305
Godin, André *Spiritualité franciscain en Flandre au XVIe siècle: L'Homéliaire de Jean Vitrier* Geneva 1971
– review of *Actes* BHR 33 (1971): 745–8
Gouwens, Kenneth 'Perceiving the Past: Renaissance Humanism after the "Cognitive Turn"' AHR 103 (1998): 55–82
Gray, Hanna H. 'Renaissance Humanism: The Pursuit of Eloquence' *Journal of the History of Ideas* 24 (1963): 497–514
Gunn, Steven 'The French Wars of Henry VIII,' in Jeremy Black (ed) *The Origins of War in Early Modern Europe* Edinburgh 1987, 28–51
Haigh, Christopher *The English Reformation Revised* Cambridge 1987
Hale, J.R. *War and Society in Renaissance Europe 1450–1620* Leicester 1985
Hamilton, Alastair *Heresy and Mysticism in Spain: The 'Alumbrados'* Cambridge 1992

Havel, Václav *Disturbing the Peace: A Conversation with Karel Hvízdala* New York 1990

Hexter, J.H. 'The Education of the Aristocracy in the Renaissance,' in *Reappraisals in History: New Views on History and Society in Early Modern Europe* New York/Evanston 1961, 45–70

Hoven, René 'In Memoriam Léon-E. Halkin (1906–1998),' in ERSY 19 (1999): 111

Huizinga, Johan *Homo Ludens: A Study of the Play-Element in Culture* London 1949

Isocrates *To Nicocles* Loeb edition 1, London/Cambridge, Mass 1966

Johnson, Roger A. (ed) *Psychohistory and Religion: The Case of Young Man Luther* Philadelphia 1977

Keane, John *Václav Havel: A Political Tragedy in Six Acts* London 2000

Keen, Maurice *Chivalry* New Haven/London 1984

Kinder, Sabine, and Ellen Presser (eds) *Die Zeit gibt die Bilder, ich spreche nur die Worte dazu: Stefan Zweig 1881–1942* Munich 1993

Kristeller, Paul Oskar 'Humanism and Scholasticism in the Italian Renaissance,' in *Renaissance Thought: The Classic, Scholastic, and Humanist Strains* New York 1961

– 'Rhetoric in Medieval and Renaissance Culture,' in Murphy *Renaissance Eloquence* 1–19

Lacan, Jacques *Ecrits: A Selection*, trans Alan Sheridan, London 1977

LaCapra, Dominick *History and Criticism* Ithaca/London 1985

– *Rethinking Intellectual History: Texts, Contexts, Language* Ithaca/London 1983

Levi, A.H.T. (ed) *Humanism in France at the End of the Middle Ages and in the Early Renaissance* Manchester/New York 1970

Logan, George M. *The Meaning of More's 'Utopia'* Princeton 1983

Mack, Peter 'Humanist Rhetoric and Dialectic,' in Jill Kraye (ed) *The Cambridge Companion to Renaissance Humanism* Cambridge 1996, 82–99

Macquarrie, John 'Blondel, Maurice,' in *Encyclopedia of Philosophy* 1 New York/London 1967, 323–4

Mann, Thomas *Briefe 1 (1889–1936)* Frankfurt-am-Main 1961

Mansfield, Bruce 'Anguish of an Erasmian: P.S. Allen and the Great War' *Parergon* New Series 14 (1996): 257–76

Marcus, Raymond 'Marcel Bataillon 1895–1977' BHR 39 (1977): 597–9

Margolin, Jean-Claude 'Hommage à Pierre Mesnard, philosophe et humaniste (1900–69)' BHR 31 (1969): 645–9

– 'Jacques Chomarat (1925–1998)' BHR 60 (1998): 815–16, ERSY 19 (1999): 111–13

– 'Tribut d'un antihumaniste aux études d'humanisme et Renaissance: Note sur l'oeuvre de Michel Foucault' BHR 29 (1967): 701–11

Maritain, Jacques *True Humanism* trans M.R. Adamson, London 1946

Moeller, Bernd 'The German Humanists and the Beginnings of the Refor-

mation,' in H.C. Erik Midelfort and Mark U. Edwards, Jr (eds) *Imperial Cities and the Reformation* Philadelphia 1972, 19–38
– *Reichstadt und Reformation* Gutersloh 1962
Mokrosch, Reinhold 'Devotio Moderna und nordeuropäischer Humanismus' TRE 8 609–12
Monfasani, John 'Humanism and Rhetoric,' in Albert Rabil Jr (ed) *Renaissance Humanism: Foundations, Forms, and Legacy* 3:171–235
Murphy, James J. (ed) *Renaissance Eloquence: Studies in the Theory and Practice of Renaissance Rhetoric* Berkeley 1983
Nauta, D. 'De Reformatie in Nederland in de Historiografie' *Serta Historica* 2 (1970): 49–66
Nierop, H.F.K. van *The Nobility of Holland: From Knights to Regents 1500–1650* Cambridge 1993
Nieto, José C. *Juan de Valdés and the Origins of the Spanish and Italian Reformations* Geneva 1970
Noordegraaf, Herman 'The Anarchopacifism of Bart de Ligt,' in Peter Brock and Thomas P. Socknat (eds) *Challenge to Mars: Essays on Pacifism from 1918 to 1945* Toronto 1999, 89–100
Oberman, H. A. *The Harvest of Medieval Theology: Gabriel Biel and Late Medieval Nominalism* Cambridge, Mass 1963
Percival, W. Keith 'Grammar and Rhetoric in the Renaissance,' in Murphy *Renaissance Eloquence* 303–30
Phillips, Margaret Mann 'P.S. Allen: A Lifetime of Letters,' in ERSY 9 (1989): 91–105
Potter, David *A History of France, 1460–1560: The Emergence of a Nation State* London 1995
Prater, D.A. *European of Yesterday: A Biography of Stefan Zweig* Oxford 1972
Quintilian *Institutio oratoria* Loeb edition 4 vols, Cambridge, Mass, 1963–8
Rahner, Karl (ed) *Encyclopedia of Theology: The Concise Sacramentum Mundi* Tunbridge Wells 1993
Renaudet, Augustin *Préréforme et humanisme à Paris pendant les premières guerres d'Italie (1494–1517)* 2nd ed, Paris 1953
– 'Paris from 1494 to 1517 – Church and University; Religious Reforms; Culture and the Humanists' Critiques,' in Werner L. Gundersheimer (ed) *French Humanism 1470–1560* London 1969, 65–89
Rice, Eugene 'John Colet and the Annihilation of the Natural' *Harvard Theological Review* 45 (1952): 141–63
Richardson, Glenn 'The Privy Chamber of Henry VIII and Anglo-French Relations, 1515–1520' *Court Historian* 4 (1999): 119–40
– *Renaissance Monarchy: The Reigns of Henry VIII, Francis I and Charles V* London 2002
Rummel, Erika *The Humanist-Scholastic Debate in the Renaissance and Reformation* Cambridge, Mass 1995
Scarisbrick, J.J. *Henry VIII* Harmondsworth 1971

– *The Reformation and the English People* Oxford 1984
Schiffman, Z.S. 'Renaissance Historicism Reconsidered' *History and Theory* 24 (1985): 170–82
Schoeck, R.J. *The Eye of a Traveller: Landscapes and Seascapes* Lewiston 1992
– 'Humanism in Renaissance England,' in Rabil (ed) *Renaissance Humanism* 2:5–38, and 'Humanism and Jurisprudence,' in ibid 3:310–26
Screech, M.A. 'Margaret Mann Phillips,' in ERSY 8 (1988): 1–4
Scribner, R.W. *For the Sake of Simple Folk: Popular Propaganda for the German Reformation* Oxford 1994
– 'Is There a Social History of the Reformation?' *Social History* 4 (1977): 483–505
Simpler, Steven H. *Roland H. Bainton: An Examination of His Reformation Historiography* Lewiston/Queenston 1985
Skinner, Quentin 'Meaning and Understanding in the History of Ideas,' in James Tully (ed) *Meaning and Context: Quentin Skinner and His Critics* Cambridge 1988, 29–67
Strand, Kenneth A. (ed) *The Dawn of Modern Civilization: Studies in Renaissance, Reformation and Other Topics to Honor Albert Hyma*, 2nd edn, Ann Arbor 1964
Thompson, Craig R. 'Three American Erasmians,' in ERSY 4 (1984): 1–36
Toews, John E. 'Intellectual History after the Linguistic Turn' AHR 92 (1987): 879–907
Tracy, James D. *A Financial Revolution in the Habsburg Netherlands: 'Renten' and 'Renteniers' in the County of Holland, 1515–1565* Berkeley 1985
– *Holland under Habsburg Rule 1506–1566: The Formation of a Body Politic* Berkeley 1990
Ward, John O. 'Renaissance Commentators on Ciceronian Rhetoric,' in Murphy *Renaissance Eloquence* 126–73
Weiler, A.G. 'Recent Historiography on the Modern Devotion: Some Debated Questions' *Archief voor de Geschiedenis van de Katholieke Kerk in Nederland* 26 (1984): 161–79
White, Hayden 'The Burden of History,' in White *Tropics of Discourse: Essays in Cultural Criticism* Baltimore 1978
Yates, Frances A. *Astraea: The Imperial Theme in the Sixteenth Century* London/Boston 1975
Zelewitz, Klaus 'Raconter l'histoire – est-ce un risque? Les biographies de Stefan Zweig,' in *Stefan Zweig 1881–1942: Actes du Colloque tenu à l'Université de Metz (décembre 1981)* Paris 1982
Zschäbitz, G. *Martin Luther: Grösse und Grenze* Berlin 1967
Zweig, Stefan *The World of Yesterday* London 1953

Index

Adam, Karl 132
Adams, Robert P.: on Erasmus and English humanism 22; on Erasmus as social critic 21; on French war 33
Aesop 215
Agricola, Rudolf 85, 159, 180
Alberti, Leon Battista 241n50
Alcalá, University of 45
Aldus Manutius 157
Aleander, Girolamo 63, 96, 112, 194–5, 211
Algiers 49
allegory 89, 145–6, 178
Allen, J.W. 17, 41
Allen, P.S. 15, 68, 80, 83, 181, 190, 208
Althusius 29
Ambrose 221
Amerbach, Bonifacius 5
American Historical Association 153
Amiel, Charles 48
Amiel, Emile 215
Ammonio, Andrea 194
Amsterdam 57, 80, 227
Anabaptism 59, 76
Anderlecht 4–5, 197
Andreas-Silvius-Stiftung, Basel 106
Anglican church 6, 84

antihumanism 88
anti-Semitism 223, 276n171
antitrinitarians, Polish 75
Antwerp 5, 38, 81, 96
Aquinas, Thomas 11, 66, 90–1, 92, 103, 121, 122, 142, 172, 174
Aretino 68
Aristotelianism 158
Aristotle 29, 91
Arminians 217
Aron, Raymond 50
Asensio, Eugenio: correction to Bataillon 48–9; without successors 238n10
Auer, Alfons: and Lortz 117, 118; and lay piety 117–18, 119; on Erasmus' anthropology 118; Kohls' critique of 118–19; compared with Hoffmann 137
Augsburg 56
Augsburg, Diet of (1530) 10, 26, 75, 129
Augustijn, Cornelis: on Erasmus' ecclesiology 103–4; on Erasmus and Reformation controversies 127–8; on free-will controversy 128; on Erasmus and Swiss Reformers 128; on Erasmus and reunion 129; on Erasmus and Luther 129; on Erasmus' dialogical theology 198; on synthesis in